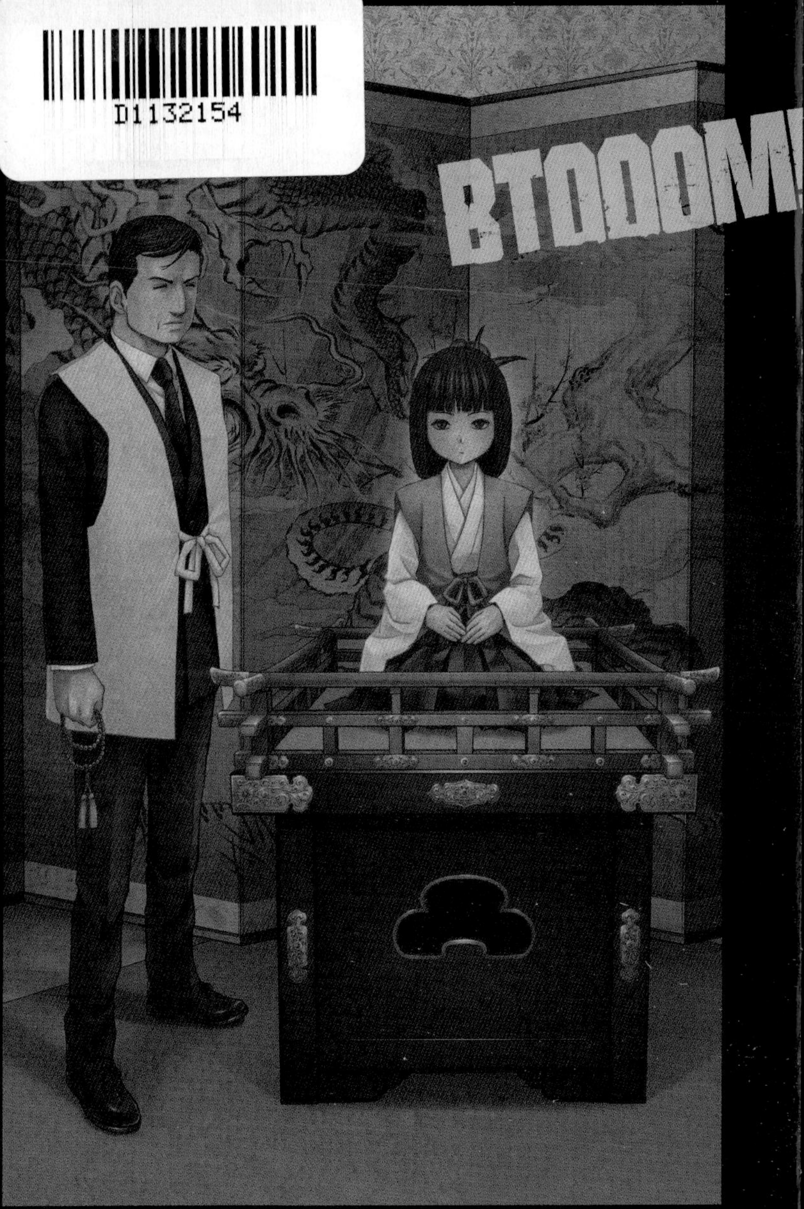
BTOOOM!

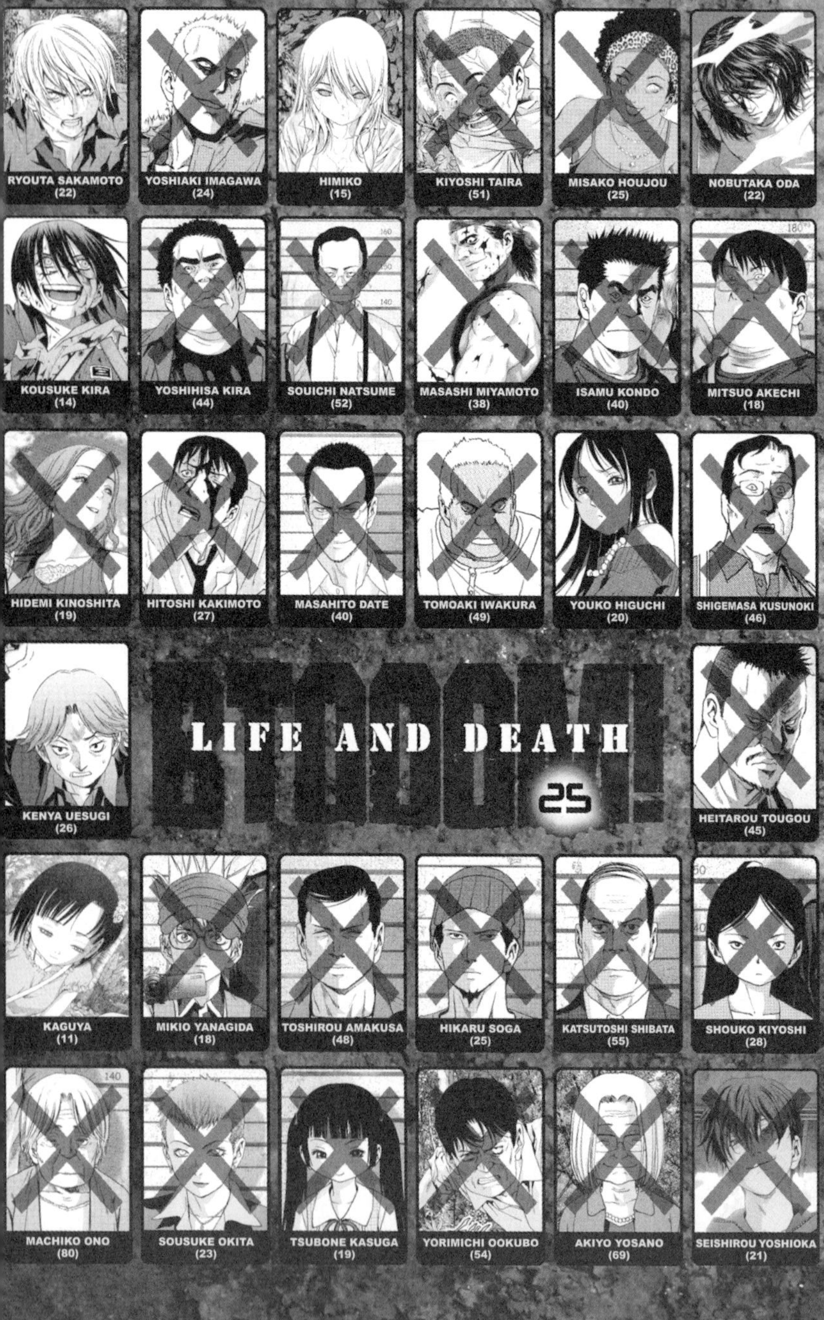

RYOUTA SAKAMOTO (22)
YOSHIAKI IMAGAWA (24)
HIMIKO (15)
KIYOSHI TAIRA (51)
MISAKO HOUJOU (25)
NOBUTAKA ODA (22)
KOUSUKE KIRA (14)
YOSHIHISA KIRA (44)
SOUICHI NATSUME (52)
MASASHI MIYAMOTO (38)
ISAMU KONDO (40)
MITSUO AKECHI (18)
HIDEMI KINOSHITA (19)
HITOSHI KAKIMOTO (27)
MASAHITO DATE (40)
TOMOAKI IWAKURA (49)
YOUKO HIGUCHI (20)
SHIGEMASA KUSUNOKI (46)
KENYA UESUGI (26)
BTOOOM!
LIFE AND DEATH
25
HEITAROU TOUGOU (45)
KAGUYA (11)
MIKIO YANAGIDA (18)
TOSHIROU AMAKUSA (48)
HIKARU SOGA (25)
KATSUTOSHI SHIBATA (55)
SHOUKO KIYOSHI (28)
MACHIKO ONO (80)
SOUSUKE OKITA (23)
TSUBONE KASUGA (19)
YORIMICHI OOKUBO (54)
AKIYO YOSANO (69)
SEISHIROU YOSHIOKA (21)

BTOOOM!

JUNYA INOUE

CHARACTER

NOBUTAKA ODA

GENDER: Male
AGE: 22
BLOOD TYPE: AB
JOB: Restaurant manager
HOME: Tokyo

Sakamoto's biggest rival and an old classmate of his from high school. His elaborate plans and surprisingly daring athleticism have helped him procure chips at a rapid pace as he plans for his own departure from the island. Engaging in life-or-death battles with his former best friend Sakamoto, he has demonstrated himself to be an unequaled master at combat.

HIMIKO

GENDER: Female
AGE: 15
BLOOD TYPE: B
JOB: High school student
HOME: Tokyo

A foreign high school girl who has teamed up with Sakamoto. She harbors a deep resentment against men after a sordid experience in her past, but after surviving some battles thanks to Sakamoto, she begins to trust him. Her character in the online version of "BTOOOM!" is actually married to Sakamoto's character, and she has fallen in love with the real Sakamoto too.

RYOUTA SAKAMOTO

GENDER: Male
AGE: 22
BLOOD TYPE: B
JOB: Unemployed
HOME: Tokyo

After spending every day cooped up in his home gaming online, he suddenly finds himself forced to participate in "BTOOOM! GAMERS," a killing game taking place on a mysterious uninhabited island. As a world ranker in the online third-person shooter "BTOOOM!", he uses his experience and natural instincts to survive and concoct a plan to get off the island with his comrades, only for it to end in failure. At the Sanctuary, he teams up with Kaguya and Soga to beat Torio.

KAGUYA

GENDER: Female
AGE: 11
BLOOD TYPE: AB
JOB: Grade schooler
HOME: Tokyo

A mysterious little girl who came across Sakamoto when he washed ashore. She doesn't speak and uses a tablet to communicate. She's the figurehead of the Order of Moonlight, a religious cult, and can see dead people. In the Sanctuary, she worked with Sakamoto and Soga to defeat the real villain behind the tragedies, Torio.

KENYA UESUGI

GENDER: Male
AGE: 26
BLOOD TYPE: AB
JOB: Office worker
HOME: Tokyo

A cowardly and easily flattered young man who used to dream of becoming an actor. He was almost killed by Kira, but he escaped thanks to Higuchi's lie-detecting ability. He was previously a part of Tougou's team.

KOUSUKE KIRA

GENDER: Male
AGE: 14
BLOOD TYPE: AB
JOB: Junior high student
HOME: Tokyo

This junior high student harbors a dark, brutal, murderous past. On the island, he blew up his own father and is genuinely enjoying this murderous game of "BTOOOM!". He's always been a big fan of the online version of the game, and his dream is to defeat "SAKAMOTO", a top world ranker. Unfortunately, he keeps failing at it. Tougou's death makes him realize for the first time ever how precious life is.

BTOOOM! 25

LONGER SCHWARITZ

GENDER: Male
AGE: 77
BLOOD TYPE: O
JOB: Capitalist
HOME: New York

A descendant of European aristocracy, he is a man of power who controls the world behind the scenes with his considerable capital. In order to more thoroughly control the online realm, he founds the THEMIS project and has high hopes for "BTOOOM! GAMERS."

XAVIERA FRANCISCA

GENDER: Female
AGE: 22
BLOOD TYPE: O
JOB: Freelancer
HOME: Washington

The operator of the drone that dropped the medicine case down on the island. Instead of BIMs, she attacks the players with a machine gun. Her skill is universally acknowledged, and in the online version of "BTOOOM!", she is the reigning world champion. However, she's never beaten Sakamoto, so she's obsessed with doing so.

TAKANOHASHI

GENDER: Male
AGE: 45
BLOOD TYPE: AB
JOB: Game planner
HOME: Hokkaido

An executive staff member at Tyrannos Japan, he is the leader behind all the development of the online and real-life versions of "BTOOOM! GAMERS." He considers Sakamoto a valuable player and debugger. As a result of Sakamoto's plan to hijack the helicopter, Takanohashi's precious game was almost forced to come to a premature end.

HISANOBU

GENDER: Male
AGE: 55
BLOOD TYPE: A
JOB: Unemployed
HOME: Tokyo

Yukie's new husband and Sakamoto's stepfather. He's worried about how much time his stepson spends up in his room and scolds him, only to be attacked. Having just been laid off, he racks up debt because of his praiseworthy efforts to preserve his family's lifestyle. However, Yukie is frail in body and mind and attempts to kill herself. Fate has dealt him an unfair card in life.

TSUNEAKI IIDA

GENDER: Male
AGE: 24
BLOOD TYPE: A
JOB: Programmer
HOME: Tokyo

An employee at Tyrannos Japan and Sakamoto's senpai from college. He's an excellent programmer and works under Takanohashi on the development of "BTOOOM! GAMERS." But he doesn't agree with the inhumane nature of the game and approached Sakamoto with the proposal and strategy to put a stop to the game's development, only for the plan to fall apart.

MATTHEW PERRIER

GENDER: Male
AGE: 27
BLOOD TYPE: O
JOB: Ex-NSA programmer, political refugee
HOME: Washington (location unknown after exile)

A former programmer with the NSA (U.S. National Security Agency), he's a capable hacker and curbed a number of cyber-crimes while with the NSA. But after learning about the government's darker side, he made off with sensitive data about the THEMIS project— in a way, the evidence of their nefarious plans—and defected to another country.

DIGEST

DAY 1

THE GAME BEGINS, AND EVERYONE'S EQUALLY CONFUSED...

DAY 2

THE EXPLOSIVE DEATH MATCH RAMPS UP, AND FIGHTS BREAK OUT ALL OVER.

DAY 3

HIMIKO IS KIDNAPPED, AND SAKAMOTO IS TESTED.

DAY 4

SAKAMOTO IS REUNITED WITH AND MUST BATTLE ODA. AND THEN...

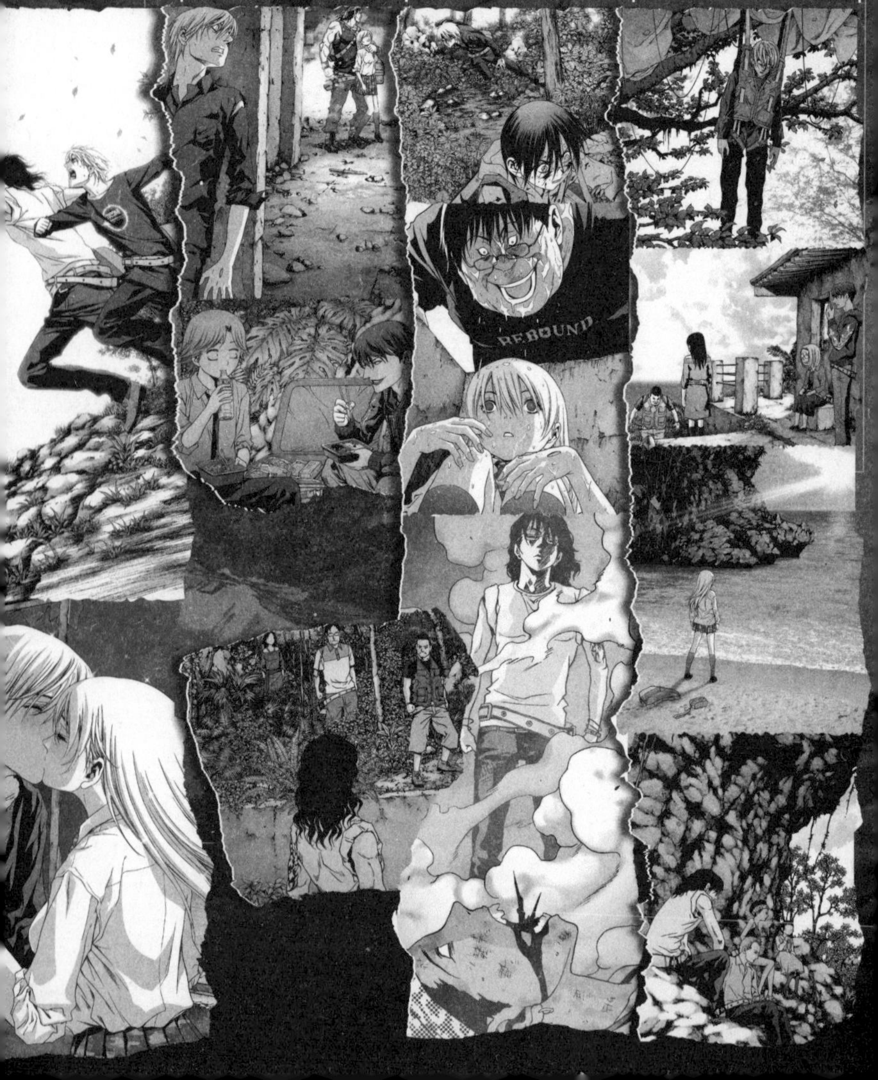
REBOUND

BTOOOM! 25

DAY 5

THE ISLAND GETS BUSY, AND SAKAMOTO AND HIS TEAM PLAN THEIR ESCAPE.

DAY 6

THE ESCAPE PLAN FAILS, AND MORE TRAGEDIES ENSUE.

DAY 7

THE FEW REMAINING SURVIVORS DWINDLE FURTHER.

DAY 8

AND NOW.........

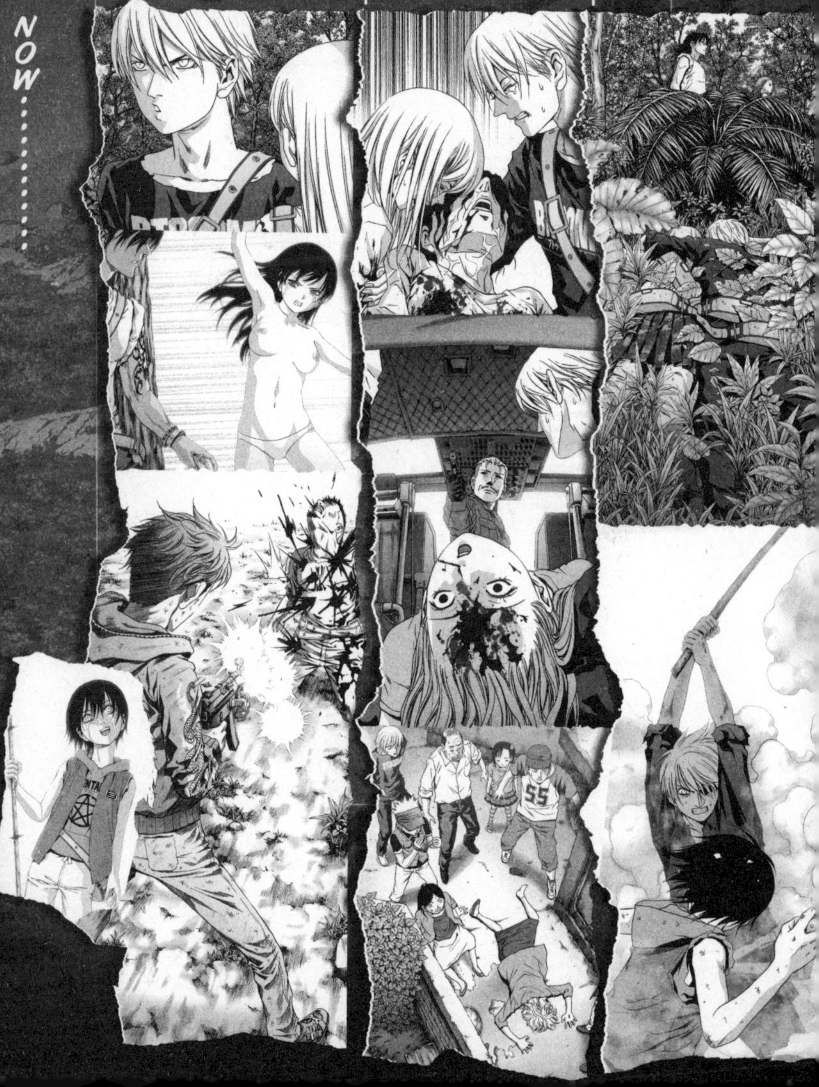

CONTENTS

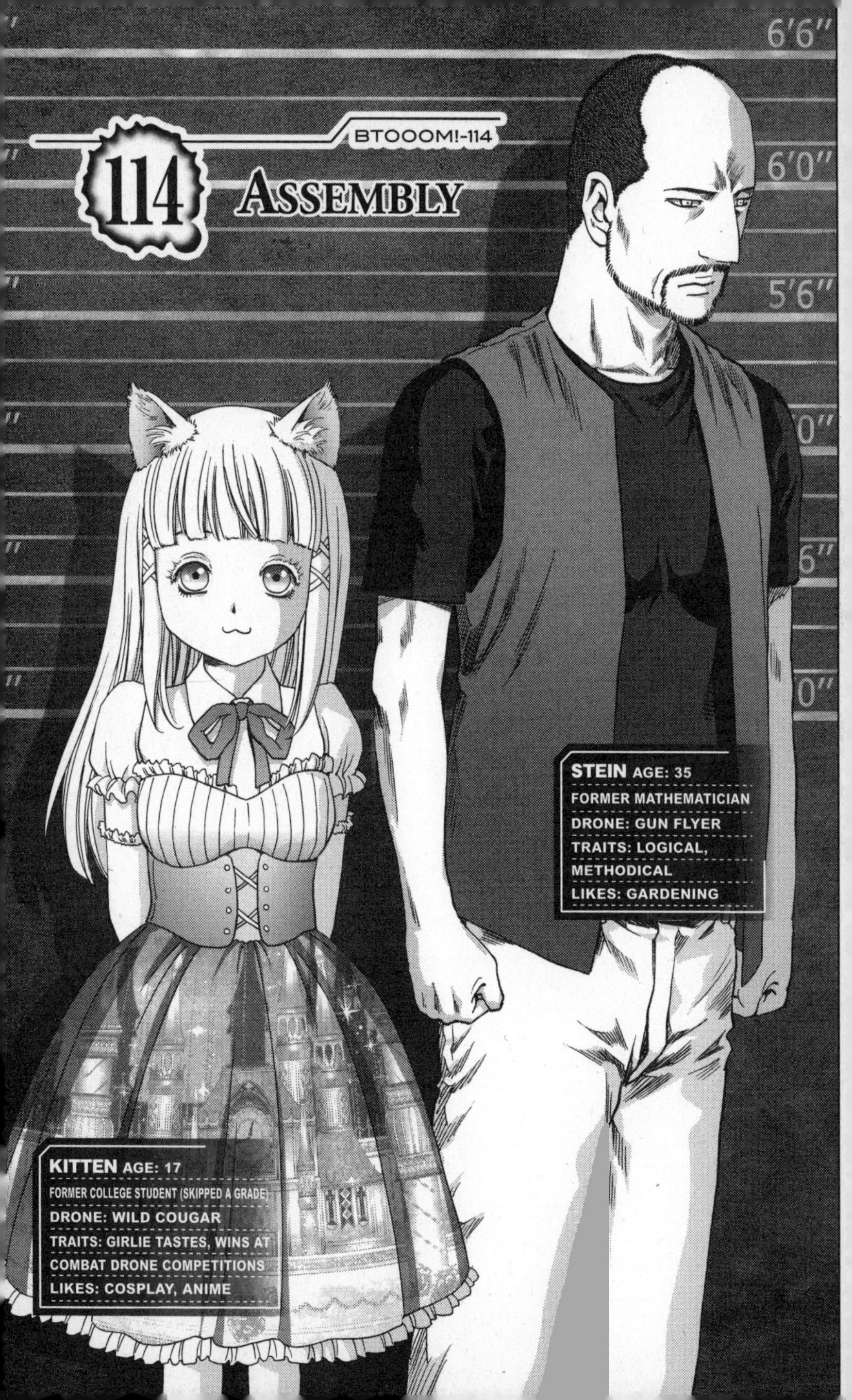
BTOOOM!-114
114
ASSEMBLY
6'6"
6'0"
5'6"
STEIN AGE: 35
FORMER MATHEMATICIAN
DRONE: GUN FLYER
TRAITS: LOGICAL, METHODICAL
LIKES: GARDENING
KITTEN AGE: 17
FORMER COLLEGE STUDENT (SKIPPED A GRADE)
DRONE: WILD COUGAR
TRAITS: GIRLIE TASTES, WINS AT COMBAT DRONE COMPETITIONS
LIKES: COSPLAY, ANIME

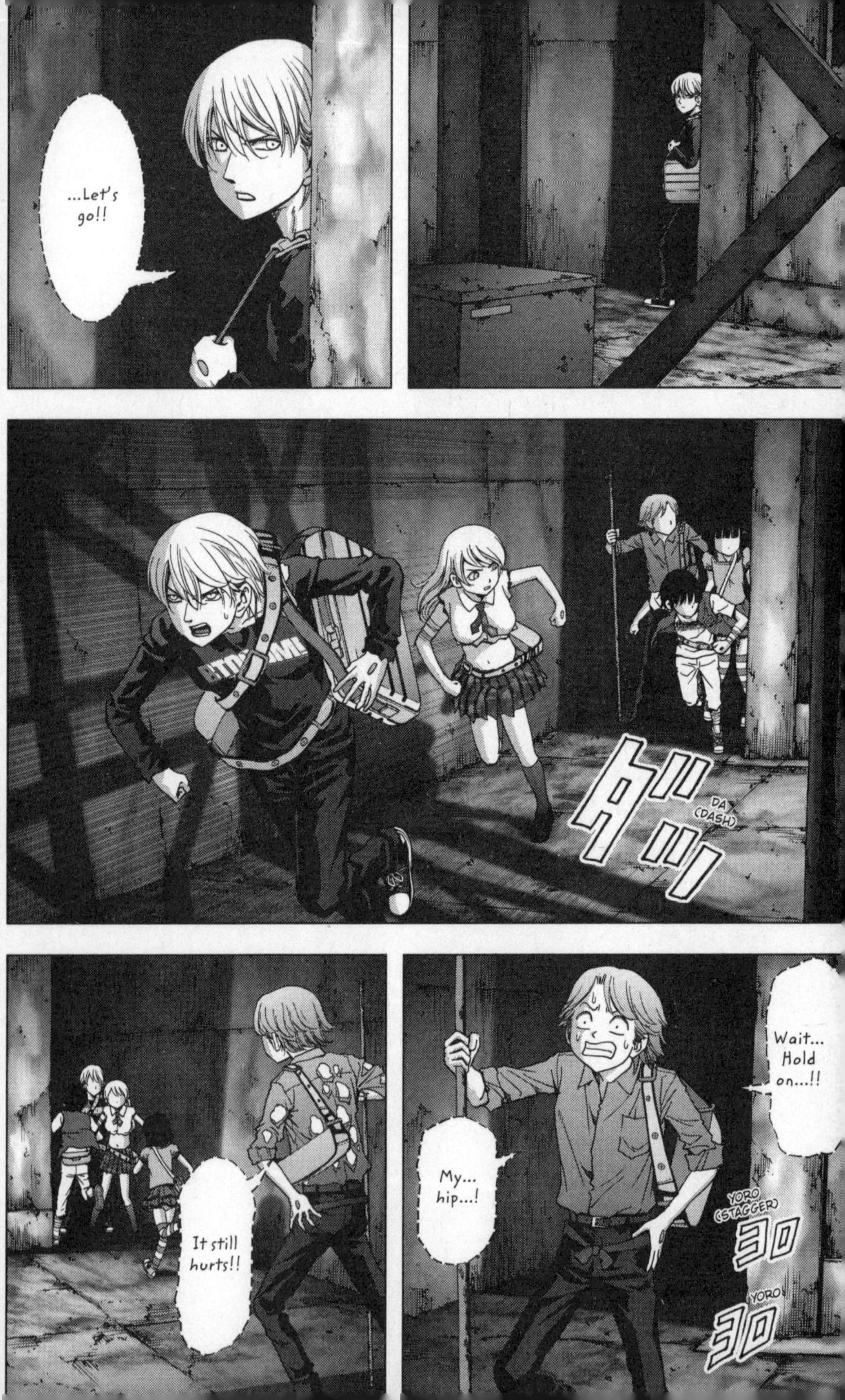
...Let's go!!
DA (DASH)
Wait... Hold on...!!
My... hip...!
YORO (STAGGER)
YORO
It still hurts!!

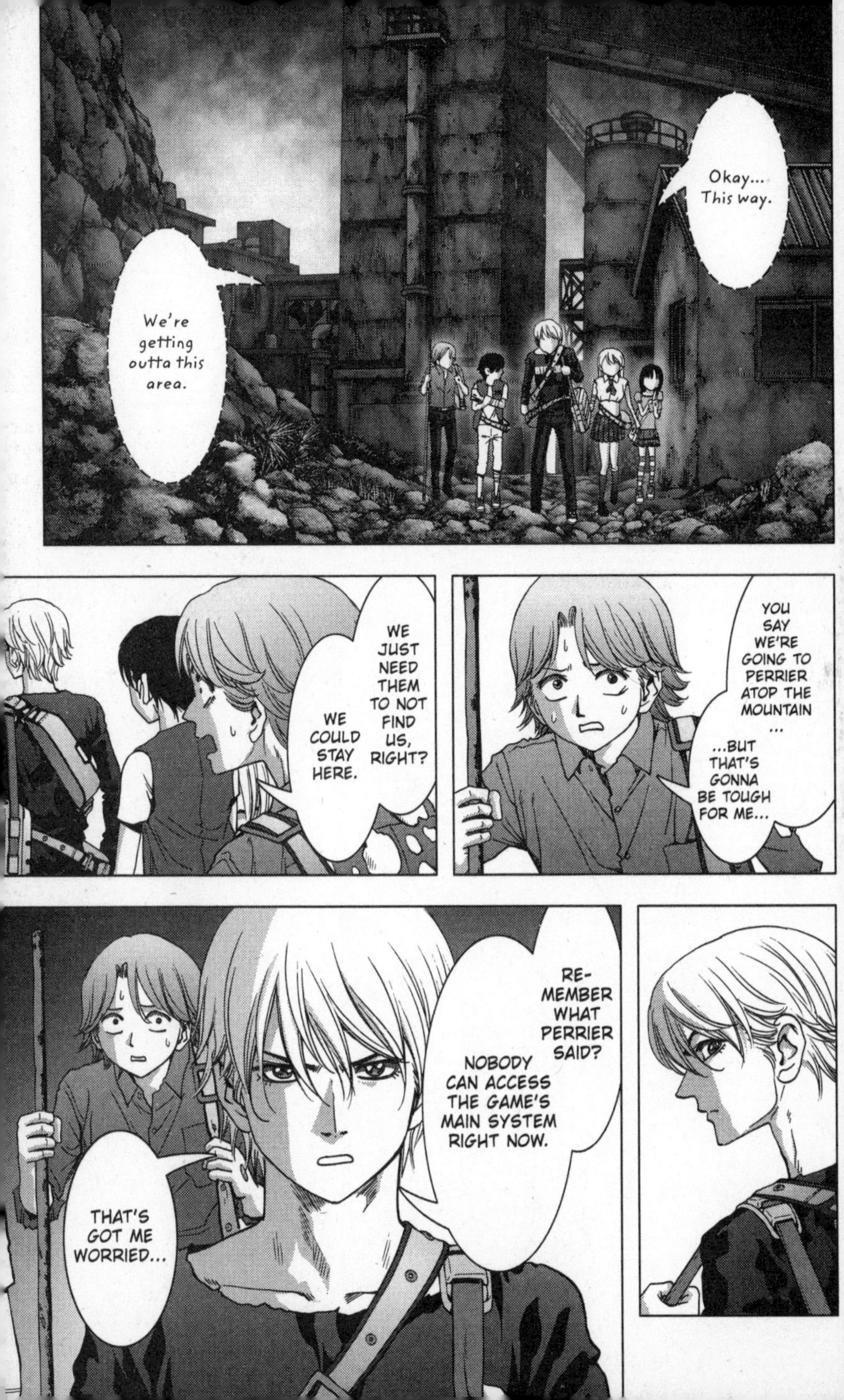
Okay... This way.
We're getting outta this area.
YOU SAY WE'RE GOING TO PERRIER ATOP THE MOUNTAIN ...
...BUT THAT'S GONNA BE TOUGH FOR ME...
WE JUST NEED THEM TO NOT FIND US, RIGHT?
WE COULD STAY HERE.
RE-MEMBER WHAT PERRIER SAID?
NOBODY CAN ACCESS THE GAME'S MAIN SYSTEM RIGHT NOW.
THAT'S GOT ME WORRIED...

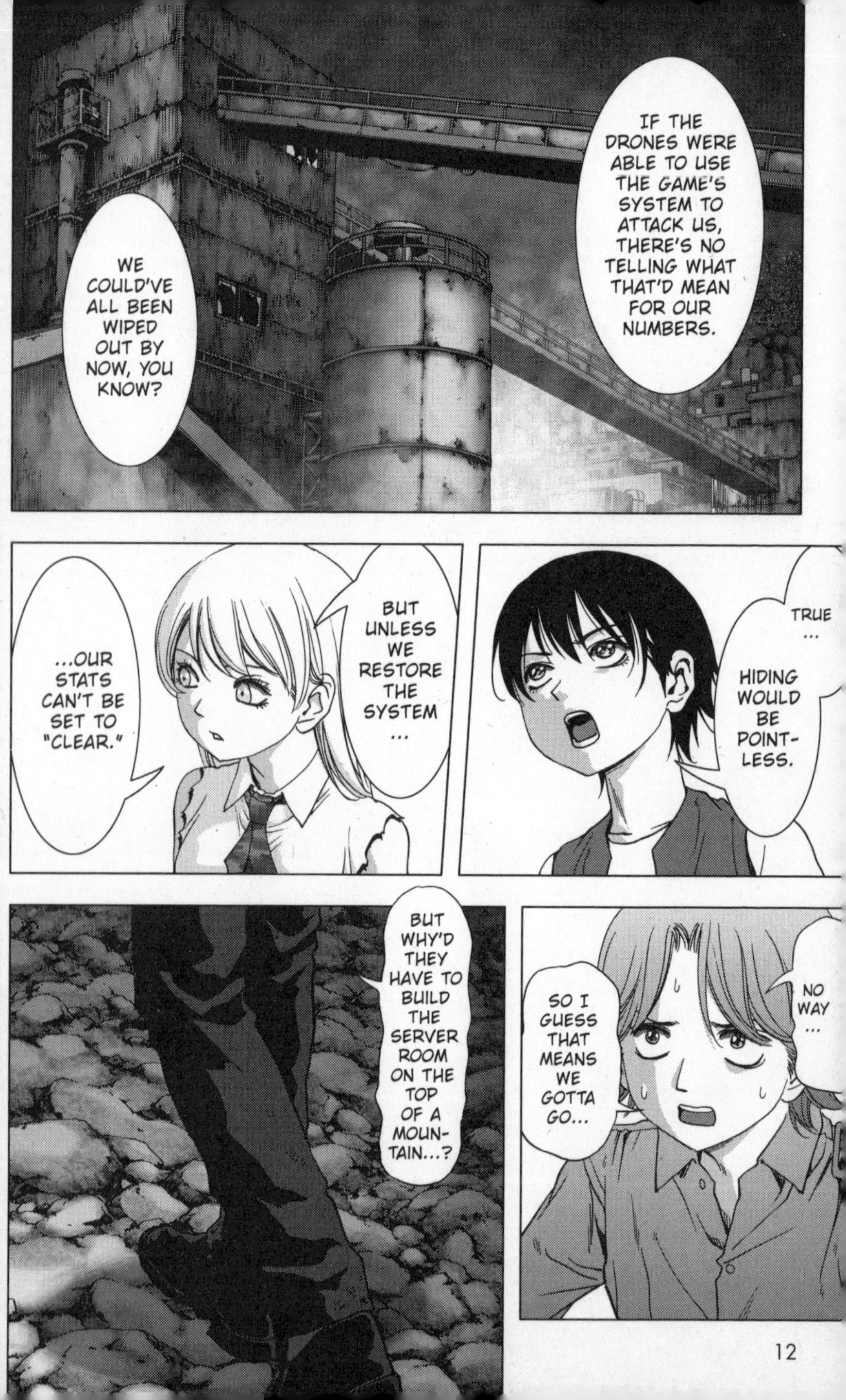

IF THE DRONES WERE ABLE TO USE THE GAME'S SYSTEM TO ATTACK US, THERE'S NO TELLING WHAT THAT'D MEAN FOR OUR NUMBERS.
WE COULD'VE ALL BEEN WIPED OUT BY NOW, YOU KNOW?
TRUE...
HIDING WOULD BE POINT-LESS.
BUT UNLESS WE RESTORE THE SYSTEM...
...OUR STATS CAN'T BE SET TO "CLEAR."
NO WAY...
SO I GUESS THAT MEANS WE GOTTA GO...
BUT WHY'D THEY HAVE TO BUILD THE SERVER ROOM ON THE TOP OF A MOUN-TAIN...?

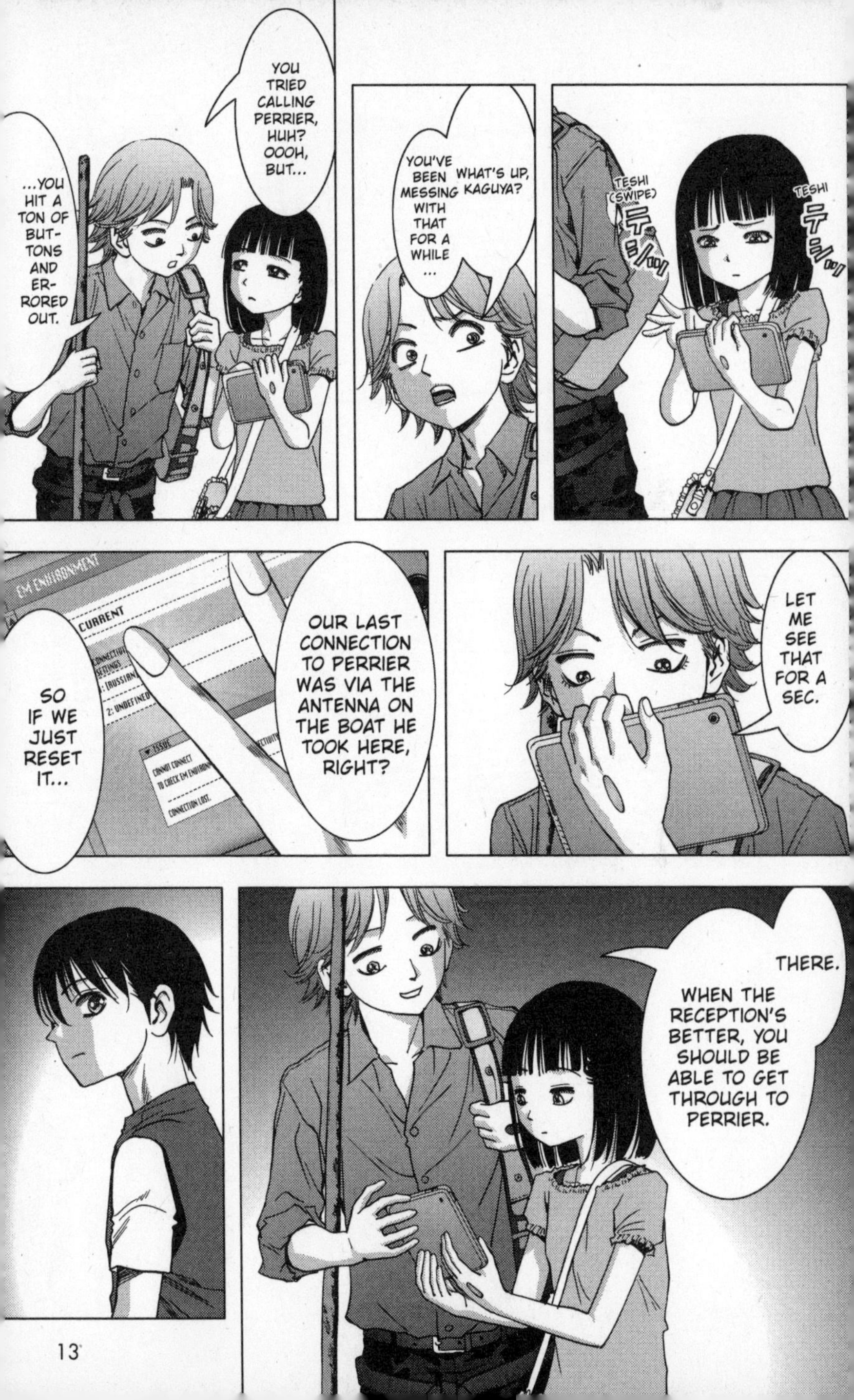
TESHI
TESHI (SWIPE)
WHAT'S UP, KAGUYA?
YOU'VE BEEN MESSING WITH THAT FOR A WHILE...
YOU TRIED CALLING PERRIER, HUH? OOOH, BUT...
...YOU HIT A TON OF BUT-TONS AND ER-RORED OUT.
LET ME SEE THAT FOR A SEC.
OUR LAST CONNECTION TO PERRIER WAS VIA THE ANTENNA ON THE BOAT HE TOOK HERE, RIGHT?
SO IF WE JUST RESET IT...
EM ENVIRONMENT
CURRENT
CONNECTION LOST.
THERE.
WHEN THE RECEPTION'S BETTER, YOU SHOULD BE ABLE TO GET THROUGH TO PERRIER.

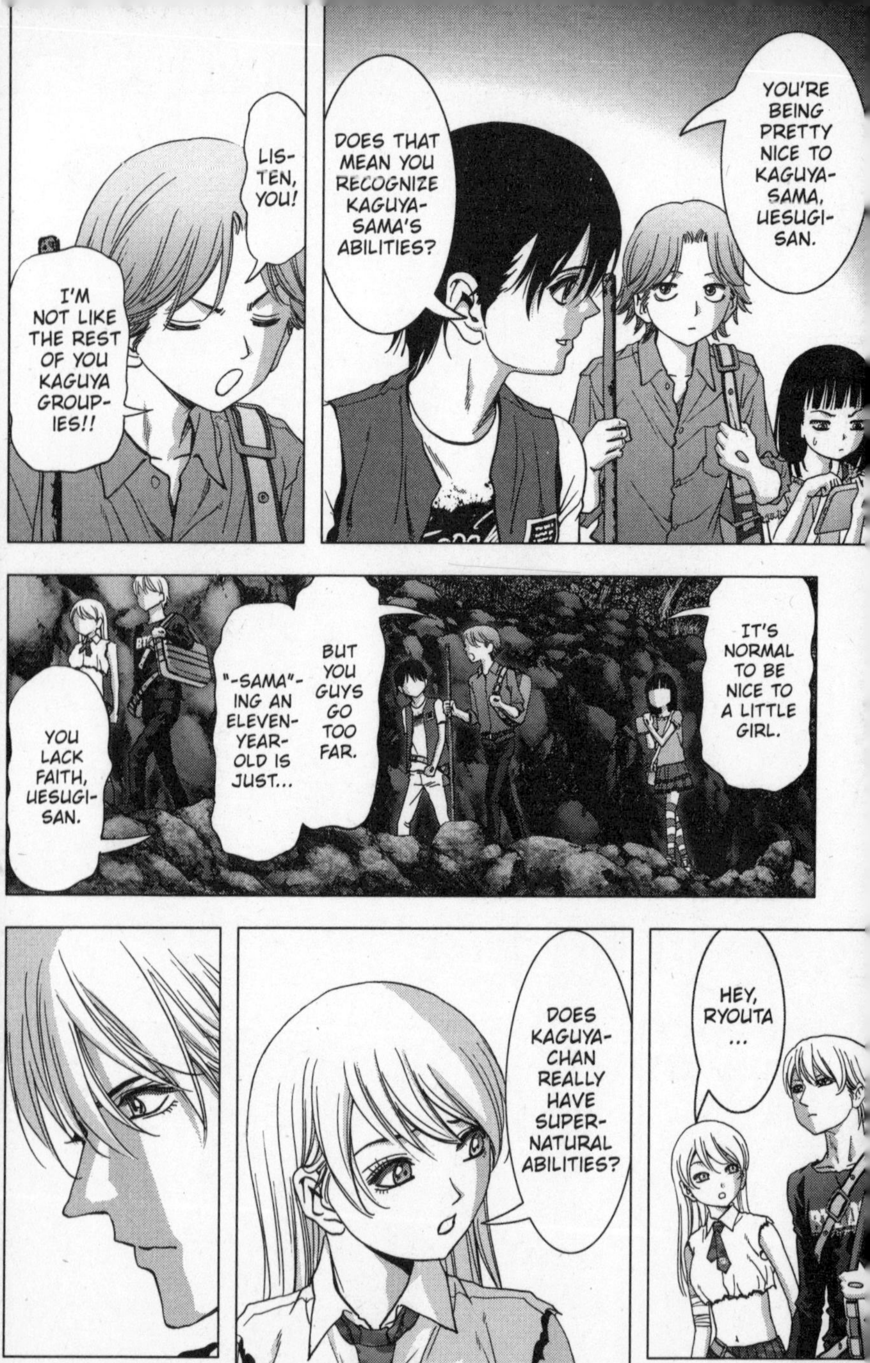
YOU'RE BEING PRETTY NICE TO KAGUYA-SAMA, UESUGI-SAN.
DOES THAT MEAN YOU RECOGNIZE KAGUYA-SAMA'S ABILITIES?
LISTEN, YOU!
I'M NOT LIKE THE REST OF YOU KAGUYA GROUPIES!!
IT'S NORMAL TO BE NICE TO A LITTLE GIRL.
BUT YOU GUYS GO TOO FAR.
"-SAMA"-ING AN ELEVEN-YEAR-OLD IS JUST...
YOU LACK FAITH, UESUGI-SAN.
HEY, RYOUTA ...
DOES KAGUYA-CHAN REALLY HAVE SUPERNATURAL ABILITIES?

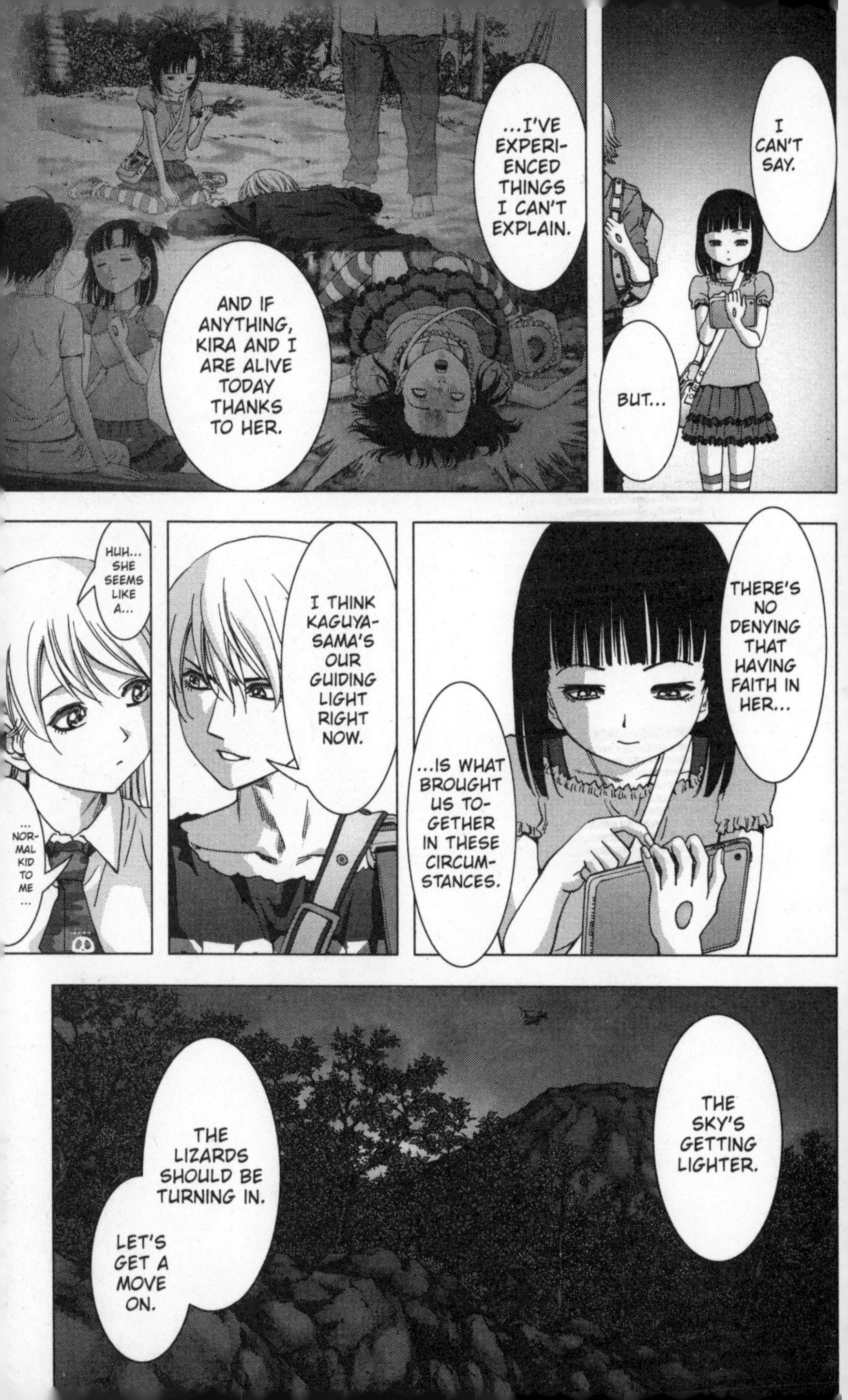
I CAN'T SAY.
BUT...
...I'VE EXPERIENCED THINGS I CAN'T EXPLAIN.
AND IF ANYTHING, KIRA AND I ARE ALIVE TODAY THANKS TO HER.
THERE'S NO DENYING THAT HAVING FAITH IN HER...
...IS WHAT BROUGHT US TOGETHER IN THESE CIRCUMSTANCES.
I THINK KAGUYA-SAMA'S OUR GUIDING LIGHT RIGHT NOW.
HUH... SHE SEEMS LIKE A...
...NORMAL KID TO ME...
THE SKY'S GETTING LIGHTER.
THE LIZARDS SHOULD BE TURNING IN.
LET'S GET A MOVE ON.

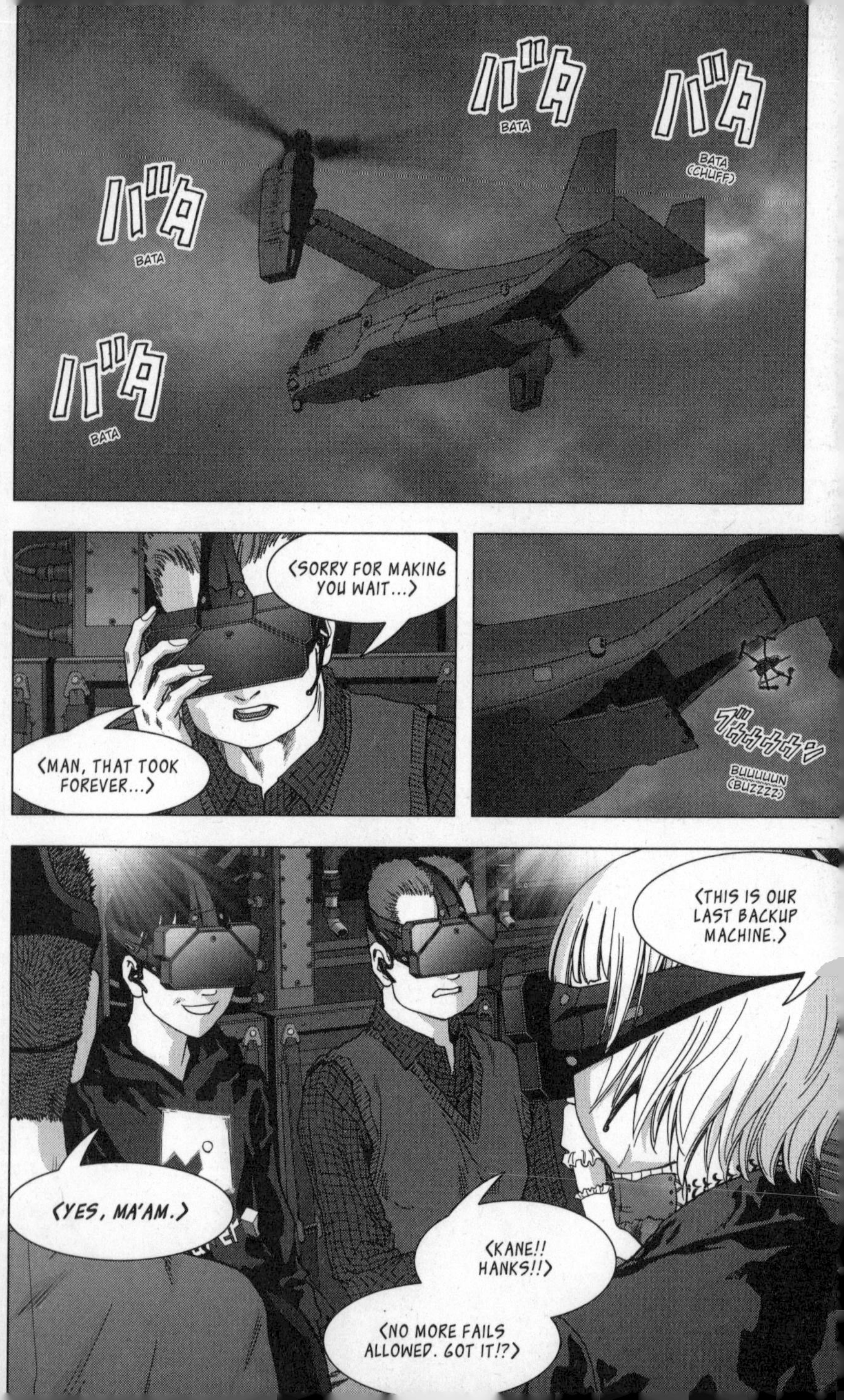
バタ
BATA
(CHUFF)
バタ
BATA
バタ
BATA
バタ
BATA
ブゥゥゥゥン
BUUUUUN
(BUZZZZ)
〈SORRY FOR MAKING YOU WAIT...〉
〈MAN, THAT TOOK FOREVER...〉
〈THIS IS OUR LAST BACKUP MACHINE.〉
〈KANE!! HANKS!!〉
〈NO MORE FAILS ALLOWED. GOT IT!?〉
〈YES, MA'AM.〉

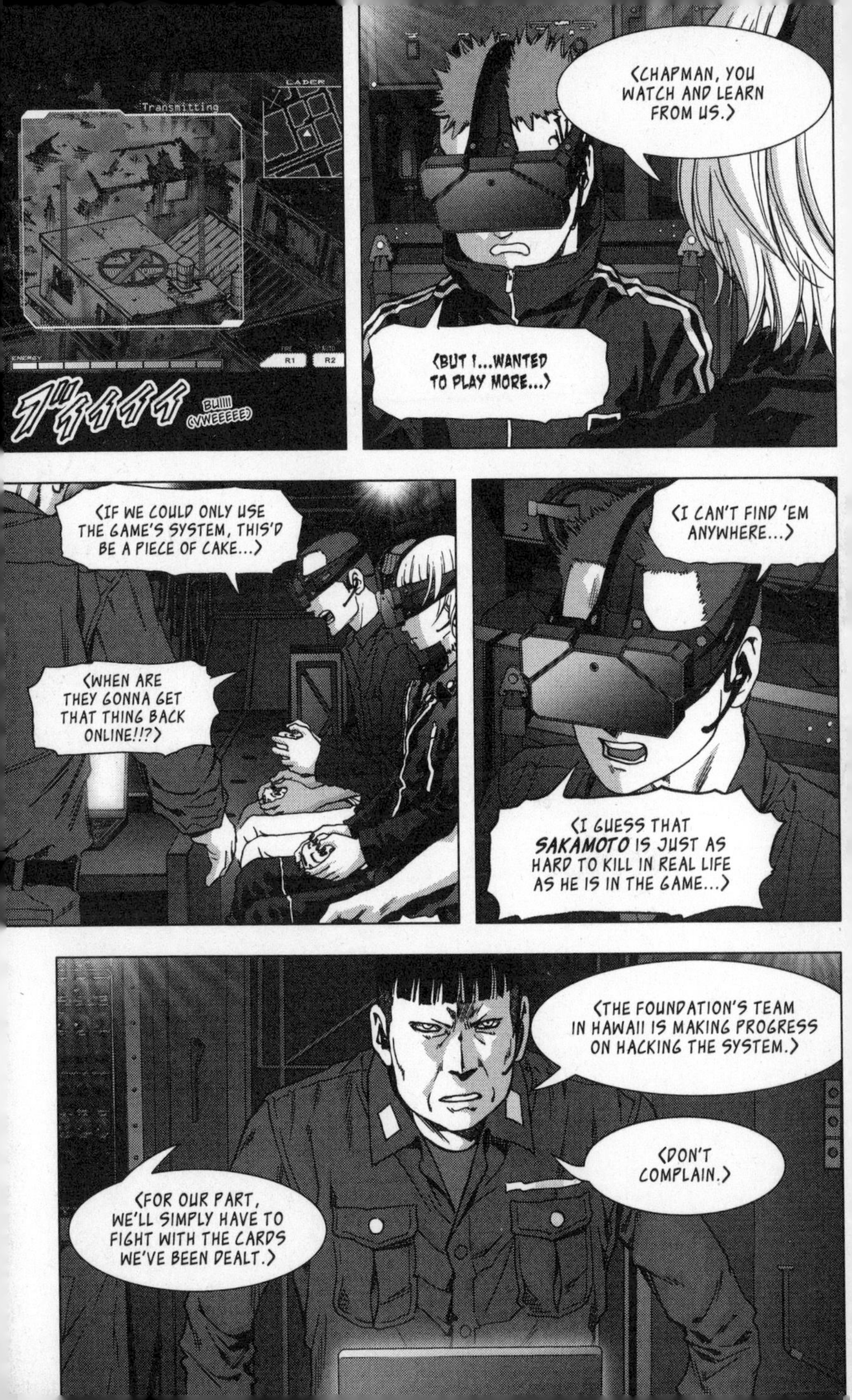
<CHAPMAN, YOU WATCH AND LEARN FROM US.>
<BUT I...WANTED TO PLAY MORE...>
Transmitting
LADER
ENEMY
FIRE
AUTO
R1
R2
ブィイイイ
BUIIII (VWEEEEE)
<I CAN'T FIND 'EM ANYWHERE...>
<I GUESS THAT SAKAMOTO IS JUST AS HARD TO KILL IN REAL LIFE AS HE IS IN THE GAME...>
<IF WE COULD ONLY USE THE GAME'S SYSTEM, THIS'D BE A PIECE OF CAKE...>
<WHEN ARE THEY GONNA GET THAT THING BACK ONLINE!!?>
<THE FOUNDATION'S TEAM IN HAWAII IS MAKING PROGRESS ON HACKING THE SYSTEM.>
<DON'T COMPLAIN.>
<FOR OUR PART, WE'LL SIMPLY HAVE TO FIGHT WITH THE CARDS WE'VE BEEN DEALT.>

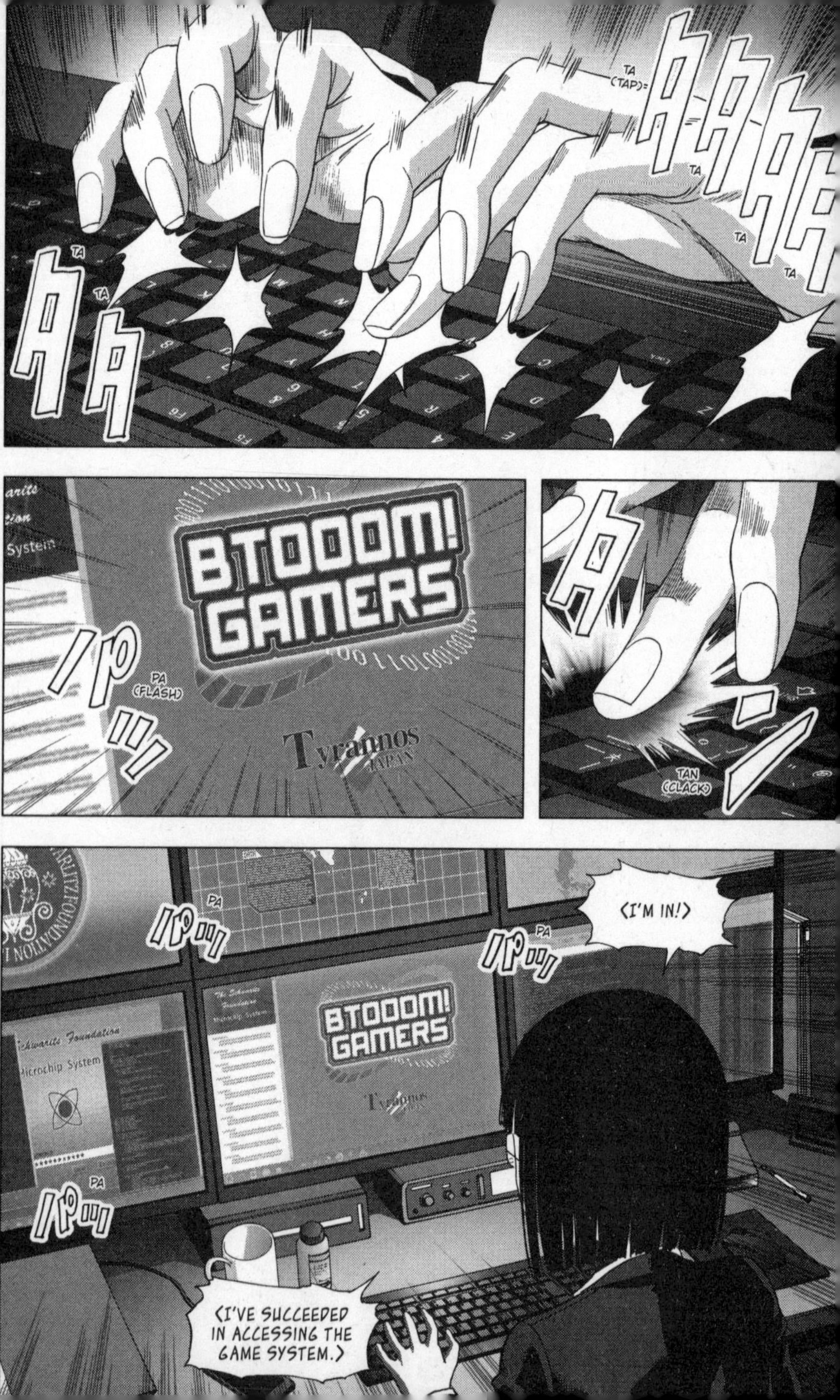
TA (TAP)
TA
TA
TA
TA
TA
TAN (CLACK)
PA (FLASH)
BTOOOM! GAMERS
Tyrannos JAPAN
System
<I'M IN!>
PA
PA
Schwarits Foundation
Microchip System
BTOOOM! GAMERS
Tyrannos
PA
<I'VE SUCCEEDED IN ACCESSING THE GAME SYSTEM.>

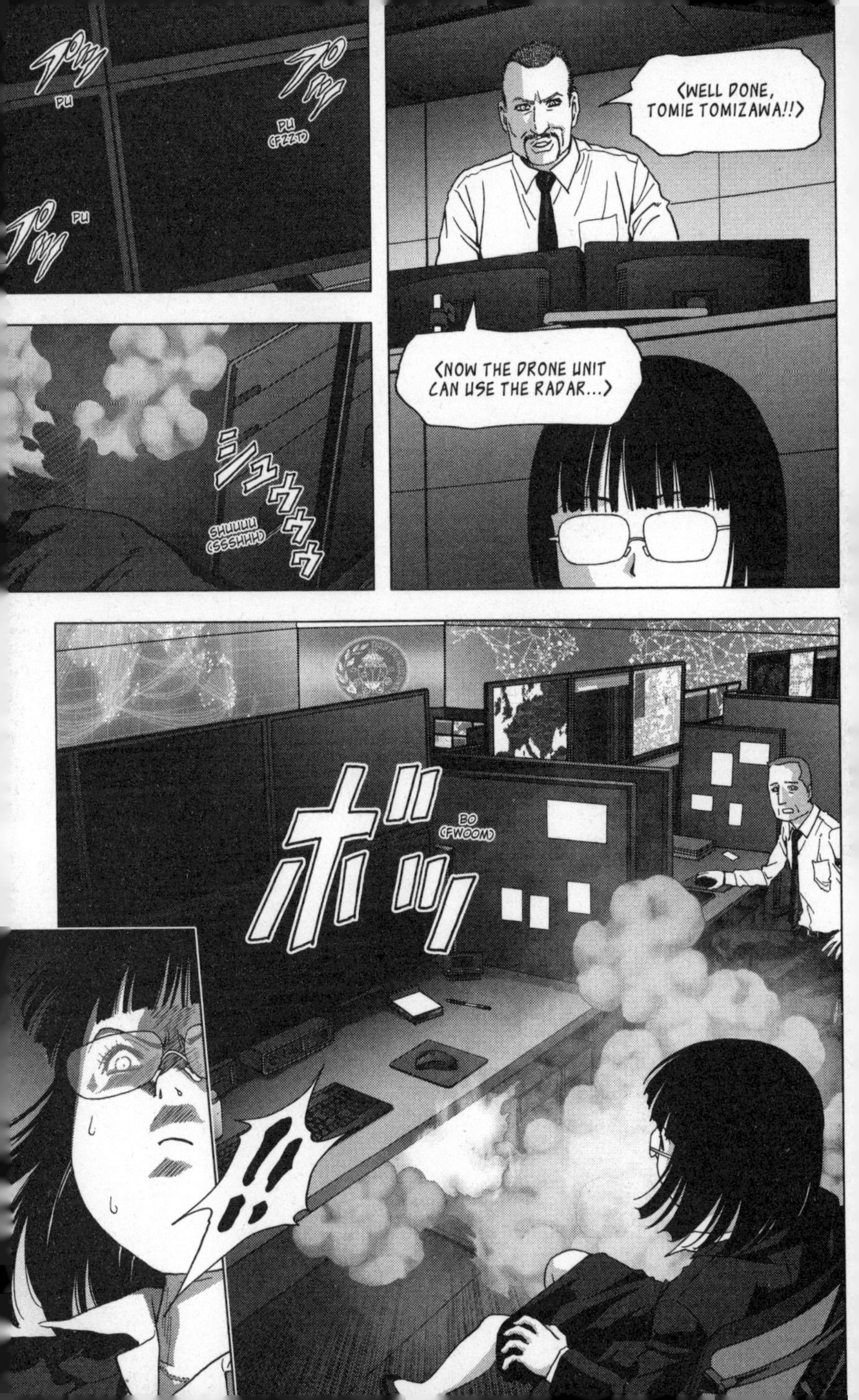

〈WELL DONE, TOMIE TOMIZAWA!!〉
PU
PU (FZZT)
PU
〈NOW THE DRONE UNIT CAN USE THE RADAR...〉
SHUUUU (SSSHHH)
BO (FWOOM)
!!

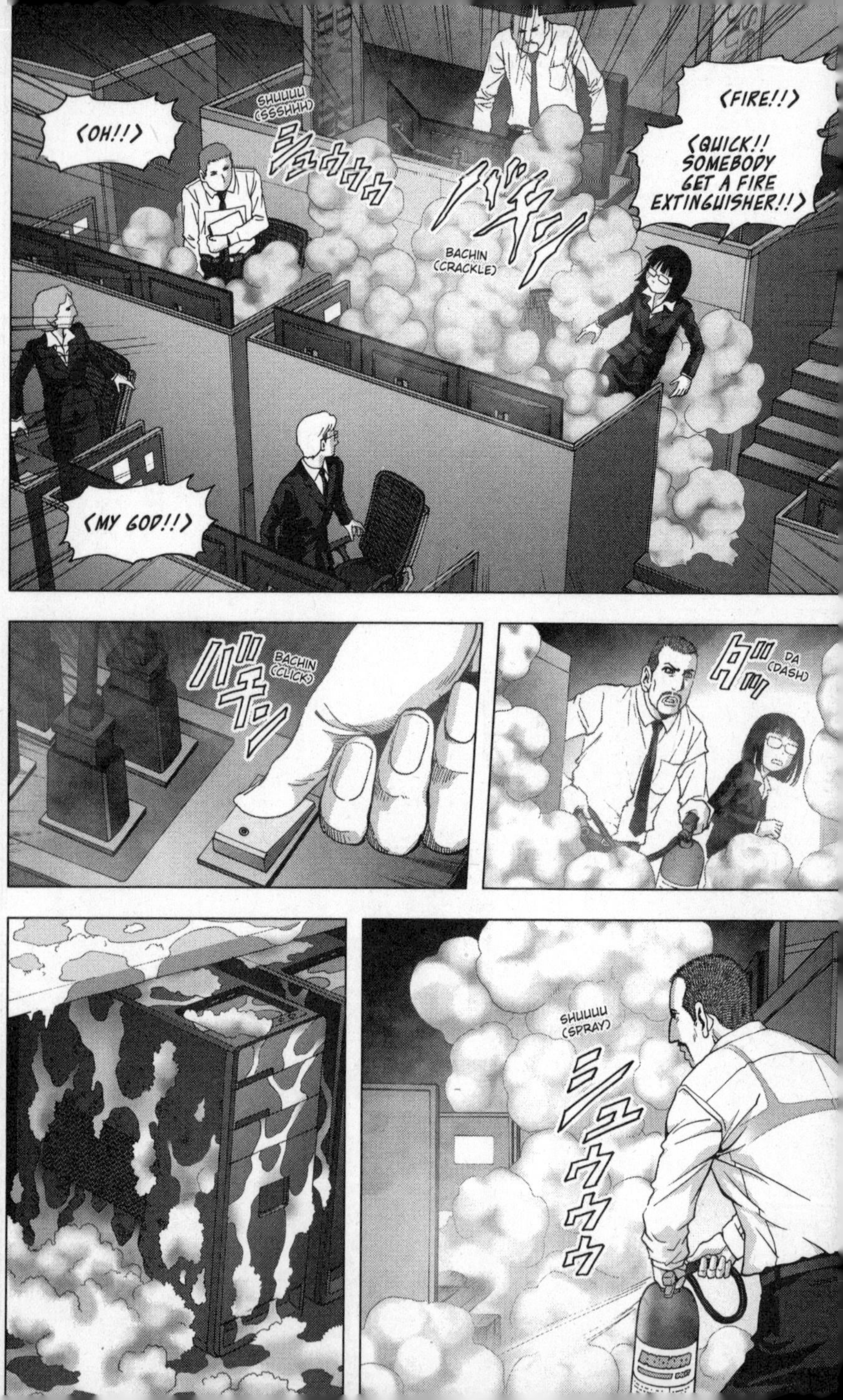
〈FIRE!!〉
〈QUICK!! SOMEBODY GET A FIRE EXTINGUISHER!!〉
BACHIN (CRACKLE)
バチン
SHUUUU (SSSHHH)
シュウウウウ
〈OH!!〉
〈MY GOD!!〉
DA (DASH)
ダッ
BACHIN (CLICK)
バチン
SHUUUU (SPRAY)
シュウウウ

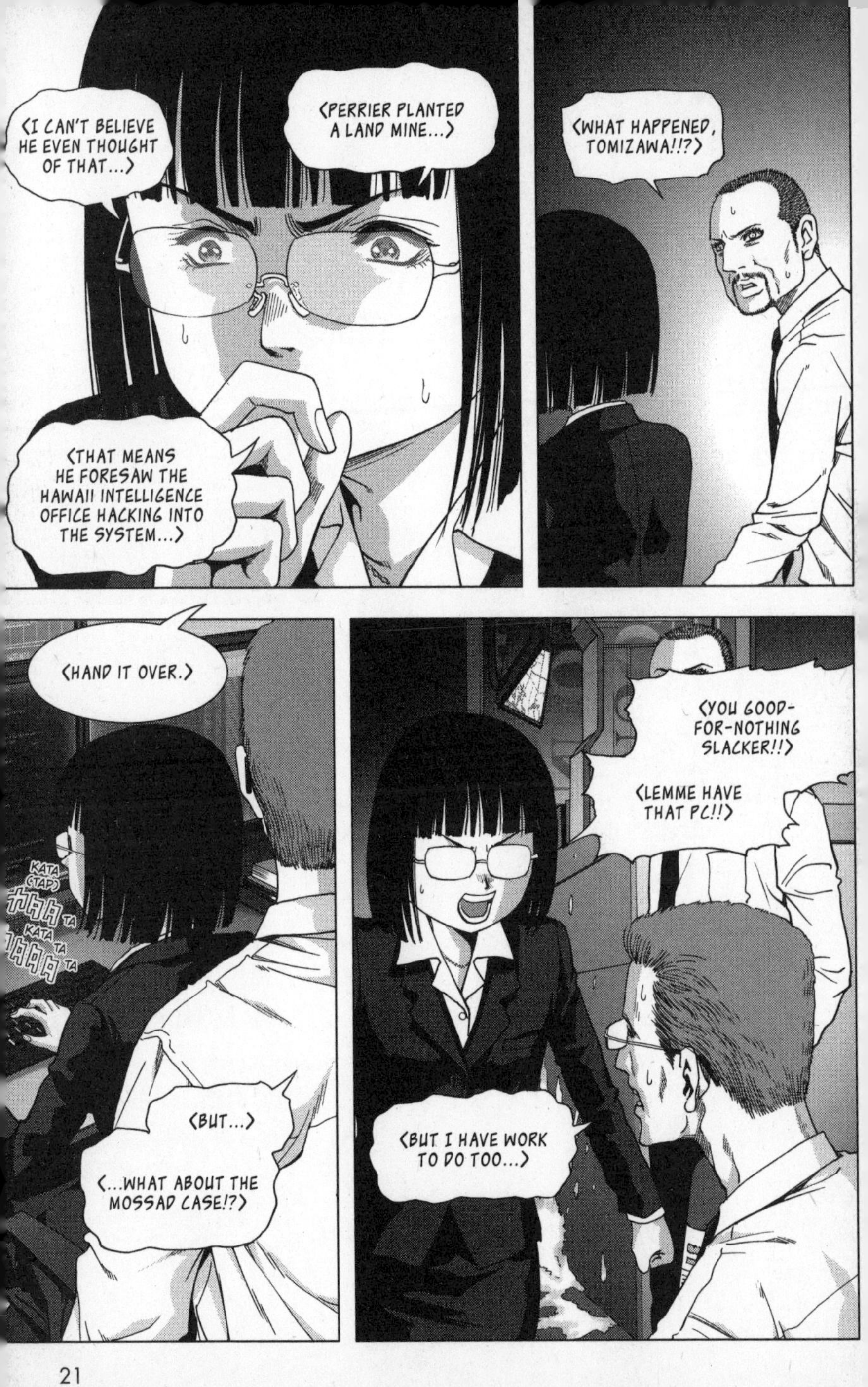
<WHAT HAPPENED, TOMIZAWA!!?>
<PERRIER PLANTED A LAND MINE...>
<I CAN'T BELIEVE HE EVEN THOUGHT OF THAT...>
<THAT MEANS HE FORESAW THE HAWAII INTELLIGENCE OFFICE HACKING INTO THE SYSTEM...>
<YOU GOOD-FOR-NOTHING SLACKER!!>
<LEMME HAVE THAT PC!!>
<BUT I HAVE WORK TO DO TOO...>
<HAND IT OVER.>
KATA (TAP) TA
KATA TA TA
<BUT...>
<...WHAT ABOUT THE MOSSAD CASE!?>

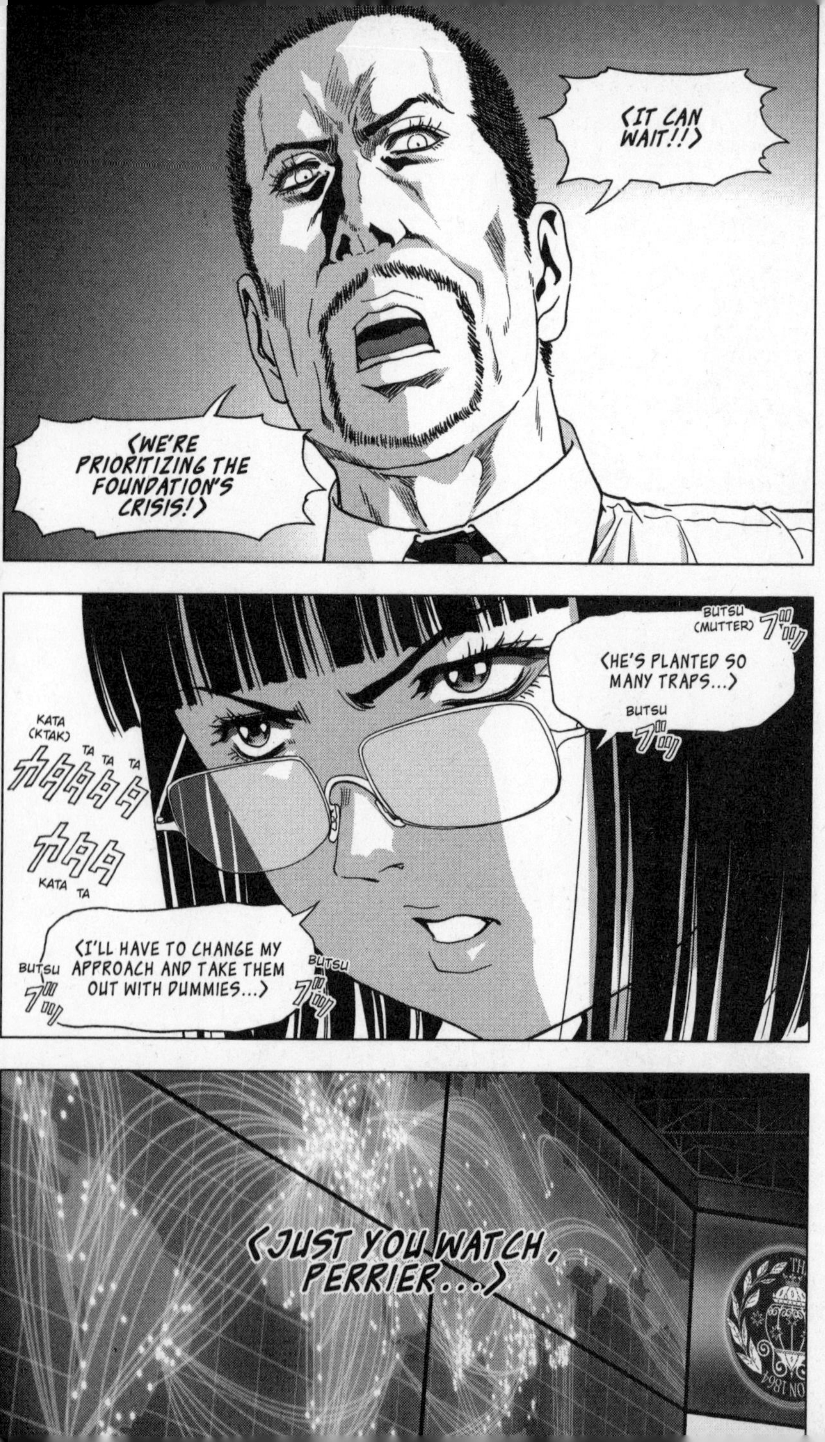
<IT CAN WAIT!!>
<WE'RE PRIORITIZING THE FOUNDATION'S CRISIS!>
BUTSU (MUTTER)
<HE'S PLANTED SO MANY TRAPS...>
BUTSU
KATA (KTAK) TA TA TA
KATA TA
<I'LL HAVE TO CHANGE MY APPROACH AND TAKE THEM OUT WITH DUMMIES...>
BUTSU
BUTSU
<JUST YOU WATCH, PERRIER...>

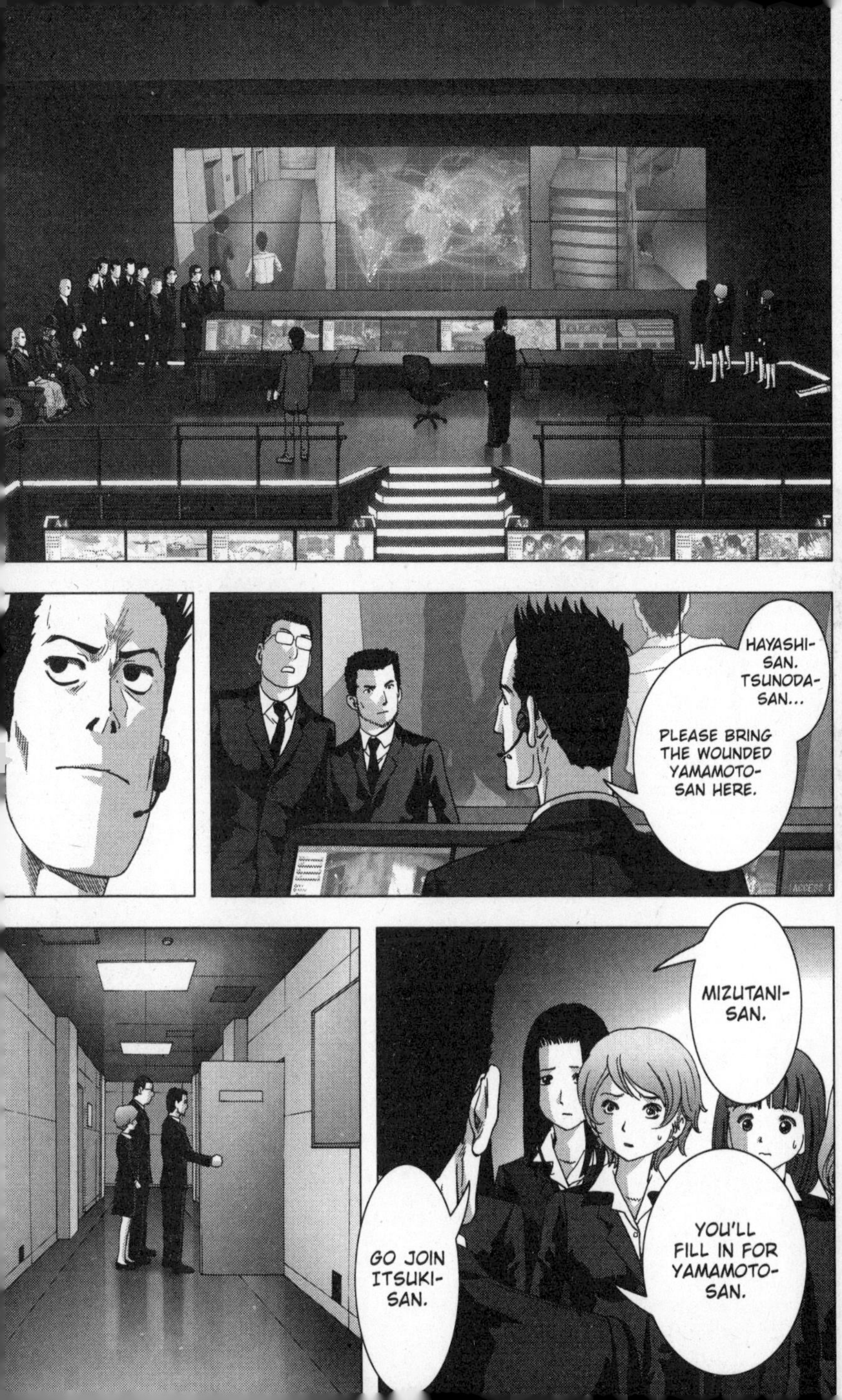
HAYASHI-SAN. TSUNODA-SAN...
PLEASE BRING THE WOUNDED YAMAMOTO-SAN HERE.
MIZUTANI-SAN.
YOU'LL FILL IN FOR YAMAMOTO-SAN.
GO JOIN ITSUKI-SAN.

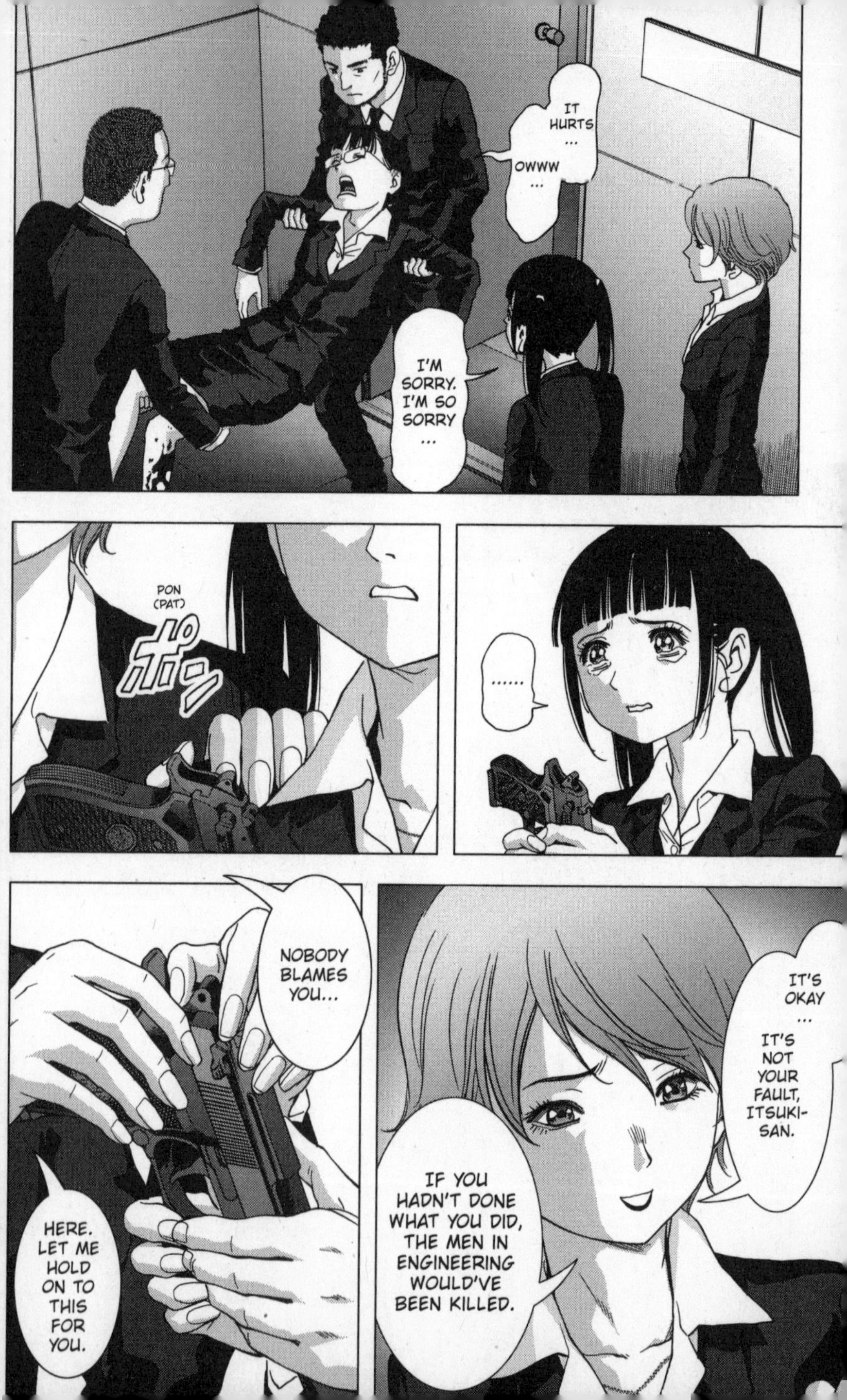
IT HURTS... OWWW...
I'M SORRY. I'M SO SORRY...
....
PON (PAT)
ポン
IT'S OKAY... IT'S NOT YOUR FAULT, ITSUKI-SAN.
IF YOU HADN'T DONE WHAT YOU DID, THE MEN IN ENGINEERING WOULD'VE BEEN KILLED.
NOBODY BLAMES YOU...
HERE. LET ME HOLD ON TO THIS FOR YOU.

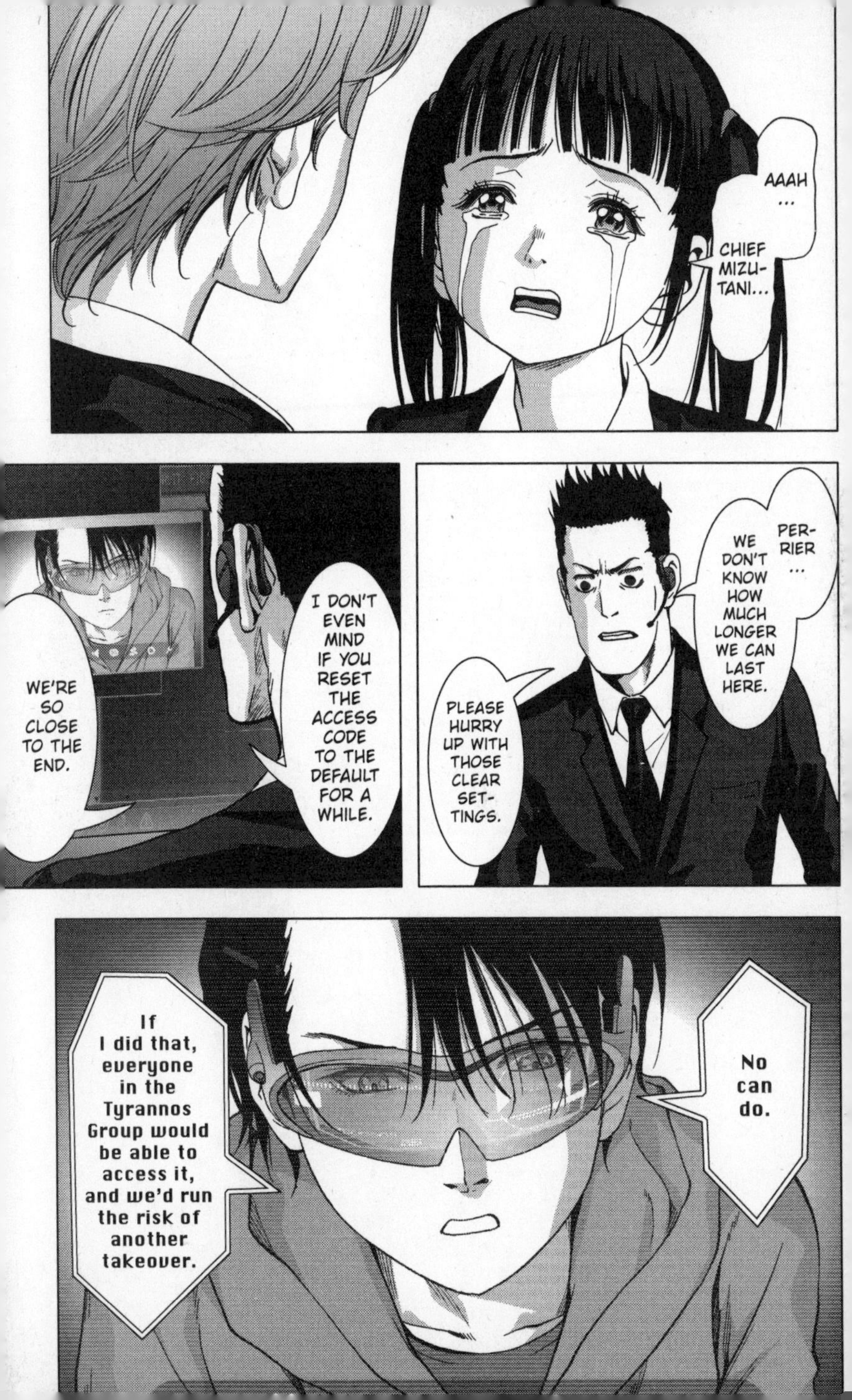
AAAH...
CHIEF MIZUTANI...
PERRIER...
WE DON'T KNOW HOW MUCH LONGER WE CAN LAST HERE.
PLEASE HURRY UP WITH THOSE CLEAR SETTINGS.
I DON'T EVEN MIND IF YOU RESET THE ACCESS CODE TO THE DEFAULT FOR A WHILE.
WE'RE SO CLOSE TO THE END.
No can do.
If I did that, everyone in the Tyrannos Group would be able to access it, and we'd run the risk of another takeover.

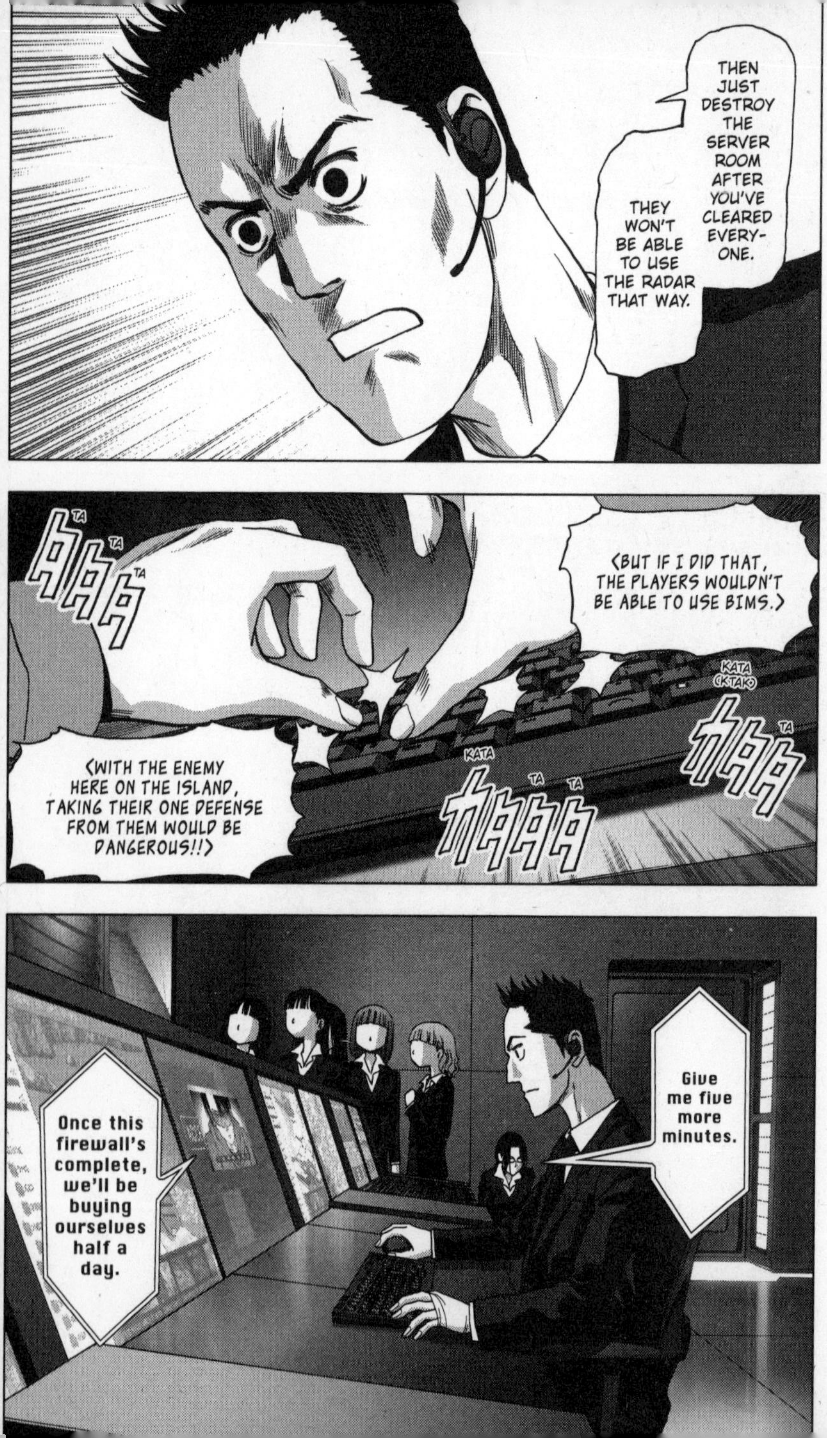
THEN JUST DESTROY THE SERVER ROOM AFTER YOU'VE CLEARED EVERY-ONE.
THEY WON'T BE ABLE TO USE THE RADAR THAT WAY.
<BUT IF I DID THAT, THE PLAYERS WOULDN'T BE ABLE TO USE BIMS.>
TA TA TA
KATA (KTAK)
TA
KATA
TA TA
<WITH THE ENEMY HERE ON THE ISLAND, TAKING THEIR ONE DEFENSE FROM THEM WOULD BE DANGEROUS!!>
Give me five more minutes.
Once this firewall's complete, we'll be buying ourselves half a day.

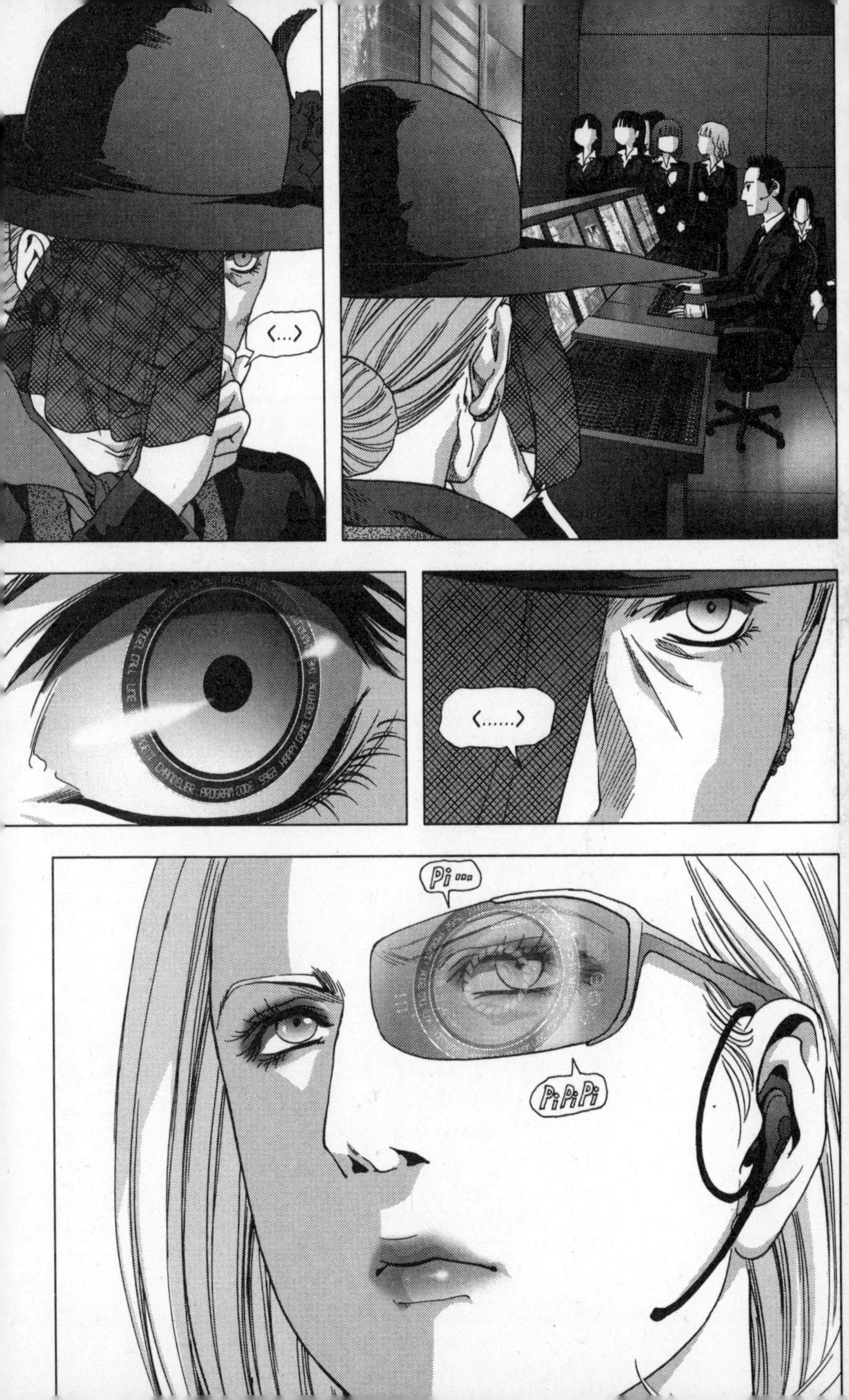
〈...〉
〈......〉
CHANDELIER PROGRAM CODE 5963 HAPPY GAME CREATOR
Pi...
PiPiPi

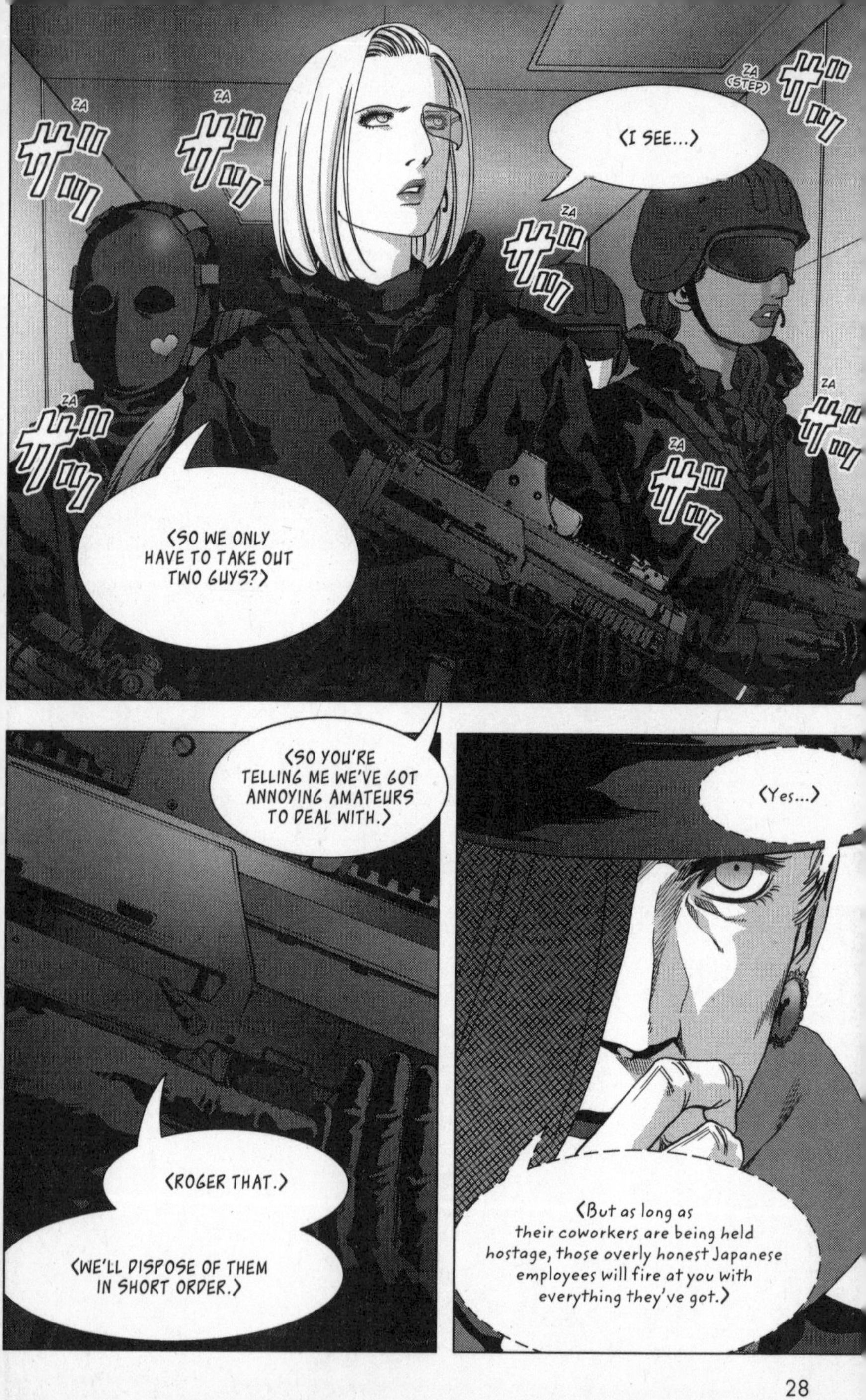
ZA (STEP)
ZA
ZA
ZA
〈I SEE...〉
ZA
ZA
ZA
〈SO WE ONLY HAVE TO TAKE OUT TWO GUYS?〉
〈Yes...〉
〈But as long as their coworkers are being held hostage, those overly honest Japanese employees will fire at you with everything they've got.〉
〈SO YOU'RE TELLING ME WE'VE GOT ANNOYING AMATEURS TO DEAL WITH.〉
〈ROGER THAT.〉
〈WE'LL DISPOSE OF THEM IN SHORT ORDER.〉

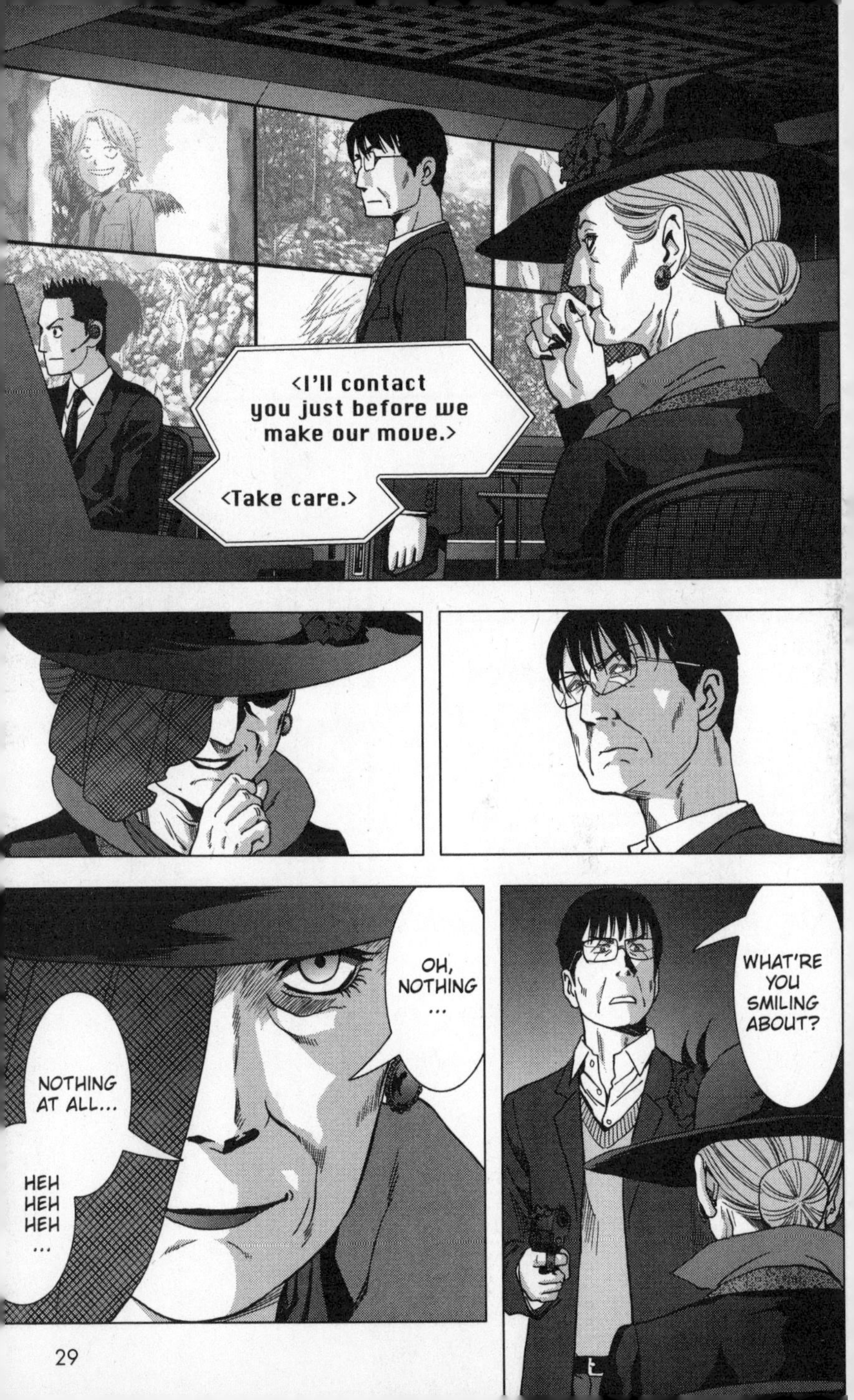
<I'll contact you just before we make our move.>
<Take care.>
WHAT'RE YOU SMILING ABOUT?
OH, NOTHING ...
NOTHING AT ALL...
HEH HEH HEH ...

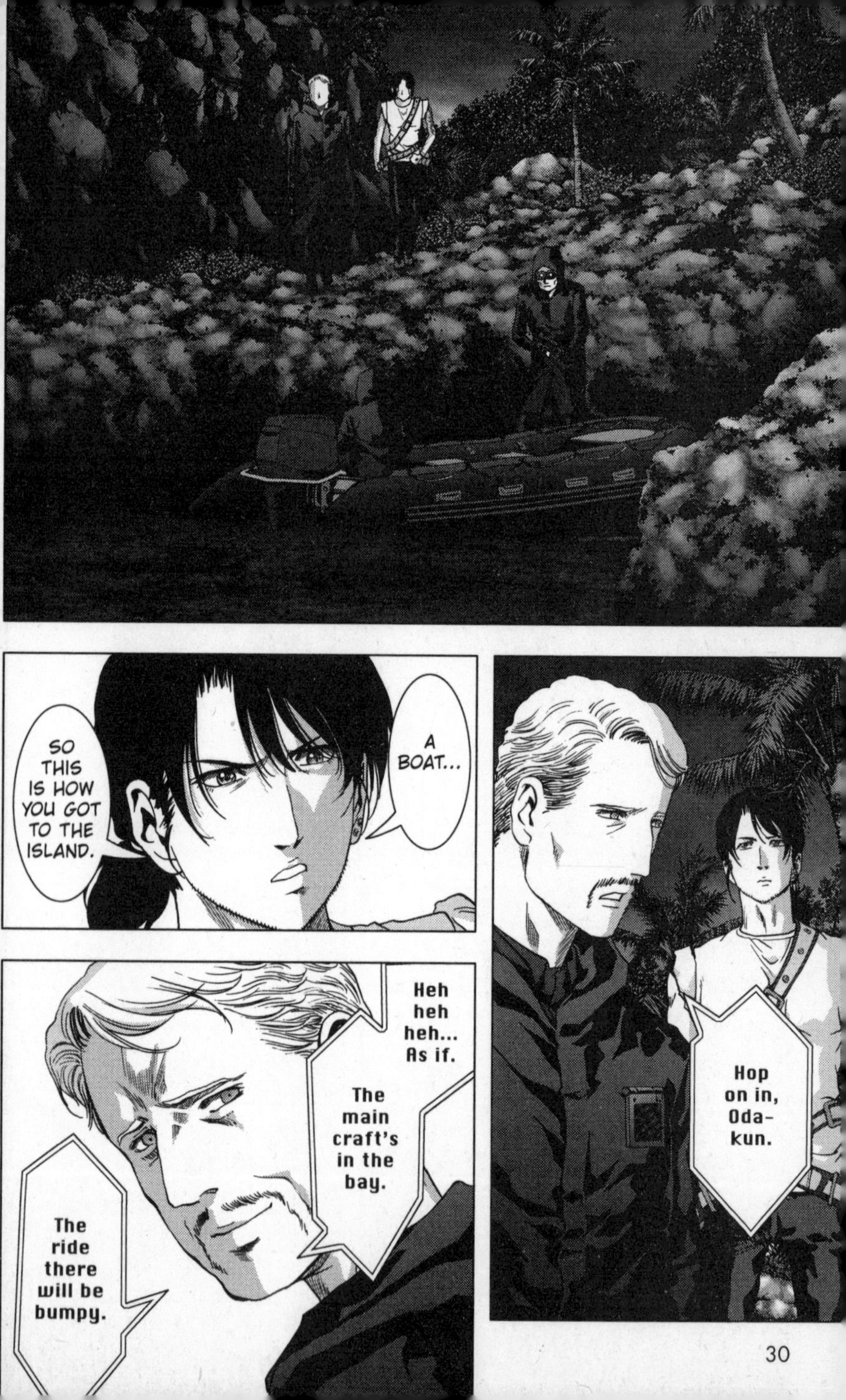
Hop on in, Oda-kun.
A BOAT...
SO THIS IS HOW YOU GOT TO THE ISLAND.
Heh heh heh... As if.
The main craft's in the bay.
The ride there will be bumpy.

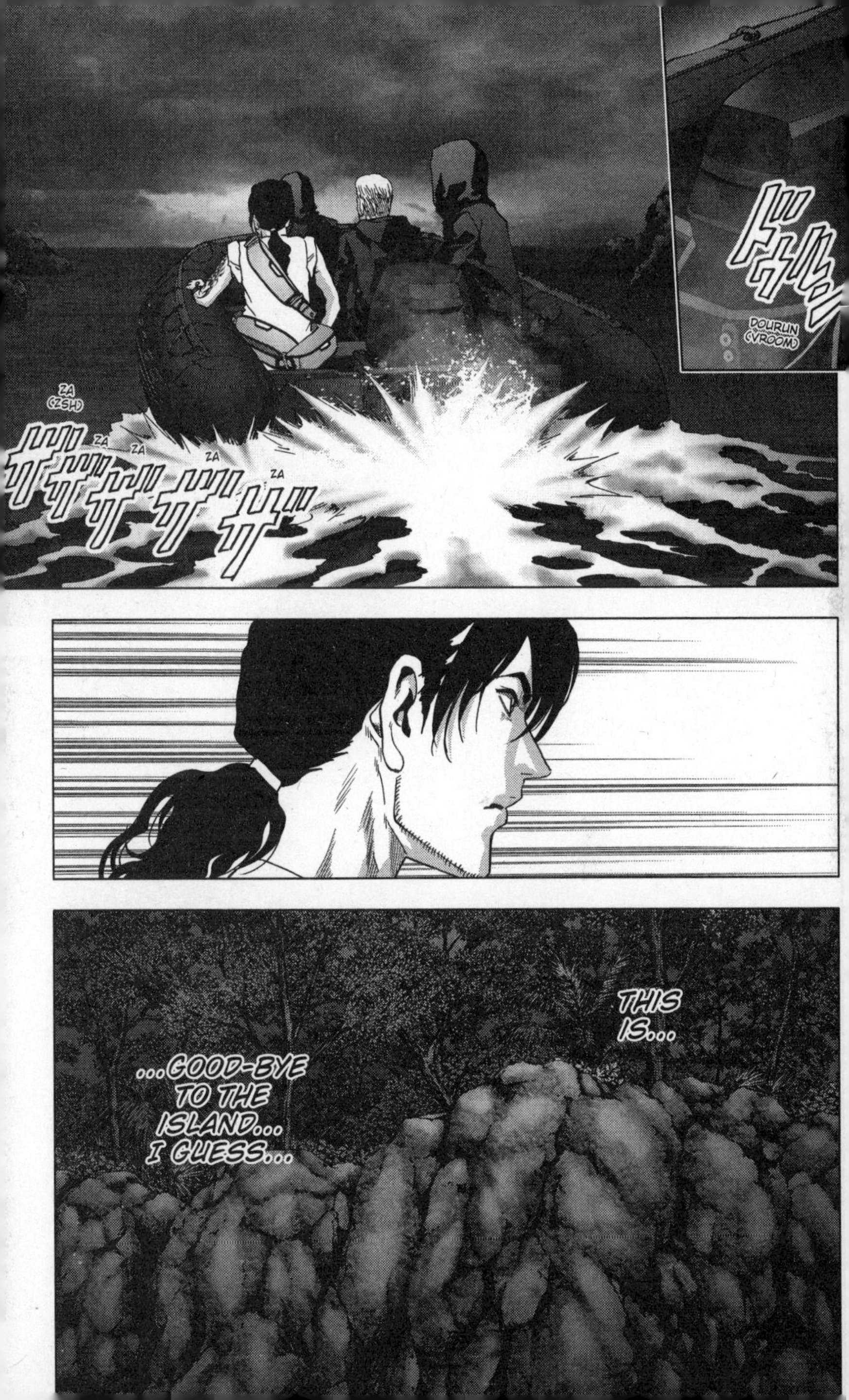
DOURUN (VROOM)
ZA (ZSHD)
ZA
ZA
ZA
ZA
THIS IS...
...GOOD-BYE TO THE ISLAND... I GUESS...

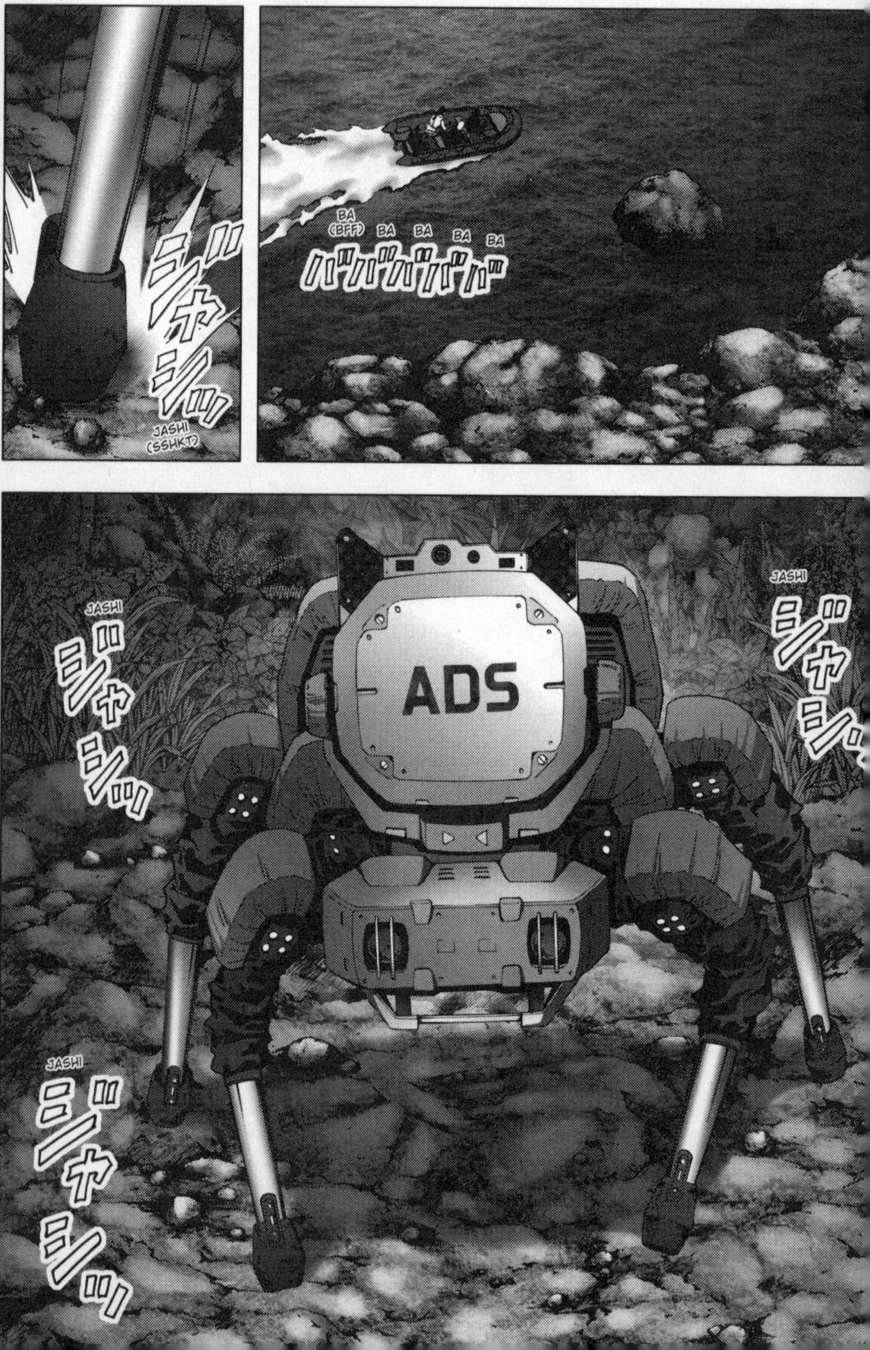
BA (BFF) BA BA BA BA
JASHI (SSHKT)
JASHI
JASHI
JASHI

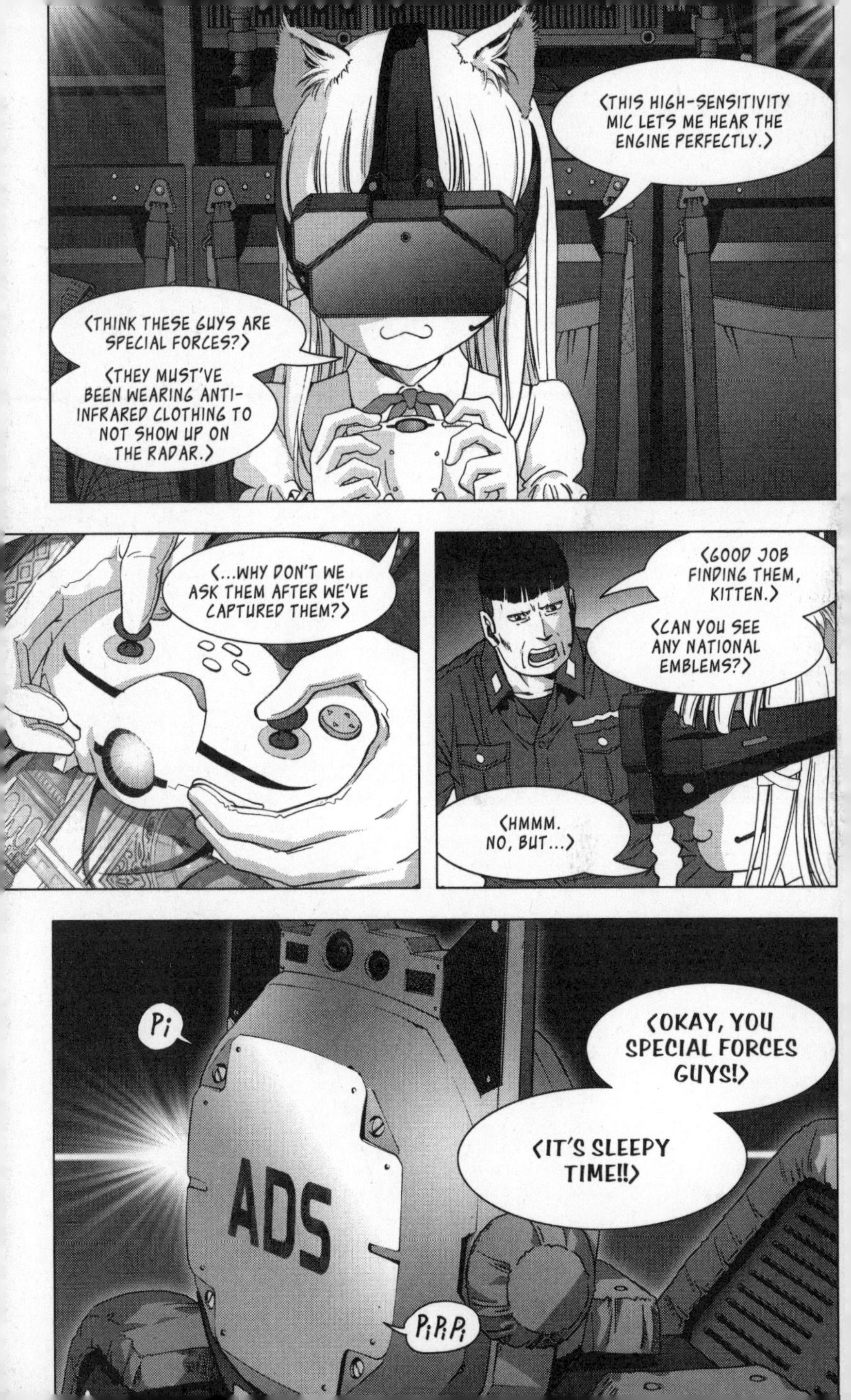
⟨THIS HIGH-SENSITIVITY MIC LETS ME HEAR THE ENGINE PERFECTLY.⟩
⟨THINK THESE GUYS ARE SPECIAL FORCES?⟩
⟨THEY MUST'VE BEEN WEARING ANTI-INFRARED CLOTHING TO NOT SHOW UP ON THE RADAR.⟩
⟨GOOD JOB FINDING THEM, KITTEN.⟩
⟨CAN YOU SEE ANY NATIONAL EMBLEMS?⟩
⟨HMMM. NO, BUT...⟩
⟨...WHY DON'T WE ASK THEM AFTER WE'VE CAPTURED THEM?⟩
⟨OKAY, YOU SPECIAL FORCES GUYS!⟩
Pi
⟨IT'S SLEEPY TIME!!⟩
ADS
PiPiPi

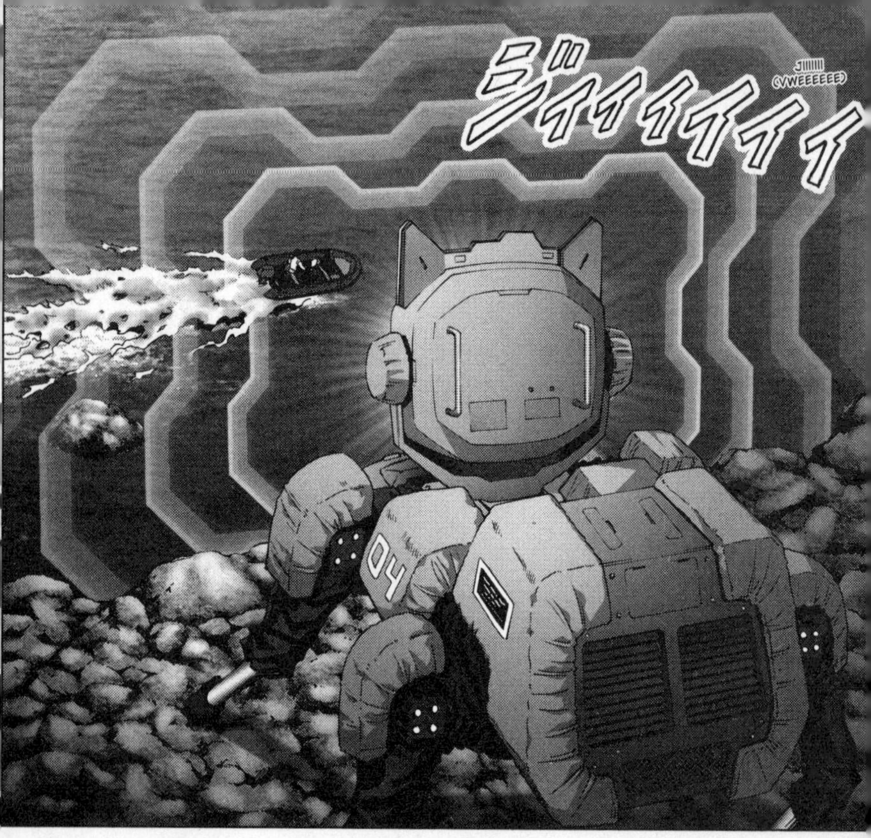
ジイイイイイイ
JIIIIIII
(VWEEEEEEE)
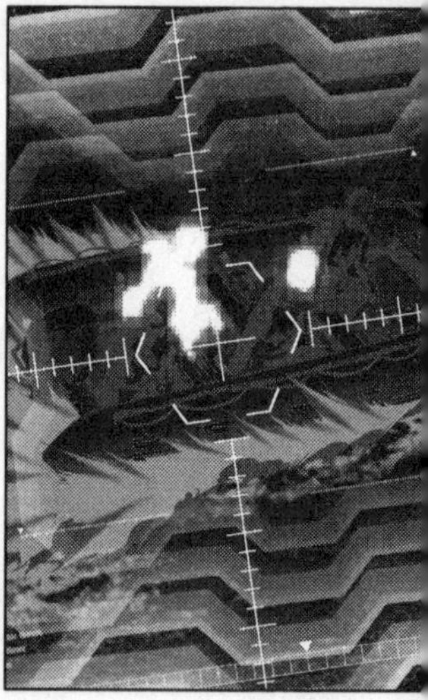
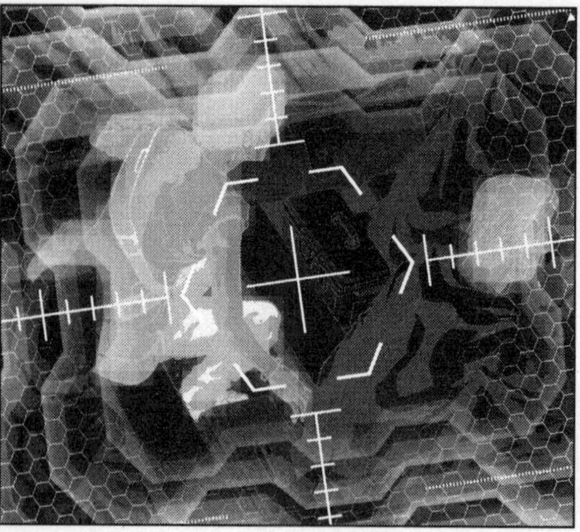

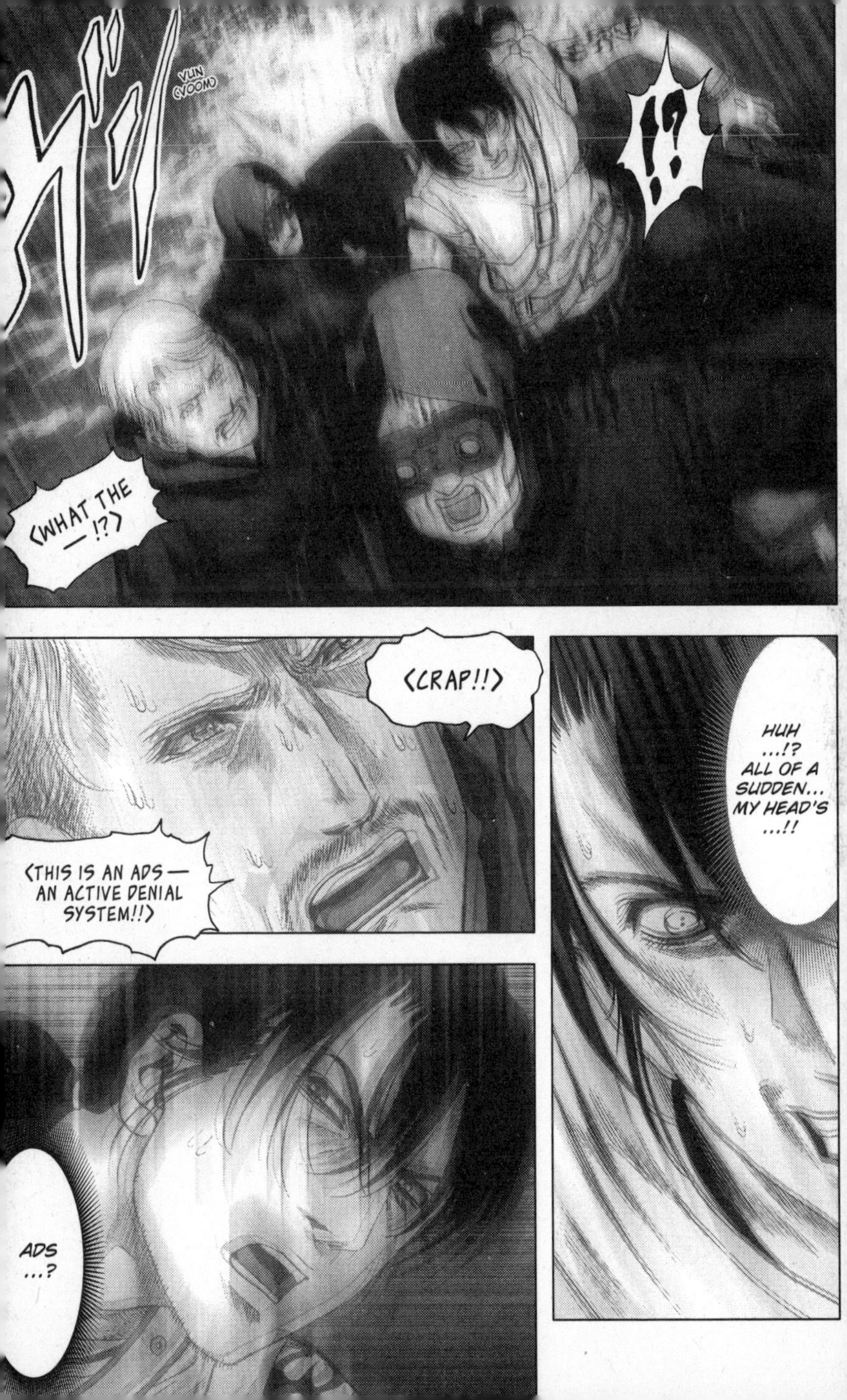
!?
VUN (VOOM)
〈WHAT THE—!?〉
HUH ...!? ALL OF A SUDDEN... MY HEAD'S ...!!
〈CRAP!!〉
〈THIS IS AN ADS— AN ACTIVE DENIAL SYSTEM!!〉
ADS ...?

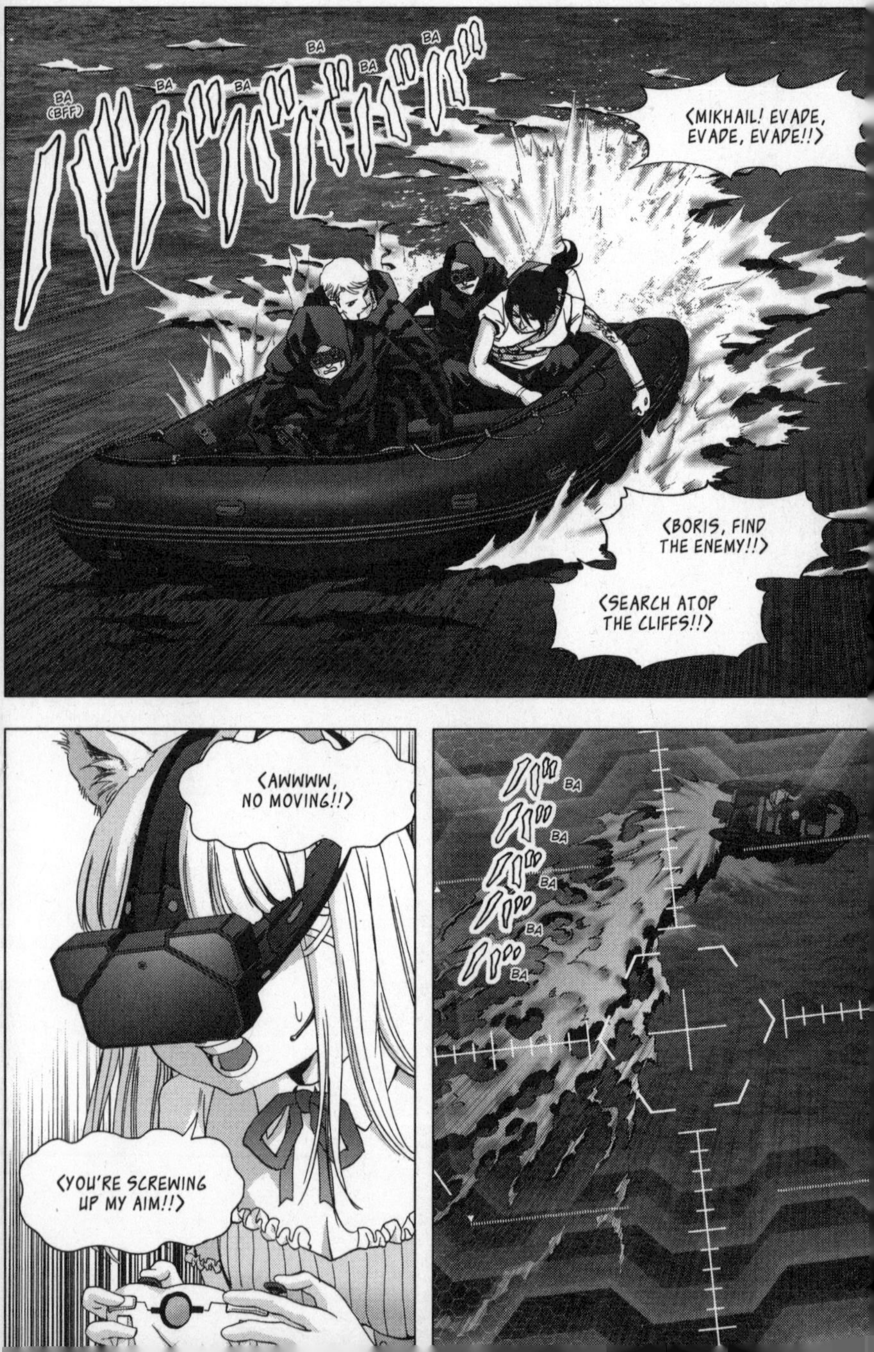

〈MIKHAIL! EVADE, EVADE, EVADE!!〉
BA
BA
BA
BA
BA
BA (BFF)
〈BORIS, FIND THE ENEMY!!〉
〈SEARCH ATOP THE CLIFFS!!〉
BA
BA
BA
BA
BA
〈AWWWW, NO MOVING!!〉
〈YOU'RE SCREWING UP MY AIM!!〉

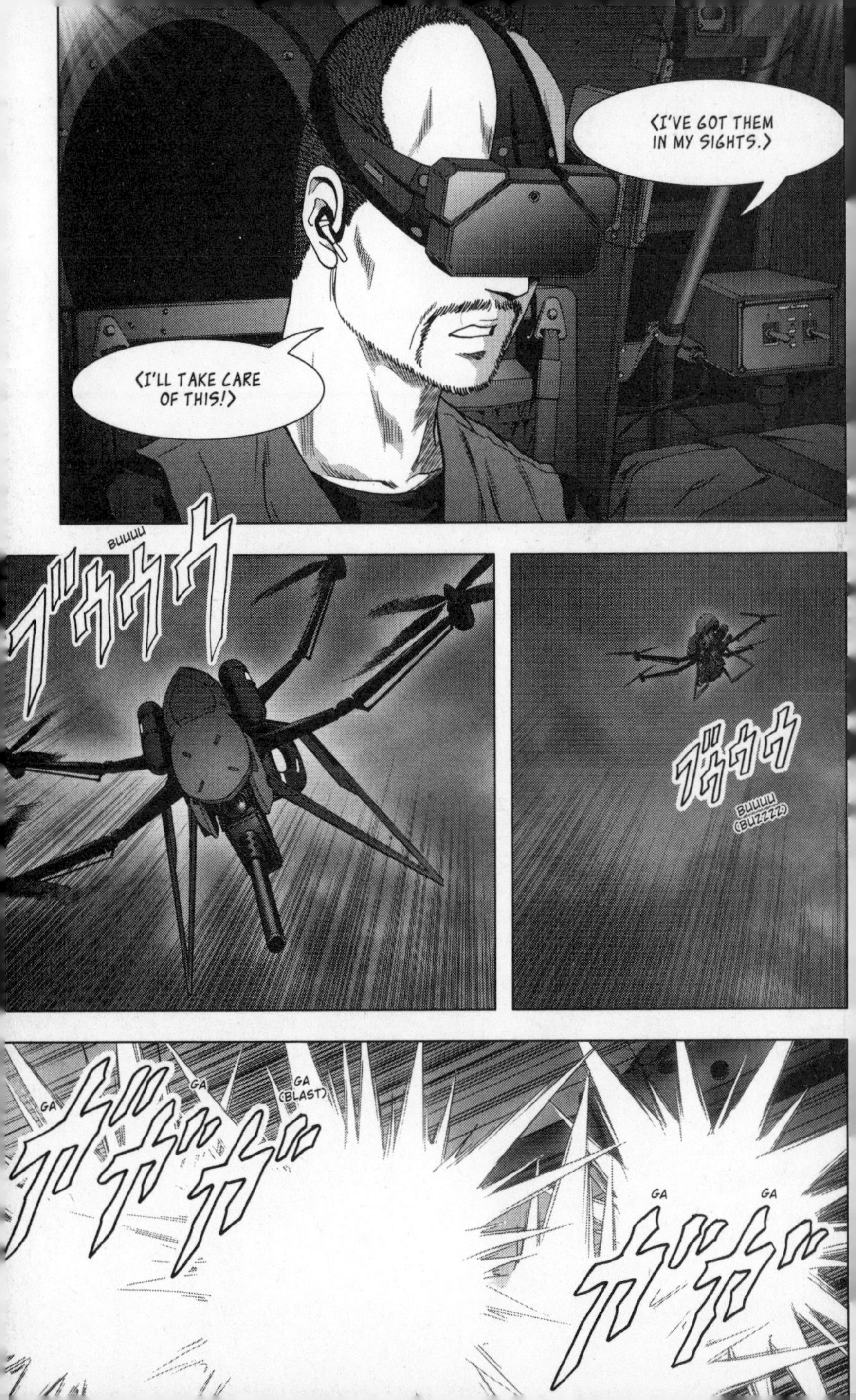
<I'VE GOT THEM IN MY SIGHTS.>
<I'LL TAKE CARE OF THIS!>
BUUUU (BUZZZZ)
BUUUU
GA
GA
GA
GA (BLAST)
GA

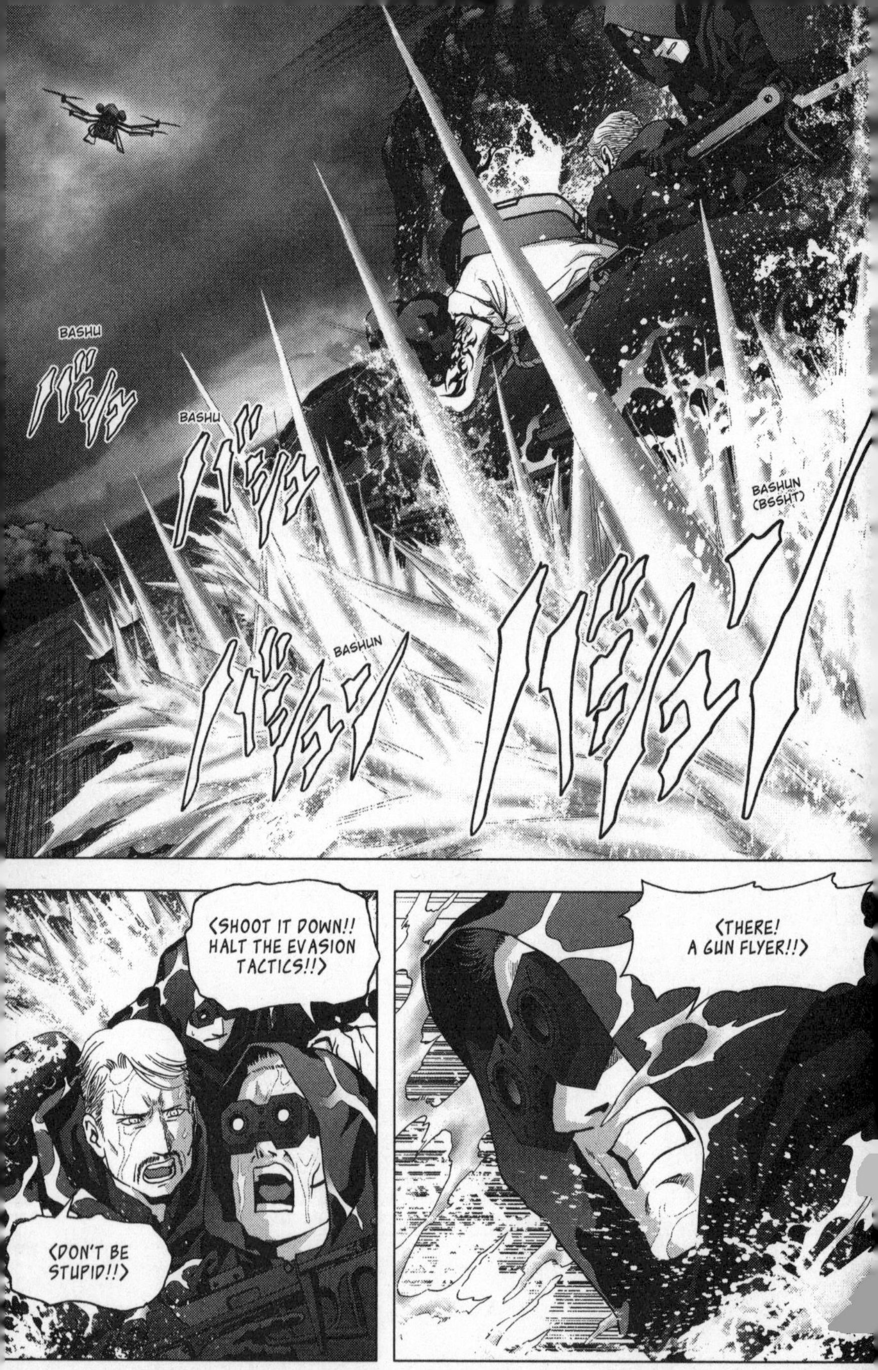
BASHUN
(BSSHT)
BASHUN
BASHU
BASHU
<THERE!
A GUN FLYER!!>
<SHOOT IT DOWN!!
HALT THE EVASION
TACTICS!!>
<DON'T BE
STUPID!!>

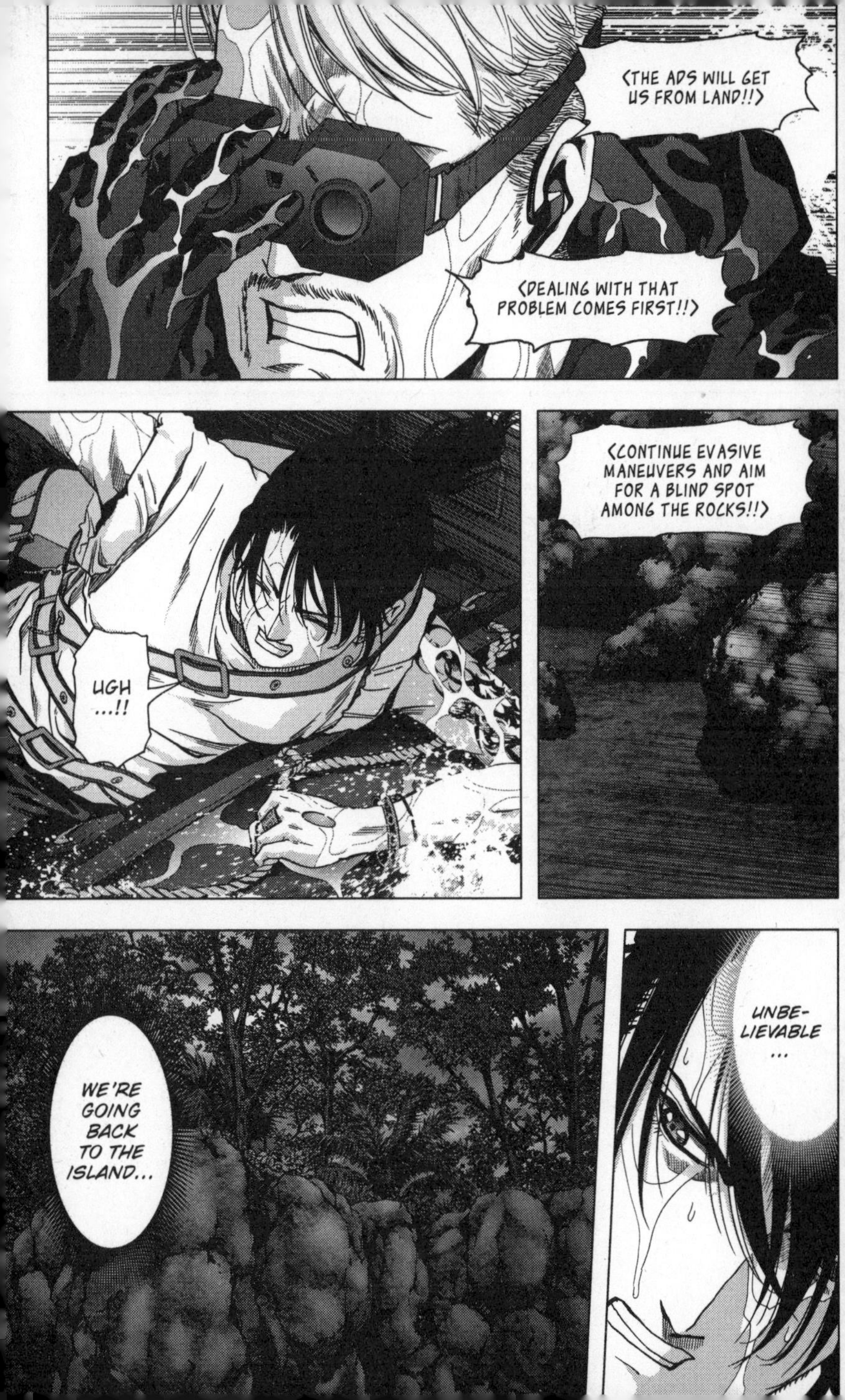
<THE ADS WILL GET US FROM LAND!!>
<DEALING WITH THAT PROBLEM COMES FIRST!!>
<CONTINUE EVASIVE MANEUVERS AND AIM FOR A BLIND SPOT AMONG THE ROCKS!!>
UGH ...!!
UNBE-LIEVABLE ...
WE'RE GOING BACK TO THE ISLAND...

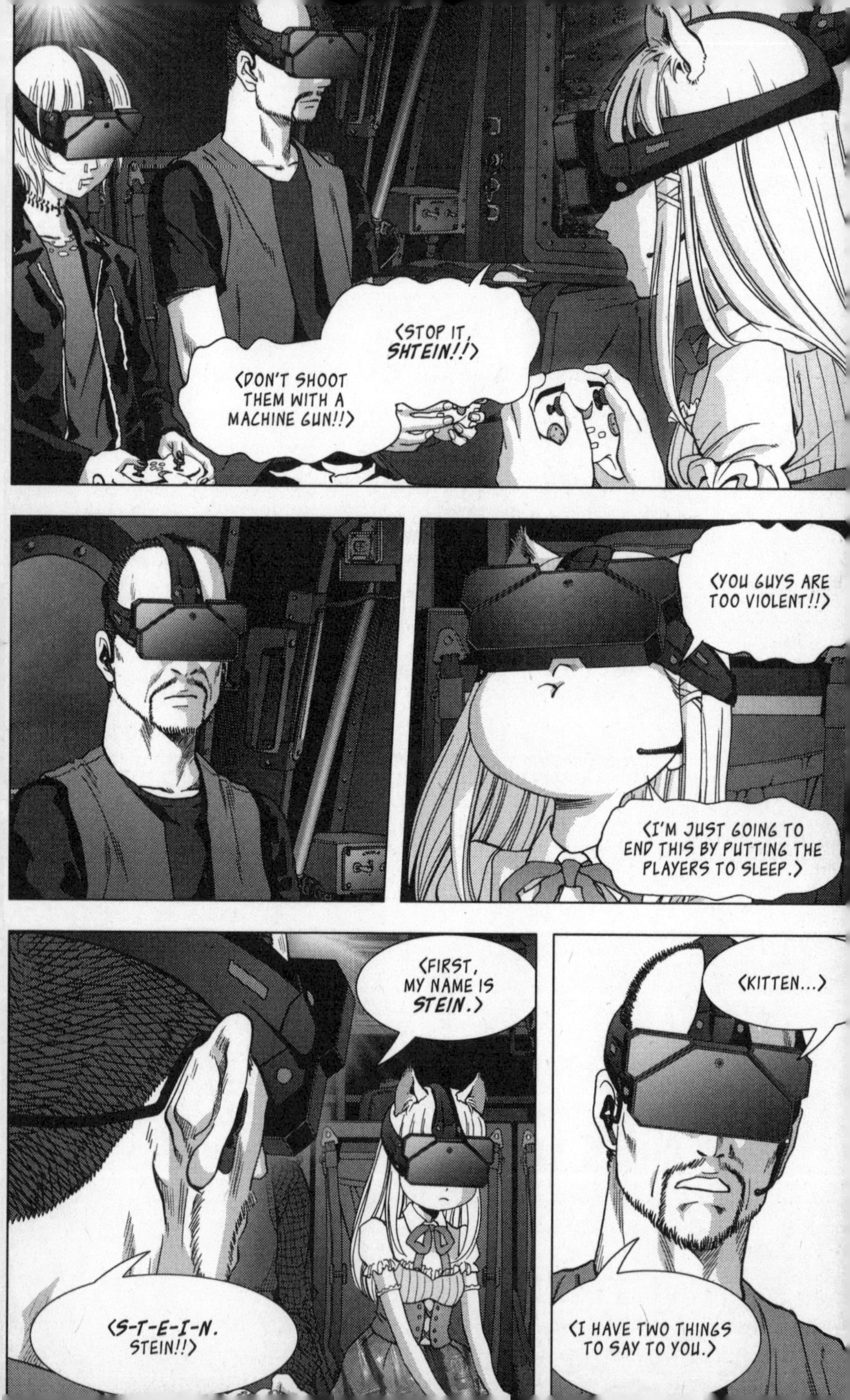
<STOP IT, SHTEIN!!>
<DON'T SHOOT THEM WITH A MACHINE GUN!!>
<YOU GUYS ARE TOO VIOLENT!!>
<I'M JUST GOING TO END THIS BY PUTTING THE PLAYERS TO SLEEP.>
<KITTEN...>
<I HAVE TWO THINGS TO SAY TO YOU.>
<FIRST, MY NAME IS STEIN.>
<S-T-E-I-N. STEIN!!>

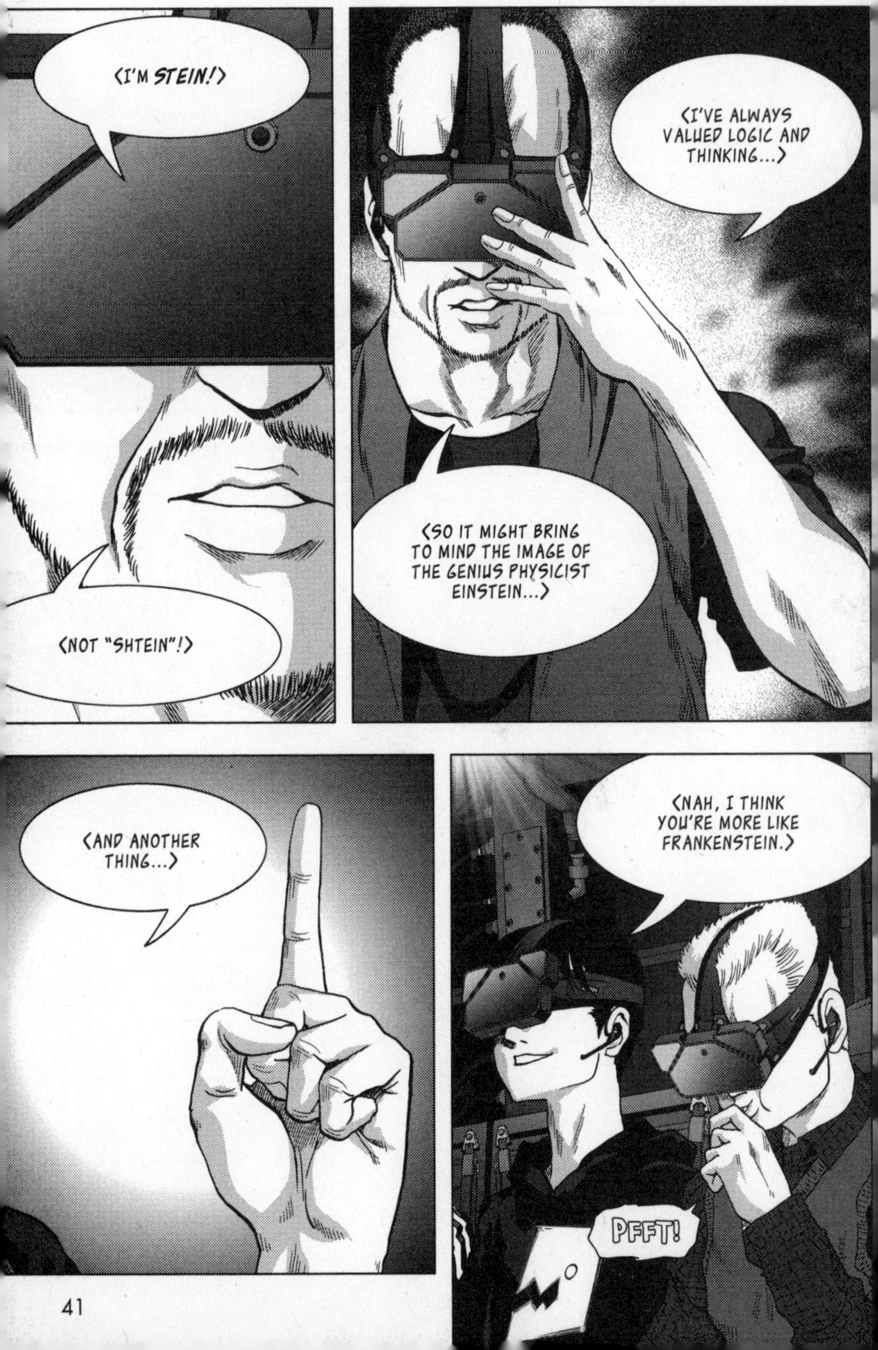

⟨I'VE ALWAYS VALUED LOGIC AND THINKING...⟩
⟨SO IT MIGHT BRING TO MIND THE IMAGE OF THE GENIUS PHYSICIST EINSTEIN...⟩
⟨I'M STEIN!⟩
⟨NOT "SHTEIN"!⟩
⟨NAH, I THINK YOU'RE MORE LIKE FRANKENSTEIN.⟩
PFFT!
⟨AND ANOTHER THING...⟩

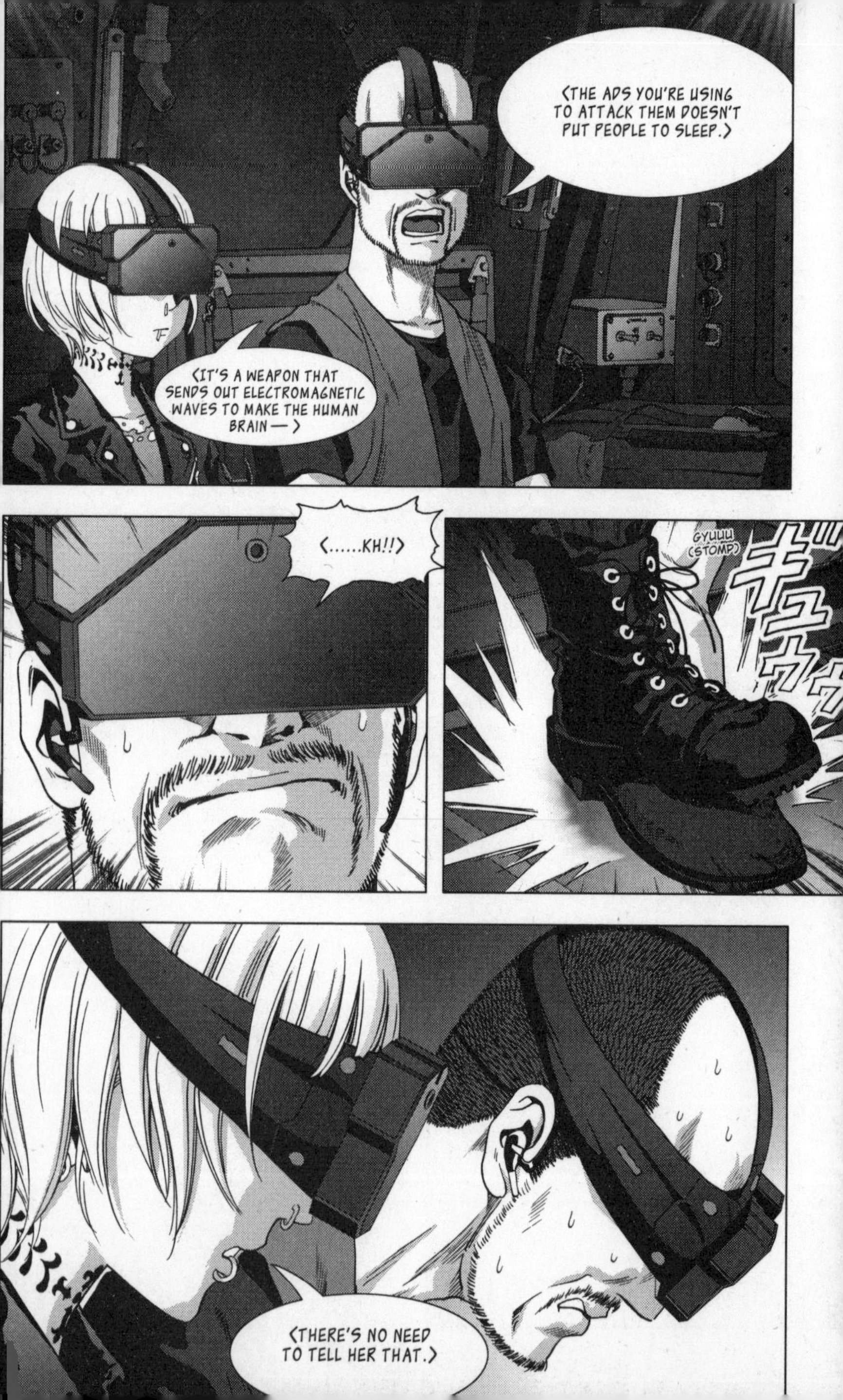

<THE ADS YOU'RE USING TO ATTACK THEM DOESN'T PUT PEOPLE TO SLEEP.>
<IT'S A WEAPON THAT SENDS OUT ELECTROMAGNETIC WAVES TO MAKE THE HUMAN BRAIN —>
GYUUU (STOMP)
<......KH!!>
<THERE'S NO NEED TO TELL HER THAT.>

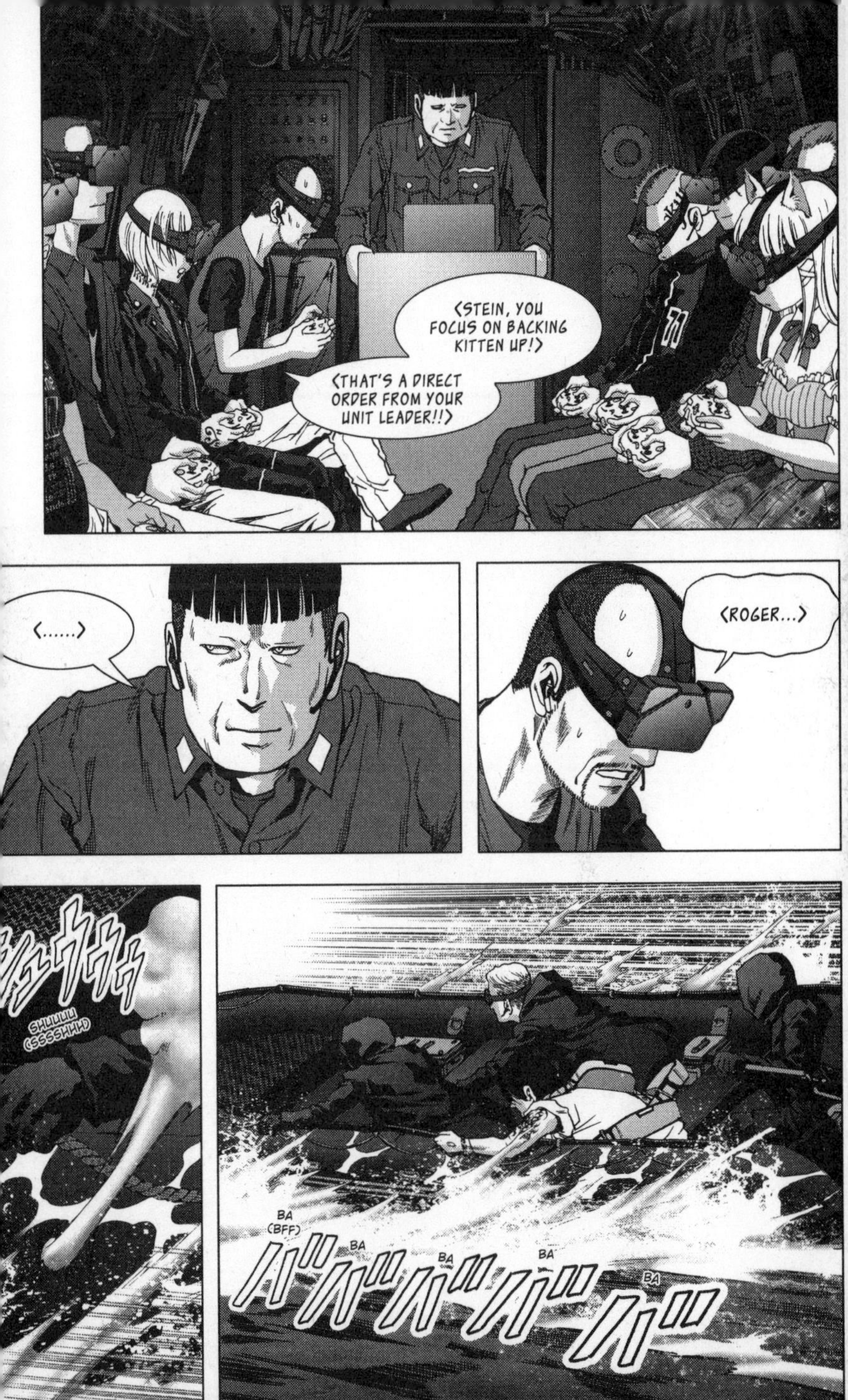
‹STEIN, YOU FOCUS ON BACKING KITTEN UP!›
‹THAT'S A DIRECT ORDER FROM YOUR UNIT LEADER!!›
‹ROGER...›
‹......›
BA (BFF)
BA
BA
BA
BA
SHUUUU (SSSSHHH)

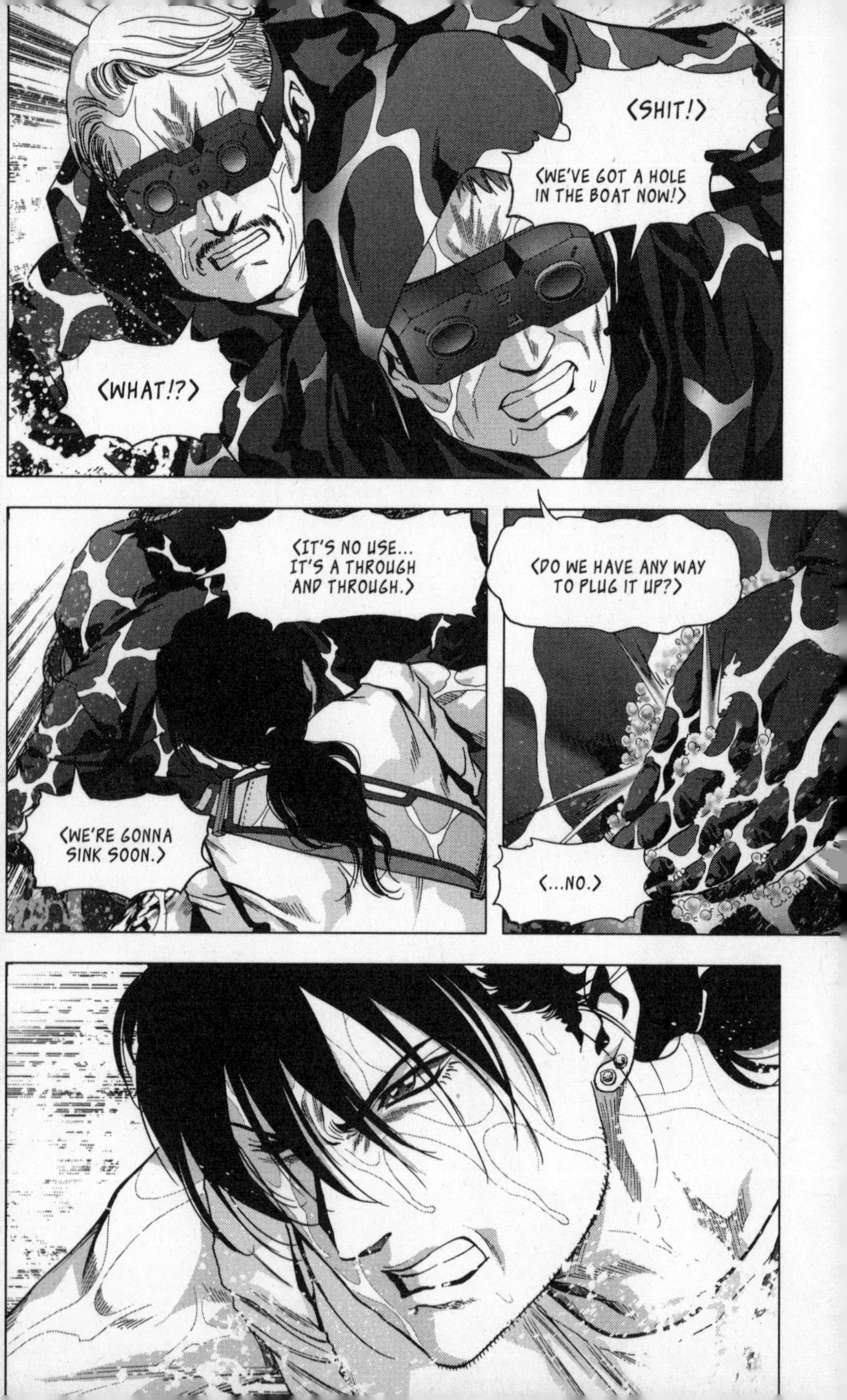
<SHIT!>
<WE'VE GOT A HOLE IN THE BOAT NOW!>
<WHAT!?>
<DO WE HAVE ANY WAY TO PLUG IT UP?>
<...NO.>
<IT'S NO USE... IT'S A THROUGH AND THROUGH.>
<WE'RE GONNA SINK SOON.>

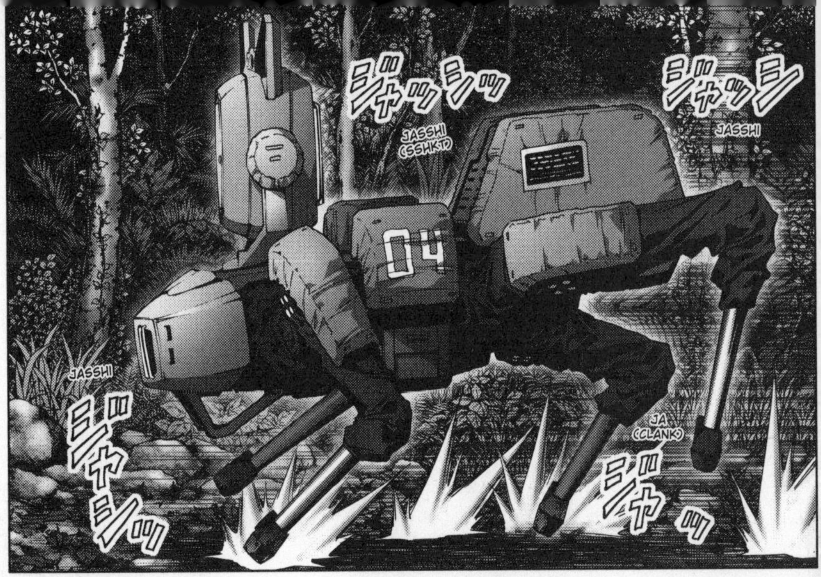
JASSHI
JASSHI
(SSHKT)
JA
(CLANK)
JASSHI

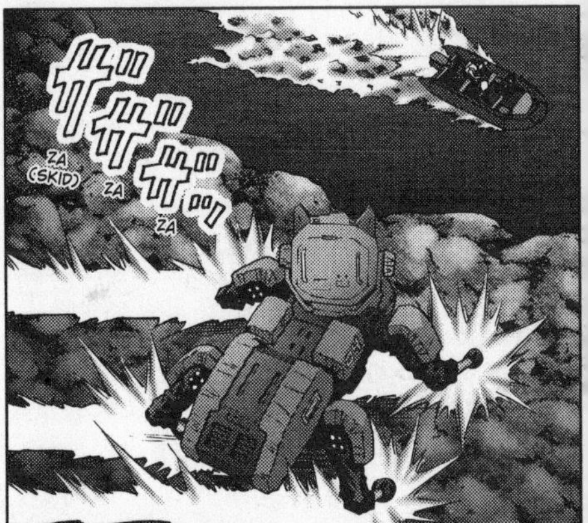
ZA
(SKID)
ZA
ZA

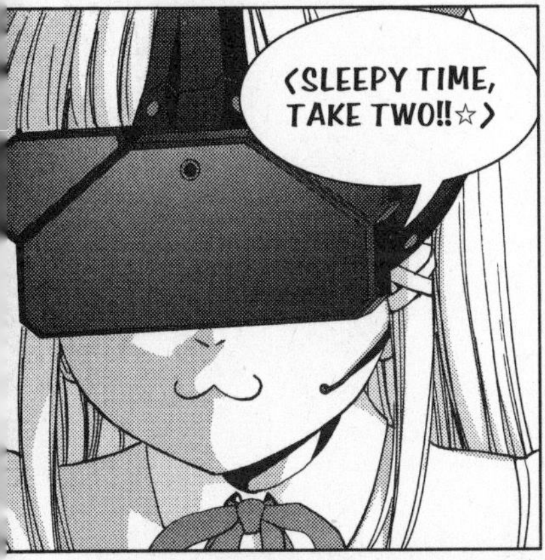
〈SLEEPY TIME, TAKE TWO!!☆〉

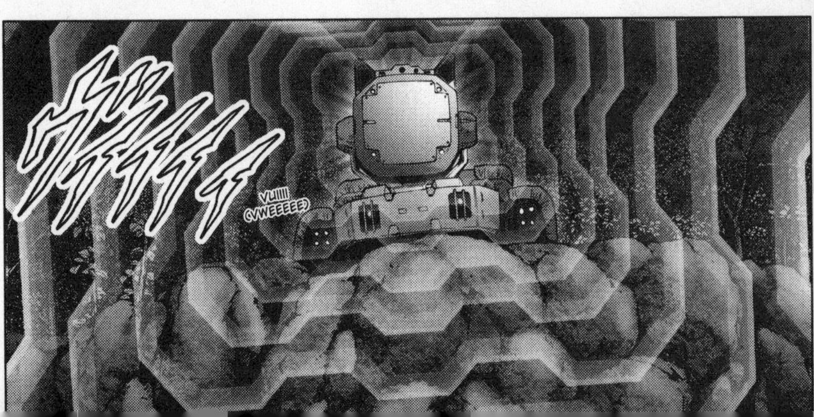
VUIIII
(VWEEEEE)

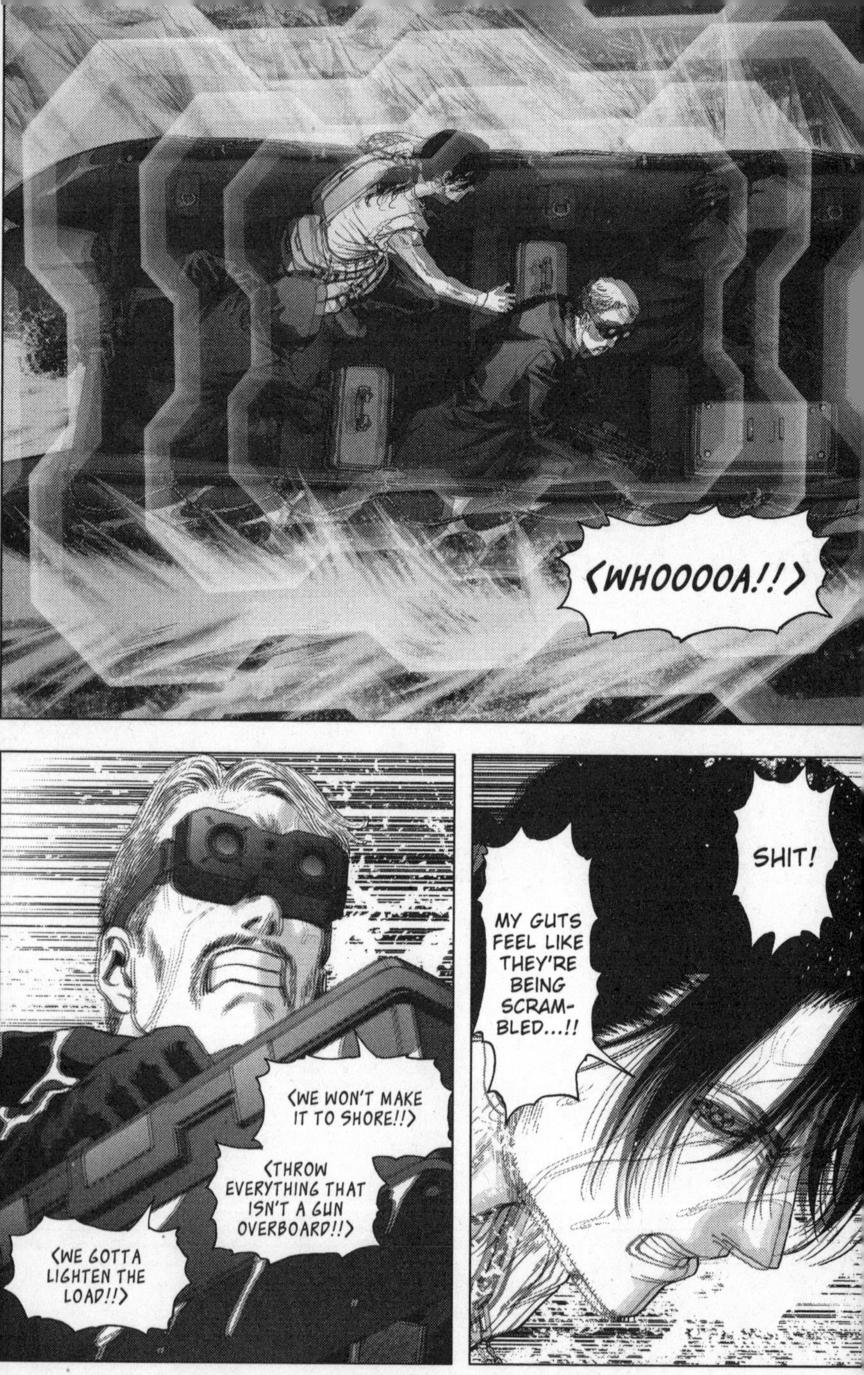
<WHOOOOA!!>
SHIT!
MY GUTS FEEL LIKE THEY'RE BEING SCRAM-BLED...!!
<WE WON'T MAKE IT TO SHORE!!>
<THROW EVERYTHING THAT ISN'T A GUN OVERBOARD!!>
<WE GOTTA LIGHTEN THE LOAD!!>

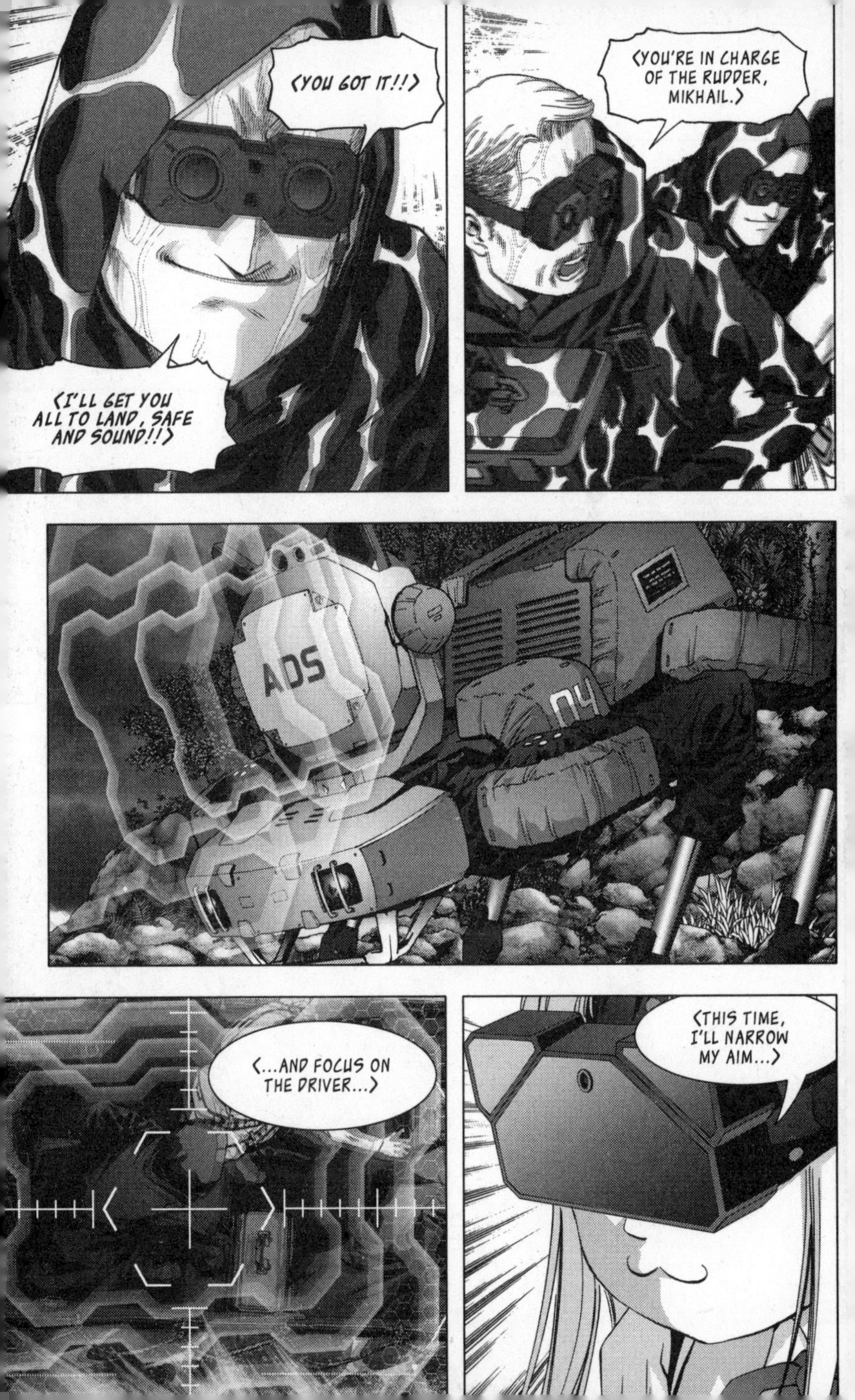
‹YOU'RE IN CHARGE OF THE RUDDER, MIKHAIL.›
‹YOU GOT IT!!›
‹I'LL GET YOU ALL TO LAND, SAFE AND SOUND!!›
ADS
04
‹THIS TIME, I'LL NARROW MY AIM...›
‹...AND FOCUS ON THE DRIVER...›

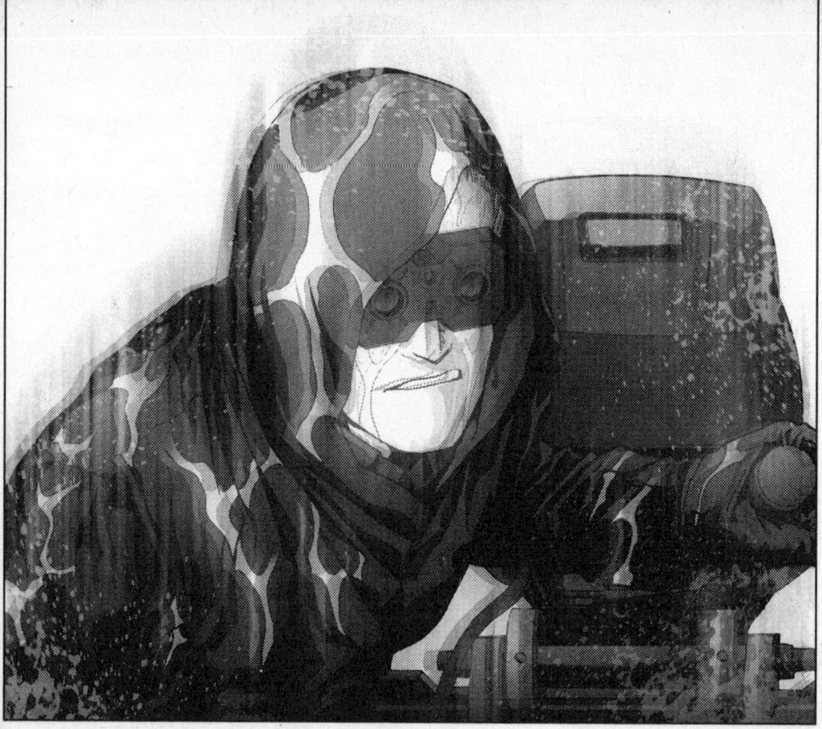

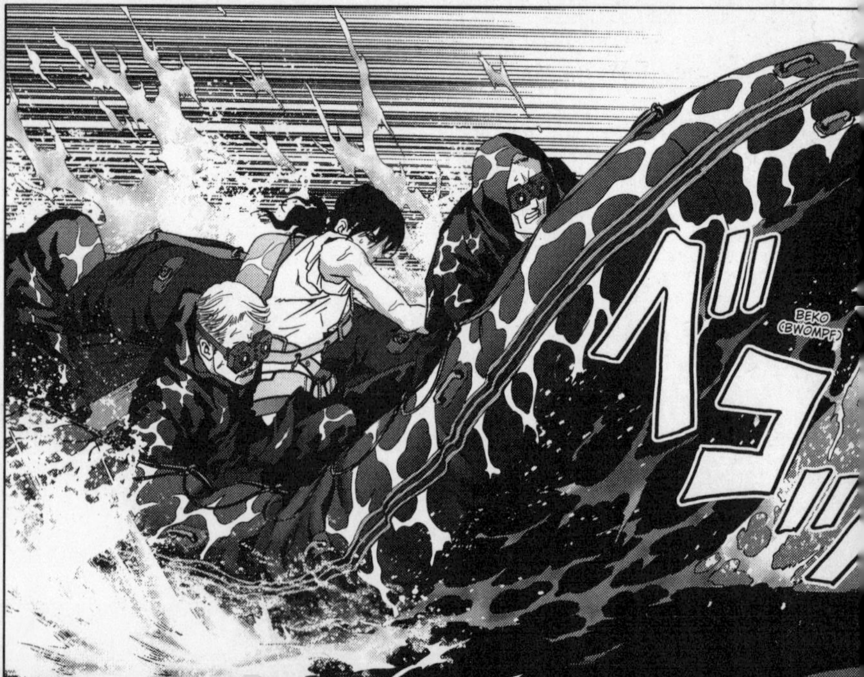
BEKO
(BWOMPF)

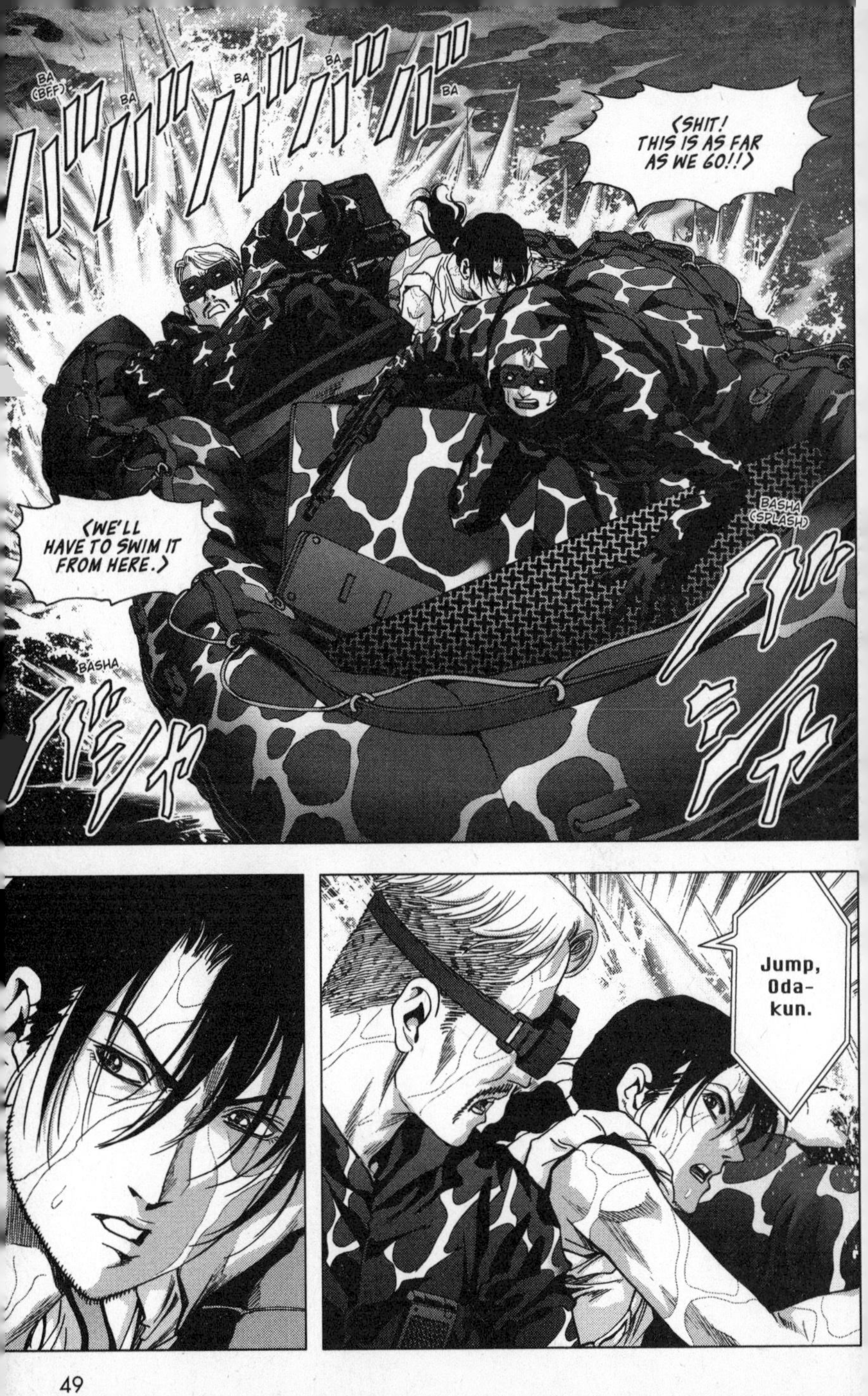

BA
BA
BA
BA
BA (BFF)
〈SHIT! THIS IS AS FAR AS WE GO!!〉
BASHA (SPLASH)
〈WE'LL HAVE TO SWIM IT FROM HERE.〉
BASHA
Jump, Oda-kun.

He pro-
tected
us.

Be grate-
ful.

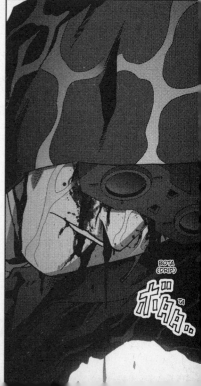

BOTA
(DRIP)

ポタ..
TA

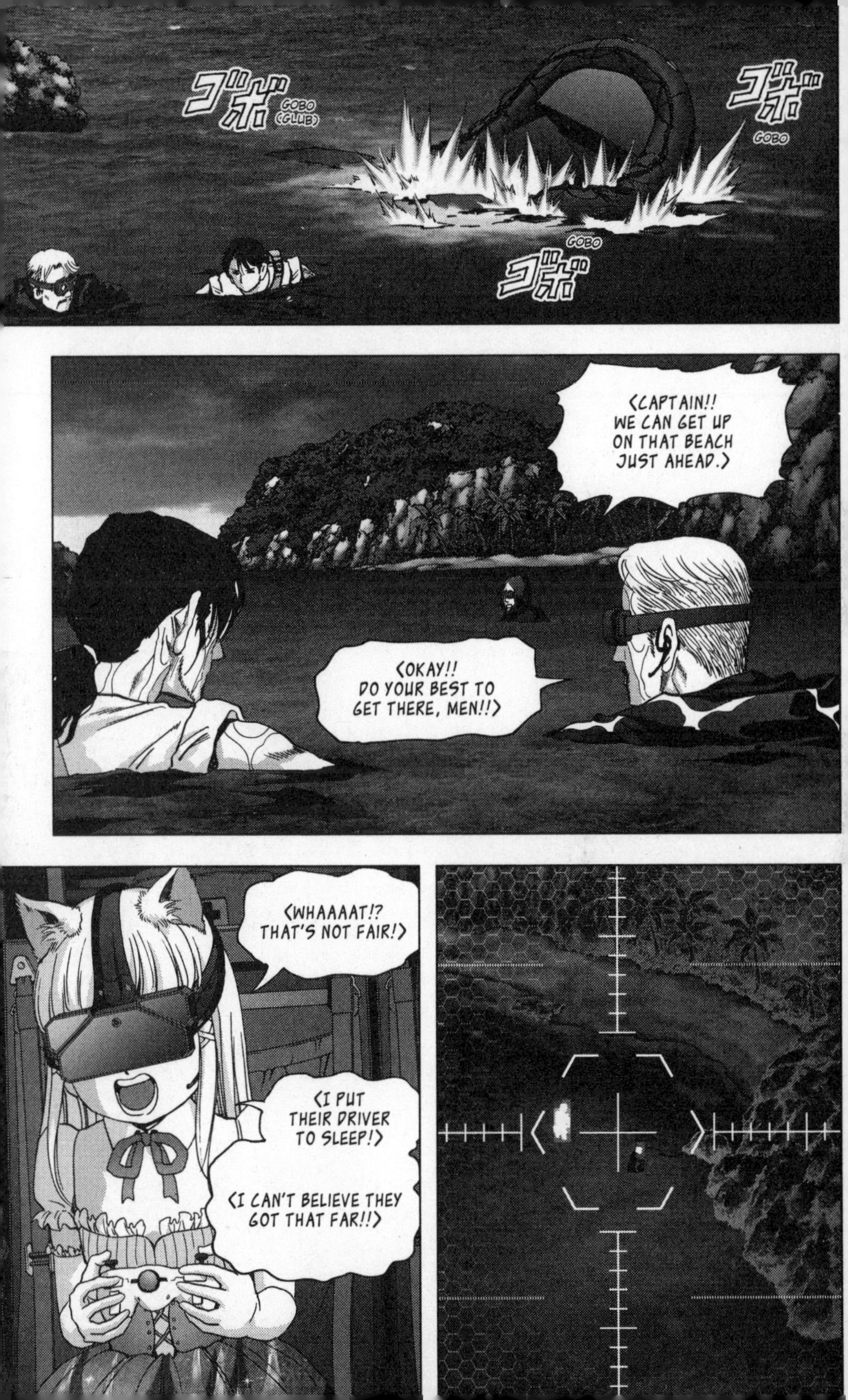
ゴボ
GOBO
ゴボ
GOBO (GLUB)
GOBO
ゴボ
<CAPTAIN!! WE CAN GET UP ON THAT BEACH JUST AHEAD.>
<OKAY!! DO YOUR BEST TO GET THERE, MEN!!>
<WHAAAAT!? THAT'S NOT FAIR!>
<I PUT THEIR DRIVER TO SLEEP!>
<I CAN'T BELIEVE THEY GOT THAT FAR!!>

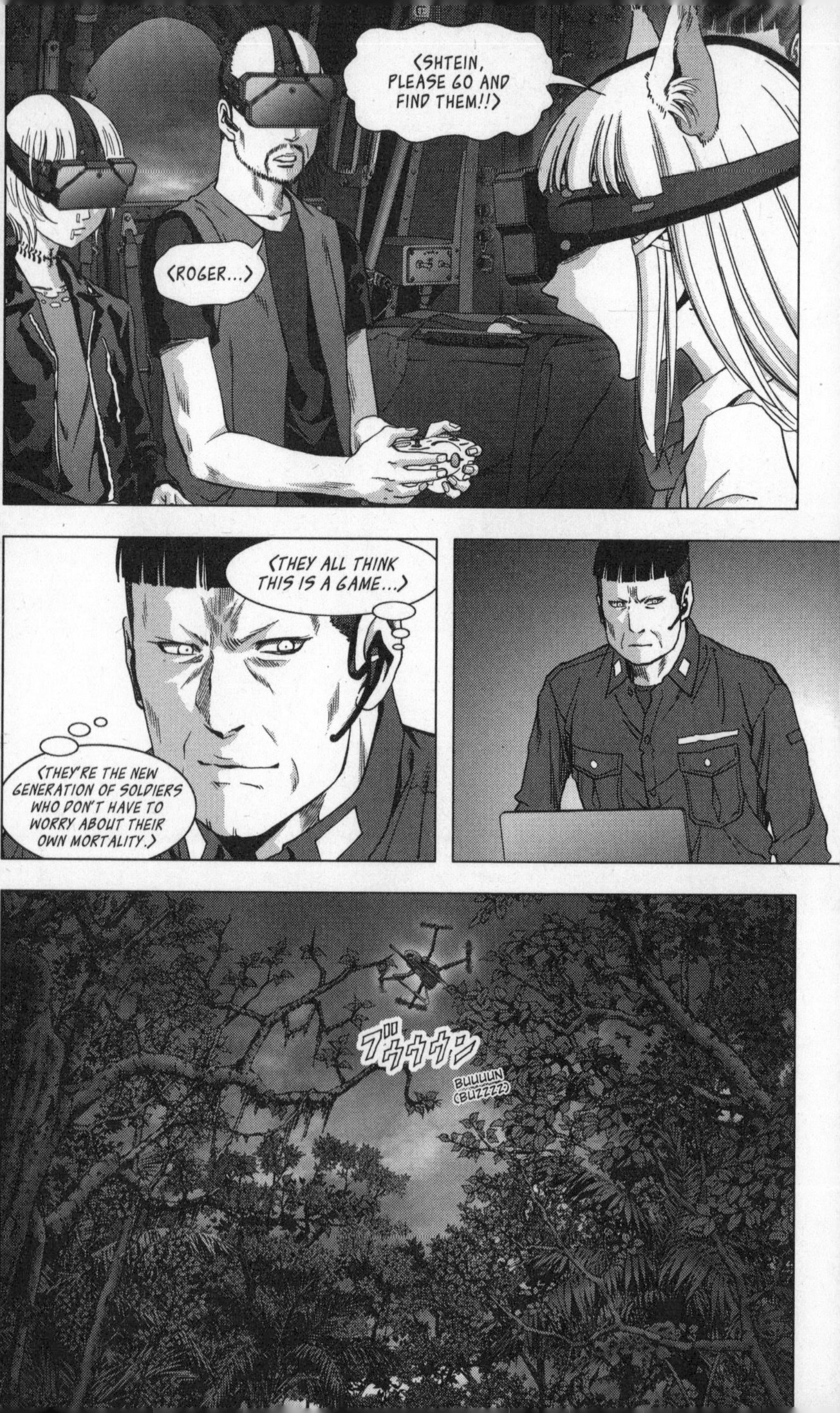
<SHTEIN, PLEASE GO AND FIND THEM!!>
<ROGER...>
<THEY ALL THINK THIS IS A GAME...>
<THEY'RE THE NEW GENERATION OF SOLDIERS WHO DON'T HAVE TO WORRY ABOUT THEIR OWN MORTALITY.>
ブゥゥゥン
BUUUUN (BUZZZZ)

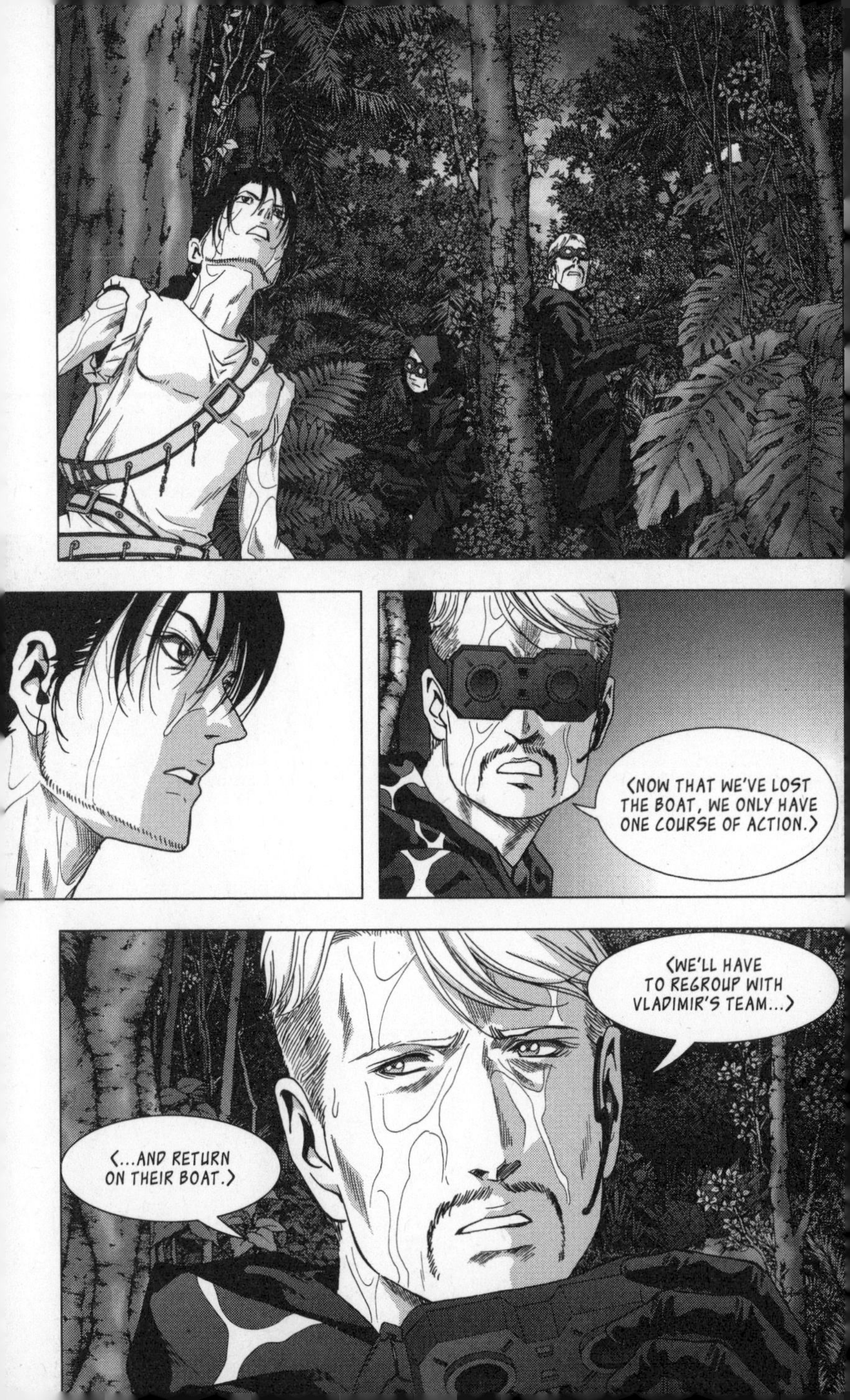
〈NOW THAT WE'VE LOST THE BOAT, WE ONLY HAVE ONE COURSE OF ACTION.〉
〈WE'LL HAVE TO REGROUP WITH VLADIMIR'S TEAM...〉
〈...AND RETURN ON THEIR BOAT.〉

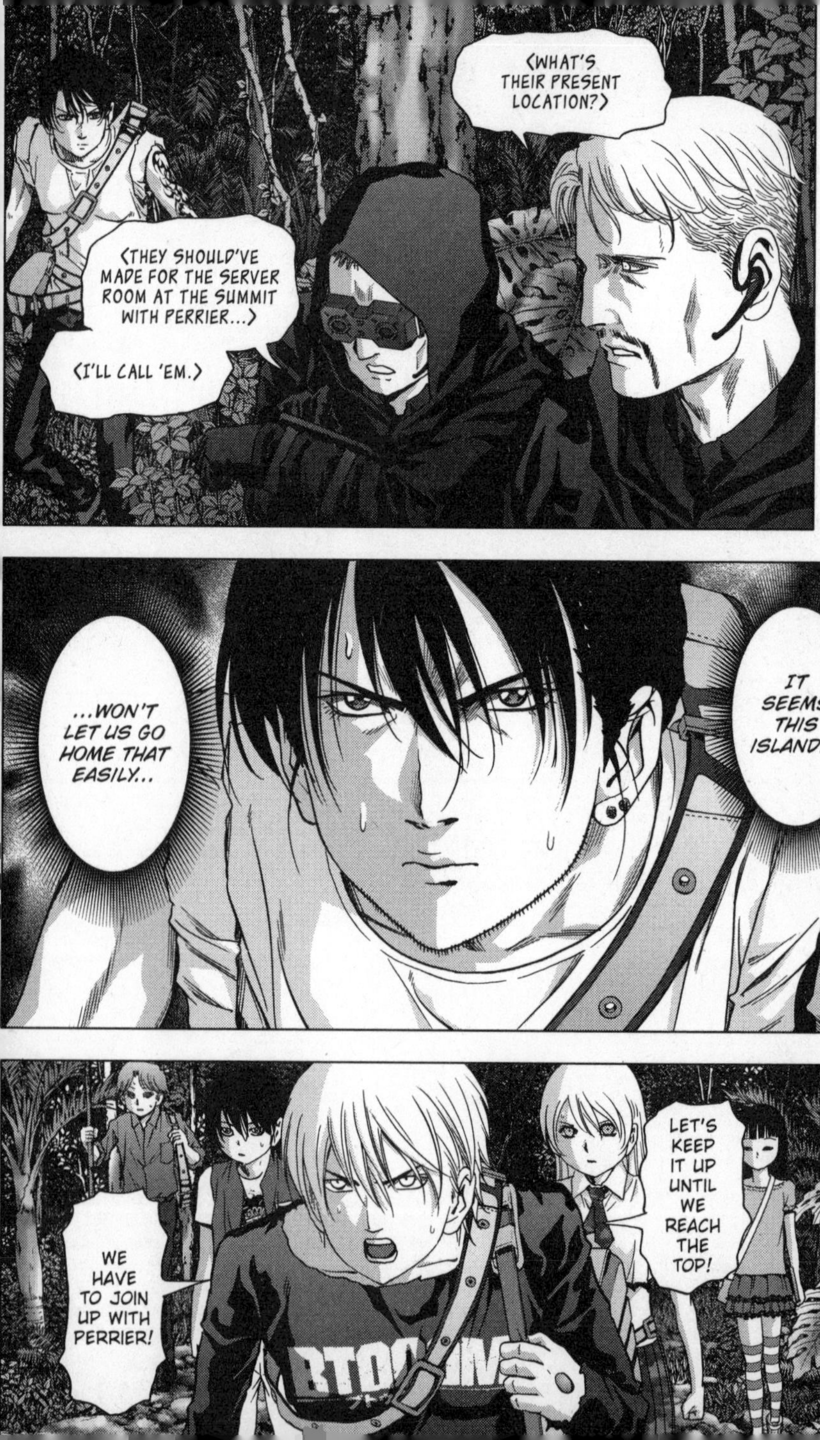
<WHAT'S THEIR PRESENT LOCATION?>
<THEY SHOULD'VE MADE FOR THE SERVER ROOM AT THE SUMMIT WITH PERRIER...>
<I'LL CALL 'EM.>
IT SEEMS THIS ISLAND...
...WON'T LET US GO HOME THAT EASILY...
LET'S KEEP IT UP UNTIL WE REACH THE TOP!
WE HAVE TO JOIN UP WITH PERRIER!

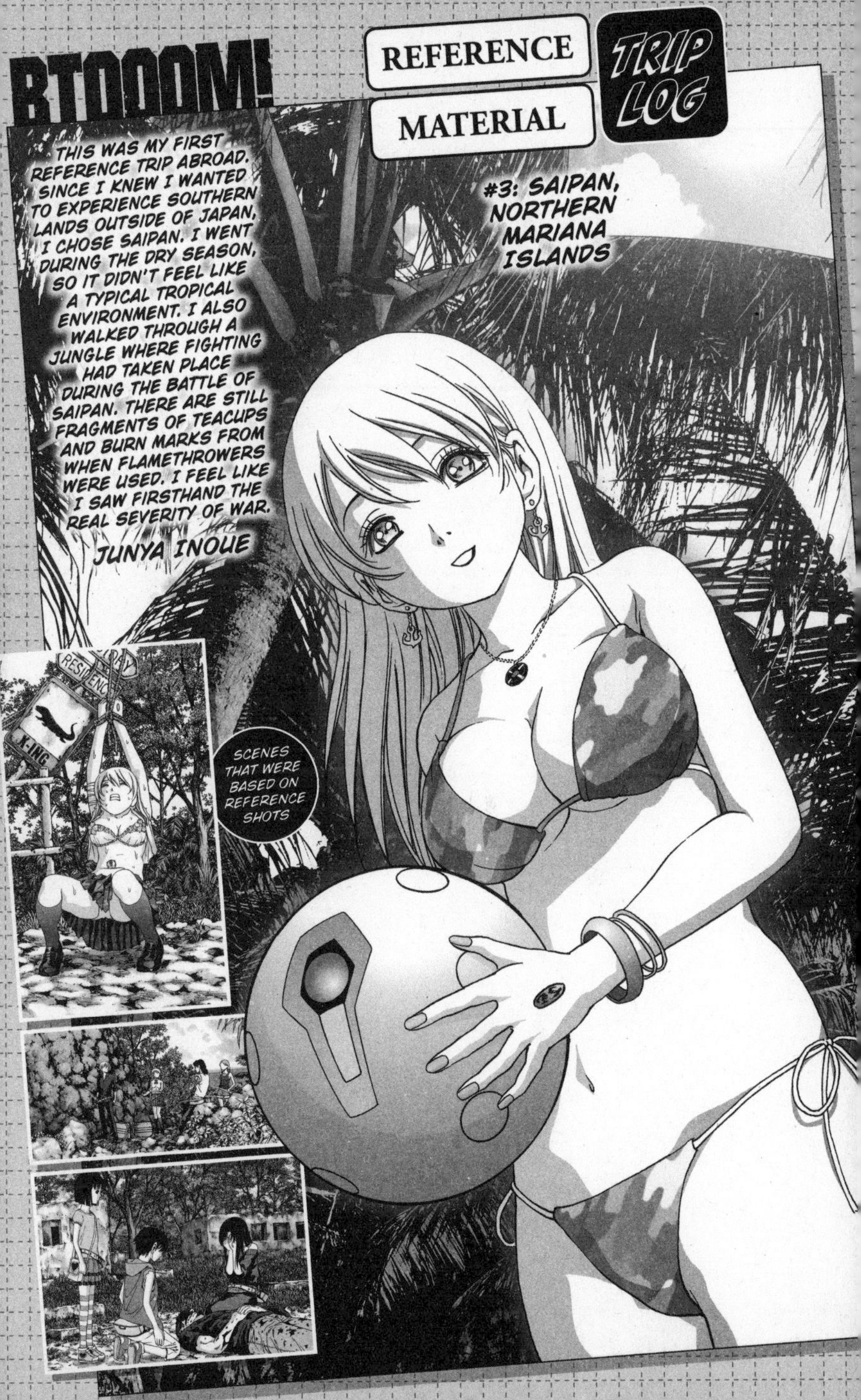
BTOOOM!
REFERENCE MATERIAL
TRIP LOG
#3: SAIPAN, NORTHERN MARIANA ISLANDS
THIS WAS MY FIRST REFERENCE TRIP ABROAD. SINCE I KNEW I WANTED TO EXPERIENCE SOUTHERN LANDS OUTSIDE OF JAPAN, I CHOSE SAIPAN. I WENT DURING THE DRY SEASON, SO IT DIDN'T FEEL LIKE A TYPICAL TROPICAL ENVIRONMENT. I ALSO WALKED THROUGH A JUNGLE WHERE FIGHTING HAD TAKEN PLACE DURING THE BATTLE OF SAIPAN. THERE ARE STILL FRAGMENTS OF TEACUPS AND BURN MARKS FROM WHEN FLAMETHROWERS WERE USED. I FEEL LIKE I SAW FIRSTHAND THE REAL SEVERITY OF WAR.
JUNYA INOUE
RESIDENCE
X-ING
SCENES THAT WERE BASED ON REFERENCE SHOTS

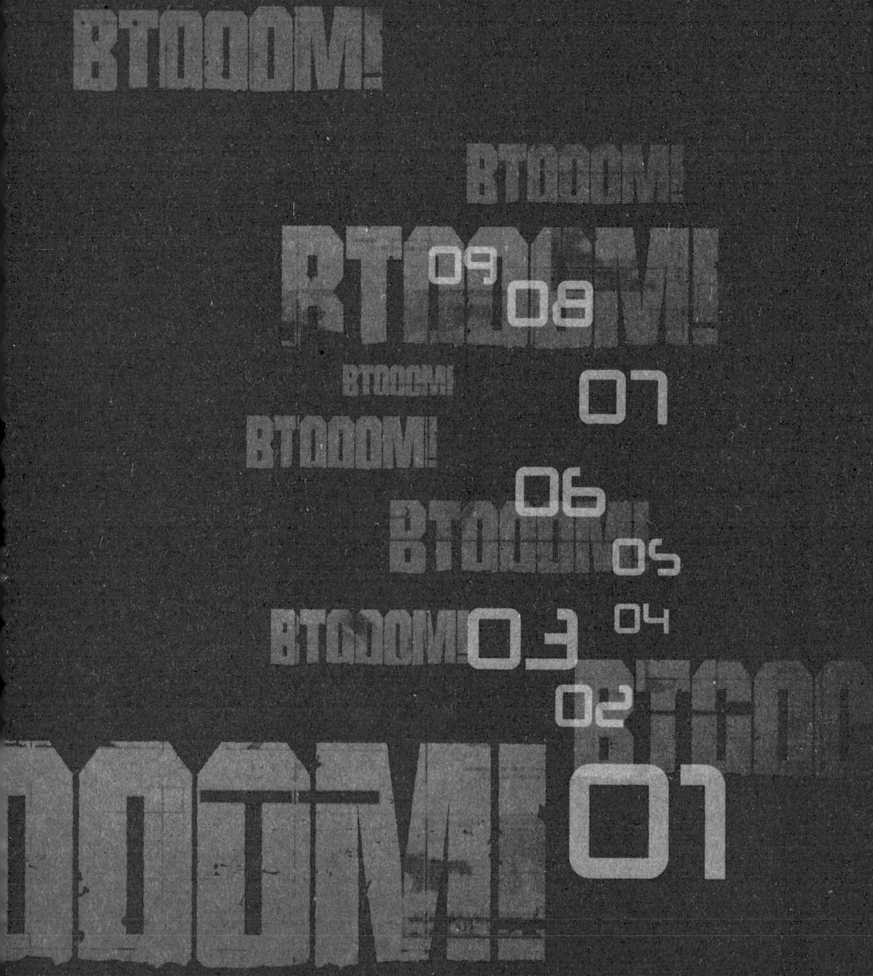
BTOOOM!
BTOOOM!
BTOOOM!
09
08
BTOOOM!
07
BTOOOM!
06
BTOOOM!
05
BTOOOM!
04
03
02
BTOOOM!
01

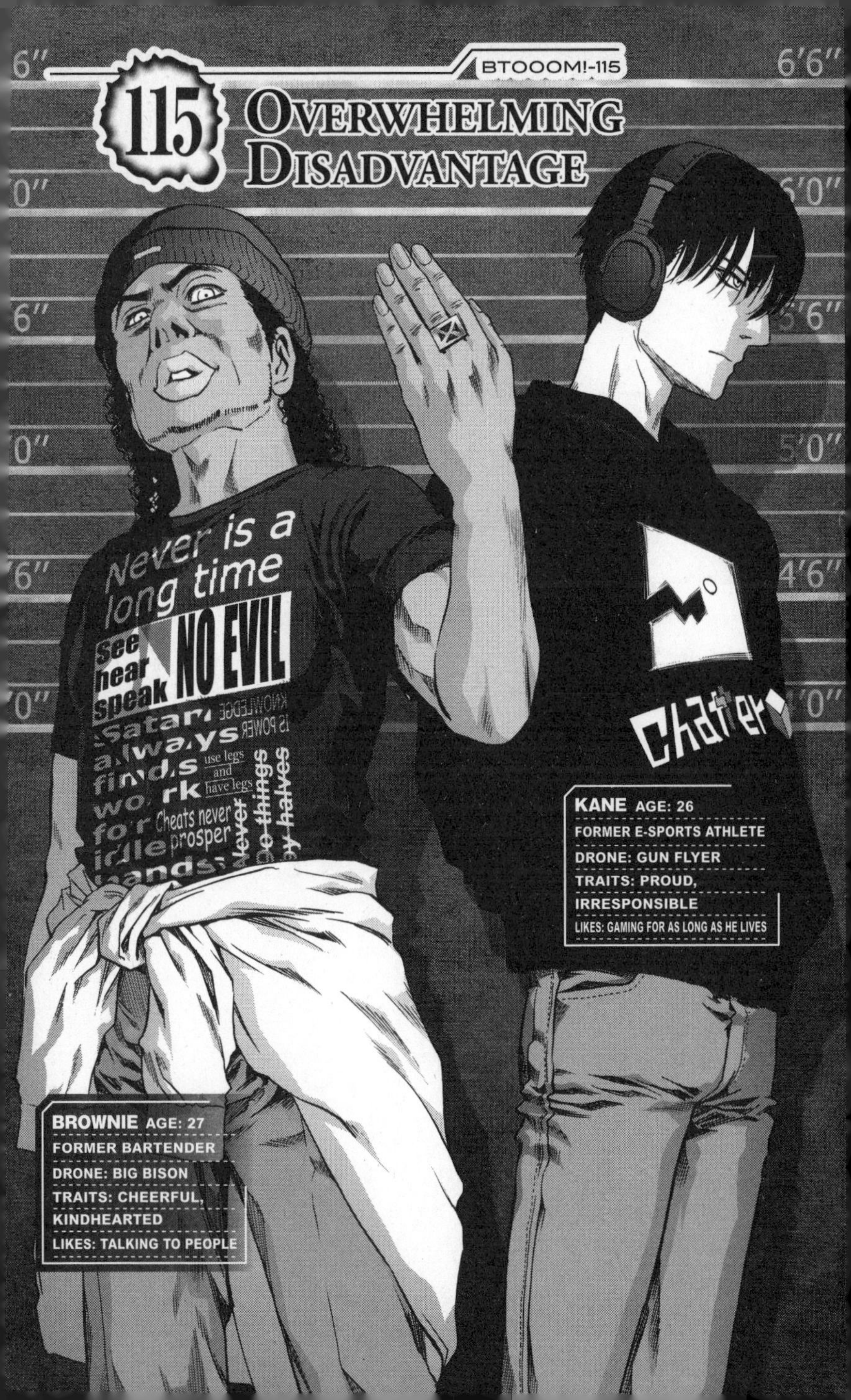
BTOOOM!-115
115
OVERWHELMING DISADVANTAGE
Never is a long time
see hear speak NO EVIL
Satan always finds work for idle hands
KNOWLEDGE IS POWER
use legs and have legs
Cheats never prosper
Chatter
KANE AGE: 26
FORMER E-SPORTS ATHLETE
DRONE: GUN FLYER
TRAITS: PROUD, IRRESPONSIBLE
LIKES: GAMING FOR AS LONG AS HE LIVES
BROWNIE AGE: 27
FORMER BARTENDER
DRONE: BIG BISON
TRAITS: CHEERFUL, KINDHEARTED
LIKES: TALKING TO PEOPLE

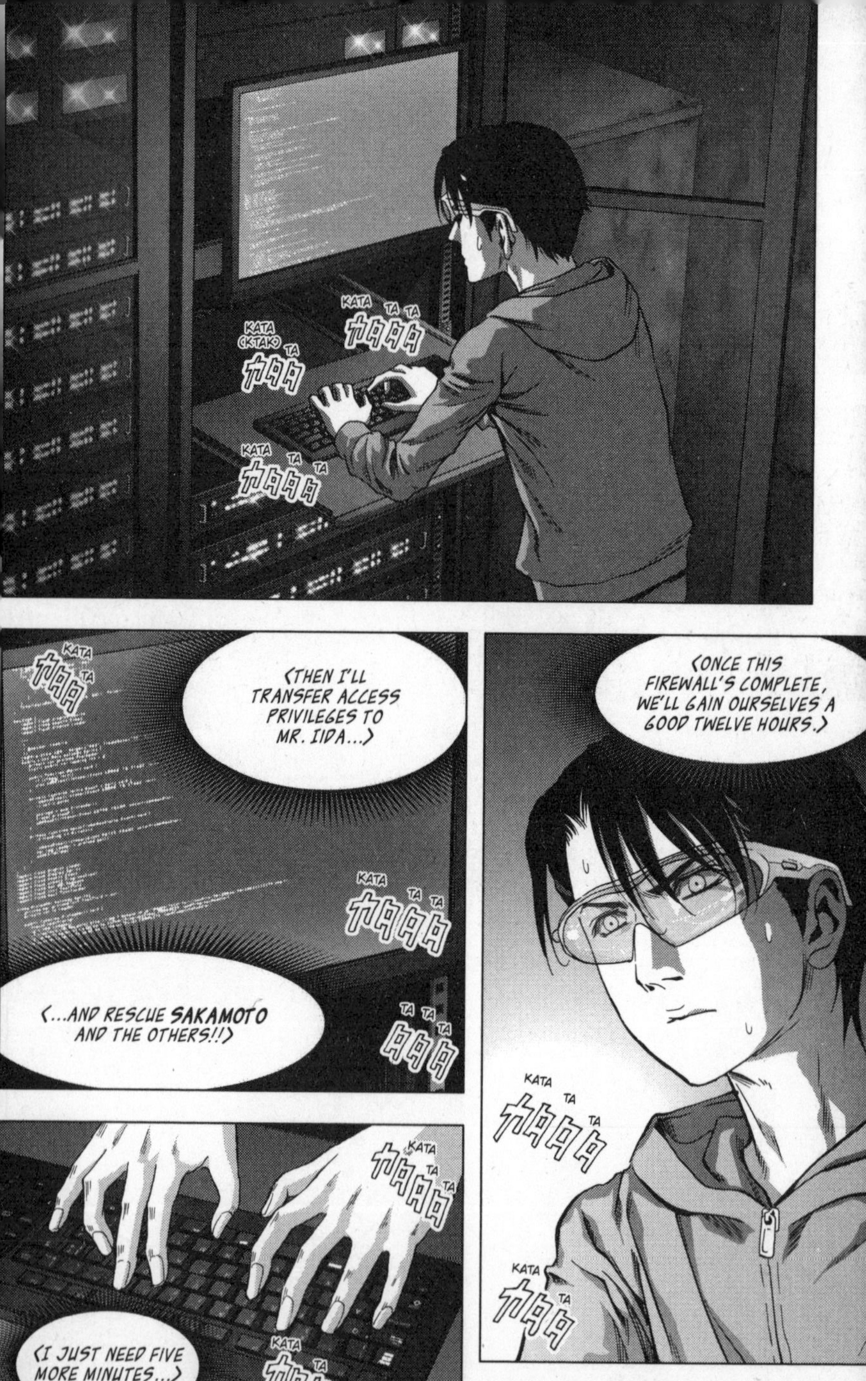
KATA TA TA カタタタ
KATA (KTAK) TA カタタ
KATA TA TA カタタタ
〈ONCE THIS FIREWALL'S COMPLETE, WE'LL GAIN OURSELVES A GOOD TWELVE HOURS.〉
KATA TA TA カタタタ
KATA TA カタタ
KATA TA カタタ
〈THEN I'LL TRANSFER ACCESS PRIVILEGES TO MR. IIDA...〉
KATA TA TA カタタタ
〈...AND RESCUE SAKAMOTO AND THE OTHERS!!〉
TA TA TA タタタ
KATA TA TA カタタタ
〈I JUST NEED FIVE MORE MINUTES...〉
KATA TA カタタ

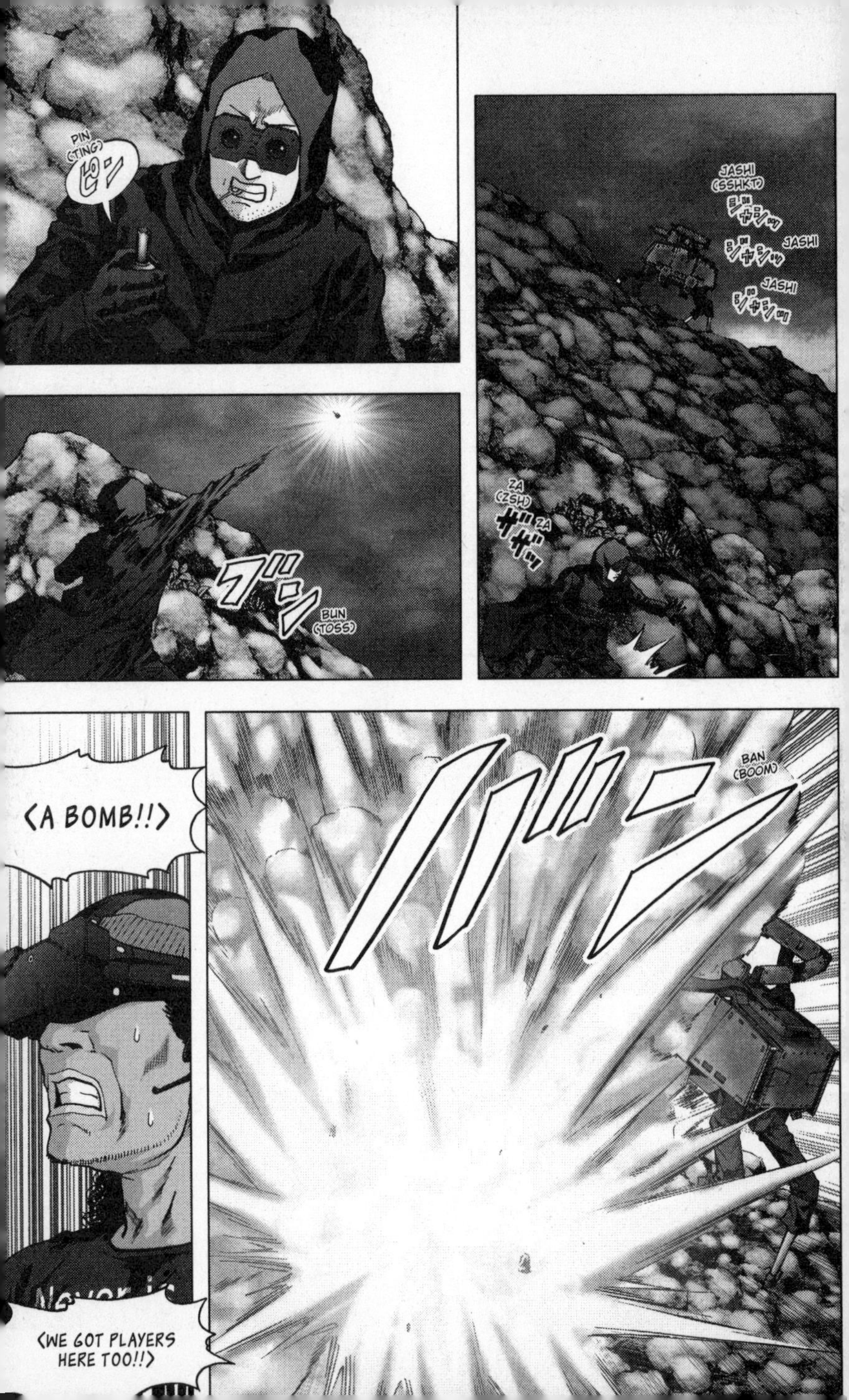
JASHI (SSHKT)
JASHI
JASHI
ZA (ZSH) ZA
PIN (TING)
BUN (TOSS)
BAN (BOOM)
〈A BOMB!!〉
〈WE GOT PLAYERS HERE TOO!!〉

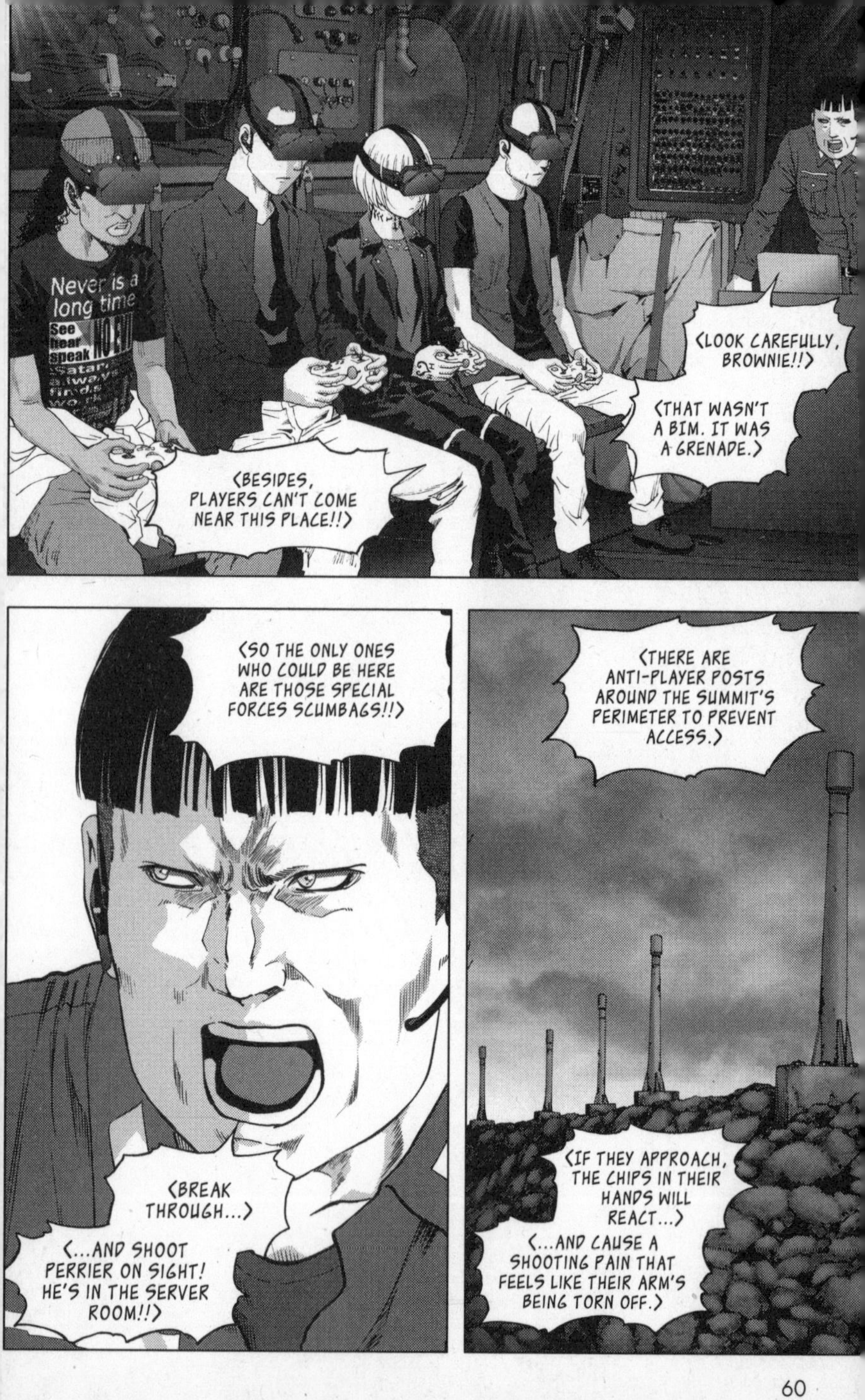

Never is a long time
‹LOOK CAREFULLY, BROWNIE!!›
‹THAT WASN'T A BIM. IT WAS A GRENADE.›
‹BESIDES, PLAYERS CAN'T COME NEAR THIS PLACE!!›
‹THERE ARE ANTI-PLAYER POSTS AROUND THE SUMMIT'S PERIMETER TO PREVENT ACCESS.›
‹IF THEY APPROACH, THE CHIPS IN THEIR HANDS WILL REACT...›
‹...AND CAUSE A SHOOTING PAIN THAT FEELS LIKE THEIR ARM'S BEING TORN OFF.›
‹SO THE ONLY ONES WHO COULD BE HERE ARE THOSE SPECIAL FORCES SCUMBAGS!!›
‹BREAK THROUGH...›
‹...AND SHOOT PERRIER ON SIGHT! HE'S IN THE SERVER ROOM!!›

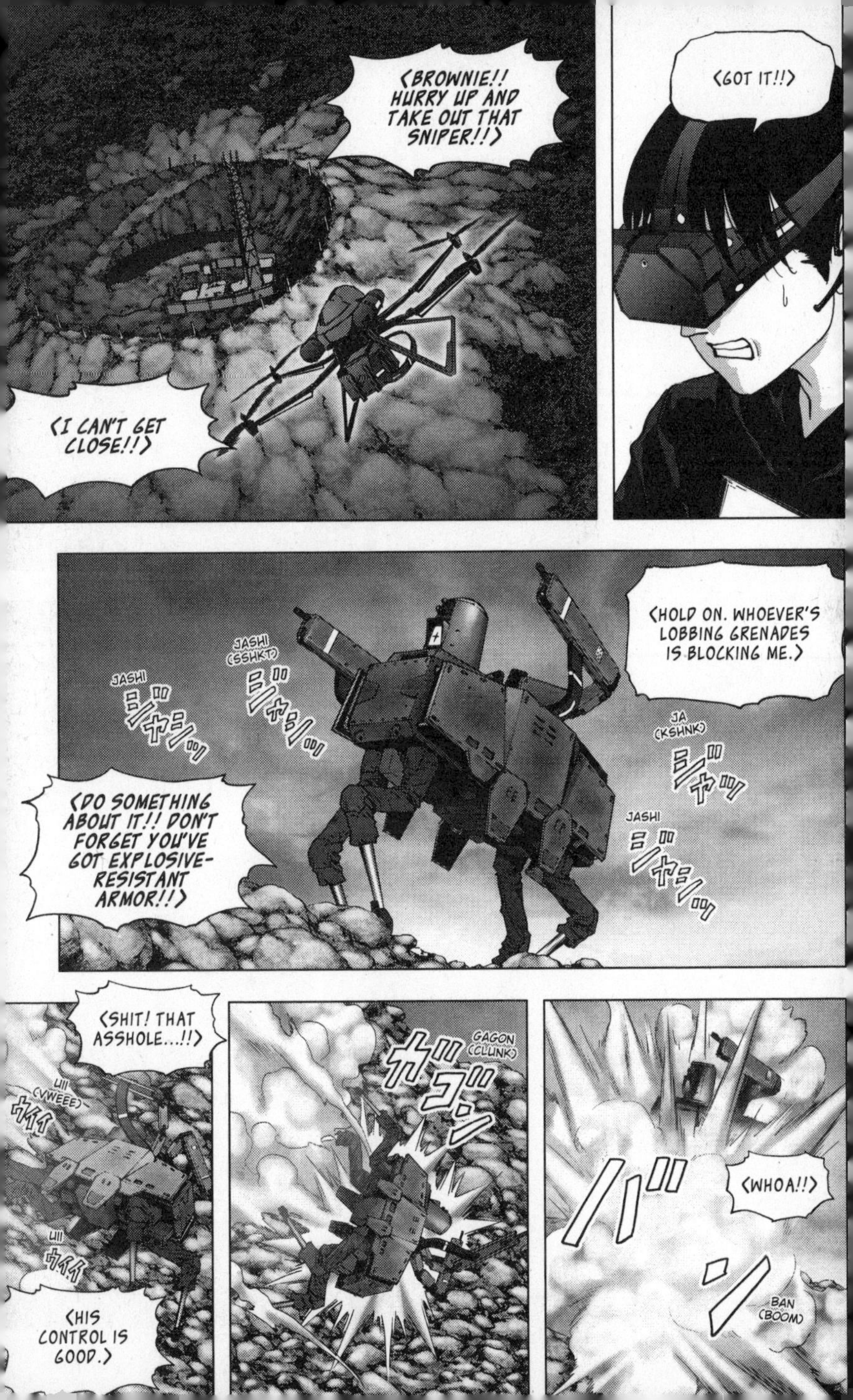

〈GOT IT!!〉
〈BROWNIE!! HURRY UP AND TAKE OUT THAT SNIPER!!〉
〈I CAN'T GET CLOSE!!〉
〈HOLD ON. WHOEVER'S LOBBING GRENADES IS BLOCKING ME.〉
JASHI (SSHKT)
JASHI
JA (KSHNK)
〈DO SOMETHING ABOUT IT!! DON'T FORGET YOU'VE GOT EXPLOSIVE-RESISTANT ARMOR!!〉
JASHI
〈WHOA!!〉
BAN (BOOM)
GAGON (CLUNK)
〈SHIT! THAT ASSHOLE...!!〉
UII (VWEEE)
UII
〈HIS CONTROL IS GOOD.〉

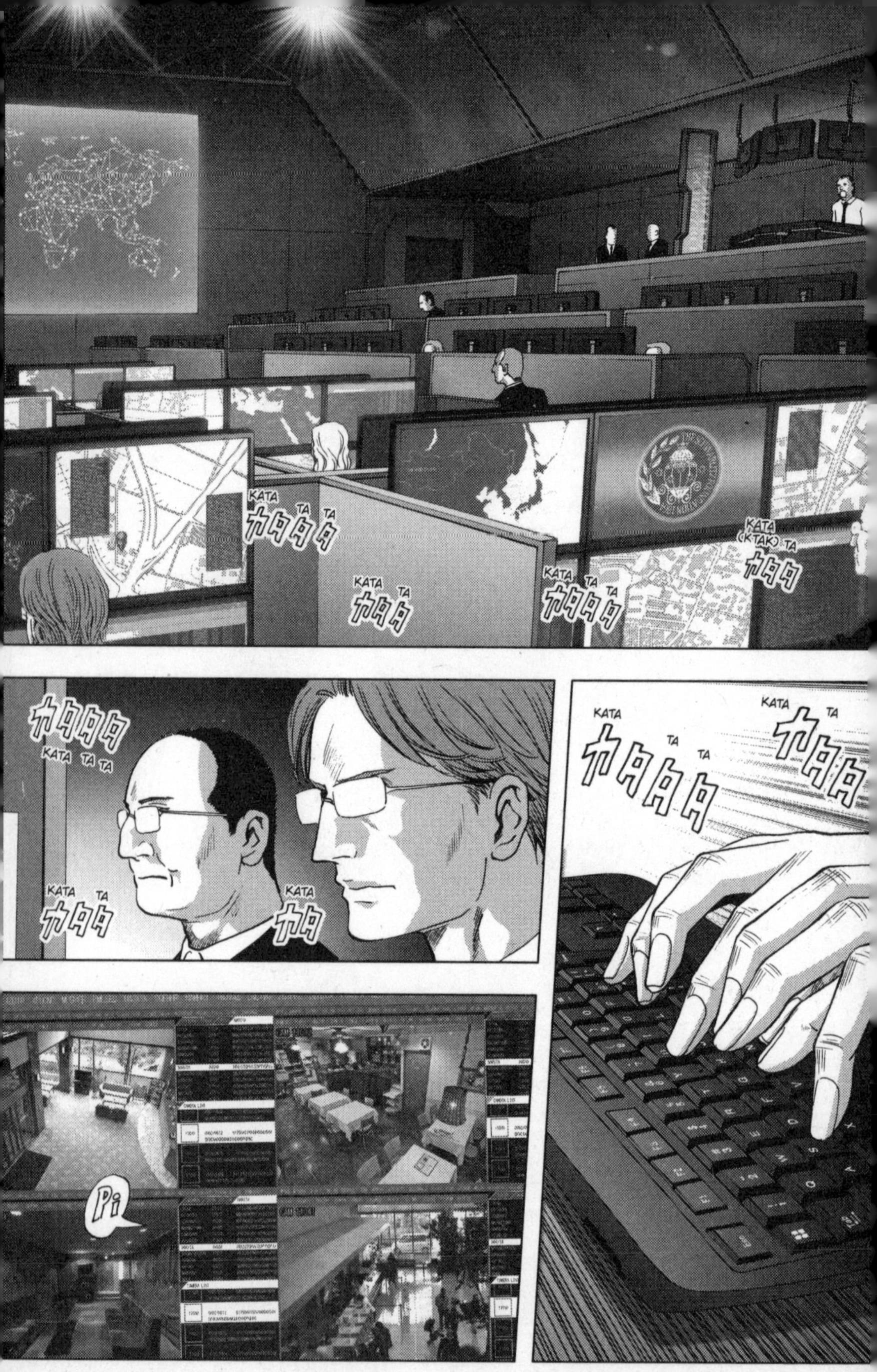
KATA (KTAK) TA
カタタ
KATA TA TA
カタタタ
KATA TA TA
カタタタ
KATA TA
カタタ
KATA TA
カタタ
KATA TA TA
カタタタ
カタタタ
KATA TA TA
KATA
カタ
KATA TA
カタタ
Pi

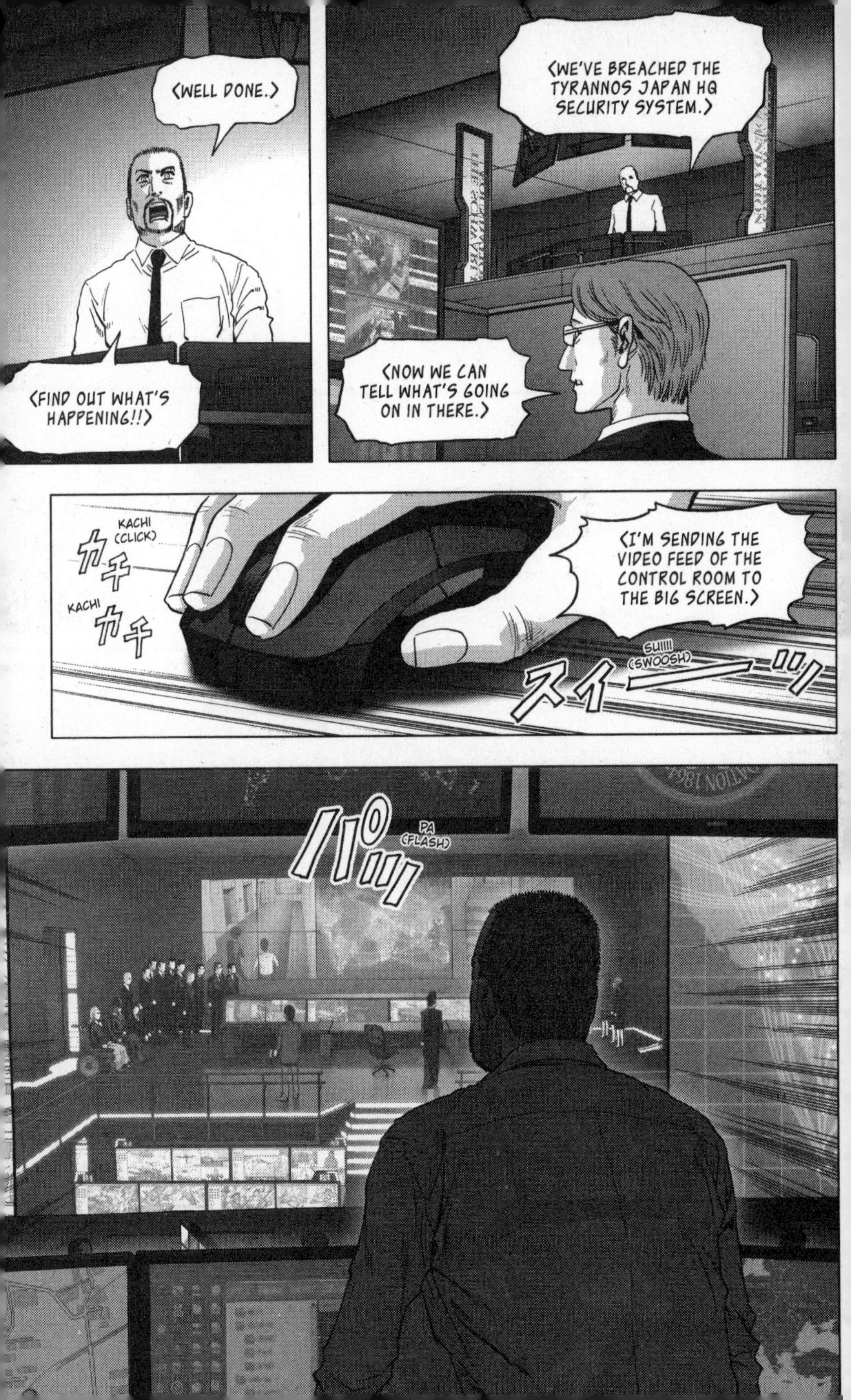

〈WE'VE BREACHED THE TYRANNOS JAPAN HQ SECURITY SYSTEM.〉
〈NOW WE CAN TELL WHAT'S GOING ON IN THERE.〉
〈WELL DONE.〉
〈FIND OUT WHAT'S HAPPENING!!〉
〈I'M SENDING THE VIDEO FEED OF THE CONTROL ROOM TO THE BIG SCREEN.〉
カチ KACHI (CLICK)
カチ KACHI
スイー SUIII (SWOOSH)
パッ PA (FLASH)

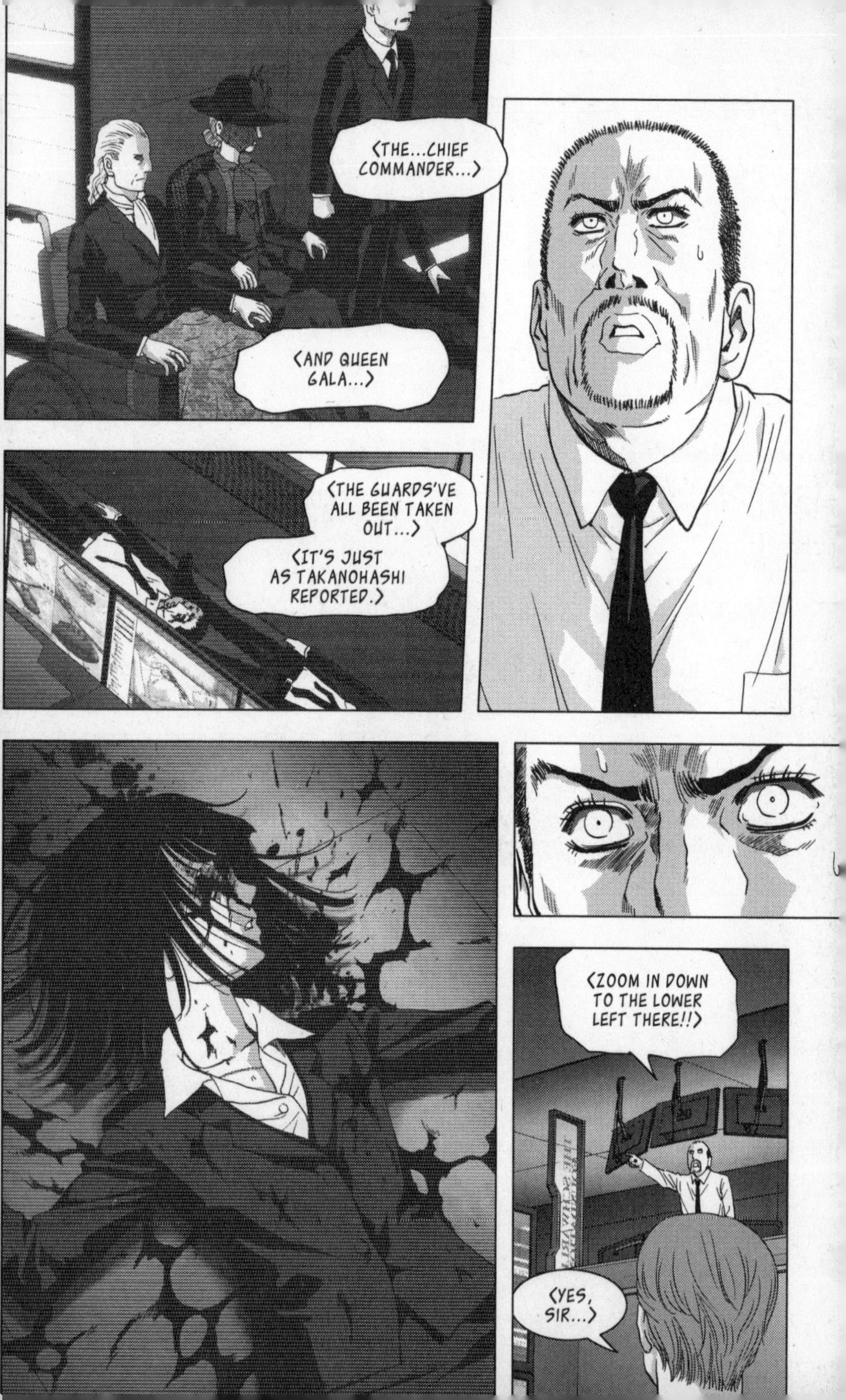
〈THE...CHIEF COMMANDER...〉
〈AND QUEEN GALA...〉
〈THE GUARDS'VE ALL BEEN TAKEN OUT...〉
〈IT'S JUST AS TAKANOHASHI REPORTED.〉
〈ZOOM IN DOWN TO THE LOWER LEFT THERE!!〉
〈YES, SIR...〉

⟨ENOUGH!! TURN IT OFF!!⟩

⟨Y-YES, SIR.⟩

⟨UH-OH!!⟩

⟨WE CAN'T LET TOMIE SEE THIS...⟩

⟨ISN'T THAT... TOMIZAWA!?⟩

⟨IS SHE DEAD!?⟩

⟨WAS MY SISTER...⟩

KATA
TA
KATA
KATA
TA

⟨...KILLED?⟩

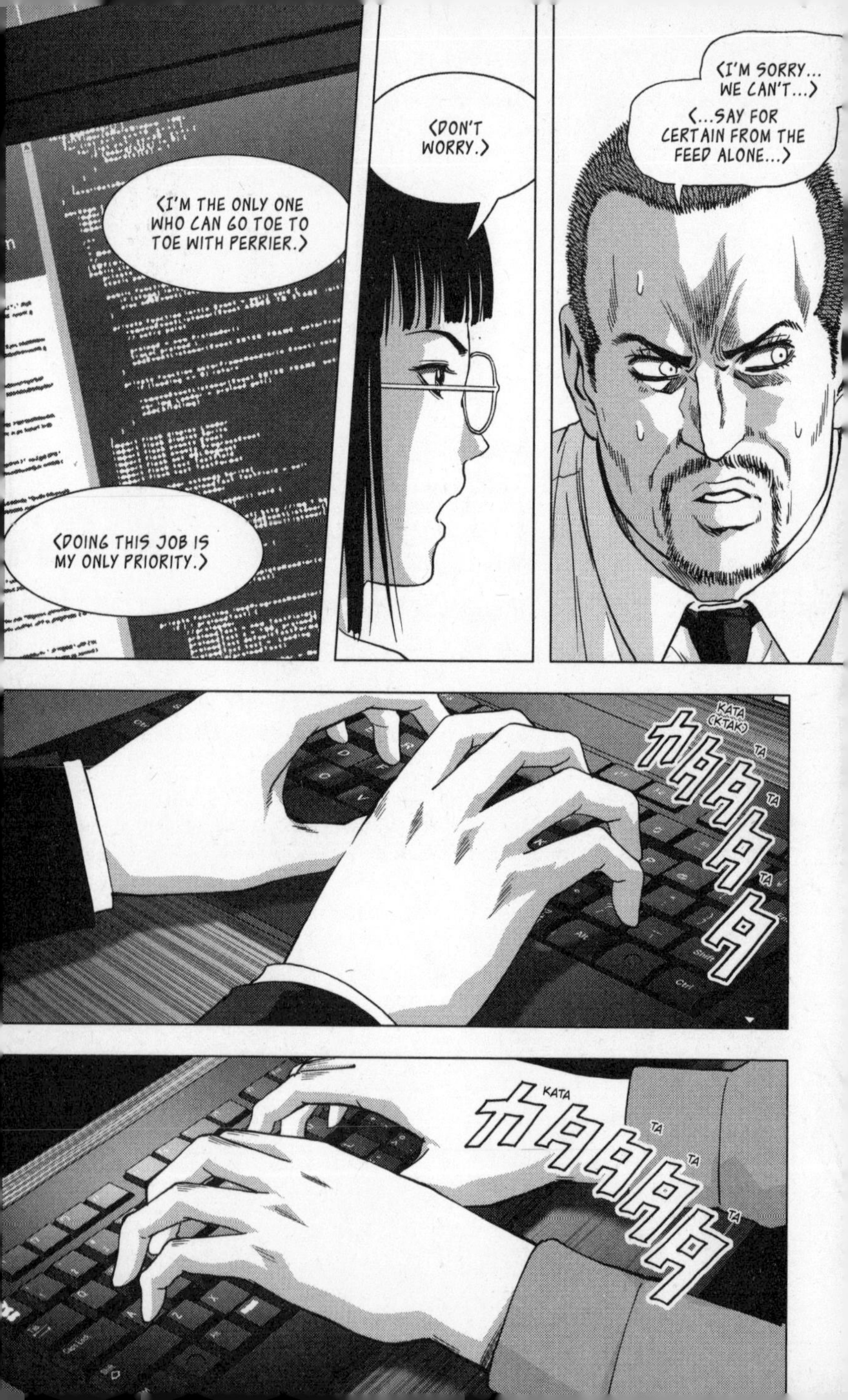
〈I'M SORRY... WE CAN'T...〉
〈...SAY FOR CERTAIN FROM THE FEED ALONE...〉
〈DON'T WORRY.〉
〈I'M THE ONLY ONE WHO CAN GO TOE TO TOE WITH PERRIER.〉
〈DOING THIS JOB IS MY ONLY PRIORITY.〉
KATA (KTAK)
TA
TA
TA
KATA
TA
TA
TA

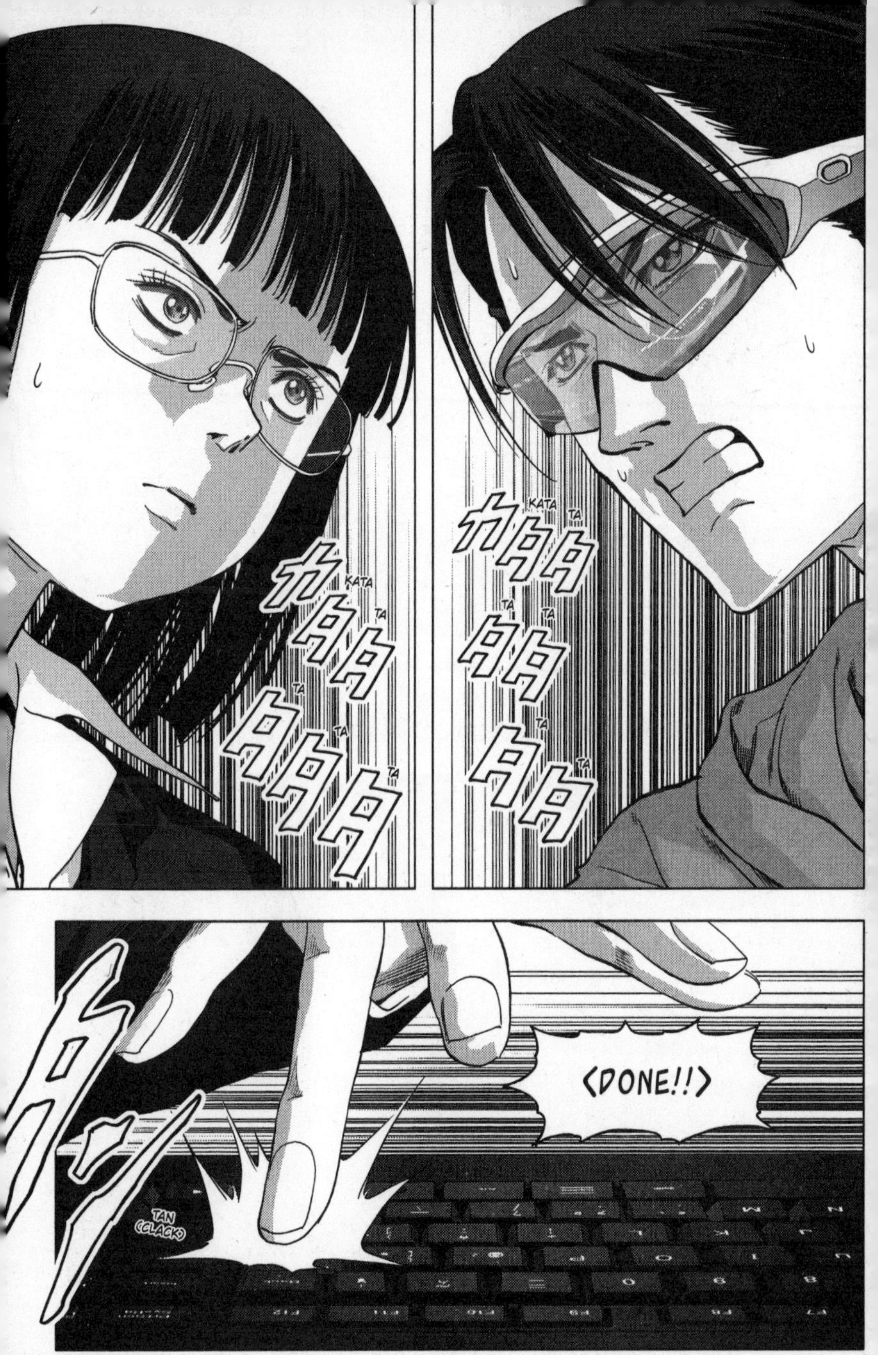
KATA
TA
TA
TA
TA
TA
KATA
TA
TA
TA
TA
⟨DONE!!⟩
TAN (CLACK)

Main System

MAIN SYSTEM CODE

		gxxj	:2j
ragE	rGzQ		
bNr	HTck	SC4A	JLXk
UsgZ	bPRX	jDAL	uTED
9m6z	DcpZ	uH2X	HzBM
QawR	PZmT	An2c	YkW8

PASS CODE

			KATA (KTAK)
rQT7	Ec6a		
hhA9	GsD3	4xzd	z75t
wtCj	8656	Auze	rARs
	GBSN	Q2cn	GdJx
	p5kF	HN93	

UNIT CODE

| | | ai3N | mCyV |

⟨ACCESS CODES HAVE BEEN RESTORED TO THEIR DEFAULTS!!⟩

⟨THE INFILTRATION IS A SUCCESS!!⟩

⟨NO TRAPS DETECTED!!⟩

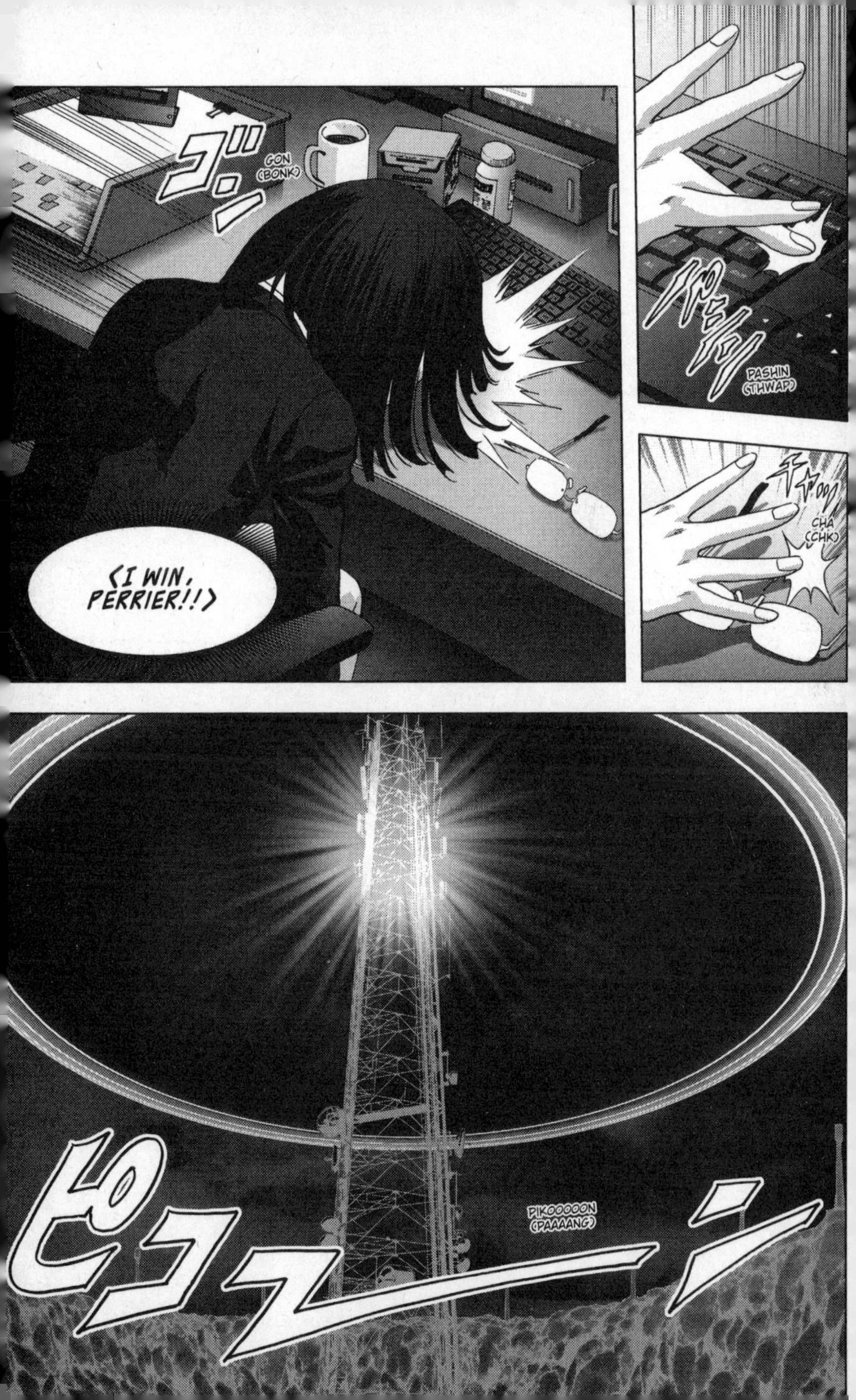
PASHIN
(THWAP)
CHA
(CHK)
GON
(BONK)
<I WIN, PERRIER!!>
PIKOOOOON
(PAAAANG)

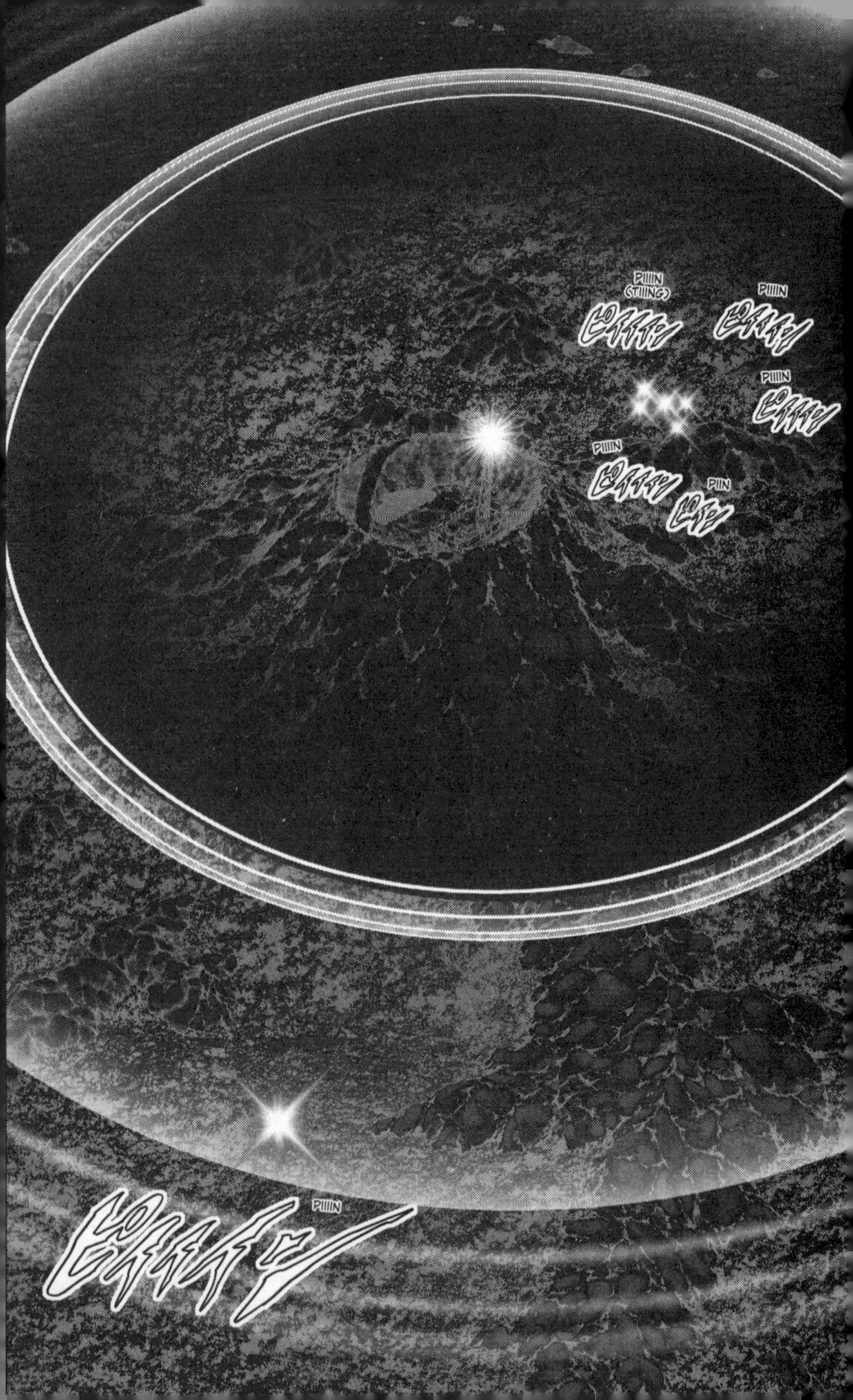

PIIIN
PIIIN (STIIING)
PIIIN
PIIIN
PIIN
PIIIN

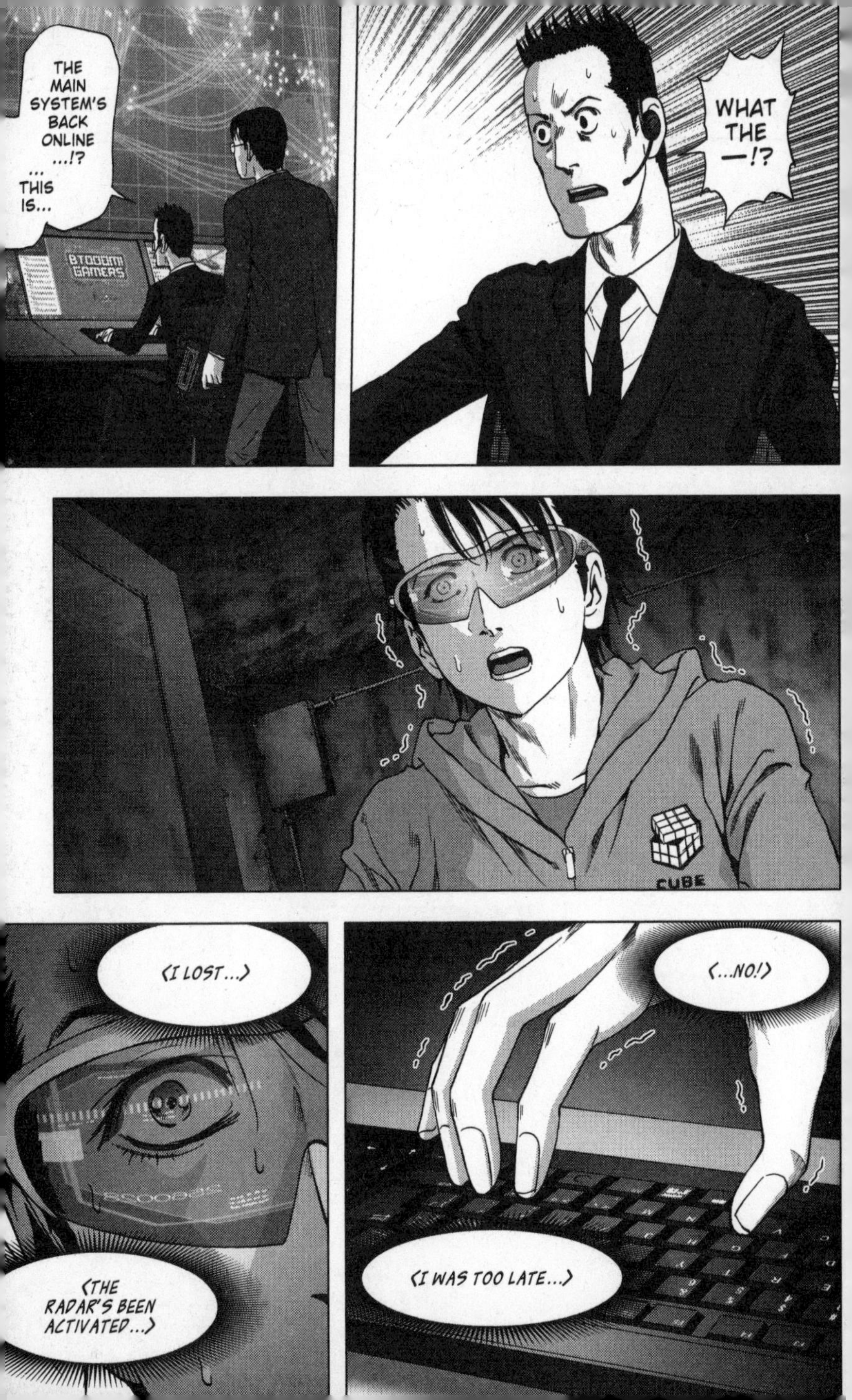
WHAT THE—!?
THE MAIN SYSTEM'S BACK ONLINE ...!?
... THIS IS...
BTOOOM! GAMERS
CUBE
〈...NO!〉
〈I WAS TOO LATE...〉
〈I LOST...〉
〈THE RADAR'S BEEN ACTIVATED...〉

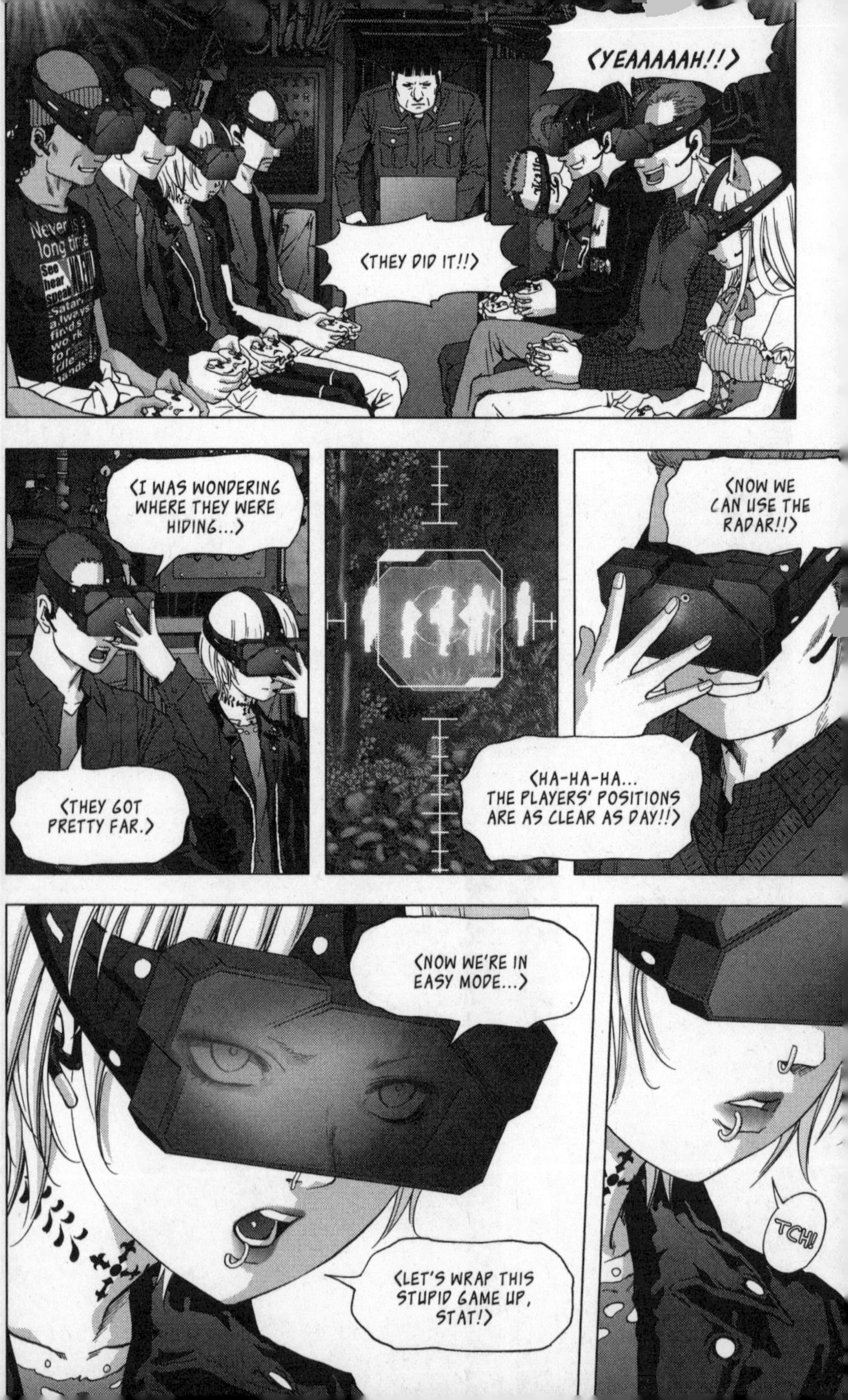
〈YEAAAAAH!!〉
〈THEY DID IT!!〉
〈NOW WE CAN USE THE RADAR!!〉
〈HA-HA-HA... THE PLAYERS' POSITIONS ARE AS CLEAR AS DAY!!〉
〈I WAS WONDERING WHERE THEY WERE HIDING...〉
〈THEY GOT PRETTY FAR.〉
TCH!
〈NOW WE'RE IN EASY MODE...〉
〈LET'S WRAP THIS STUPID GAME UP, STAT!〉

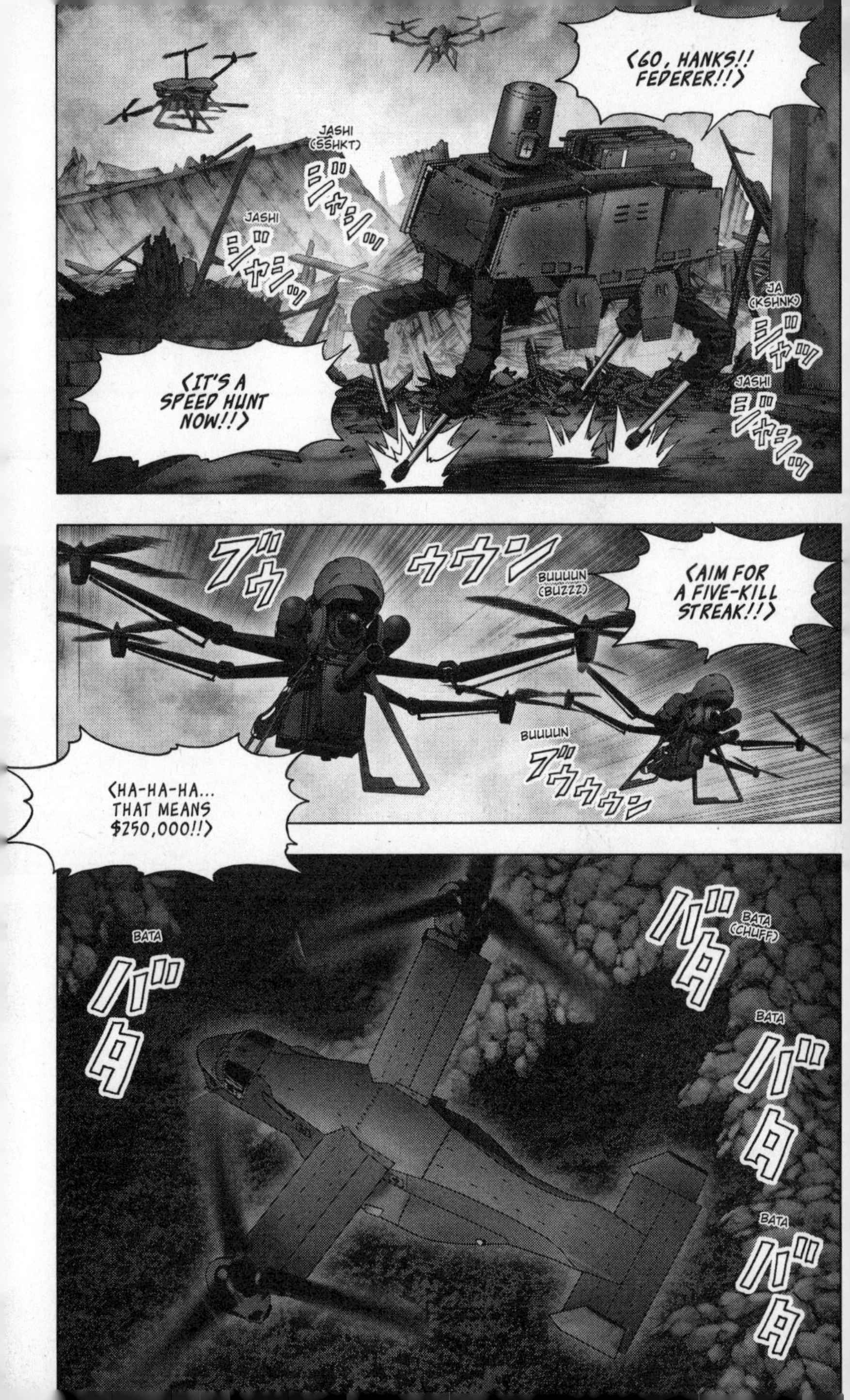
〈GO, HANKS!! FEDERER!!〉
JA (KSHNK)
ジャッ
JASHI
ジャシッ
JASHI (SSHKT)
ジャシッ
JASHI
ジャシッ
〈IT'S A SPEED HUNT NOW!!〉
〈AIM FOR A FIVE-KILL STREAK!!〉
ブウウウン
BUUUUN (BUZZZ)
BUUUUN
ブウウウン
〈HA-HA-HA... THAT MEANS $250,000!!〉
BATA (CHUFF)
バタ
BATA
バタ
BATA
バタ
BATA
バタ

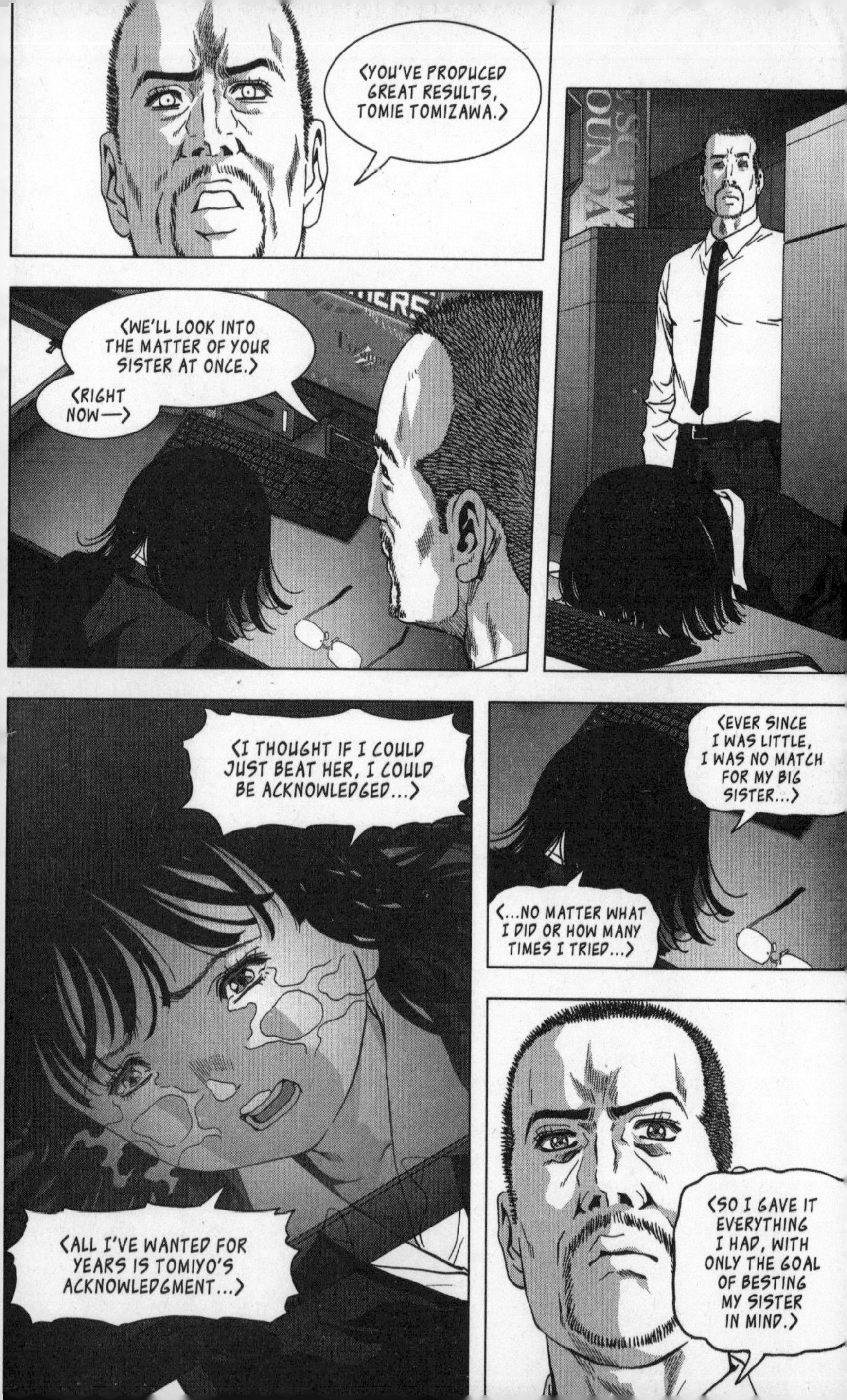
<YOU'VE PRODUCED GREAT RESULTS, TOMIE TOMIZAWA.>
<WE'LL LOOK INTO THE MATTER OF YOUR SISTER AT ONCE.>
<RIGHT NOW—>
<EVER SINCE I WAS LITTLE, I WAS NO MATCH FOR MY BIG SISTER...>
<...NO MATTER WHAT I DID OR HOW MANY TIMES I TRIED...>
<SO I GAVE IT EVERYTHING I HAD, WITH ONLY THE GOAL OF BESTING MY SISTER IN MIND.>
<I THOUGHT IF I COULD JUST BEAT HER, I COULD BE ACKNOWLEDGED...>
<ALL I'VE WANTED FOR YEARS IS TOMIYO'S ACKNOWLEDGMENT...>

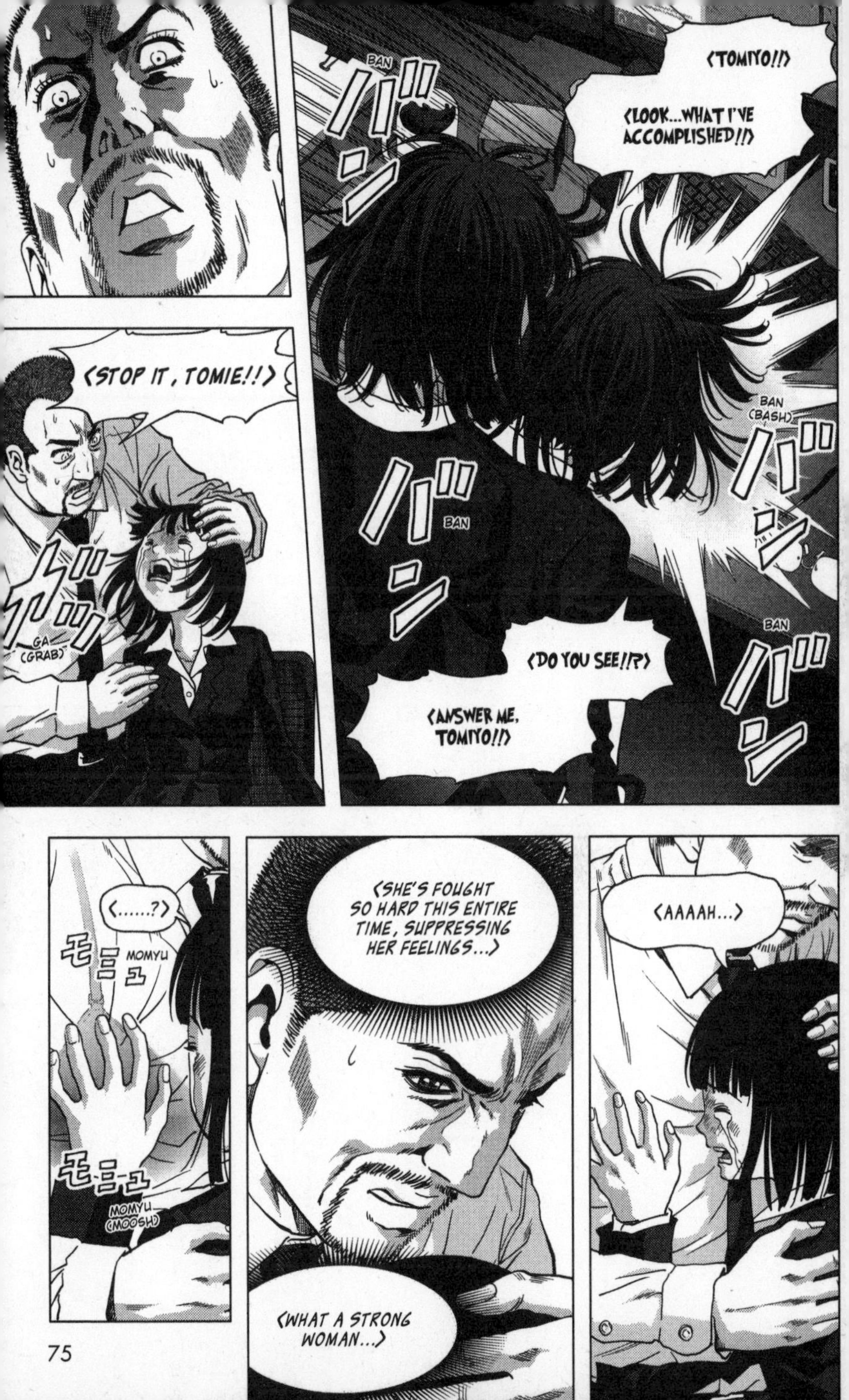
‹TOMIYO!!›
‹LOOK...WHAT I'VE ACCOMPLISHED!!›
BAN
BAN (BASH)
BAN
BAN
‹DO YOU SEE!!?›
‹ANSWER ME, TOMIYO!!›
‹STOP IT, TOMIE!!›
GA (GRAB)
‹AAAAH...›
‹SHE'S FOUGHT SO HARD THIS ENTIRE TIME, SUPPRESSING HER FEELINGS...›
‹WHAT A STRONG WOMAN...›
‹......?›
MOMYU
MOMYU (MOOSH)

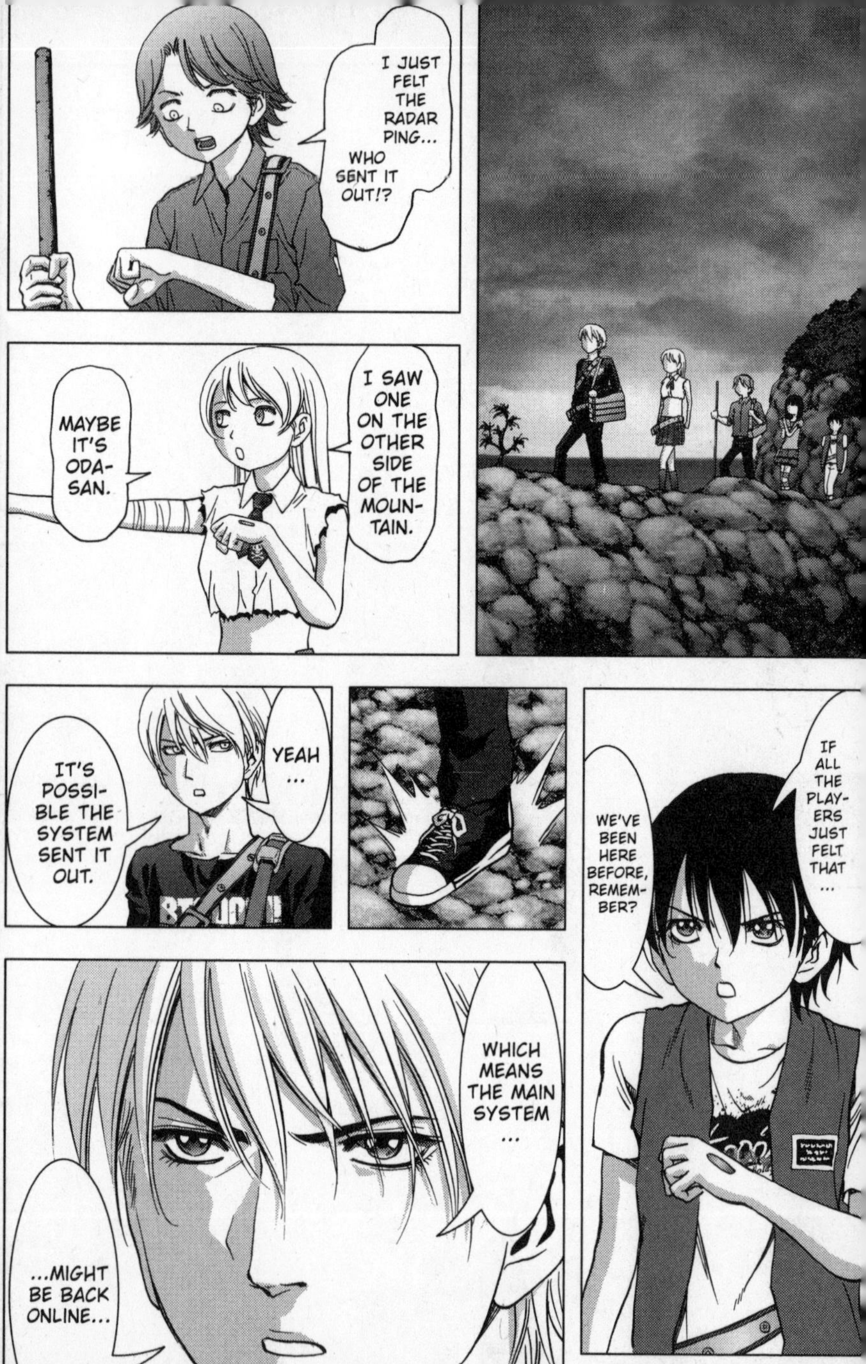
I JUST FELT THE RADAR PING...
WHO SENT IT OUT!?
I SAW ONE ON THE OTHER SIDE OF THE MOUN-TAIN.
MAYBE IT'S ODA-SAN.
IF ALL THE PLAY-ERS JUST FELT THAT...
WE'VE BEEN HERE BEFORE, REMEM-BER?
YEAH...
IT'S POSSI-BLE THE SYSTEM SENT IT OUT.
WHICH MEANS THE MAIN SYSTEM...
...MIGHT BE BACK ONLINE...

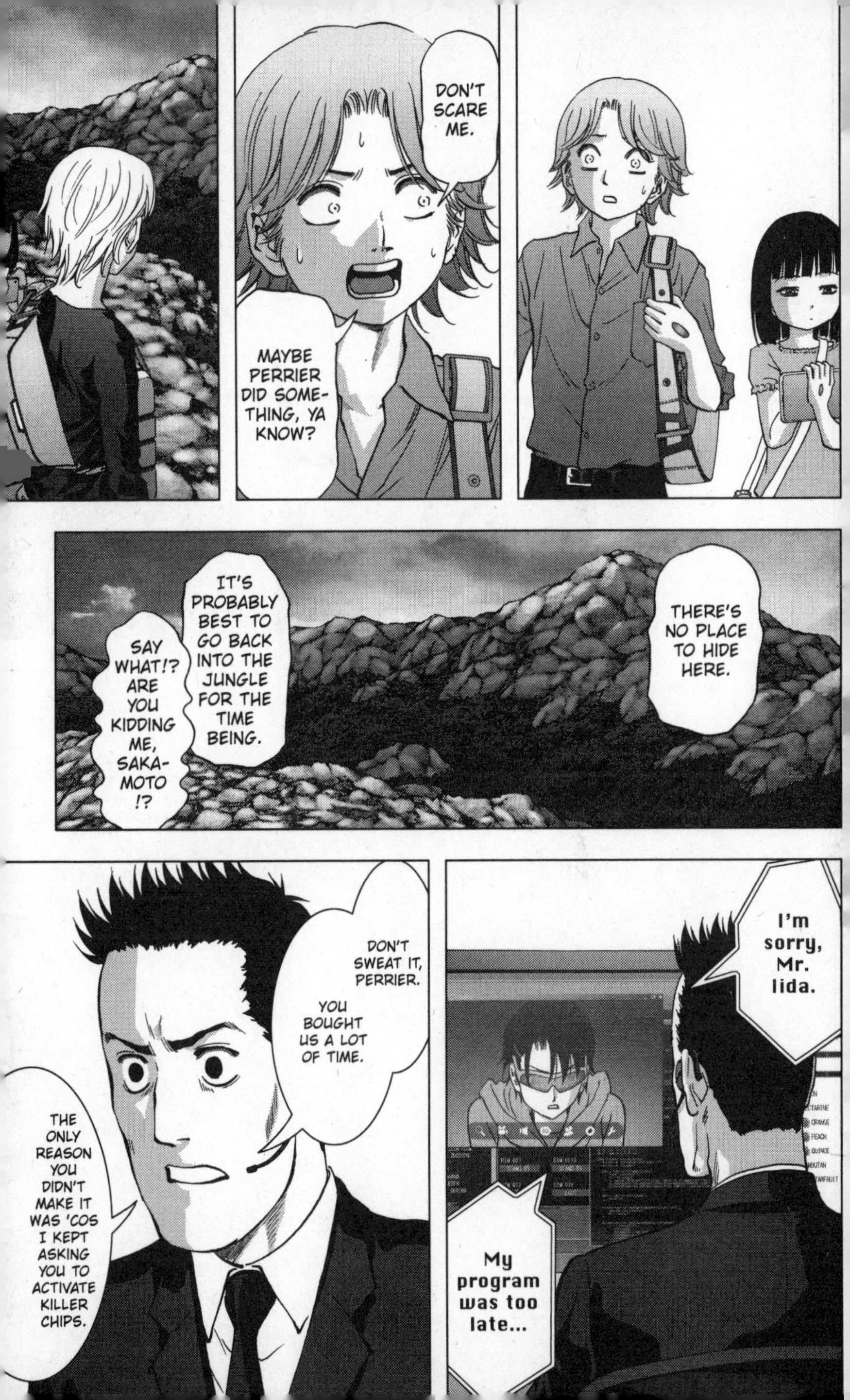
DON'T SCARE ME.
MAYBE PERRIER DID SOME-THING, YA KNOW?
THERE'S NO PLACE TO HIDE HERE.
IT'S PROBABLY BEST TO GO BACK INTO THE JUNGLE FOR THE TIME BEING.
SAY WHAT!? ARE YOU KIDDING ME, SAKA-MOTO!?
I'm sorry, Mr. Iida.
My program was too late...
DON'T SWEAT IT, PERRIER.
YOU BOUGHT US A LOT OF TIME.
THE ONLY REASON YOU DIDN'T MAKE IT WAS 'COS I KEPT ASKING YOU TO ACTIVATE KILLER CHIPS.

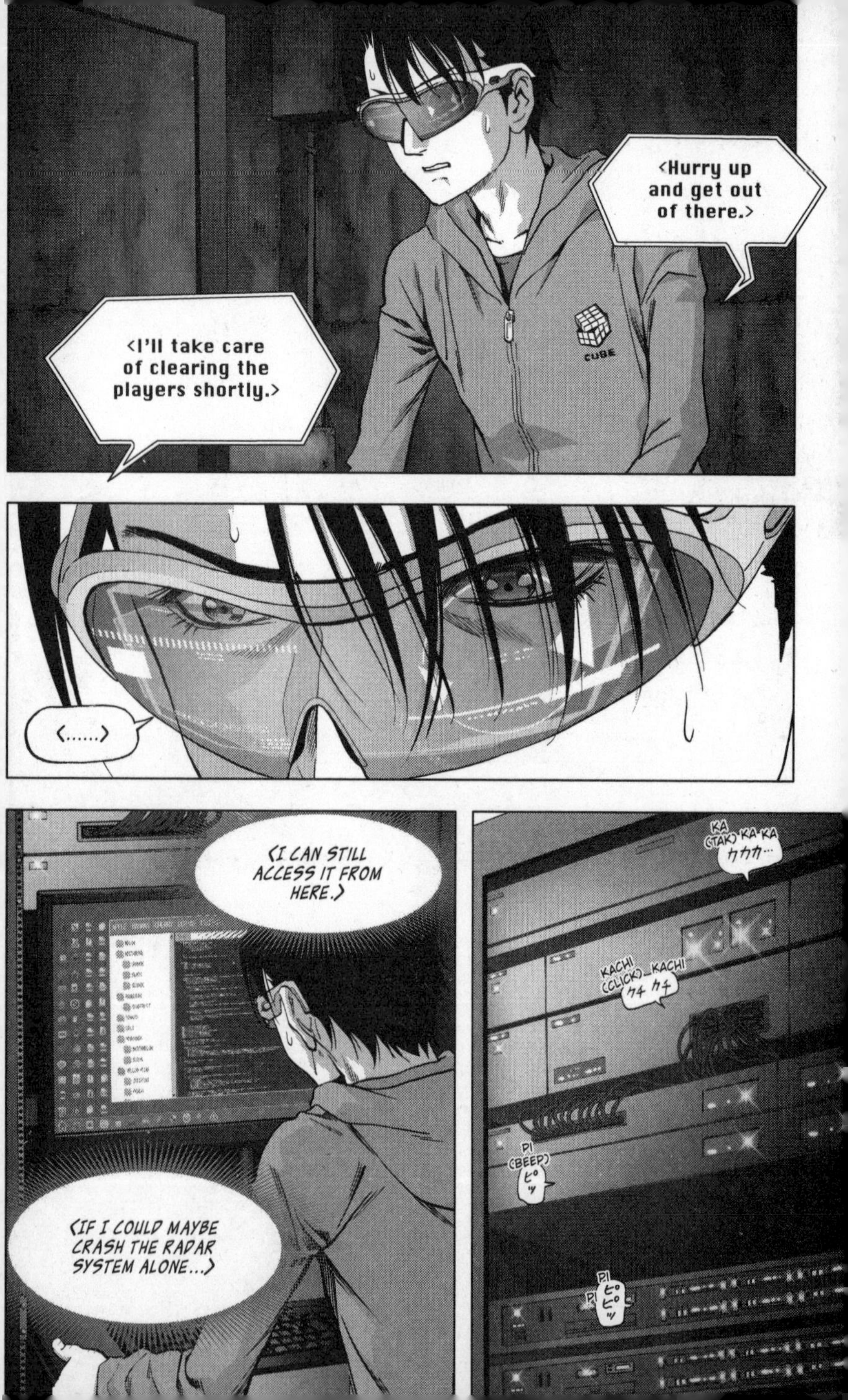
<Hurry up and get out of there.>
<I'll take care of clearing the players shortly.>
<......>
KA (TAK) KA KA カカカ…
KACHI (CLICK) KACHI カチ カチ
PI (BEEP) ピッ
PI PI ピピッ
<I CAN STILL ACCESS IT FROM HERE.>
<IF I COULD MAYBE CRASH THE RADAR SYSTEM ALONE...>

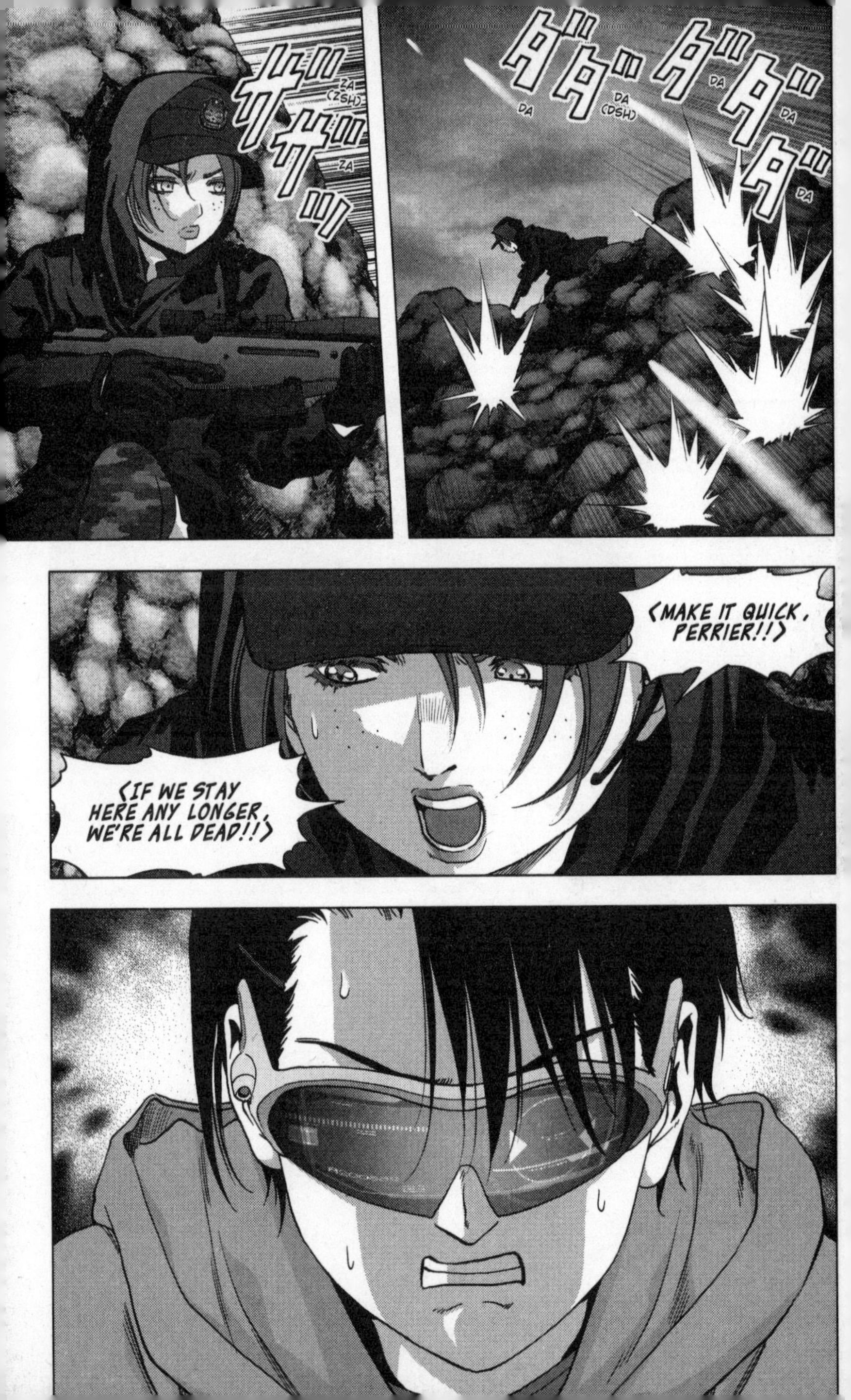
DA
DA (DSH)
DA
DA
DA
ZA (ZSH)
ZA
〈MAKE IT QUICK, PERRIER!!〉
〈IF WE STAY HERE ANY LONGER, WE'RE ALL DEAD!!〉

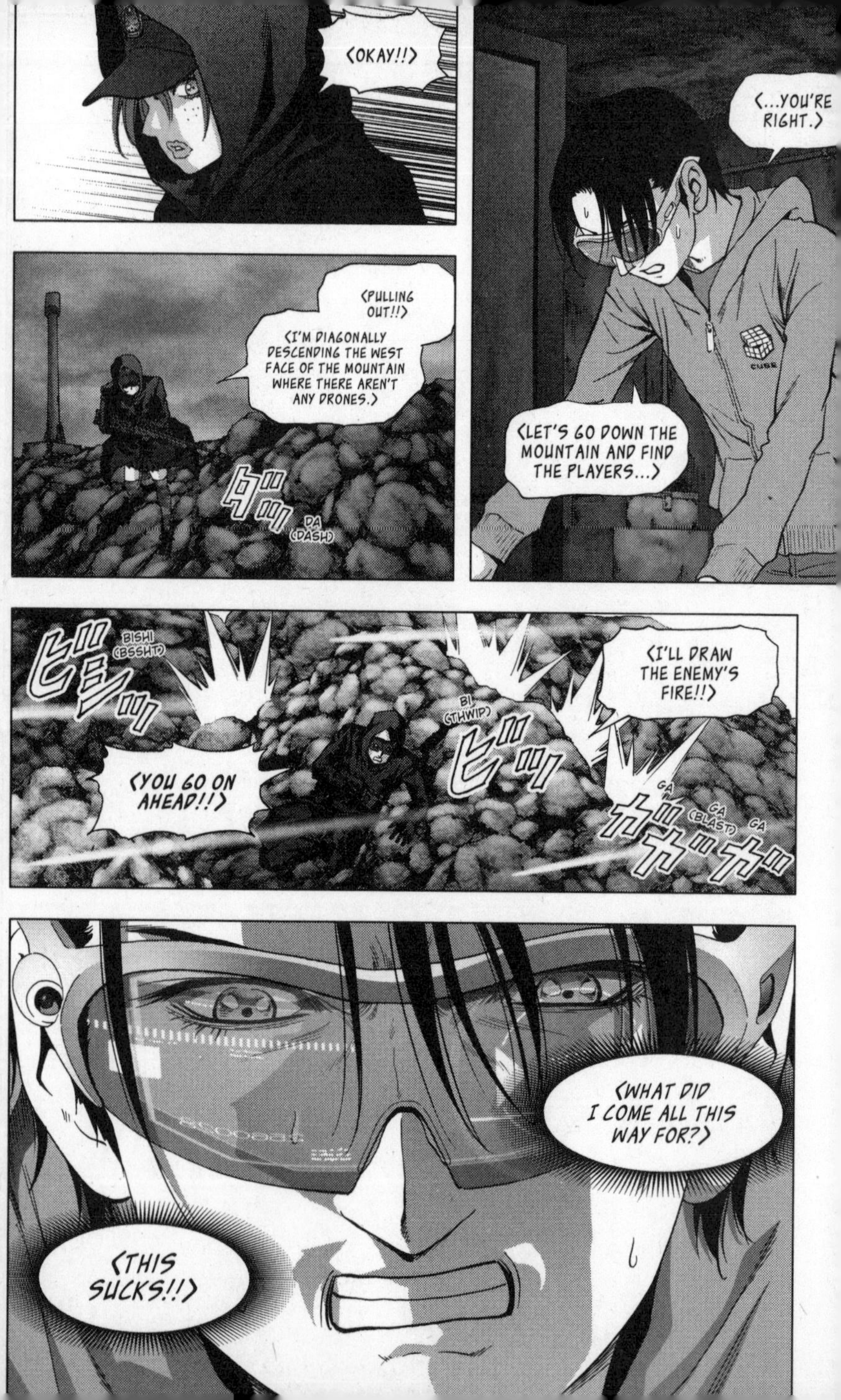
〈...YOU'RE RIGHT.〉
〈LET'S GO DOWN THE MOUNTAIN AND FIND THE PLAYERS...〉
〈OKAY!!〉
〈PULLING OUT!!〉
〈I'M DIAGONALLY DESCENDING THE WEST FACE OF THE MOUNTAIN WHERE THERE AREN'T ANY DRONES.〉
DA (DASH)
〈I'LL DRAW THE ENEMY'S FIRE!!〉
GA GA (BLAST) GA
BI (THWIP)
BISHI (BSSHT)
〈YOU GO ON AHEAD!!〉
〈WHAT DID I COME ALL THIS WAY FOR?〉
〈THIS SUCKS!!〉

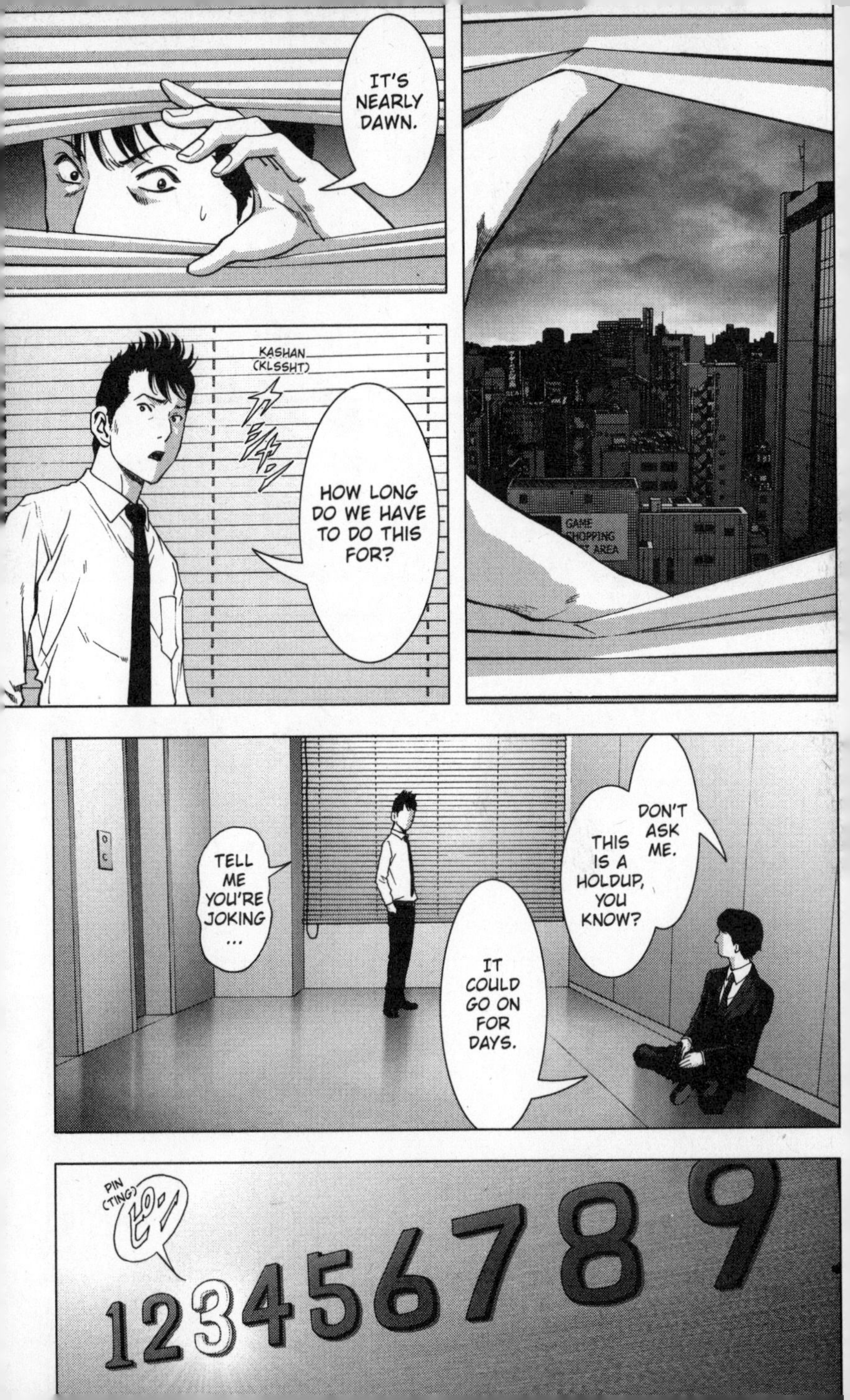
GAME
IT'S NEARLY DAWN.
KASHAN (KLSSHT)
HOW LONG DO WE HAVE TO DO THIS FOR?
DON'T ASK ME.
THIS IS A HOLDUP, YOU KNOW?
IT COULD GO ON FOR DAYS.
TELL ME YOU'RE JOKING ...
PIN (TING)
123456789

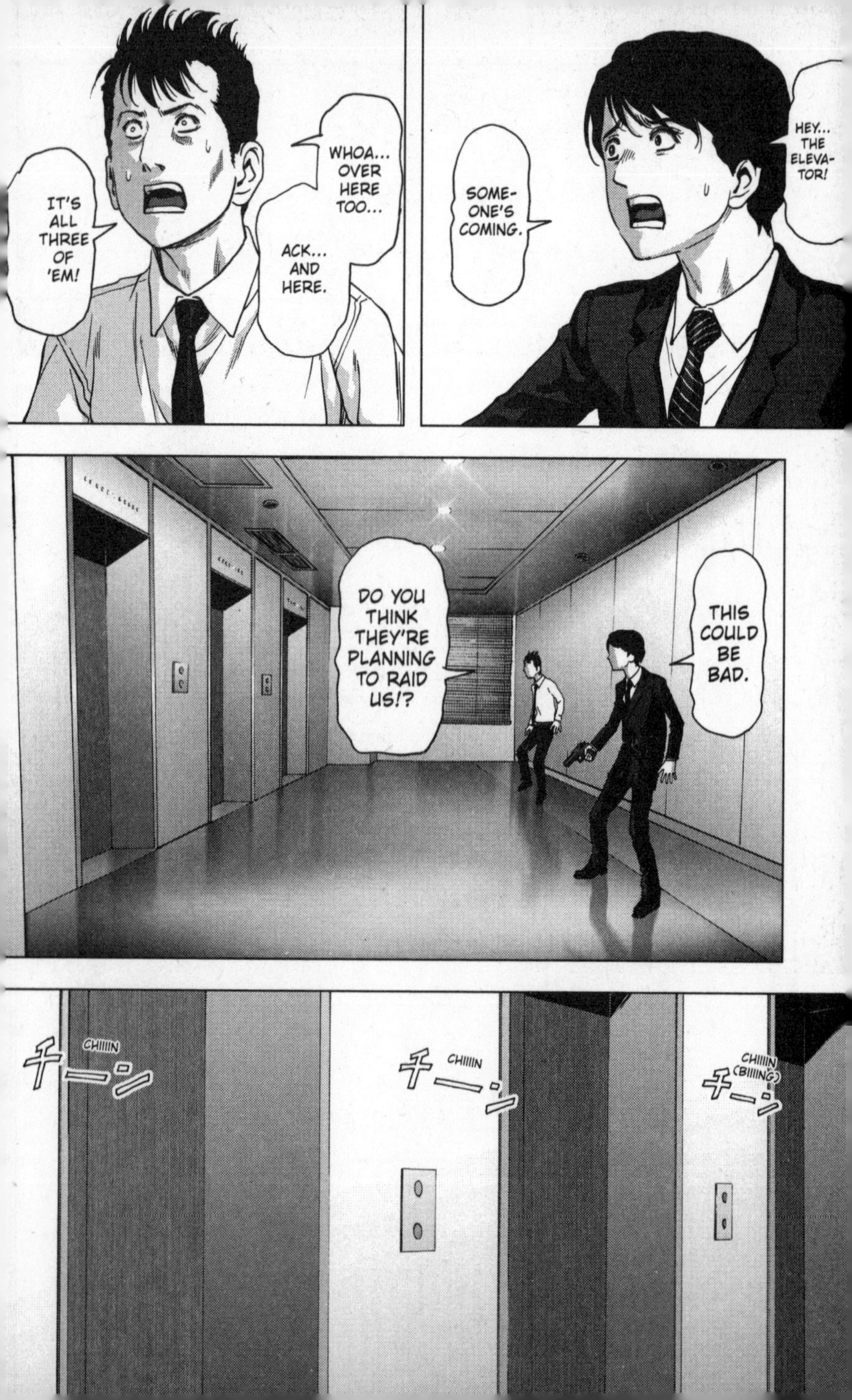
HEY... THE ELEVA-TOR!
SOME-ONE'S COMING.
WHOA... OVER HERE TOO...
ACK... AND HERE.
IT'S ALL THREE OF 'EM!
THIS COULD BE BAD.
DO YOU THINK THEY'RE PLANNING TO RAID US!?
チーン
CHIIIN (BIIIING)
チーン
CHIIIN
チーン
CHIIIIN

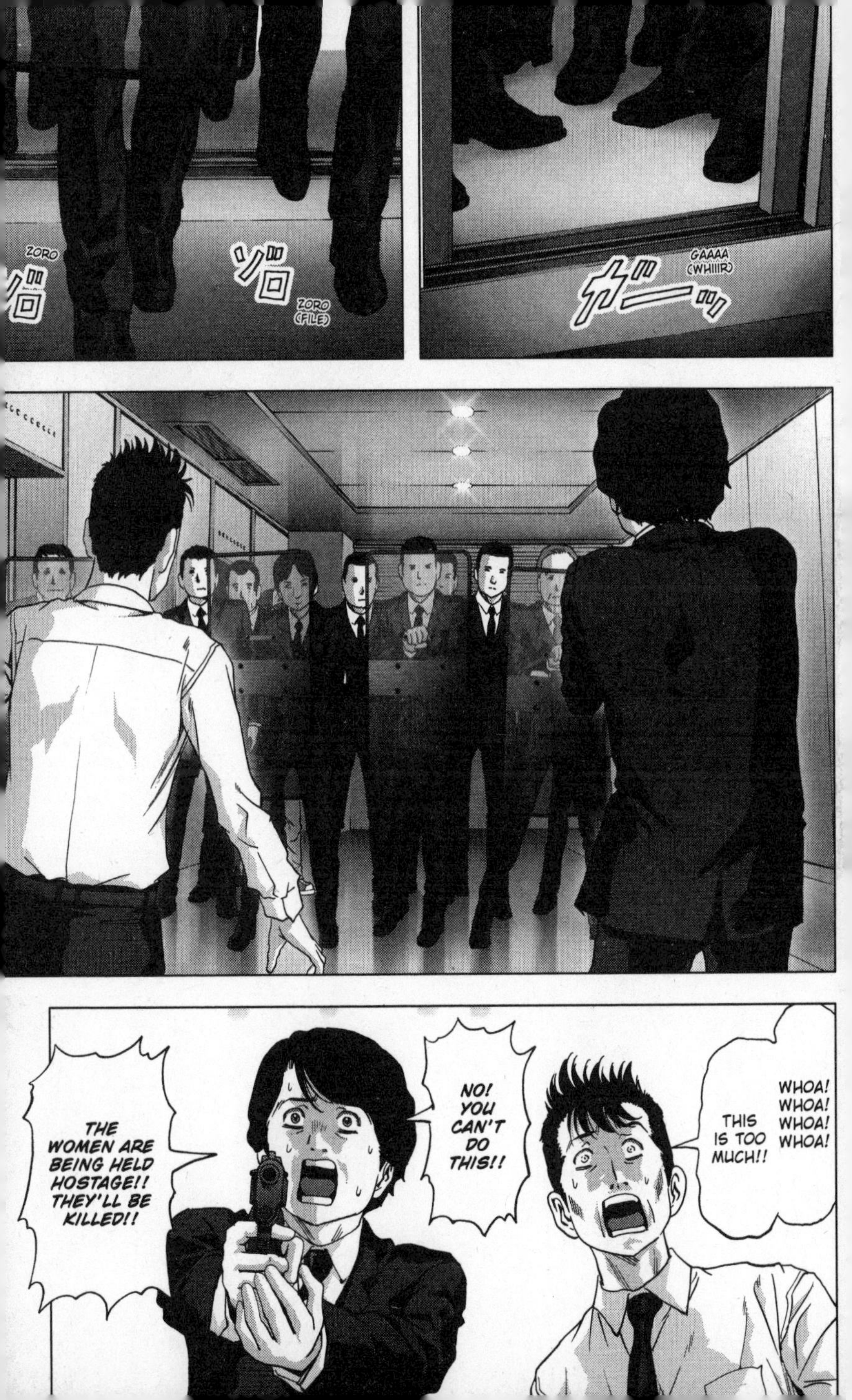
ガーッ
GAAAA (WHIIIR)
ゾロ
ZORO (FILE)
ZORO
ゾロ
WHOA! WHOA! WHOA! WHOA!
THIS IS TOO MUCH!!
NO! YOU CAN'T DO THIS!!
THE WOMEN ARE BEING HELD HOSTAGE!! THEY'LL BE KILLED!!

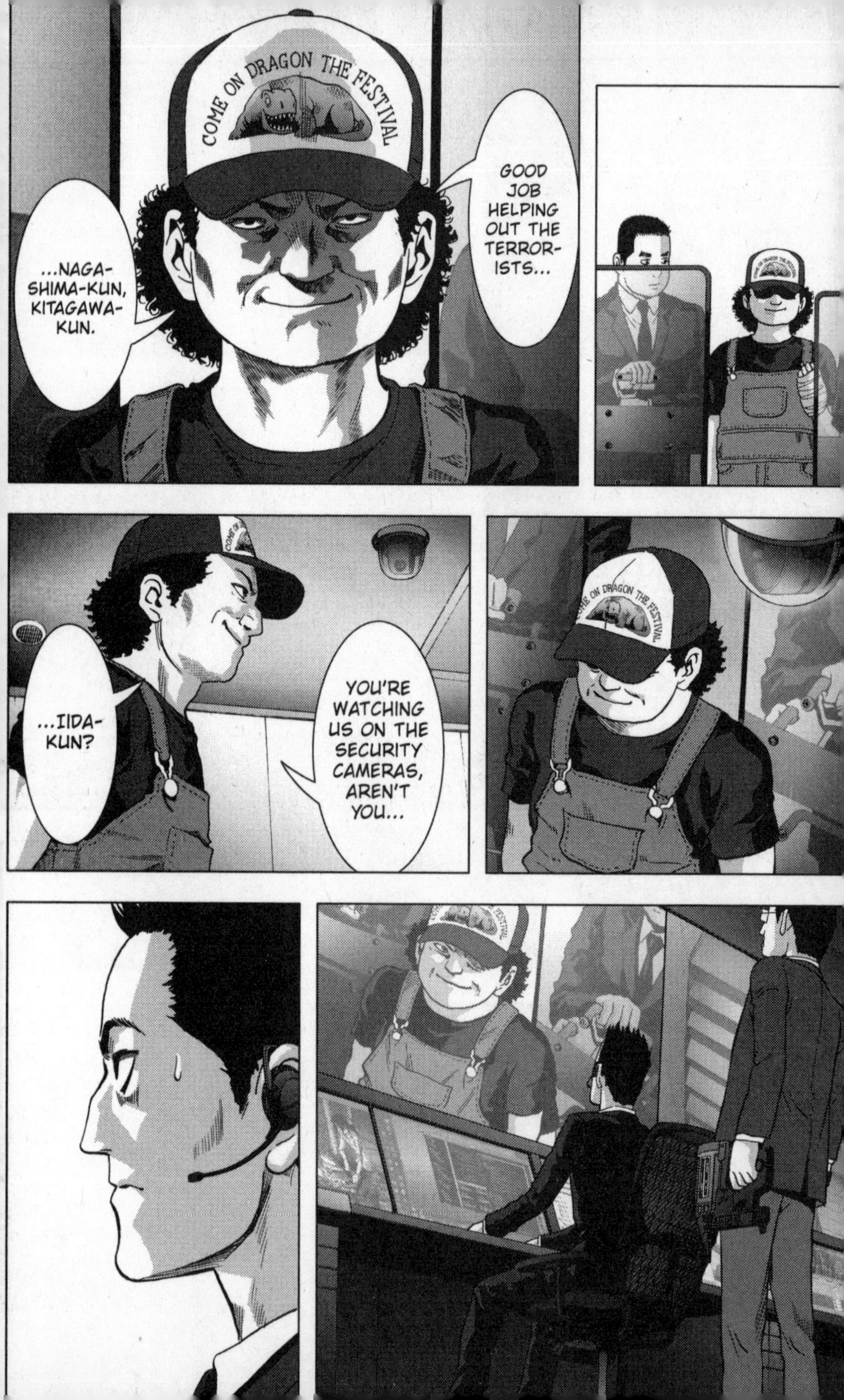
COME ON DRAGON THE FESTIVAL
GOOD JOB HELPING OUT THE TERRORISTS...
...NAGASHIMA-KUN, KITAGAWA-KUN.
YOU'RE WATCHING US ON THE SECURITY CAMERAS, AREN'T YOU...
...IIDA-KUN?

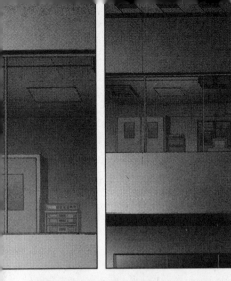

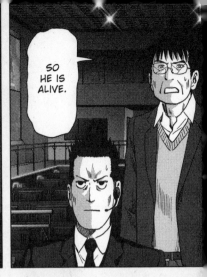

SO HE IS ALIVE.
Iida-kun ...
Did you think I'd kick the bucket that easy?
Sorry.
You're not the only one ready to die.
HE'S CLEARLY PROVOKING ME!!

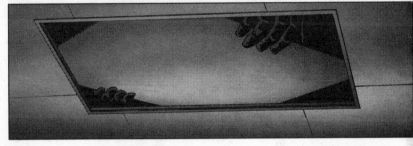

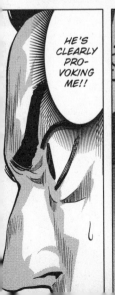

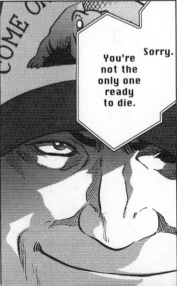

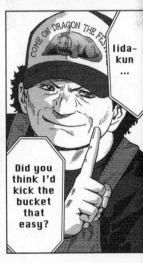

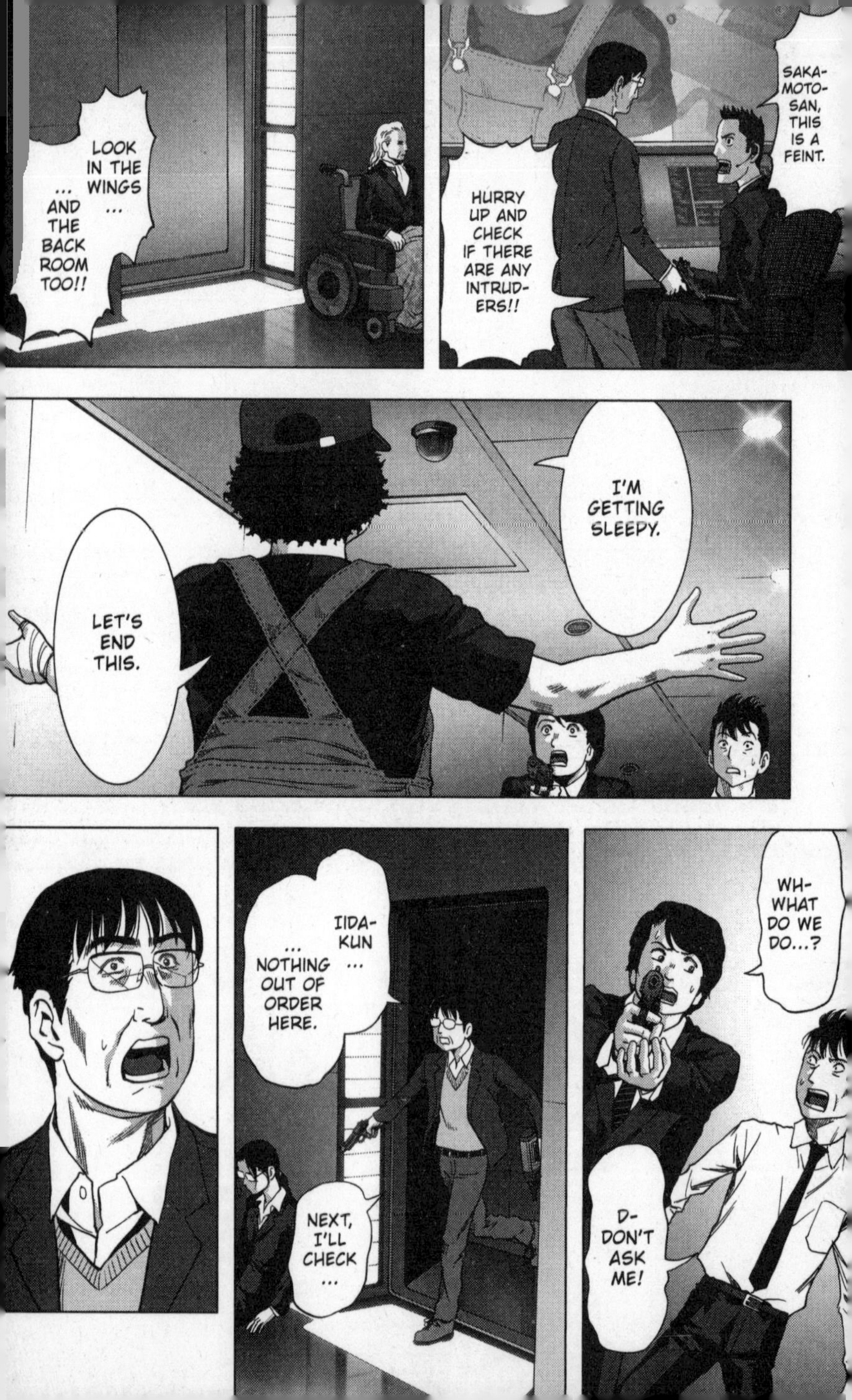
SAKA-MOTO-SAN, THIS IS A FEINT.
HURRY UP AND CHECK IF THERE ARE ANY INTRUD-ERS!!
LOOK IN THE WINGS ...
... AND THE BACK ROOM TOO!!
I'M GETTING SLEEPY.
LET'S END THIS.
WH-WHAT DO WE DO...?
D-DON'T ASK ME!
IIDA-KUN ...
... NOTHING OUT OF ORDER HERE.
NEXT, I'LL CHECK ...

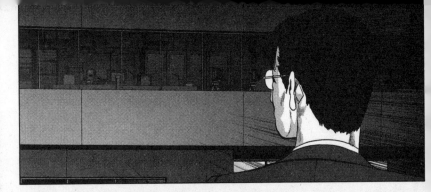

TAUN
(BLAM)

DO YOUR
STUFF!!

QUEEN'S
ANGELS
GIRLS!

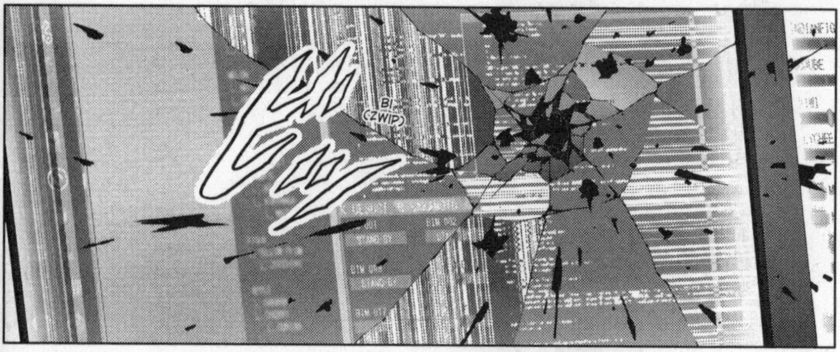
BI
(ZWIP)
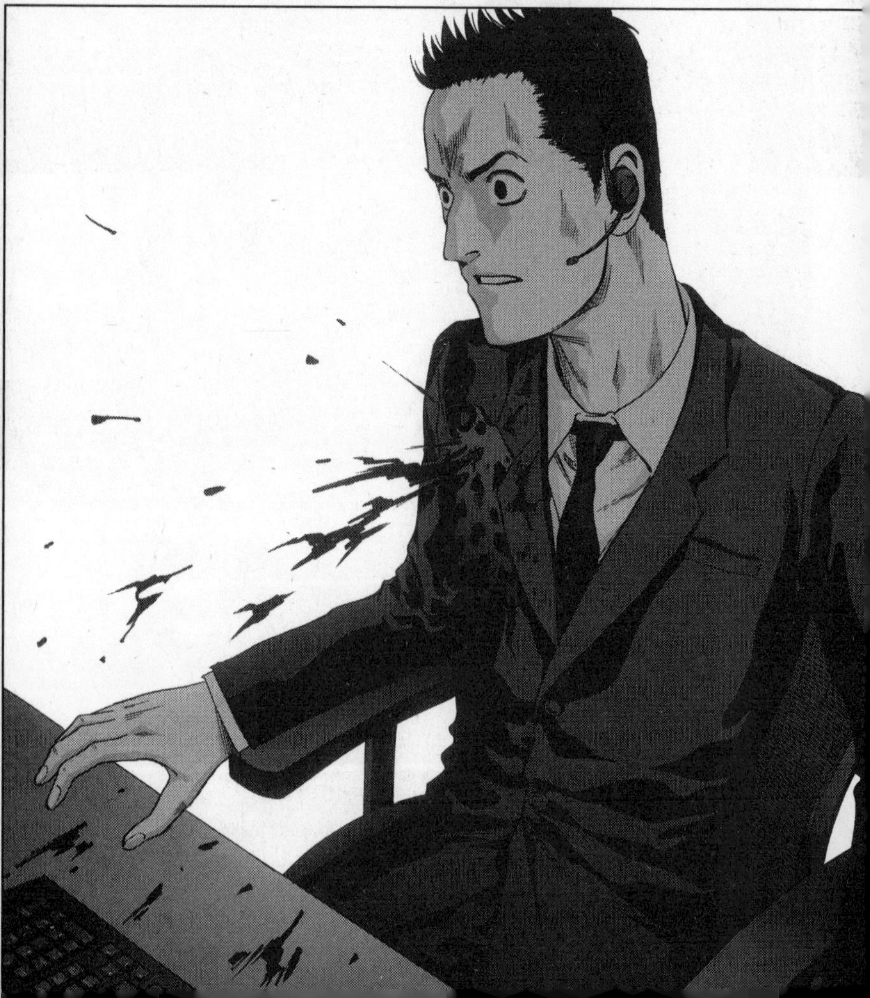

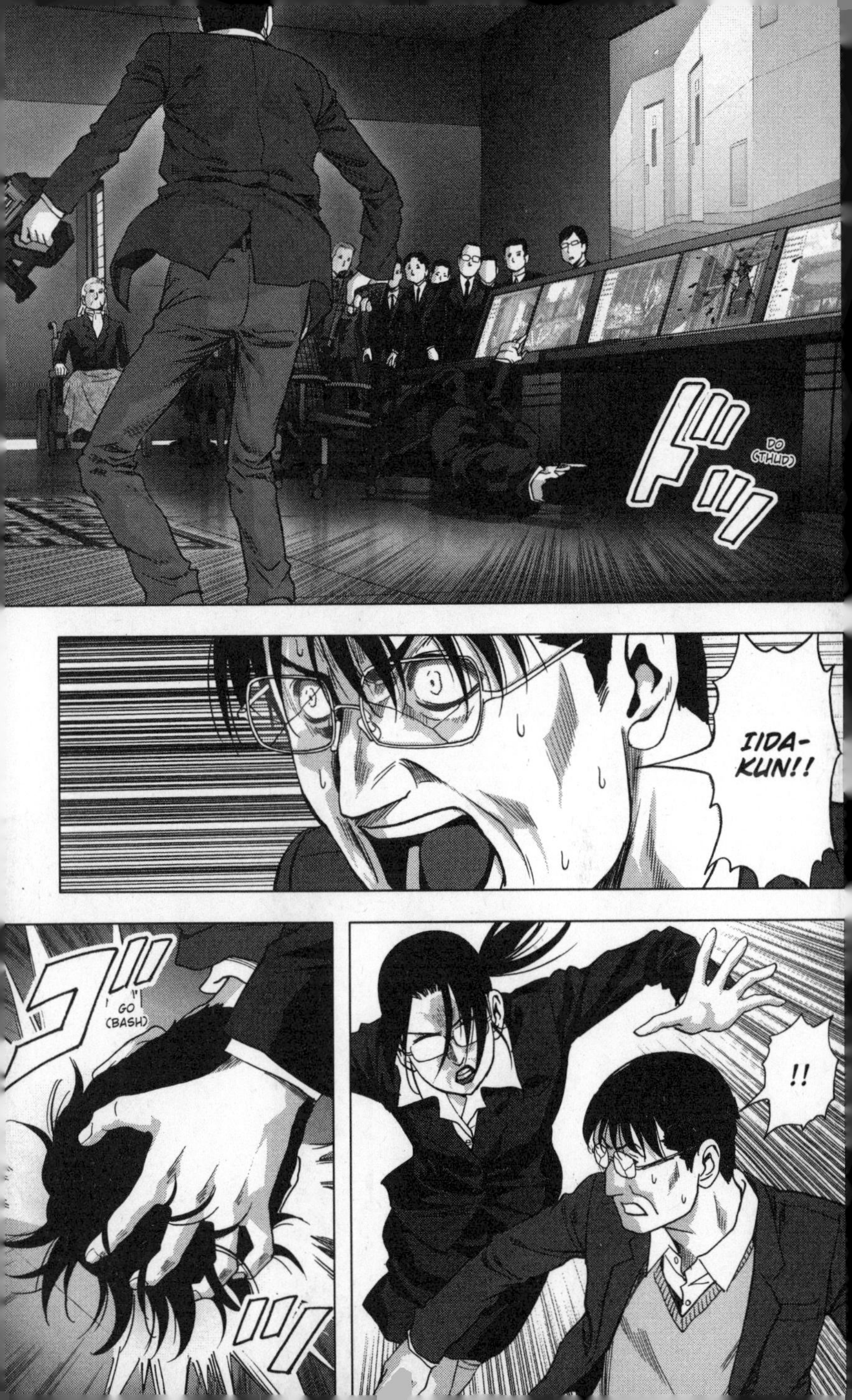
DO
(THUD)
IIDA-KUN!!
!!
GO
(BASH)

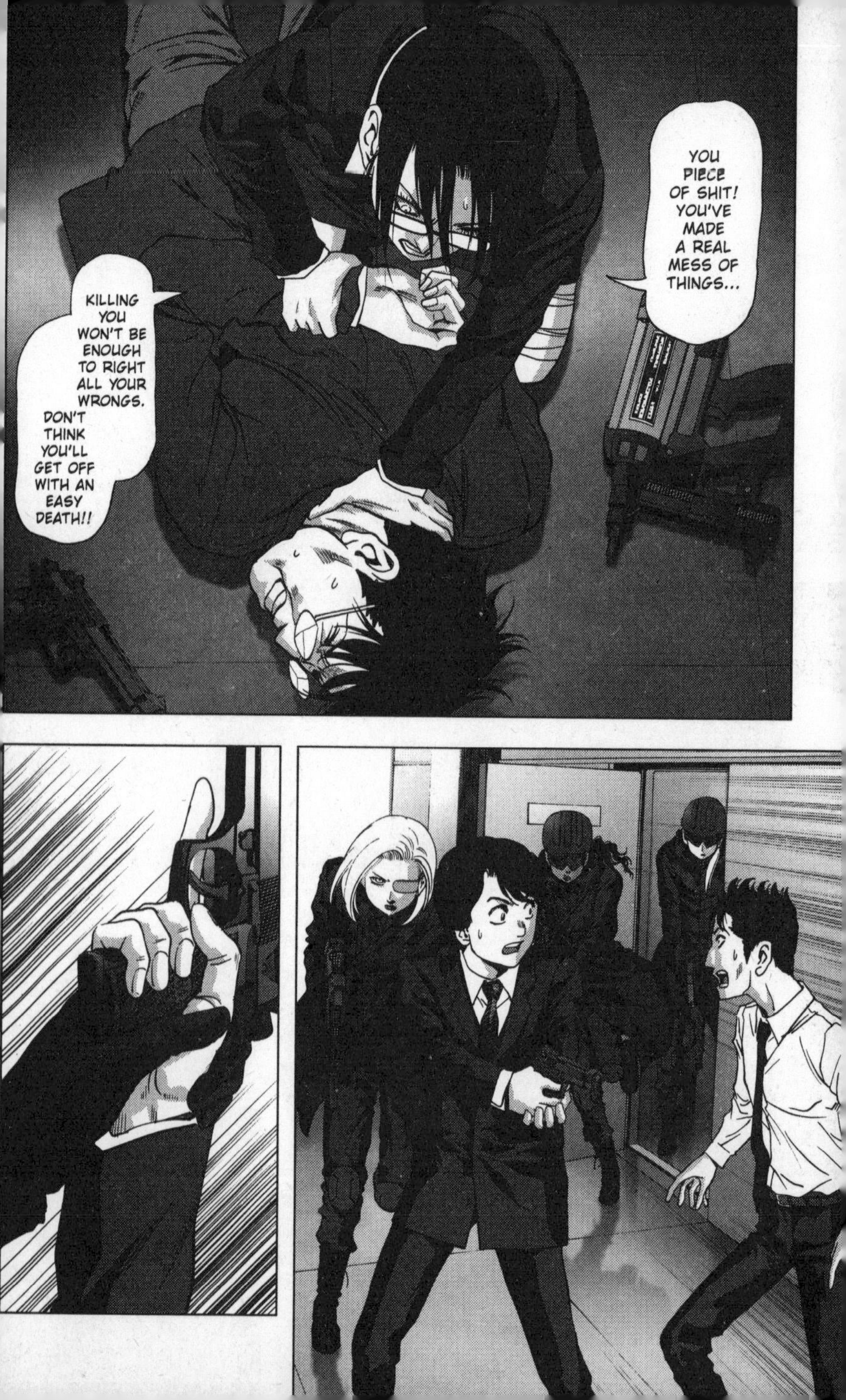
YOU PIECE OF SHIT! YOU'VE MADE A REAL MESS OF THINGS...
KILLING YOU WON'T BE ENOUGH TO RIGHT ALL YOUR WRONGS. DON'T THINK YOU'LL GET OFF WITH AN EASY DEATH!!

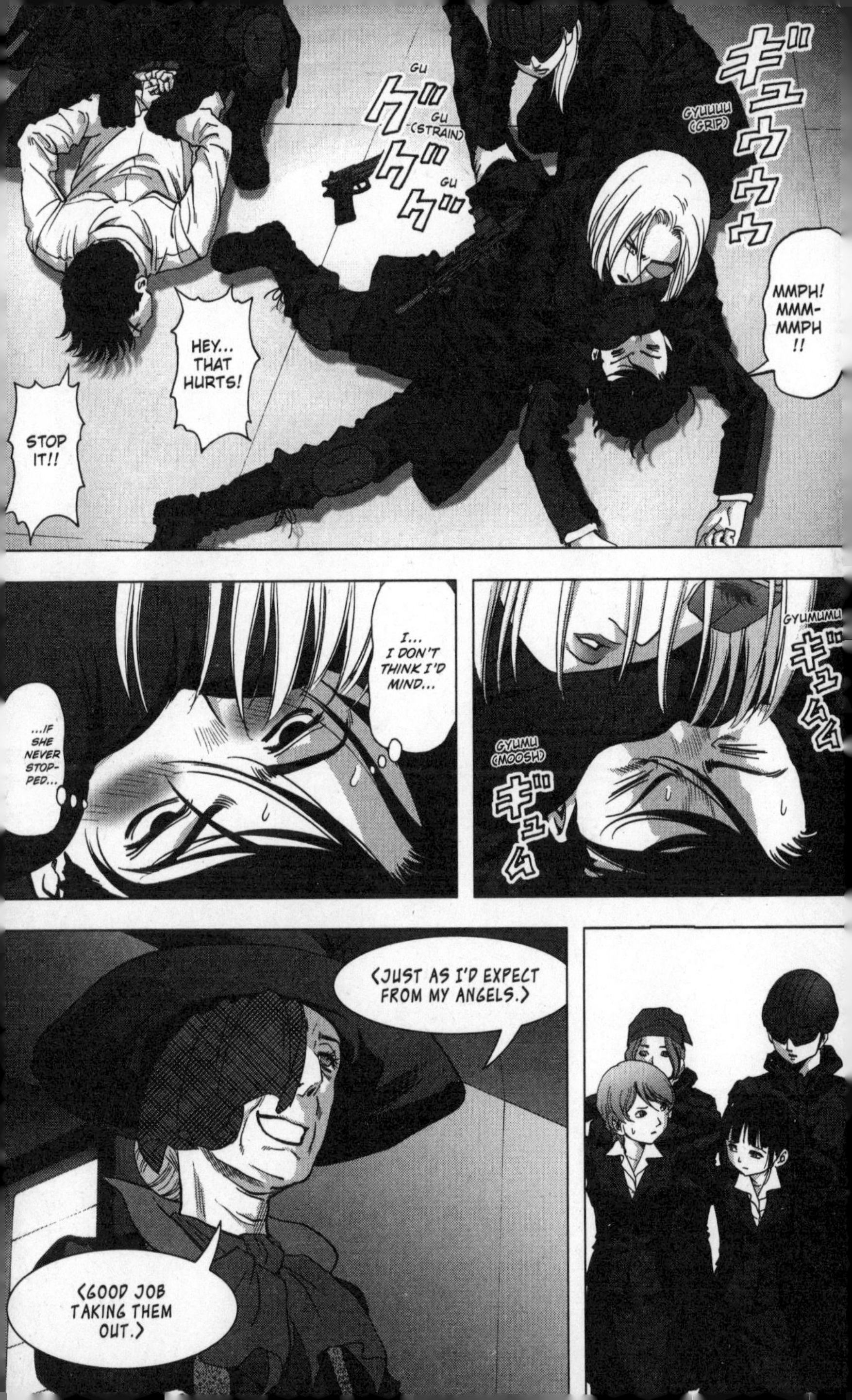
GYUUUU (GRIP)
MMPH! MMM-MMPH!!
GU GU (STRAIN) GU
HEY... THAT HURTS!
STOP IT!!
GYUMUMU
GYUMU (MOOSH)
I... I DON'T THINK I'D MIND...
...IF SHE NEVER STOPPED...
<JUST AS I'D EXPECT FROM MY ANGELS.>
<GOOD JOB TAKING THEM OUT.>

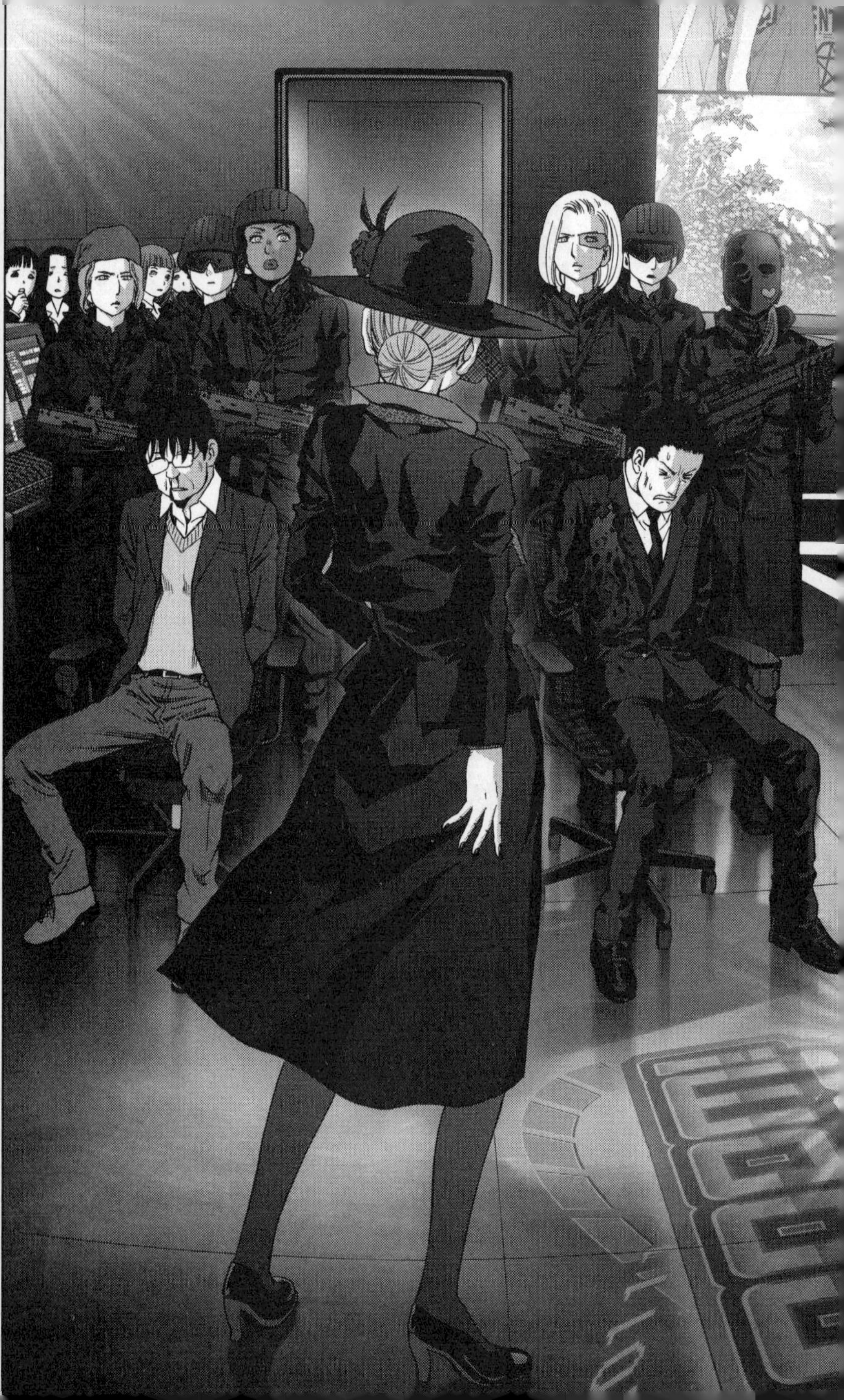

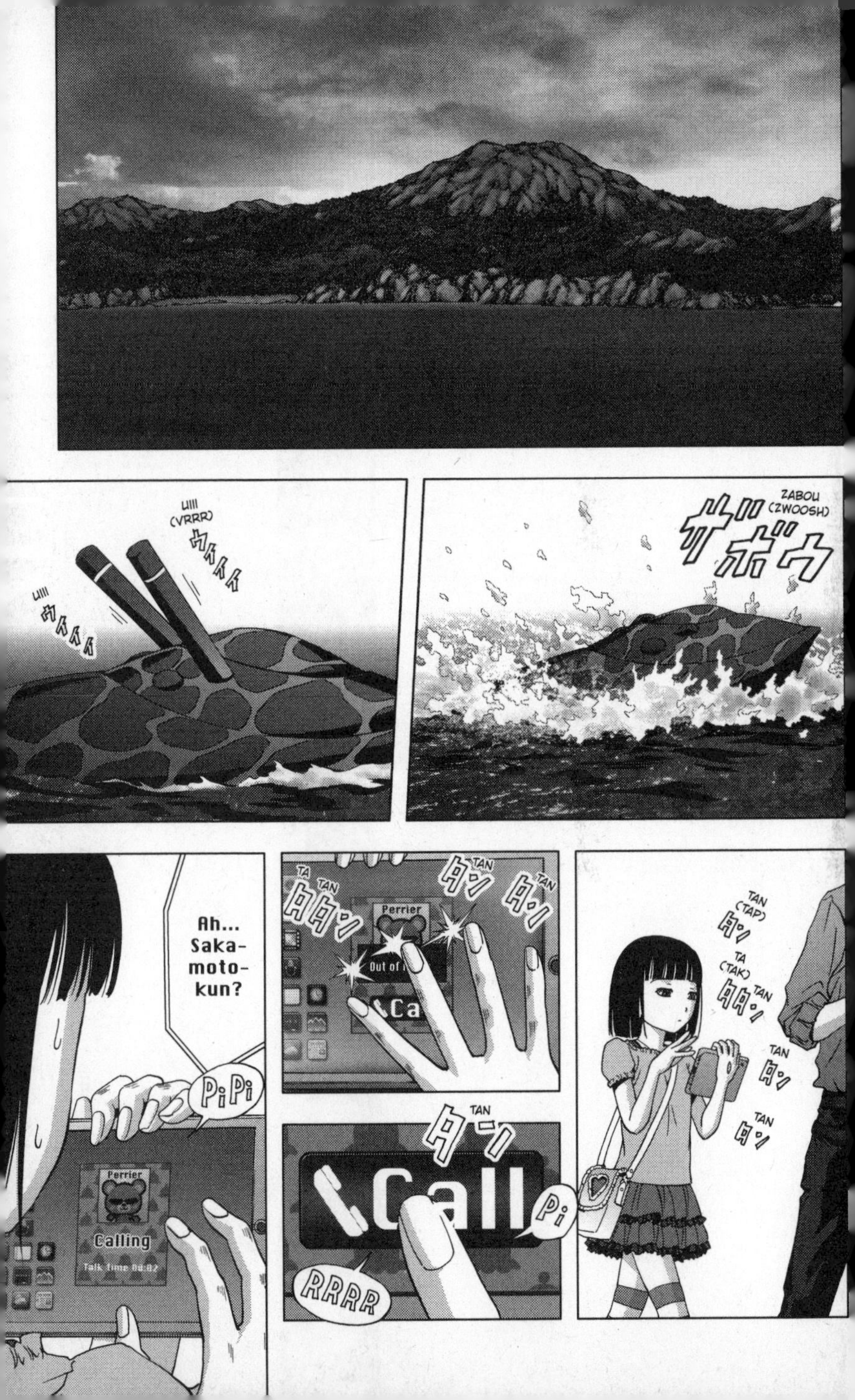
ZABOU (ZWOOSH)
ザボウ
UIII (VRRR)
ウィィィ
UIII
ウィィィ
TAN (TAP)
タン
TA (TAK) TAN
タタン
TAN
タン
TAN
タン
TA TAN
タタン
TAN
タン
TAN
タン
Perrier
Call
TAN
ターン
Call
Pi
RRRR
Ah... Sakamoto-kun?
PiPi
Perrier
Calling

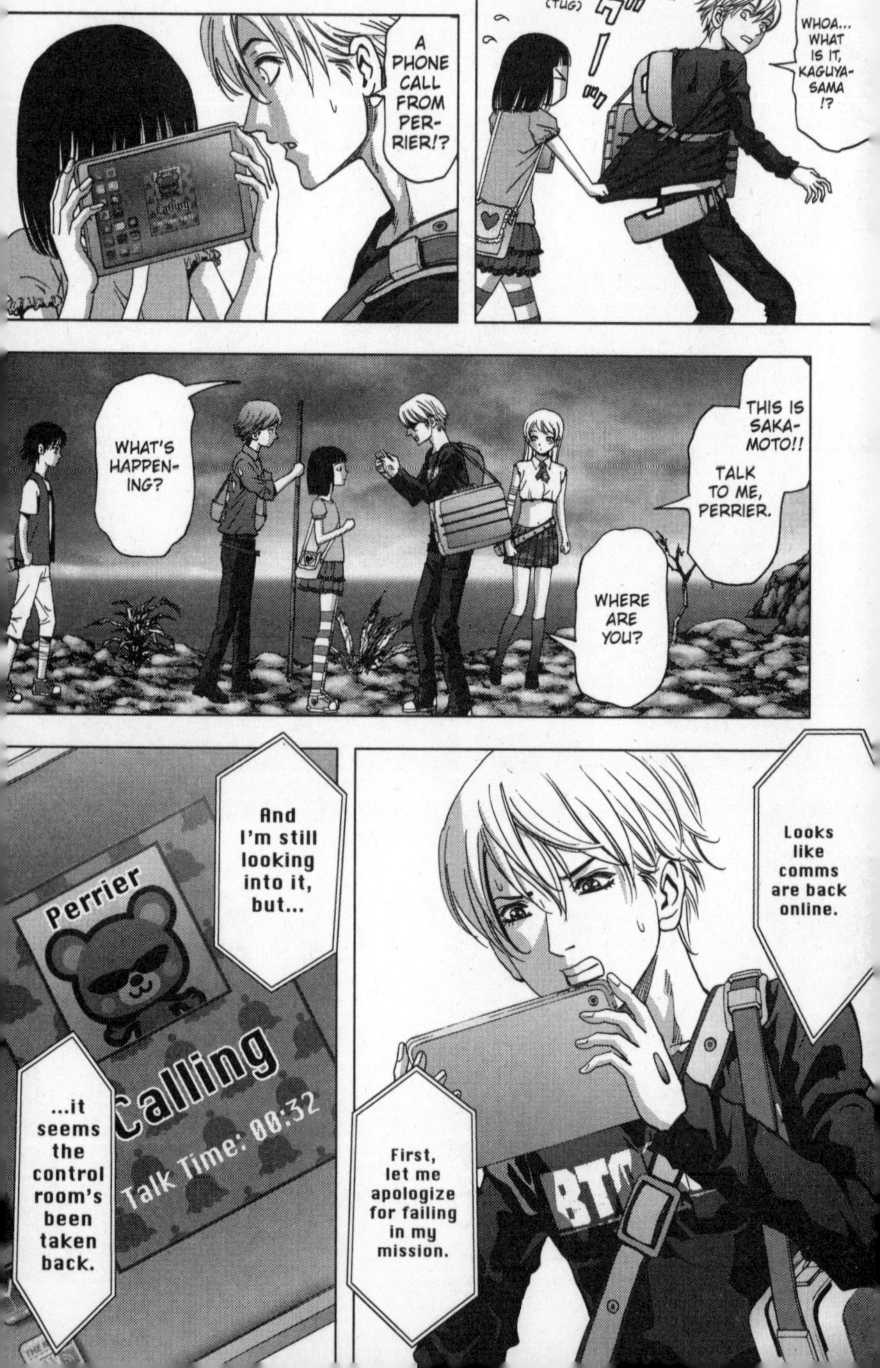
GU (TUG)
GUUUU
WHOA... WHAT IS IT, KAGUYA-SAMA!?
A PHONE CALL FROM PER-RIER!?
THIS IS SAKA-MOTO!!
TALK TO ME, PERRIER.
WHERE ARE YOU?
WHAT'S HAPPEN-ING?
Looks like comms are back online.
First, let me apologize for failing in my mission.
And I'm still looking into it, but...
...it seems the control room's been taken back.
Perrier
Calling
Talk Time: 00:32

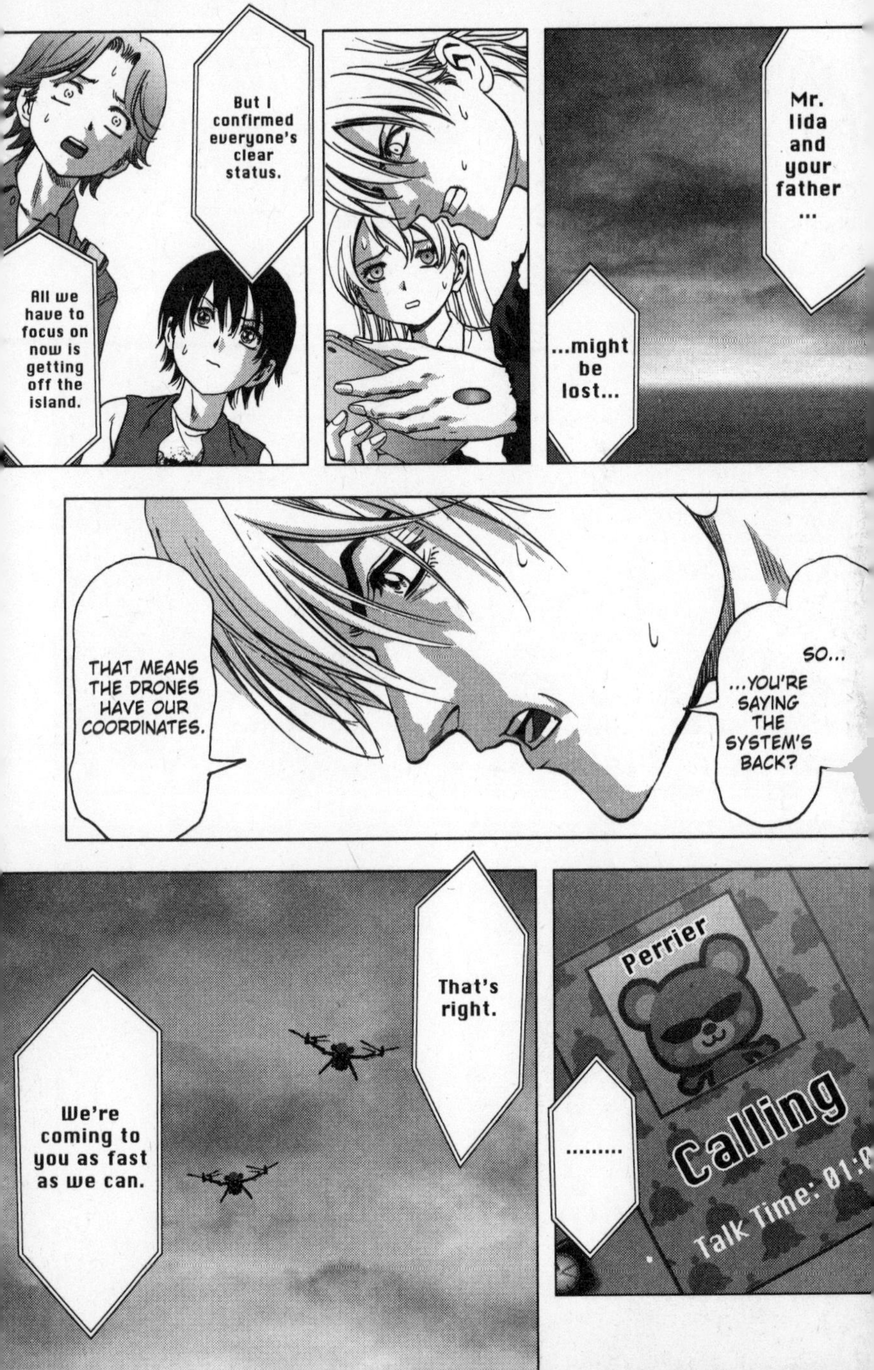
Mr. Iida and your father...
...might be lost...
But I confirmed everyone's clear status.
All we have to focus on now is getting off the island.
SO...
...YOU'RE SAYING THE SYSTEM'S BACK?
THAT MEANS THE DRONES HAVE OUR COORDINATES.
Perrier
Calling
Talk Time: 01:0
....
That's right.
We're coming to you as fast as we can.

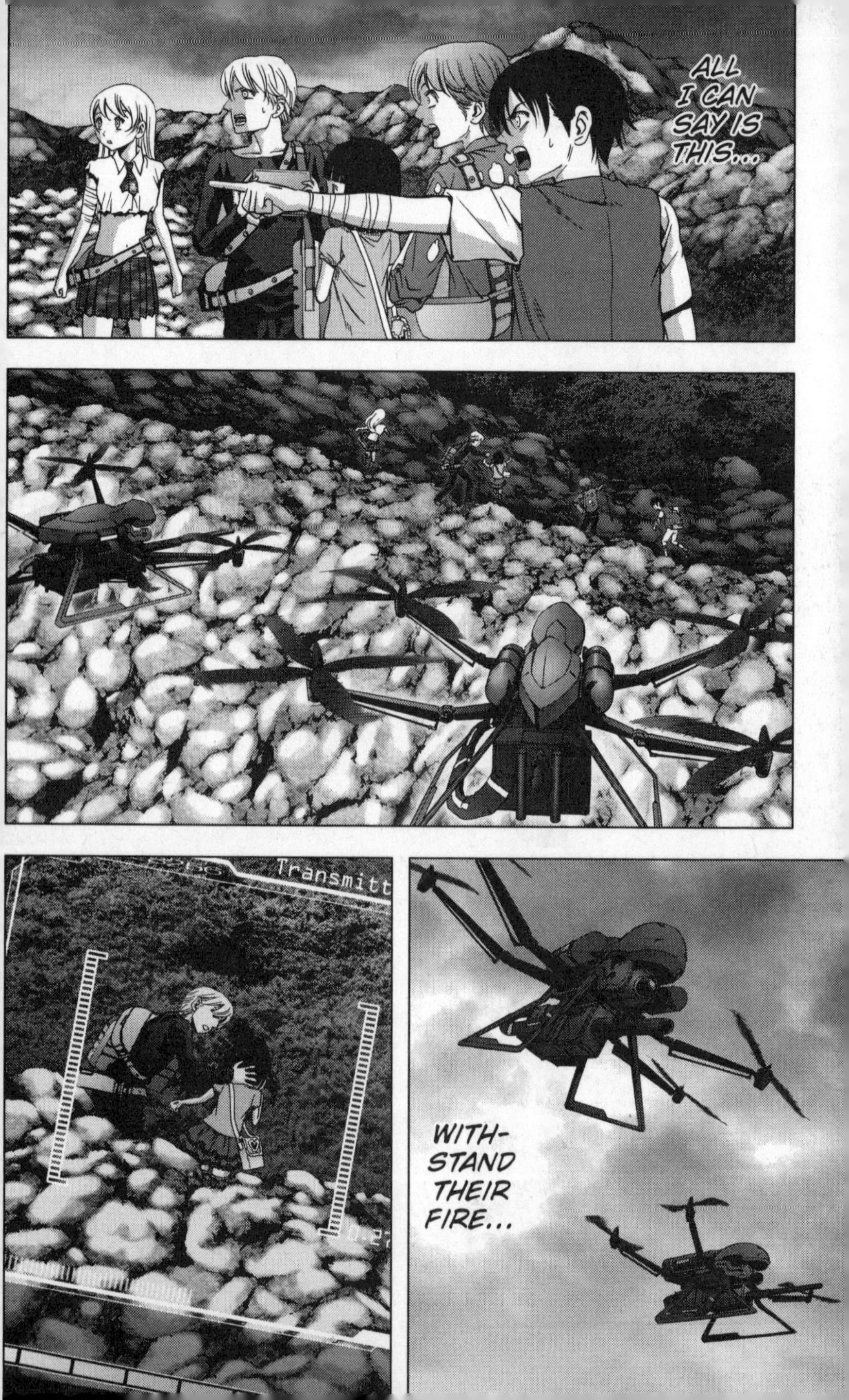
ALL I CAN SAY IS THIS...
WITH-STAND THEIR FIRE...
Transmitt

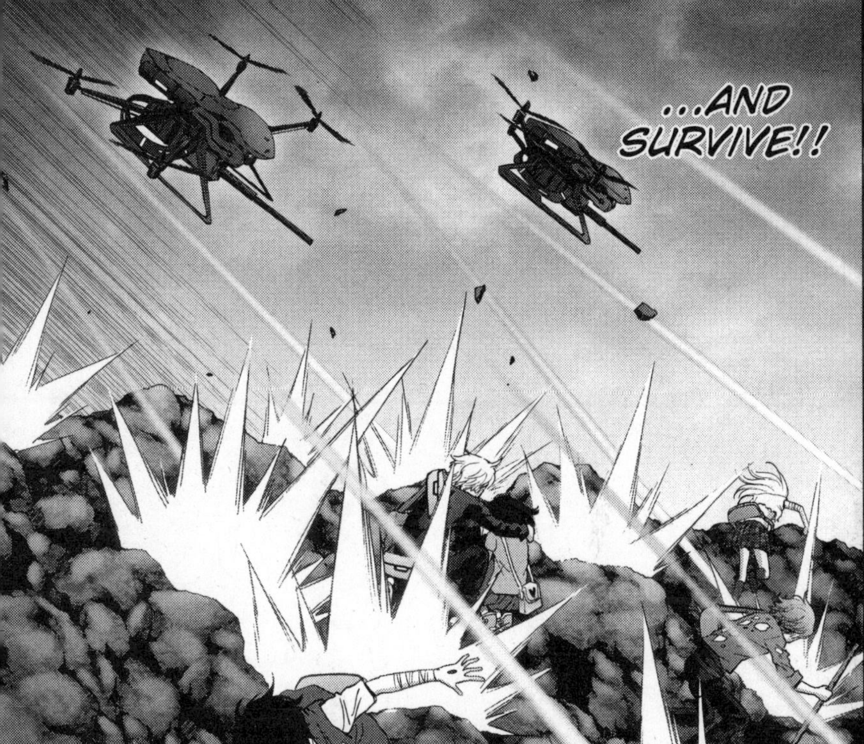
...AND SURVIVE!!
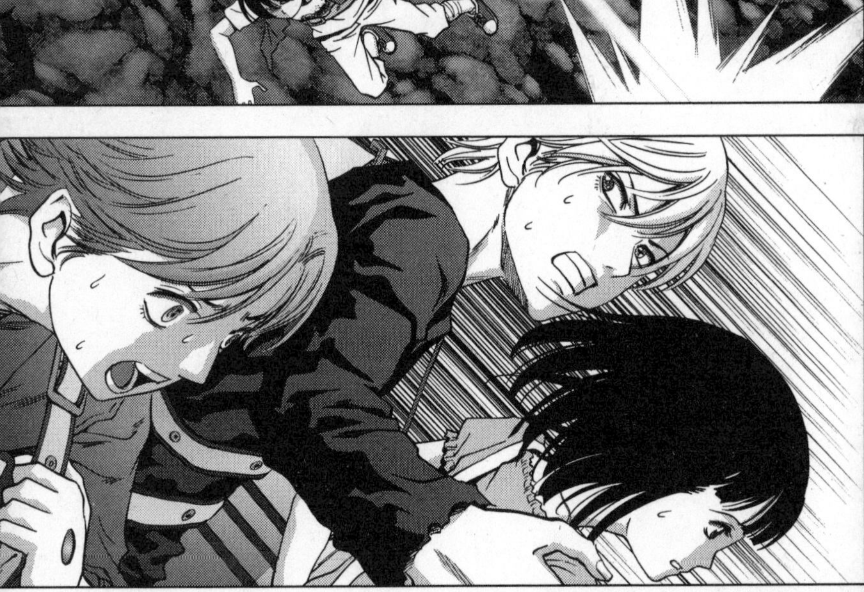

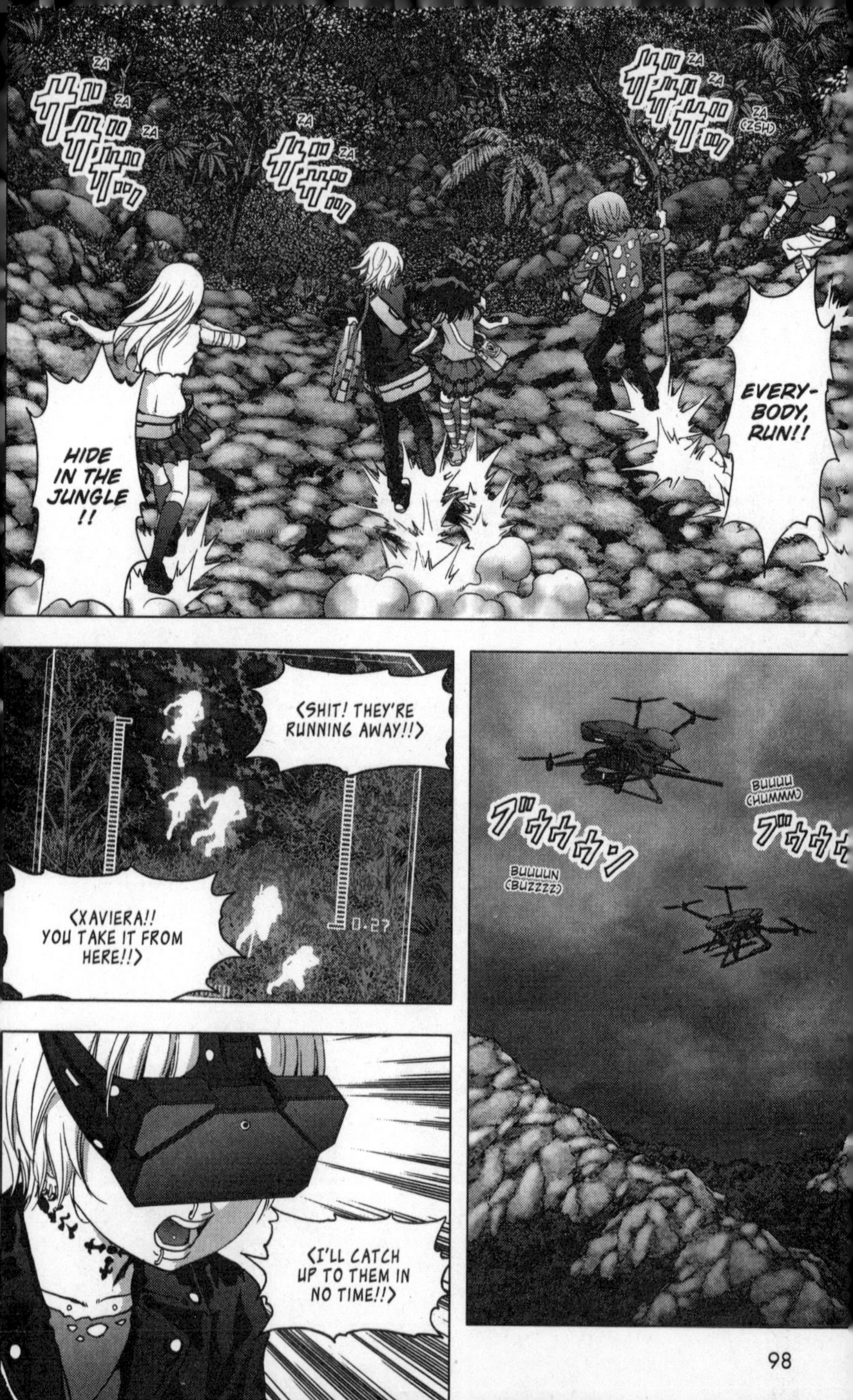
ZA ZA ZA (ZSH)
EVERY-BODY, RUN!!
ZA ZA
ZA ZA ZA
HIDE IN THE JUNGLE!!
BUUUU (HUMMM)
BUUUUN (BUZZZZ)
<SHIT! THEY'RE RUNNING AWAY!!>
0-27
<XAVIERA!! YOU TAKE IT FROM HERE!!>
<I'LL CATCH UP TO THEM IN NO TIME!!>

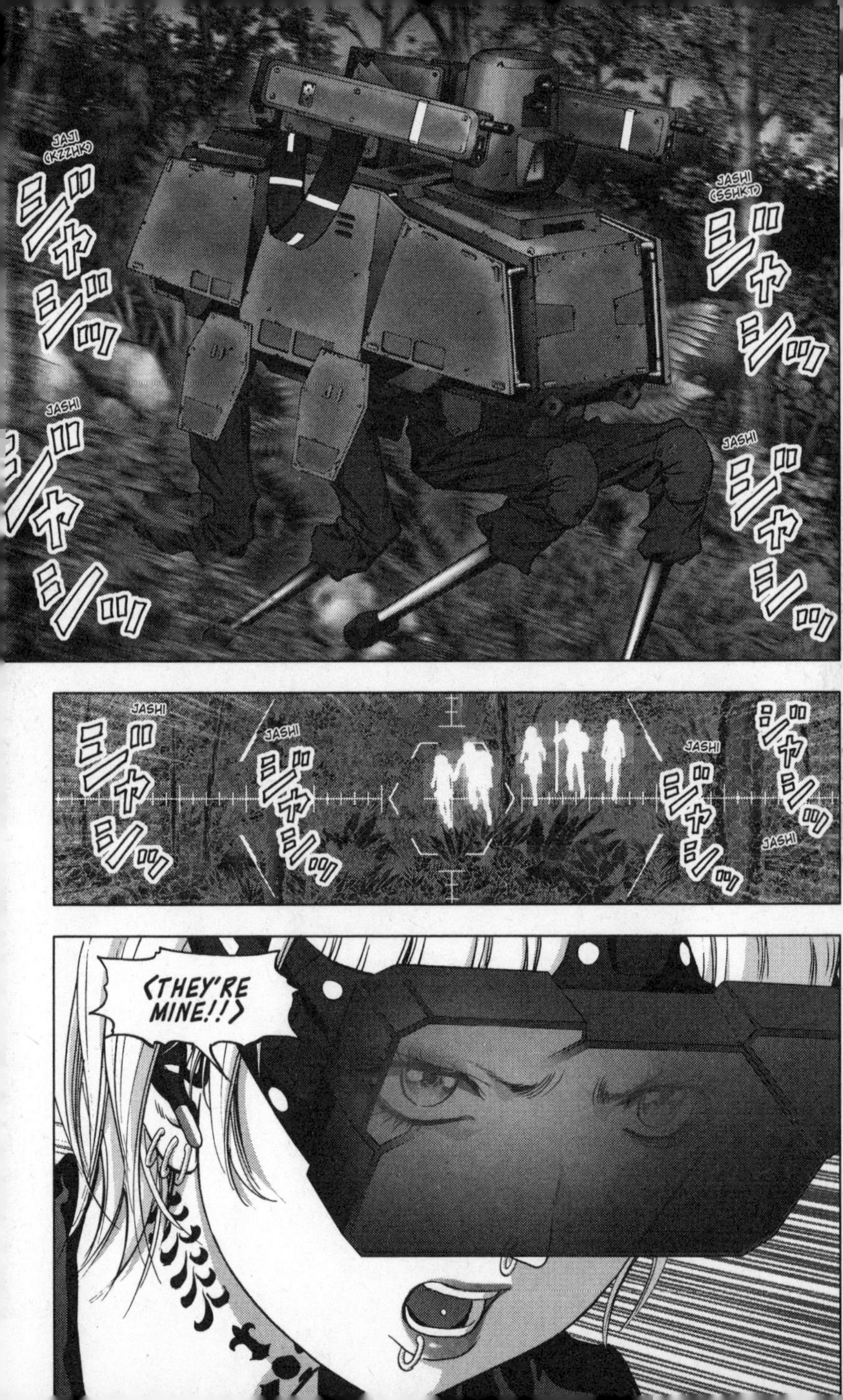
JASHI (SSHKT)
JASHI
JAJI (KZZHK)
JASHI
JASHI
JASHI
JASHI
JASHI
JASHI
〈THEY'RE MINE!!〉

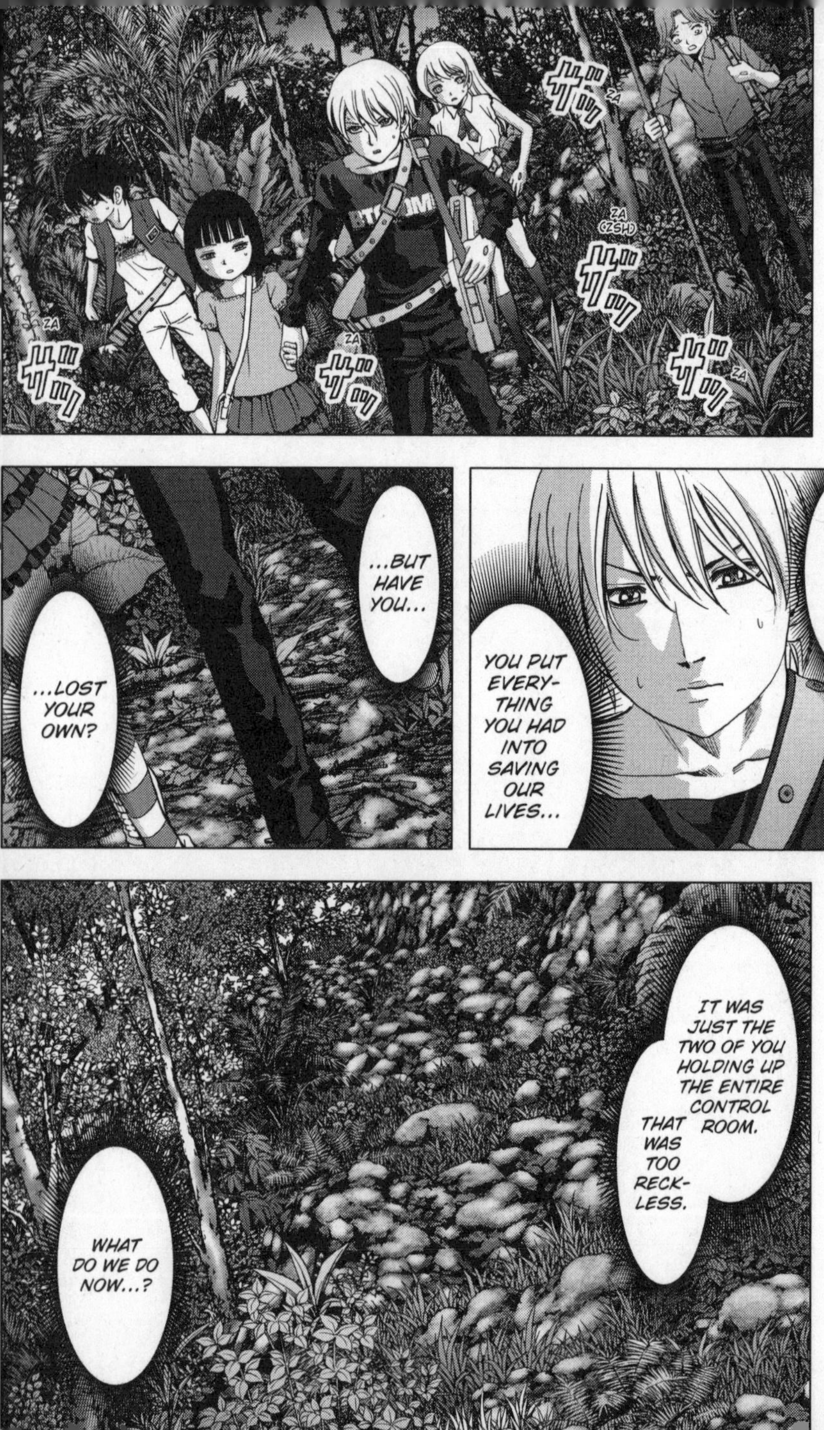

ZA
ZA (ZSH)
ZA
ZA
ZA
SENPAI!...
YOU PUT EVERYTHING YOU HAD INTO SAVING OUR LIVES...
...BUT HAVE YOU...
...LOST YOUR OWN?
IT WAS JUST THE TWO OF YOU HOLDING UP THE ENTIRE CONTROL ROOM.
THAT WAS TOO RECKLESS.
WHAT DO WE DO NOW...?

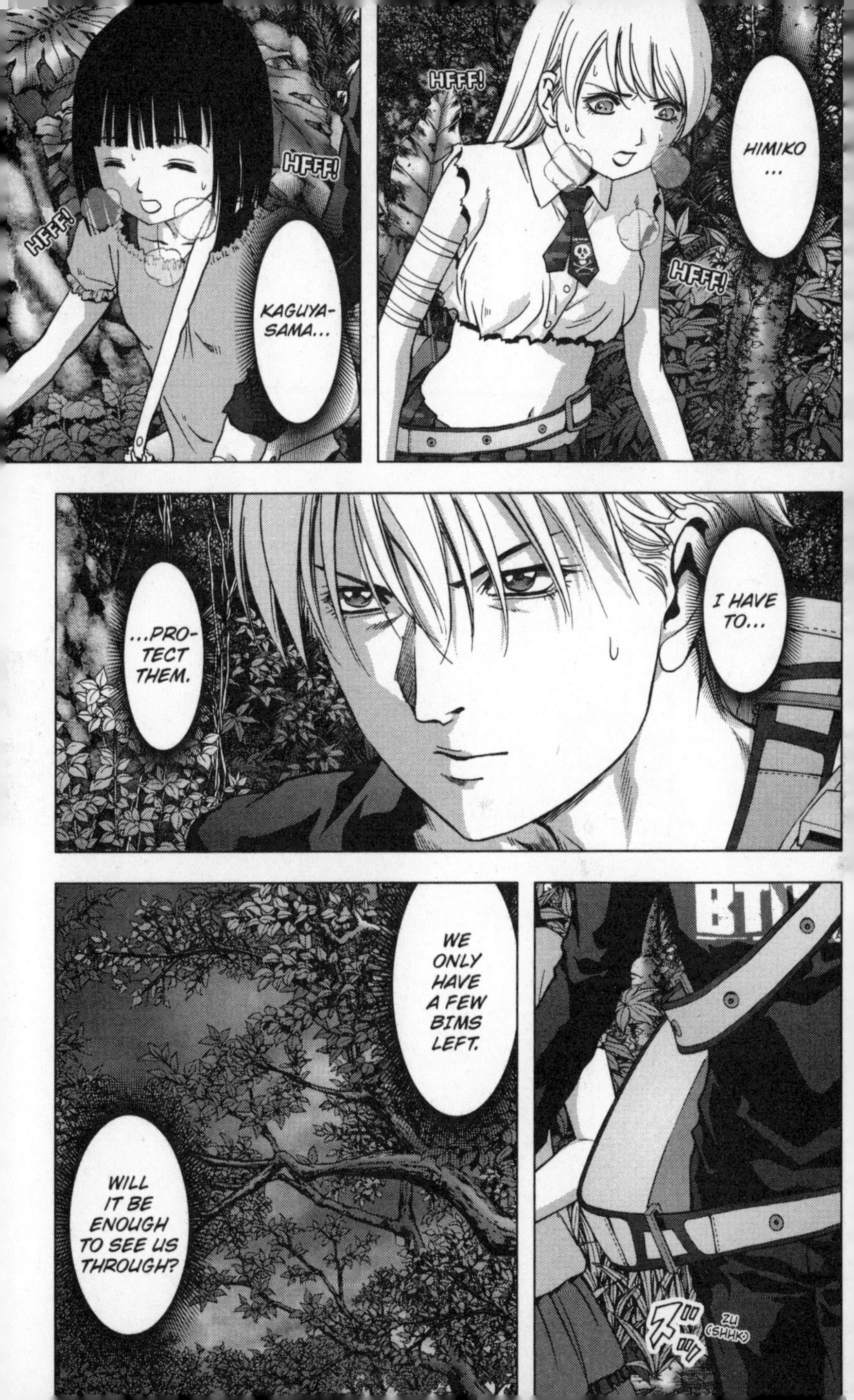
HFFF!
HIMIKO...
HFFF!
HFFF!
HFFF!
KAGUYA-SAMA...
I HAVE TO...
...PROTECT THEM.
ZU (SHHK)
WE ONLY HAVE A FEW BIMS LEFT.
WILL IT BE ENOUGH TO SEE US THROUGH?

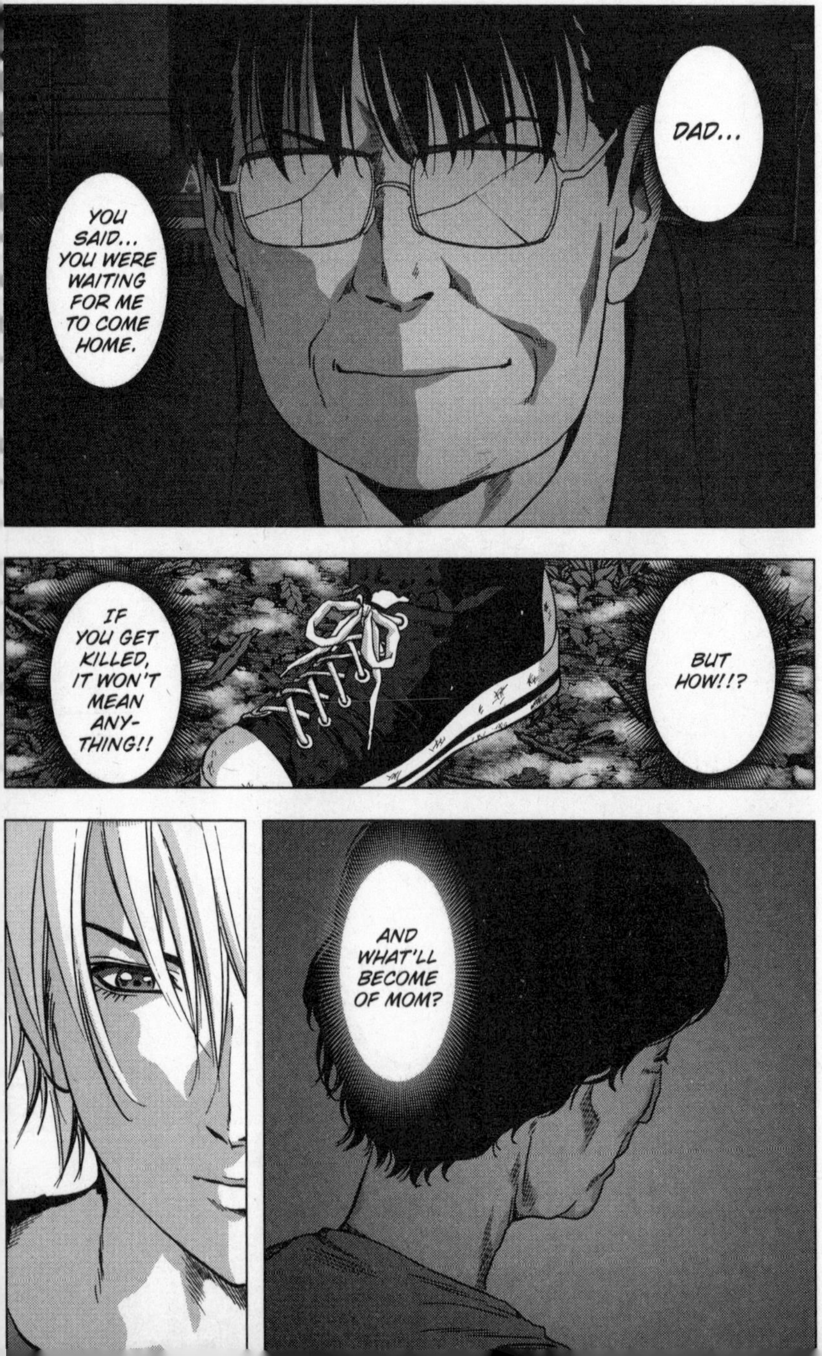
DAD...
YOU SAID... YOU WERE WAITING FOR ME TO COME HOME.
BUT HOW!!?
IF YOU GET KILLED, IT WON'T MEAN ANY-THING!!
AND WHAT'LL BECOME OF MOM?

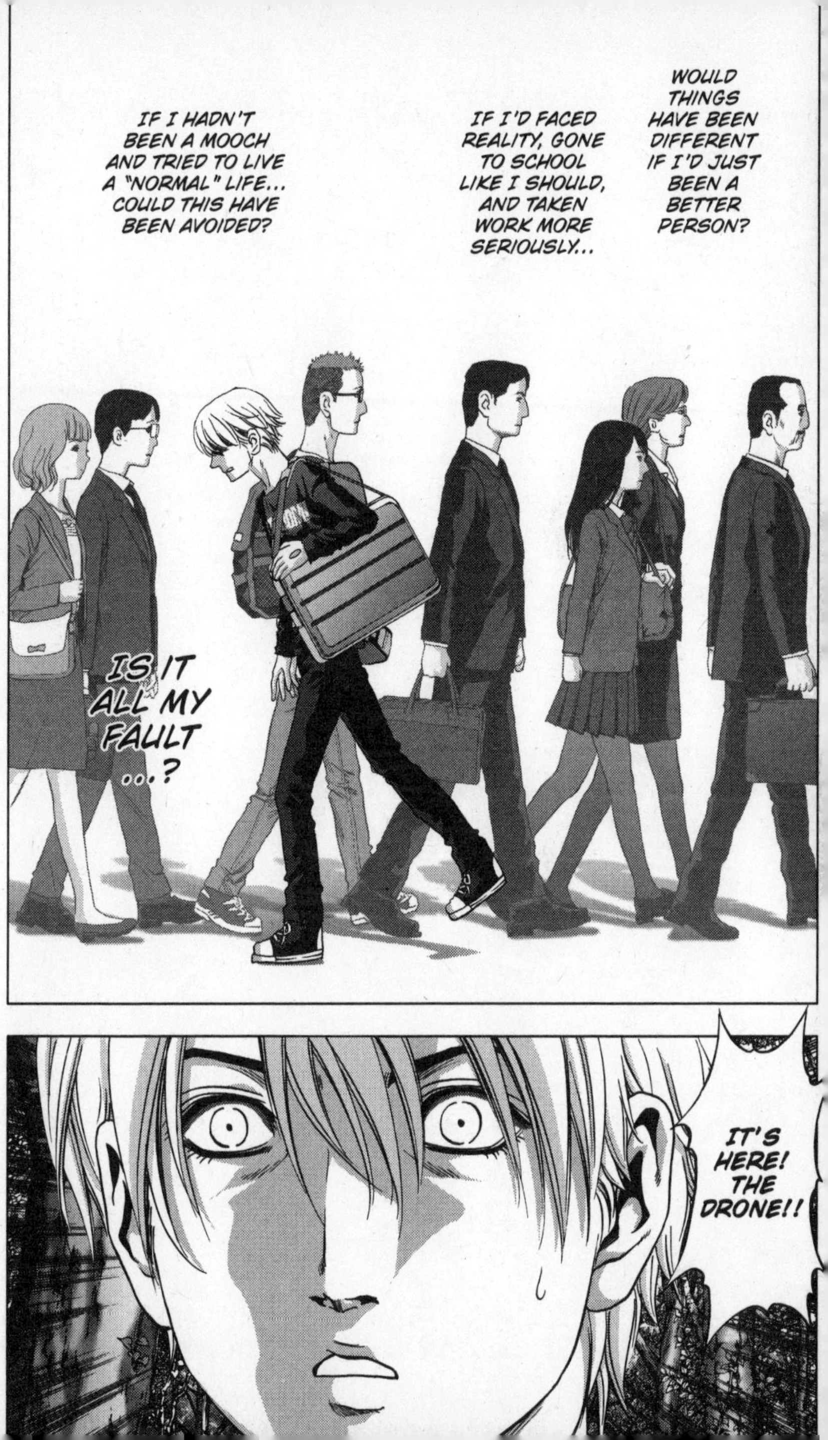
WOULD THINGS HAVE BEEN DIFFERENT IF I'D JUST BEEN A BETTER PERSON?
IF I'D FACED REALITY, GONE TO SCHOOL LIKE I SHOULD, AND TAKEN WORK MORE SERIOUSLY...
IF I HADN'T BEEN A MOOCH AND TRIED TO LIVE A "NORMAL" LIFE... COULD THIS HAVE BEEN AVOIDED?
IS IT ALL MY FAULT ...?
IT'S HERE! THE DRONE!!

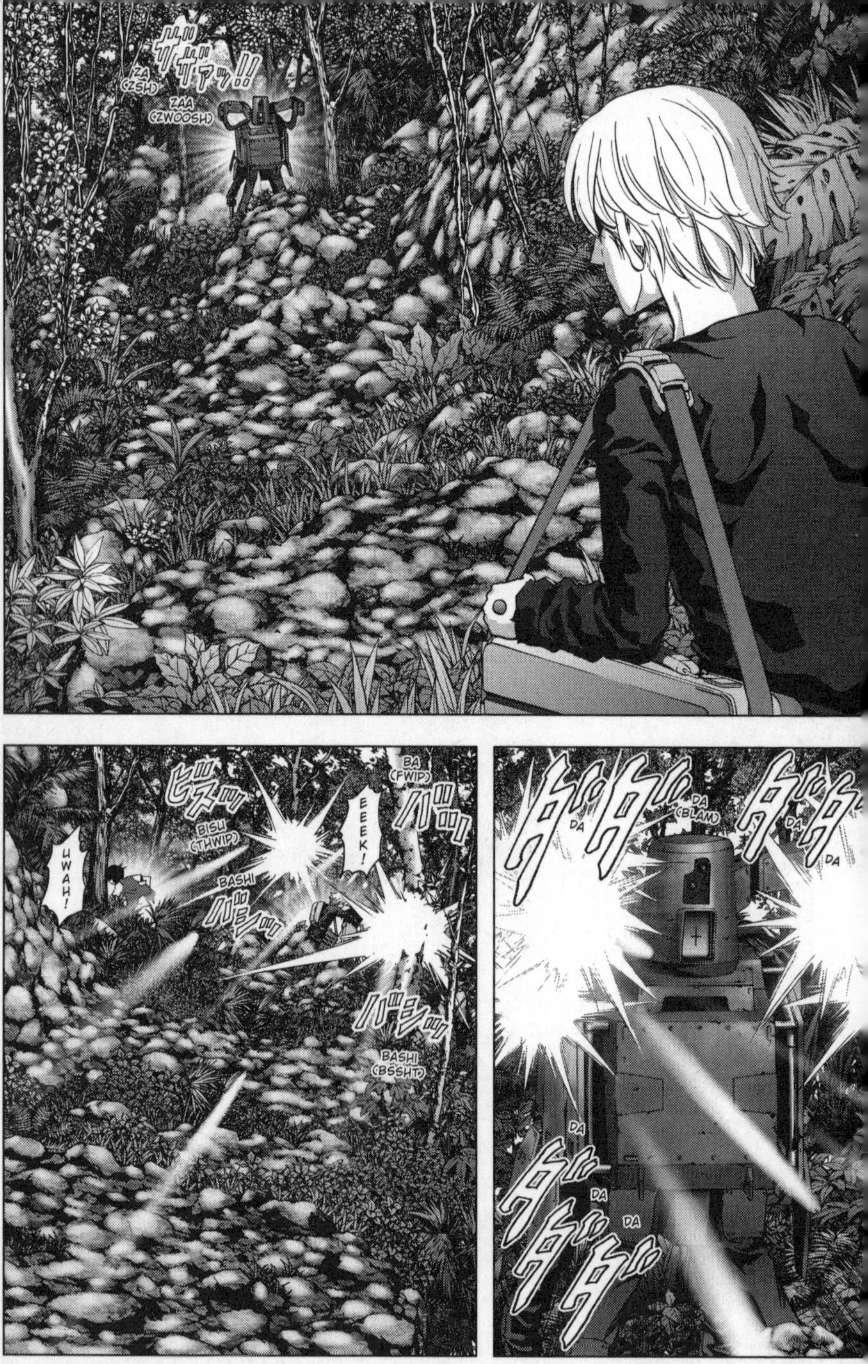
ZA (ZSH)
ZAA (ZWOOSH)
DA (BLAM)
DA
DA
DA
DA
DA
DA
BA (FWIP)
EEEK!
BISU (THWIP)
UWAH!
BASHI
BASHI (BSSHT)

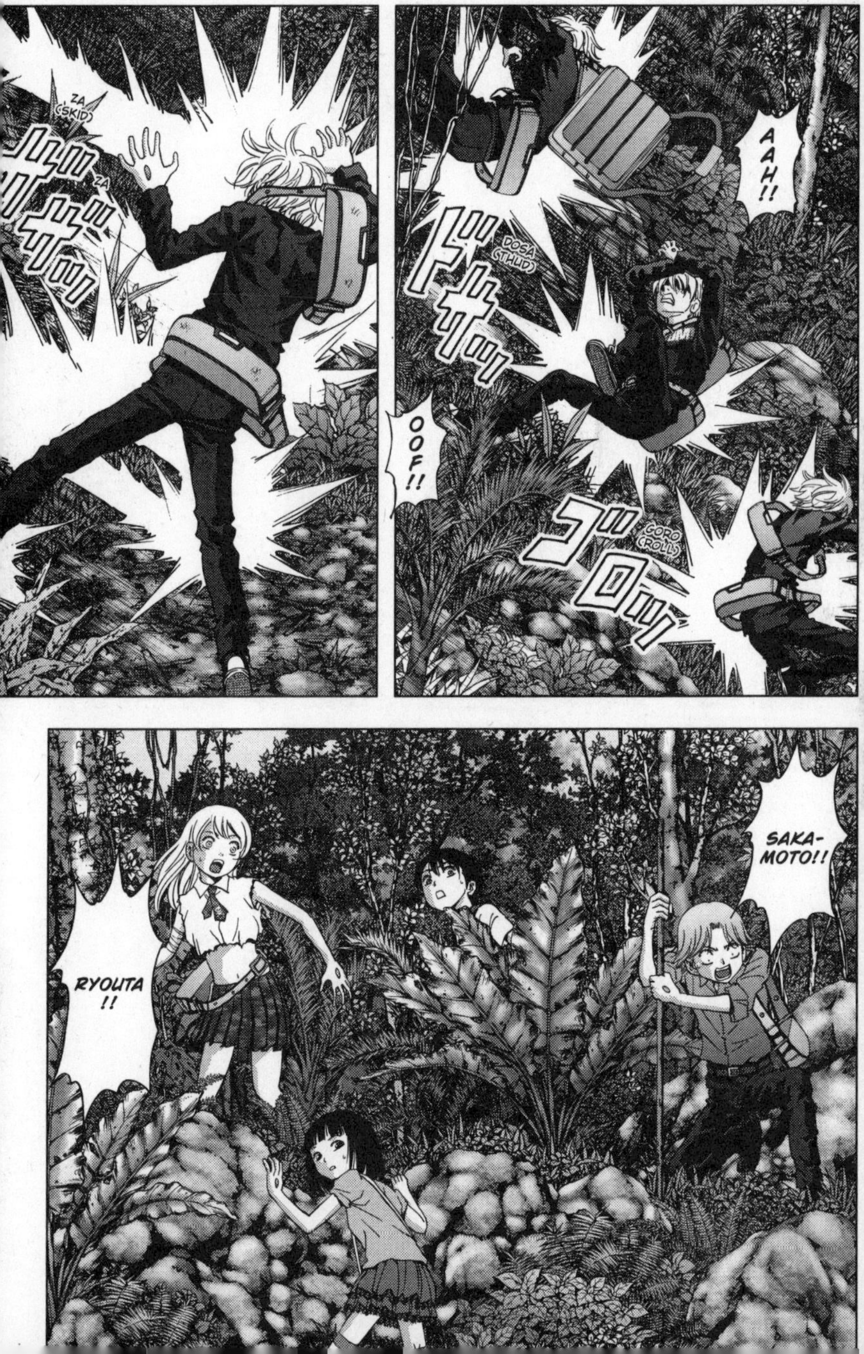
AAAH!!
DOSA (THUD)
OOF!!
GORO (ROLL)
ZA (SKID)
ZA
SAKA-MOTO!!
RYOUTA !!

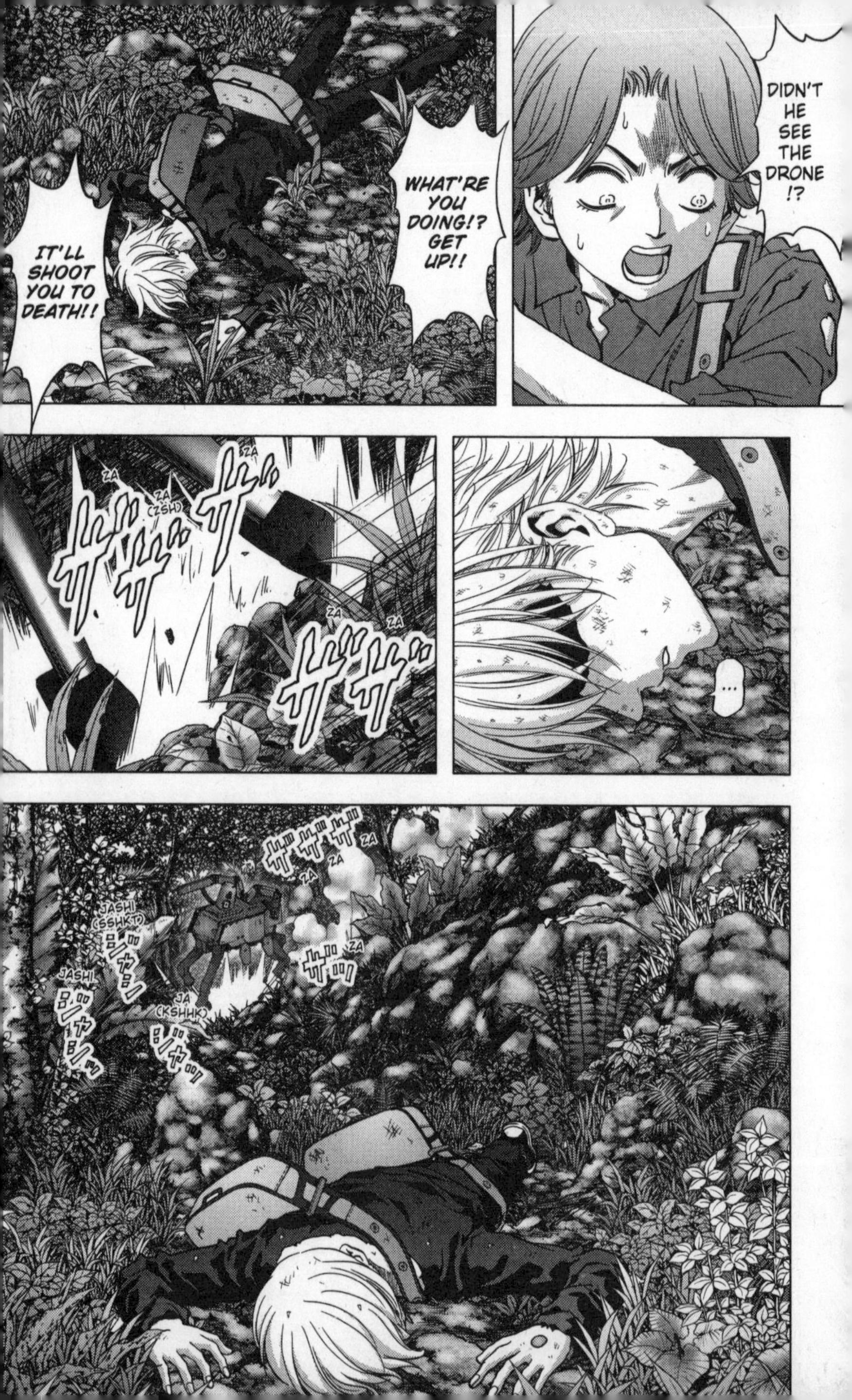
DIDN'T HE SEE THE DRONE!?
WHAT'RE YOU DOING!? GET UP!!
IT'LL SHOOT YOU TO DEATH!!
...
ZA
ZA
ZA (ZSHD)
ZA
ZA
ZA
ZA
ZA
JASHI (SSHKT)
ZA
JASHI
JA (KSHHK)

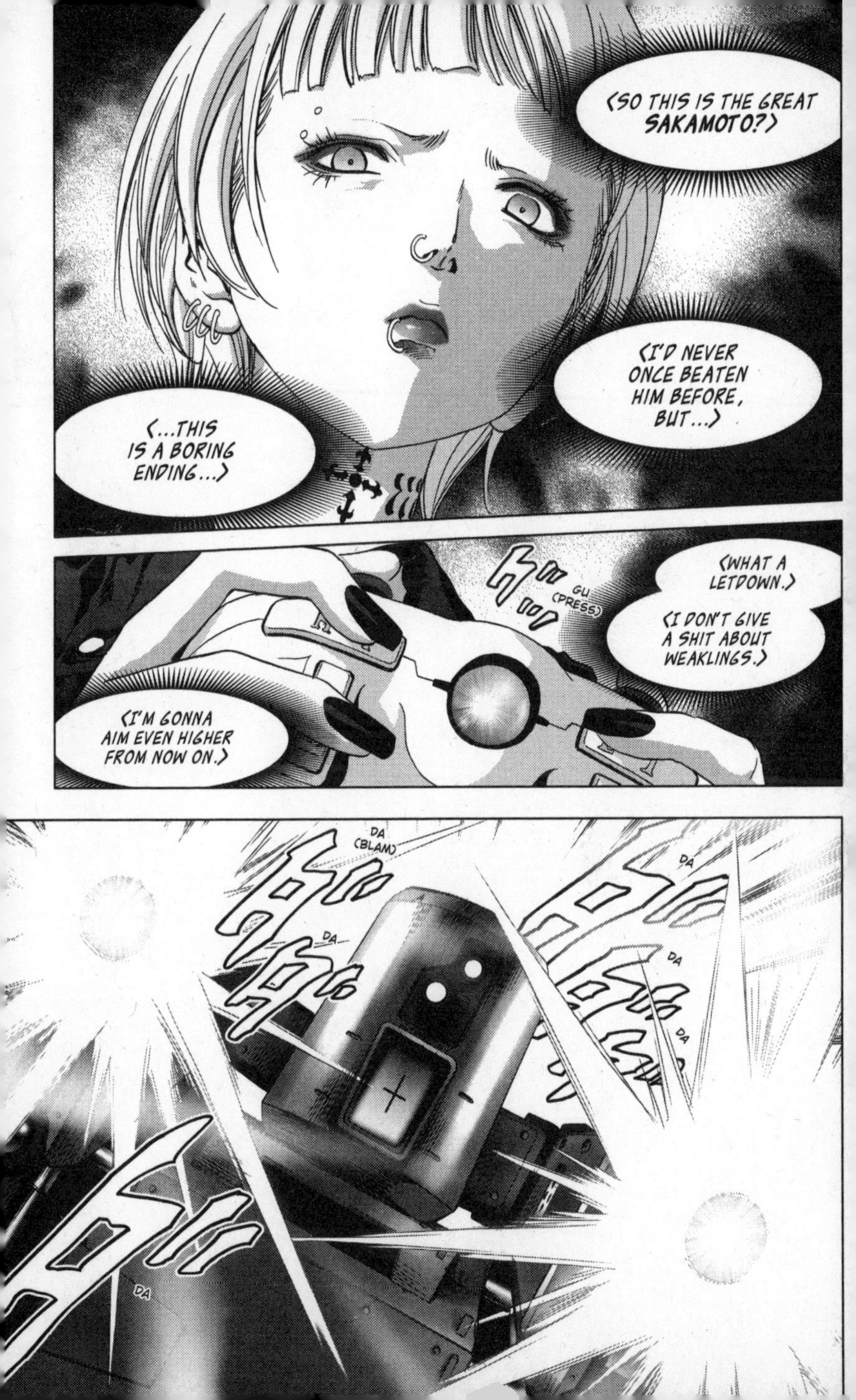

<SO THIS IS THE GREAT SAKAMOTO?>
<I'D NEVER ONCE BEATEN HIM BEFORE, BUT...>
<...THIS IS A BORING ENDING...>
GU (PRESS)
<WHAT A LETDOWN.>
<I DON'T GIVE A SHIT ABOUT WEAKLINGS.>
<I'M GONNA AIM EVEN HIGHER FROM NOW ON.>
DA
DA (BLAM)
DA
DA
DA
DA

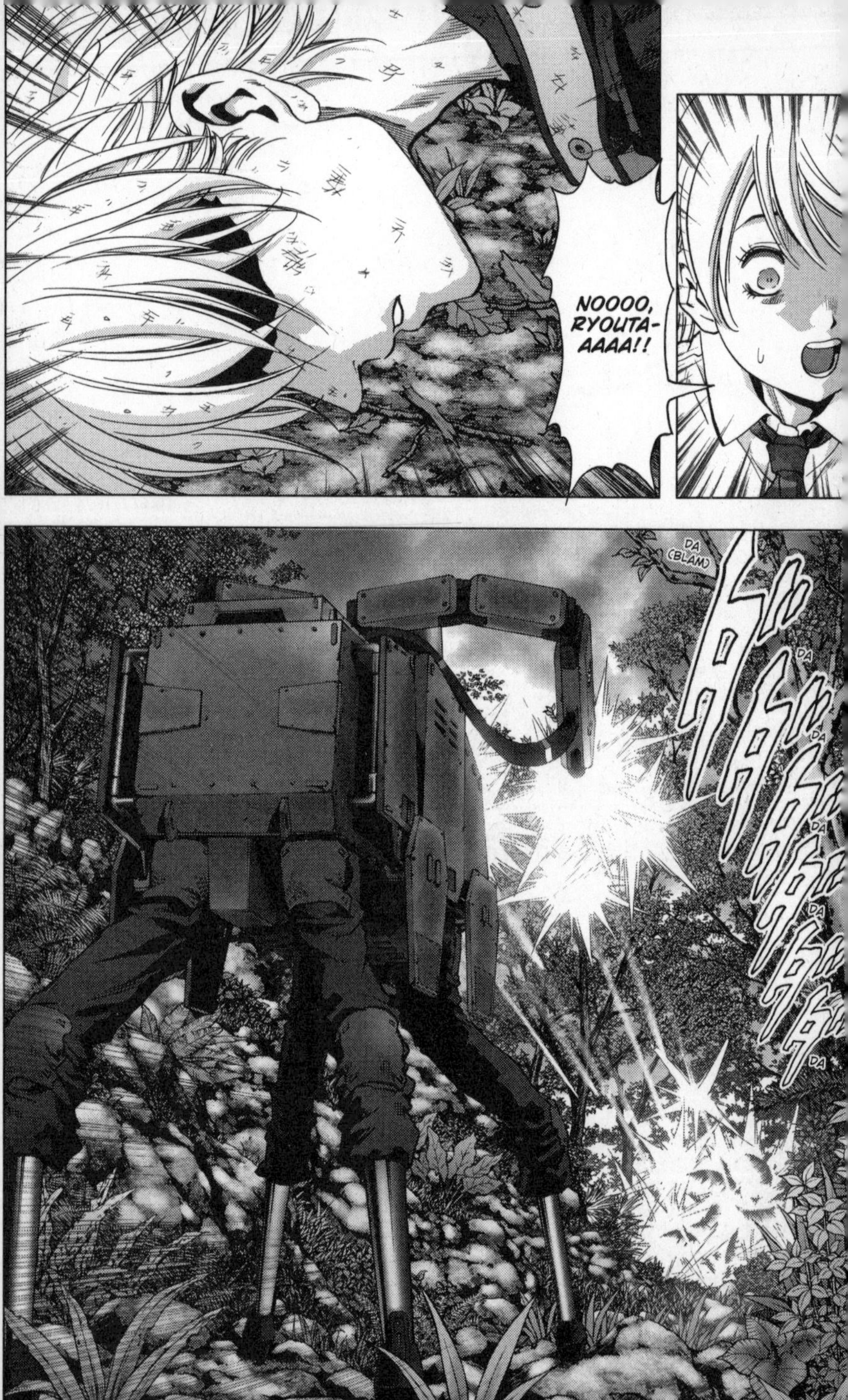
NOOOO, RYOUTA-AAAA!!
DA (BLAM)
DA
DA
DA
DA
DA

BTOOOM! REFERENCE MATERIAL TRIP LOG

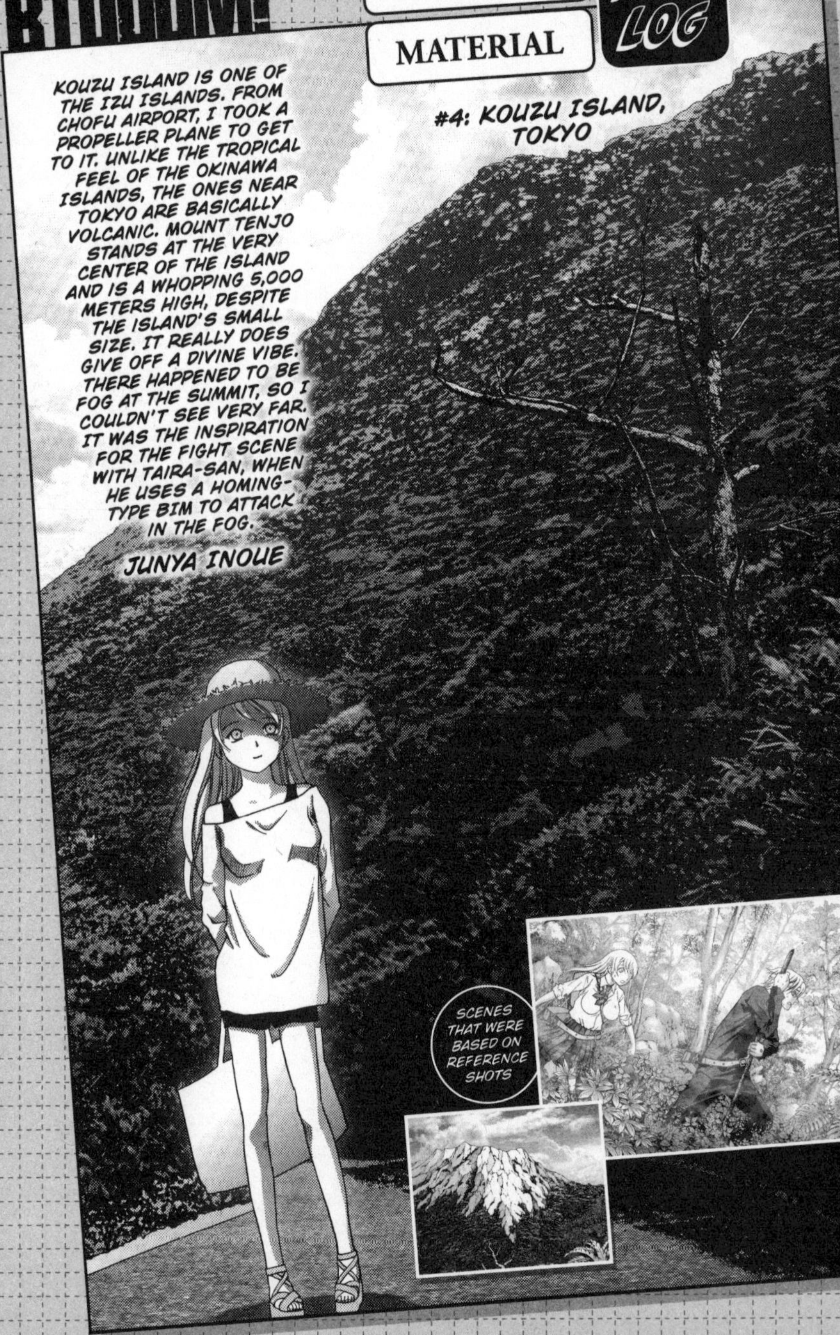
#4: KOUZU ISLAND, TOKYO
KOUZU ISLAND IS ONE OF THE IZU ISLANDS. FROM CHOFU AIRPORT, I TOOK A PROPELLER PLANE TO GET TO IT. UNLIKE THE TROPICAL FEEL OF THE OKINAWA ISLANDS, THE ONES NEAR TOKYO ARE BASICALLY VOLCANIC. MOUNT TENJO STANDS AT THE VERY CENTER OF THE ISLAND AND IS A WHOPPING 5,000 METERS HIGH, DESPITE THE ISLAND'S SMALL SIZE. IT REALLY DOES GIVE OFF A DIVINE VIBE. THERE HAPPENED TO BE FOG AT THE SUMMIT, SO I COULDN'T SEE VERY FAR. IT WAS THE INSPIRATION FOR THE FIGHT SCENE WITH TAIRA-SAN, WHEN HE USES A HOMING-TYPE BIM TO ATTACK IN THE FOG.
JUNYA INOUE
SCENES THAT WERE BASED ON REFERENCE SHOTS

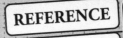

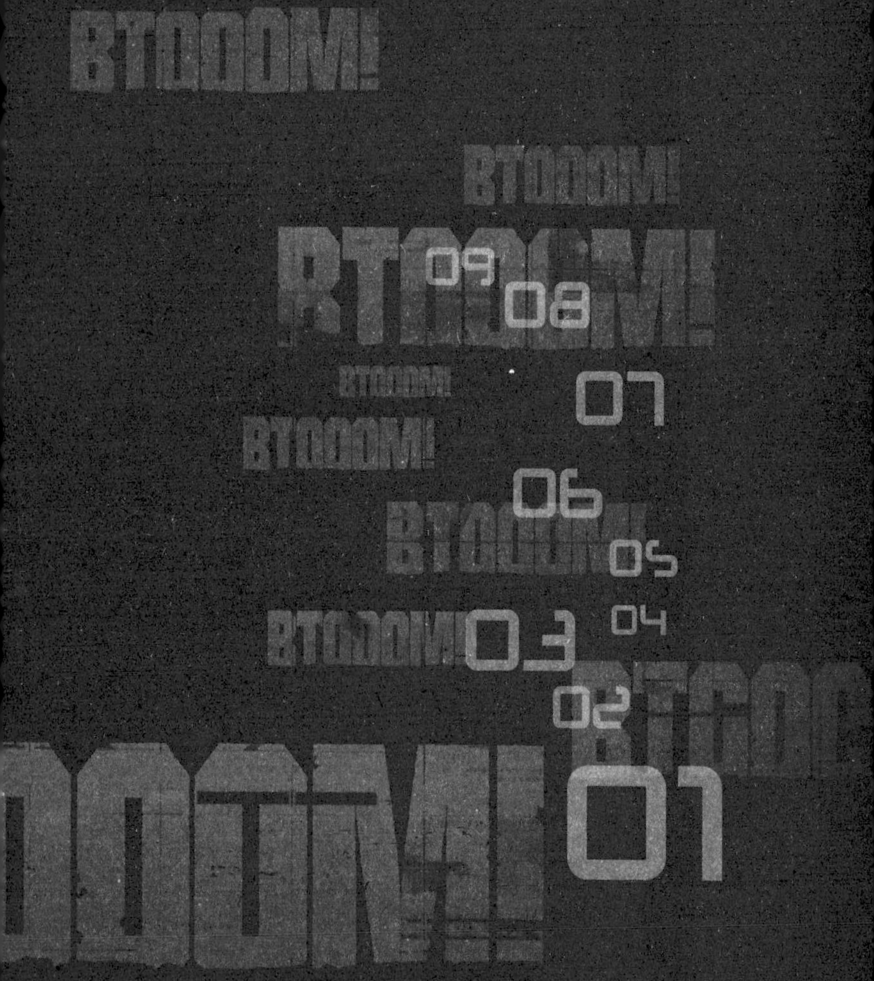
BTOOOM!
09
08
07
06
05
04
03
02
01

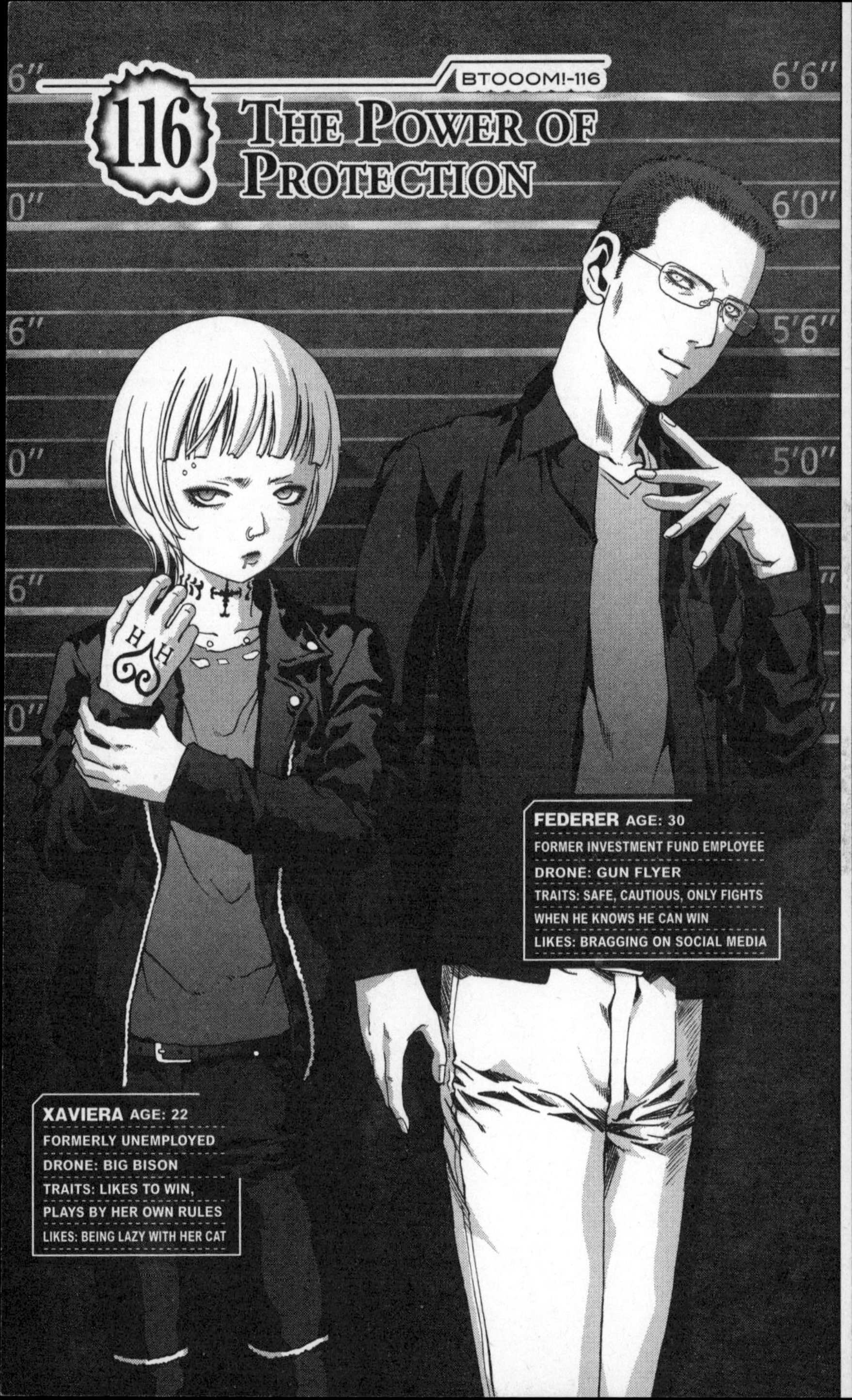
BTOOOM!-116
116 THE POWER OF PROTECTION
6'6"
6'0"
5'6"
5'0"
FEDERER AGE: 30
FORMER INVESTMENT FUND EMPLOYEE
DRONE: GUN FLYER
TRAITS: SAFE, CAUTIOUS, ONLY FIGHTS WHEN HE KNOWS HE CAN WIN
LIKES: BRAGGING ON SOCIAL MEDIA
XAVIERA AGE: 22
FORMERLY UNEMPLOYED
DRONE: BIG BISON
TRAITS: LIKES TO WIN, PLAYS BY HER OWN RULES
LIKES: BEING LAZY WITH HER CAT

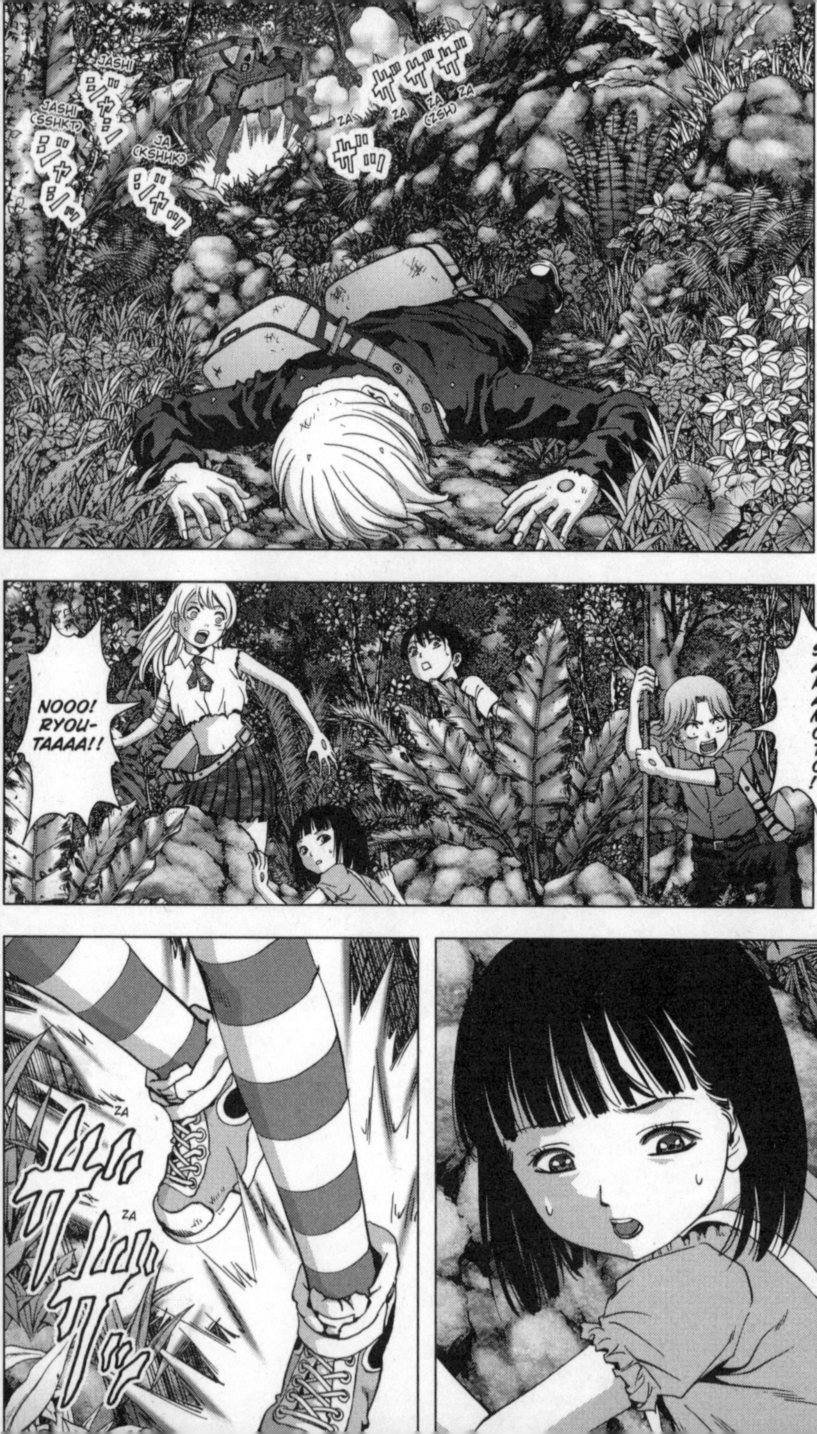
ZA ZA ZA (ZSH)
ZA
JASHI
JASHI (SSHKT)
JA (KSHHK)
SAKAMOTO!?
NOOO! RYOU-TAAAA!!
ZA
ZA

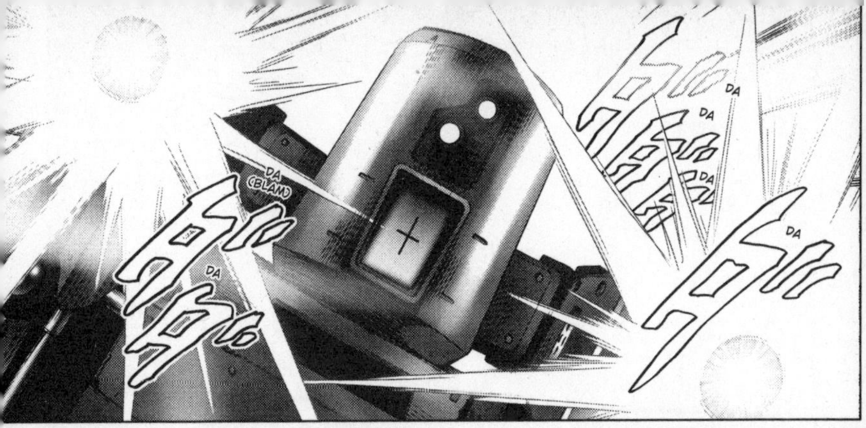

DA
DA
DA
DA
DA
DA
(BLAM)
DA

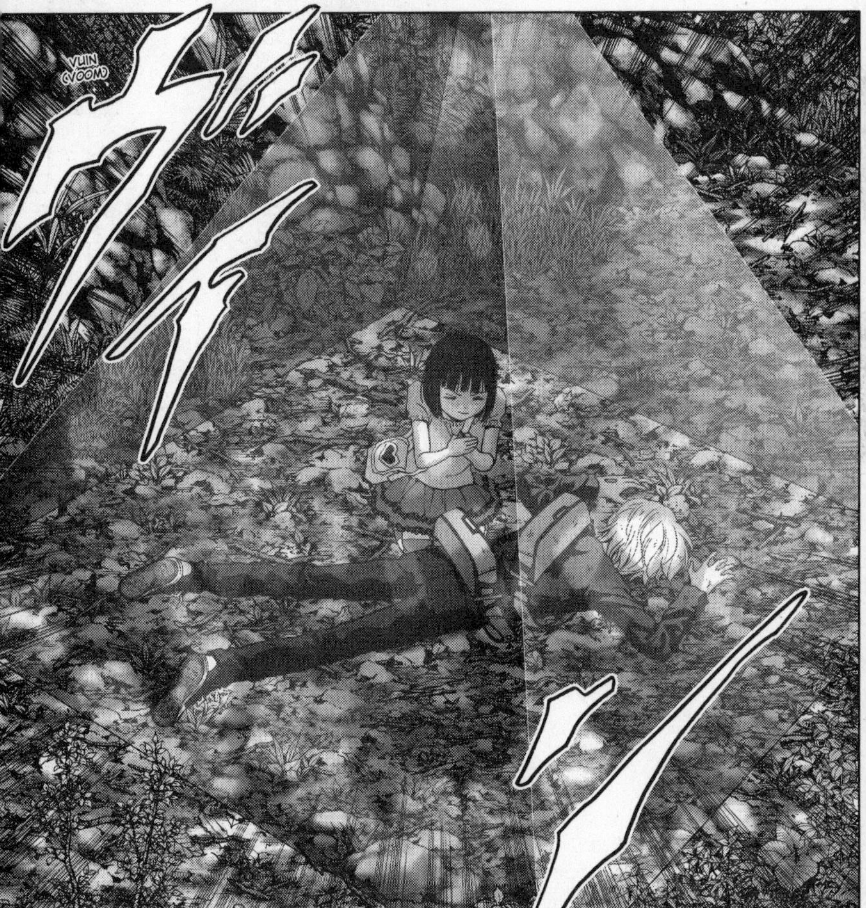

VUIN
(VOOM)

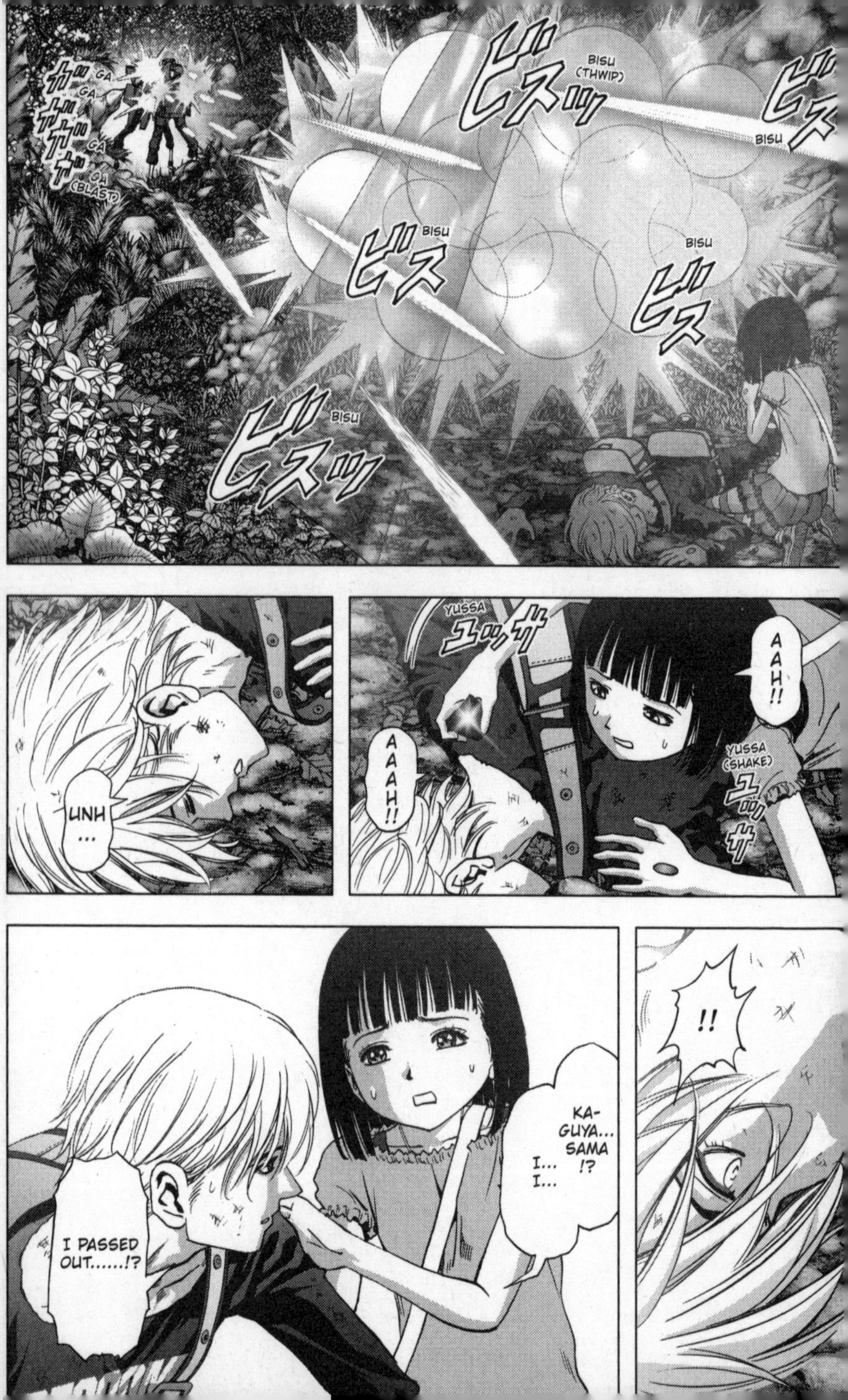
ビス
BISU
ビスッ
BISU (THWIP)
ガガガガ
GA GA GA GA (BLAST)
ビス
BISU
ビス
BISU
ビスッ
BISU
ユッサ
YUSSA
AAH!!
YUSSA (SHAKE)
ユッサ
AAAH!!
UNH...
!!
KAGUYA... SAMA!?
I... I...
I PASSED OUT.......!?

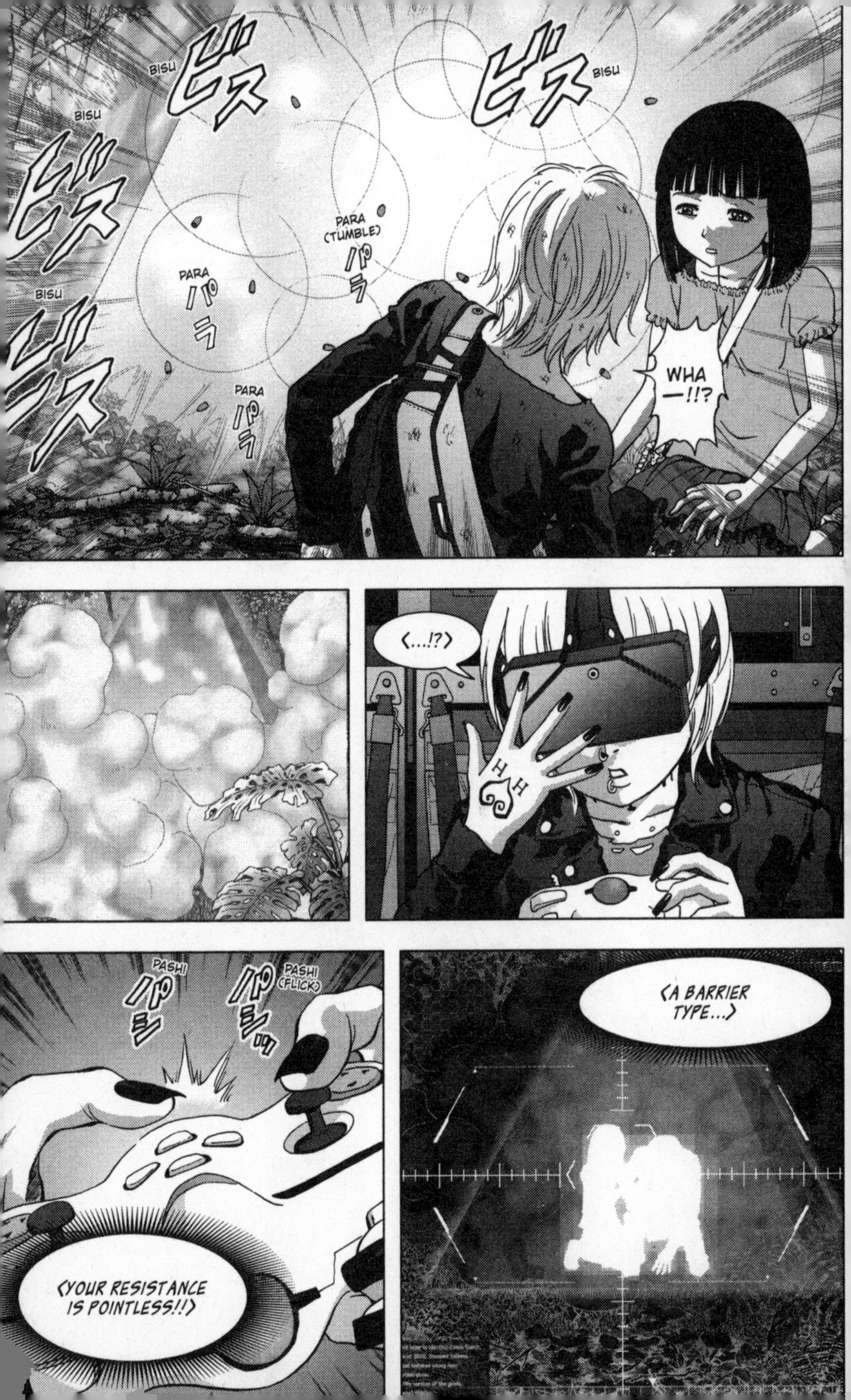
BISU ビス
BISU ビス
BISU ビス
PARA (TUMBLE) パラ
WHA—!!?
PARA パラ
BISU ビス
PARA パラ
〈...!?〉
〈A BARRIER TYPE...〉
PASHI (FLICK) パシッ
PASHI パシ
〈YOUR RESISTANCE IS POINTLESS!!〉

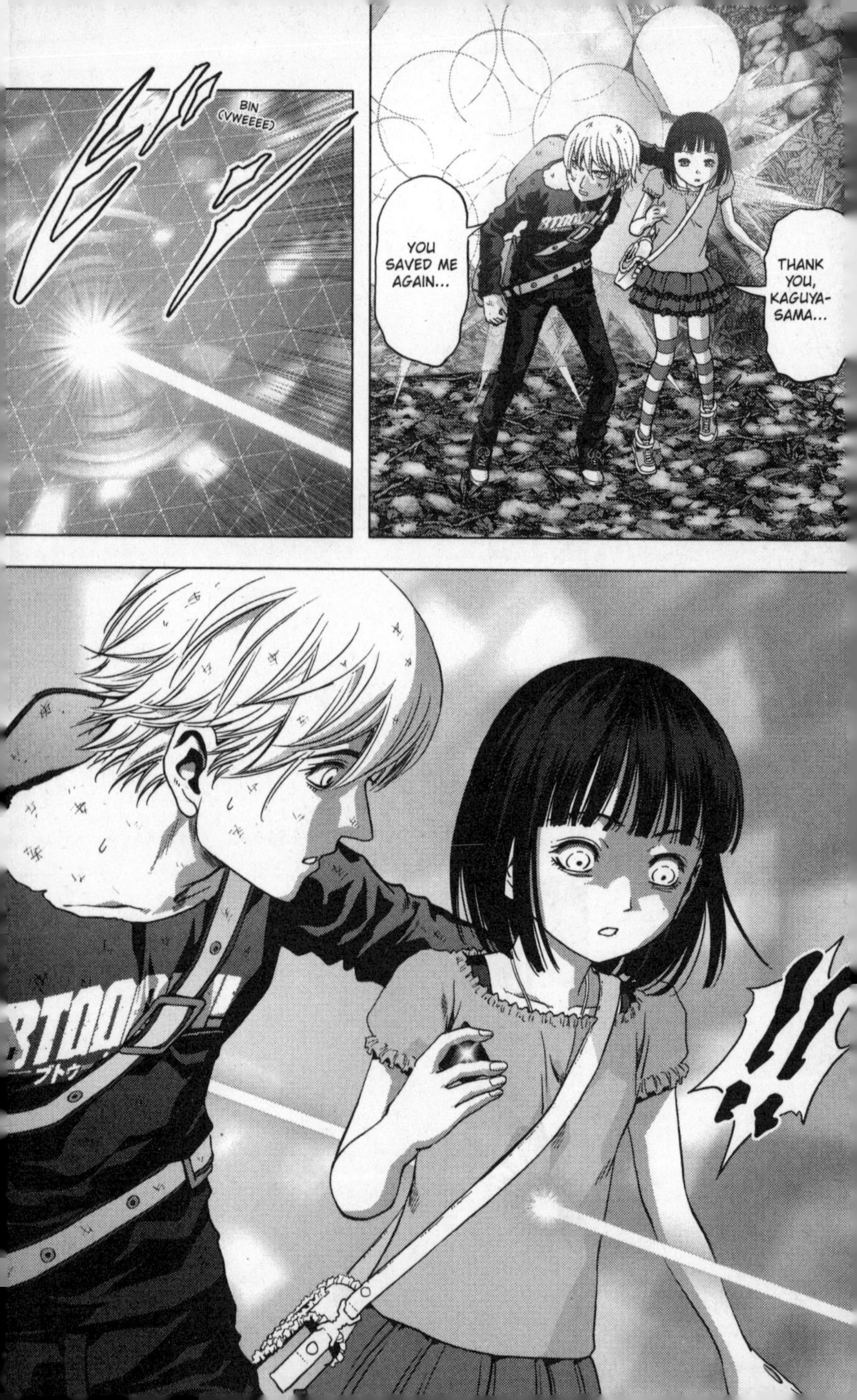

THANK YOU, KAGUYA-SAMA...
YOU SAVED ME AGAIN...
BIN (VWEEEE)

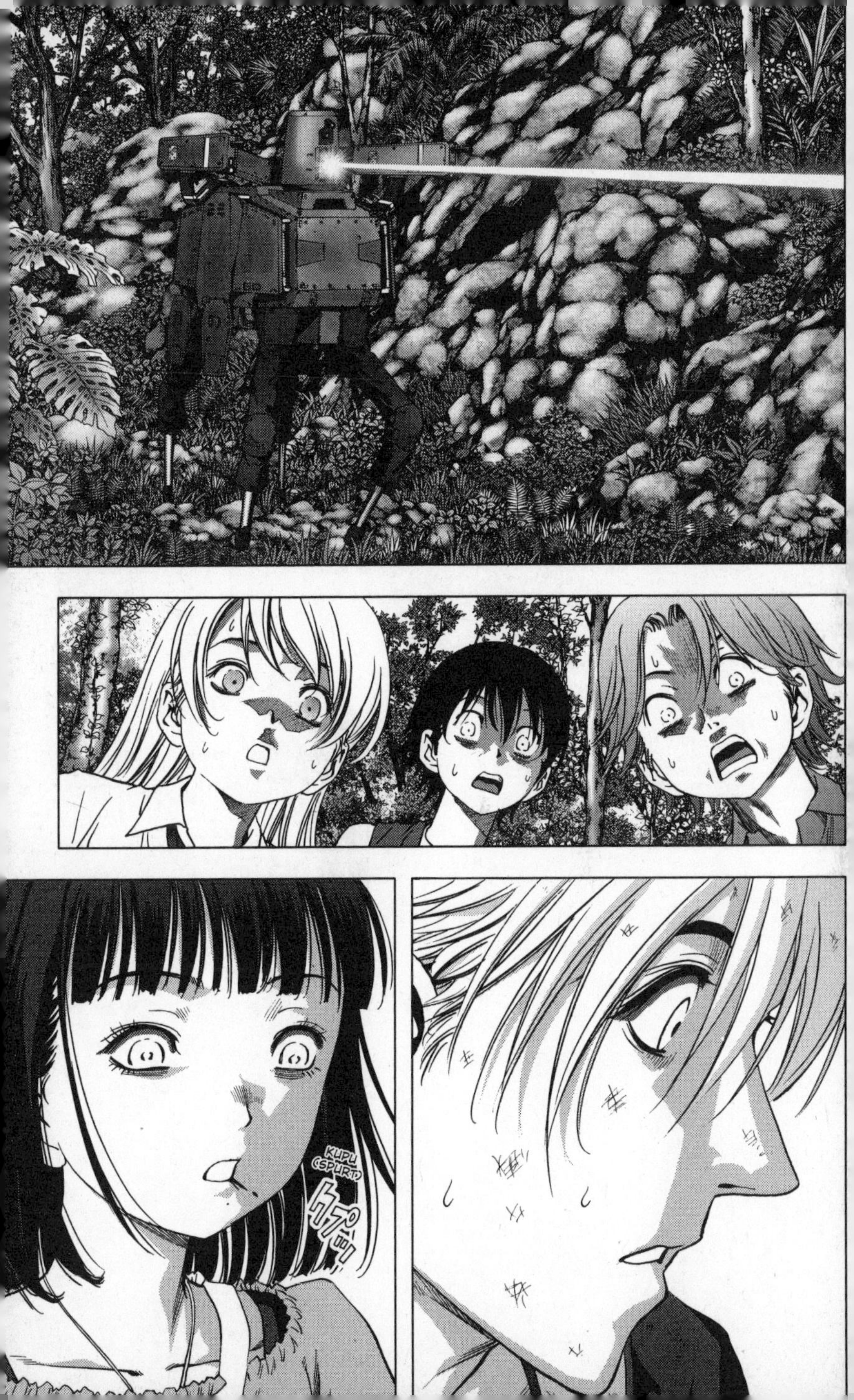
KUPU (SPURT)

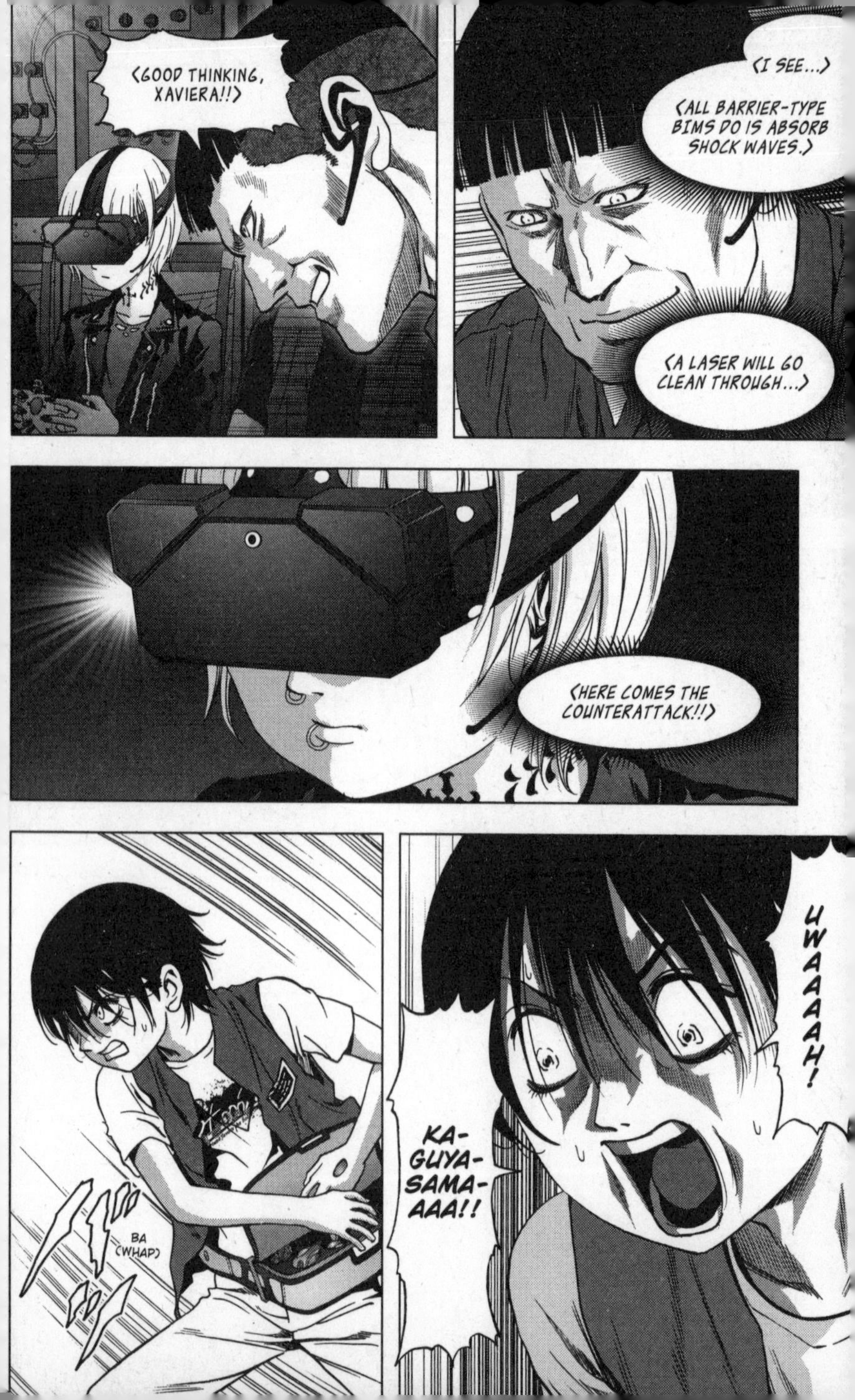
⟨I SEE...⟩
⟨ALL BARRIER-TYPE BIMS DO IS ABSORB SHOCK WAVES.⟩
⟨A LASER WILL GO CLEAN THROUGH...⟩
⟨GOOD THINKING, XAVIERA!!⟩
⟨HERE COMES THE COUNTERATTACK!!⟩
UWAAAAAAH!
KA-GUYA-SAMA-AAA!!
BA (WHAP)

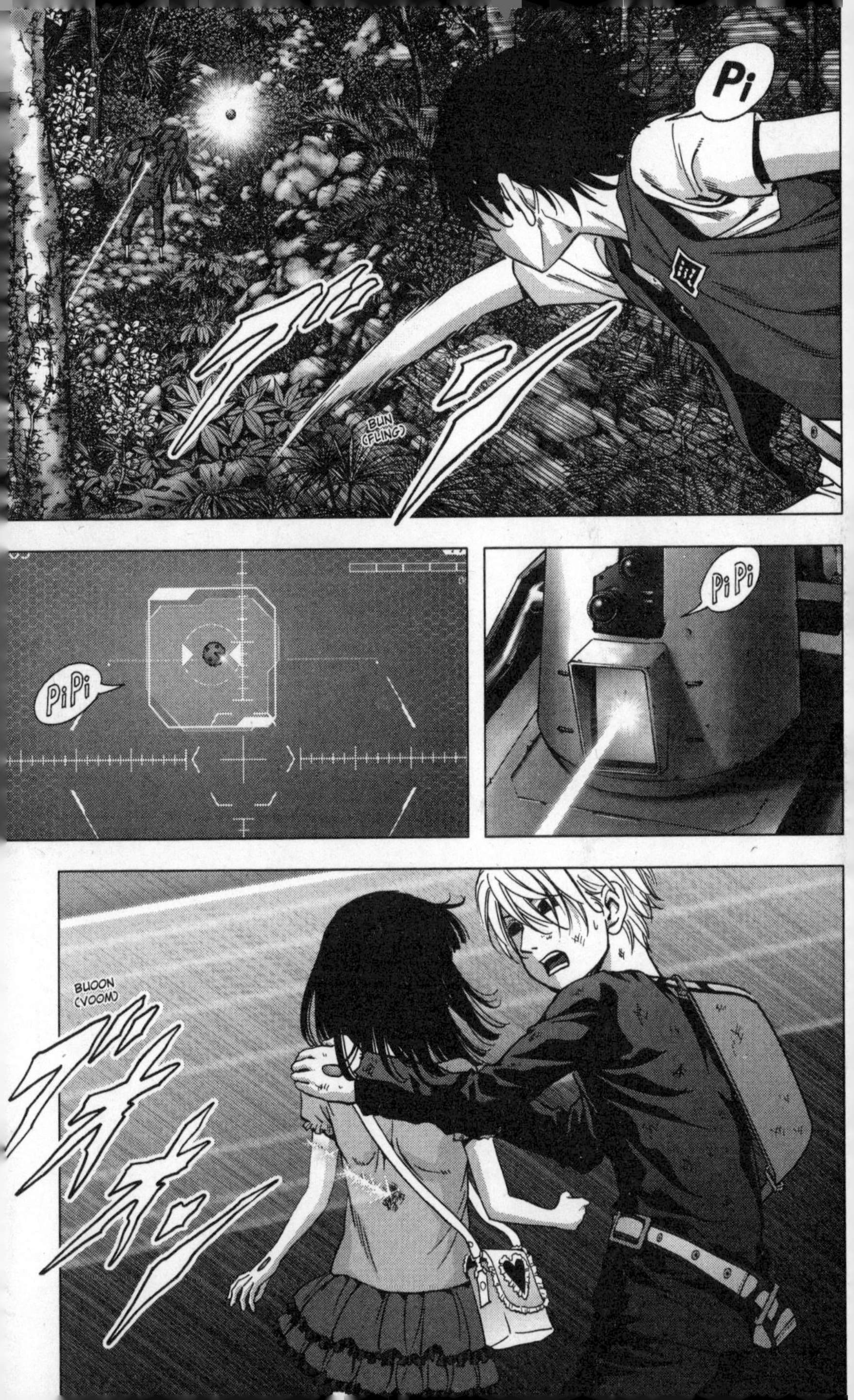
Pi
BUN (FLING)
Pi Pi
Pi Pi
BUOON (VOOM)

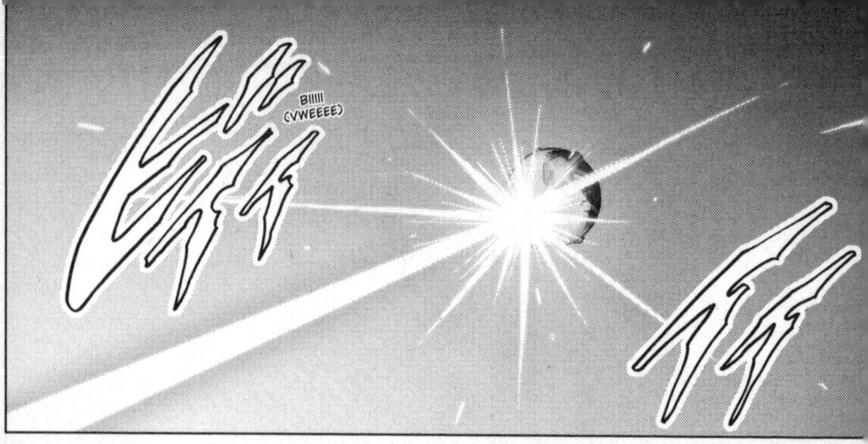
BIIIII
(VWEEEEE)
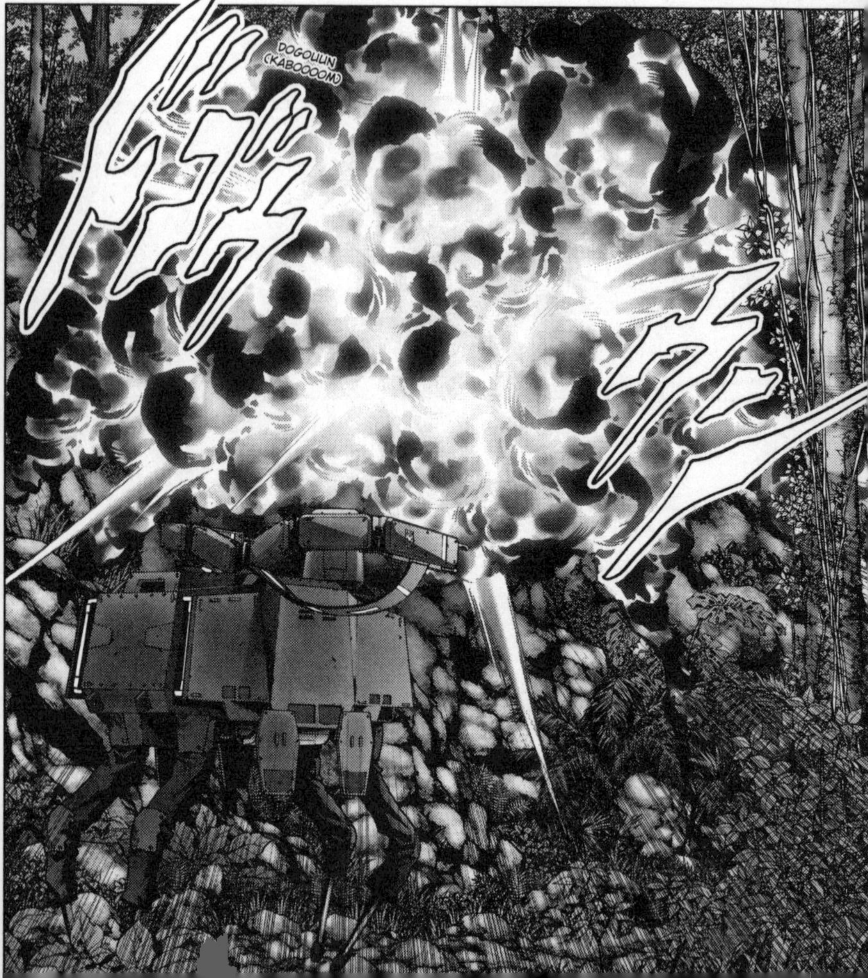
DOGOUUN
(KABOOOOM)

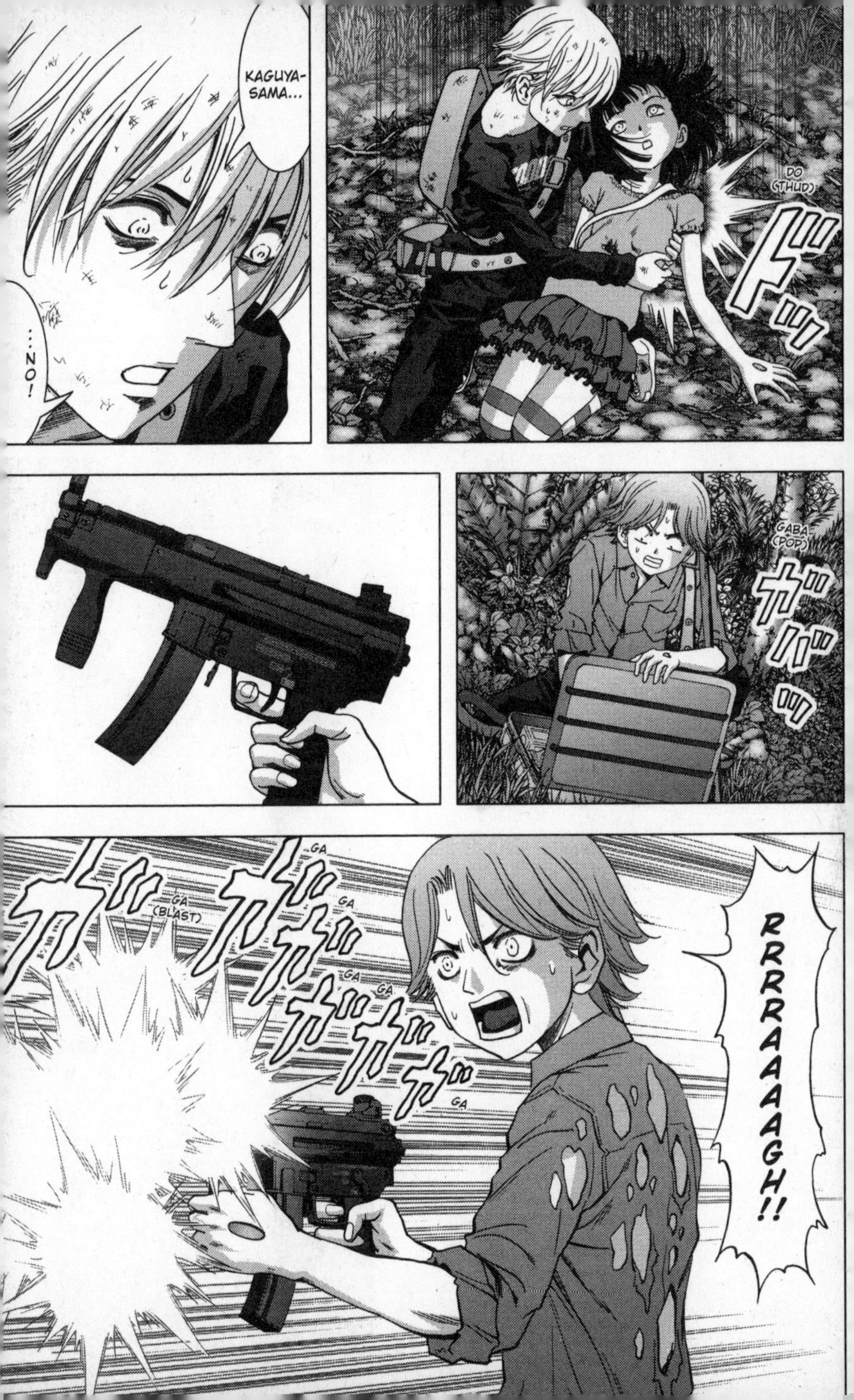
DO (THUD)
KAGUYA-SAMA...
...NO!
GABA (POP)
RRRRAAAAAGH!!
GA
GA
GA (BLAST)
GA
GA
GA

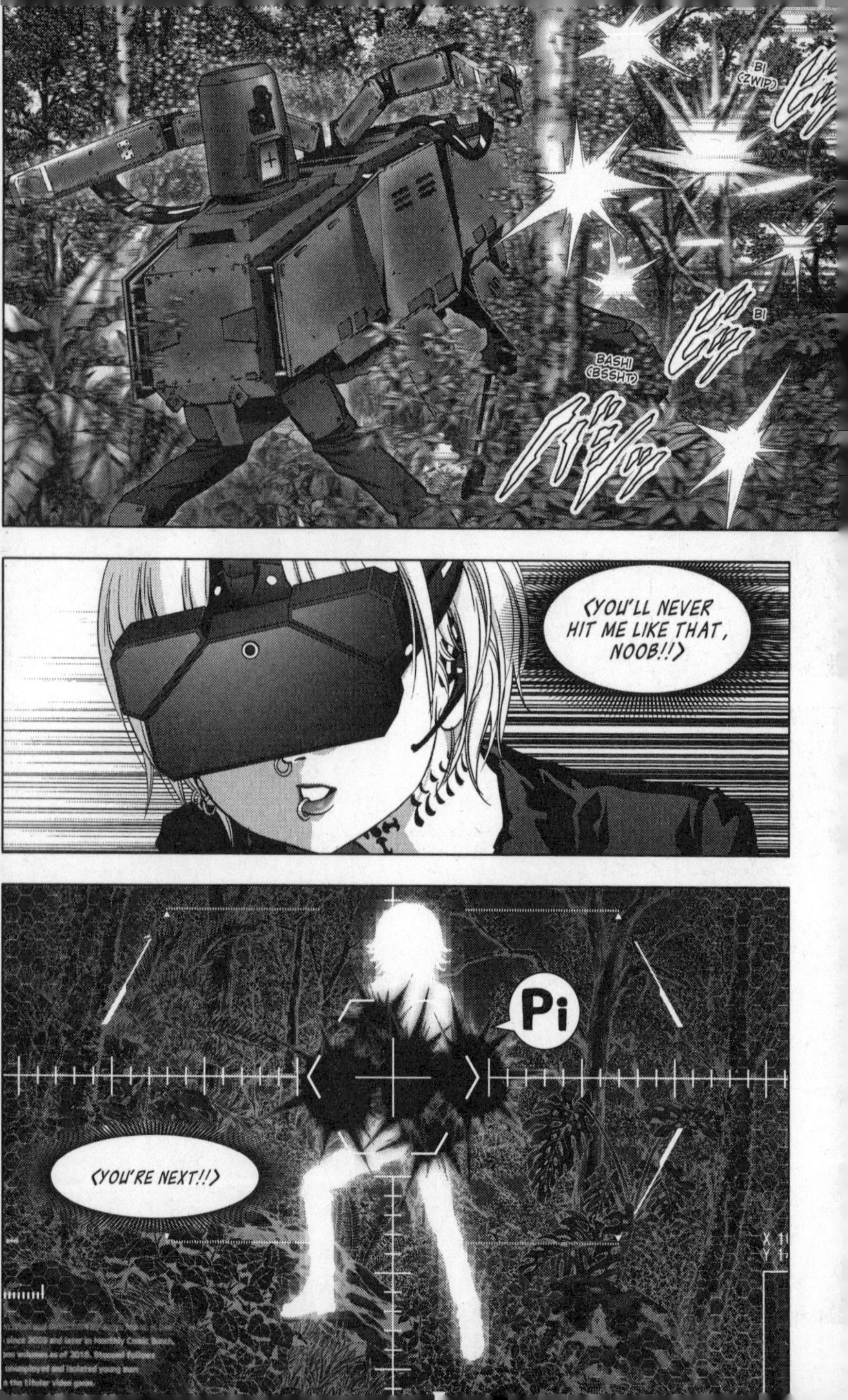
BI (ZWIP)
BI
BASHI (BSSHT)
⟨YOU'LL NEVER HIT ME LIKE THAT, NOOB!!⟩
Pi
⟨YOU'RE NEXT!!⟩

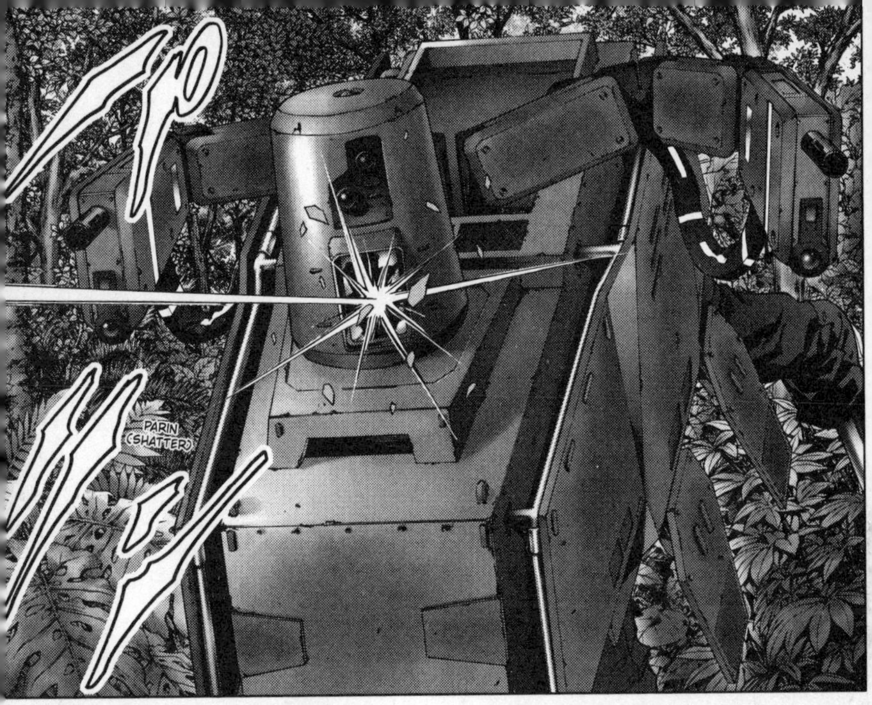
PARIN
(SHATTER)
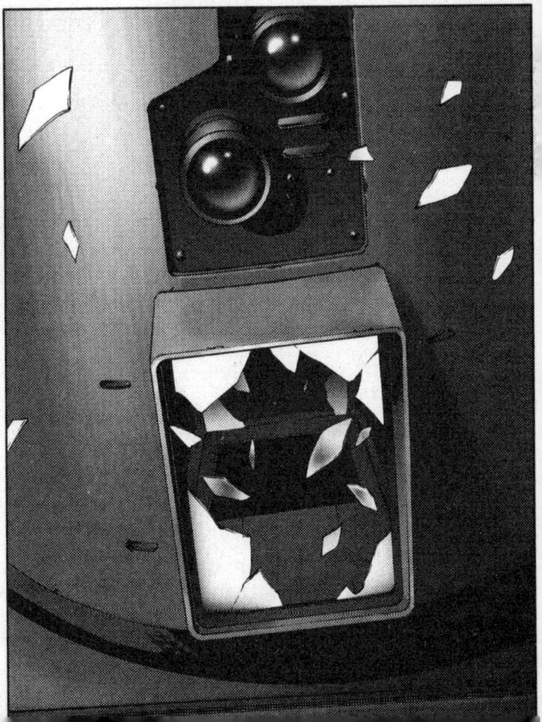
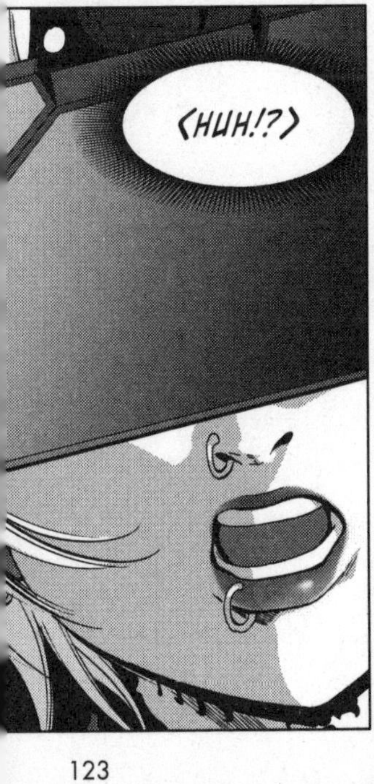
<HUH!?>

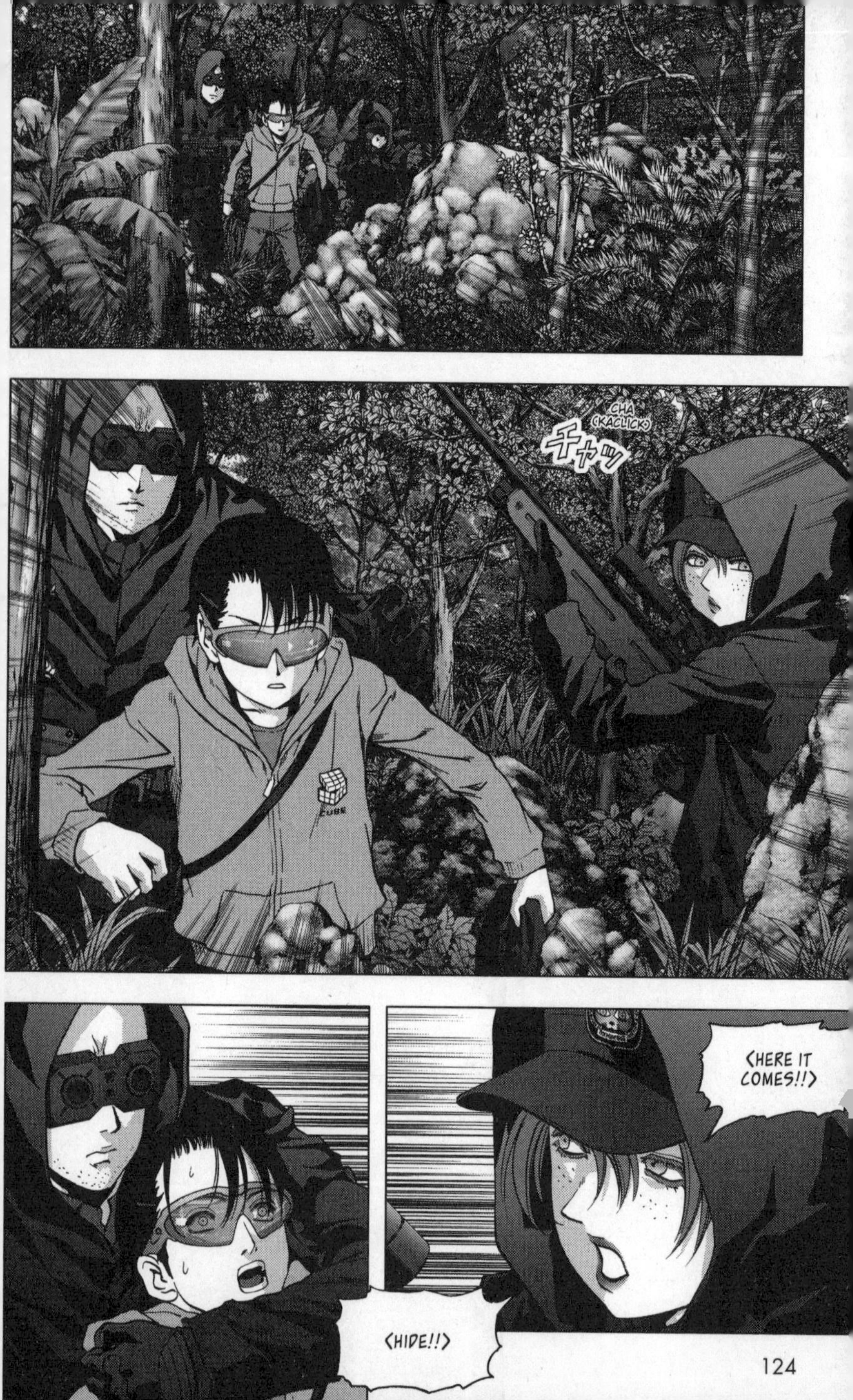
チャッ
CHA (KACLICK)
⟨HERE IT COMES!!⟩
⟨HIDE!!⟩

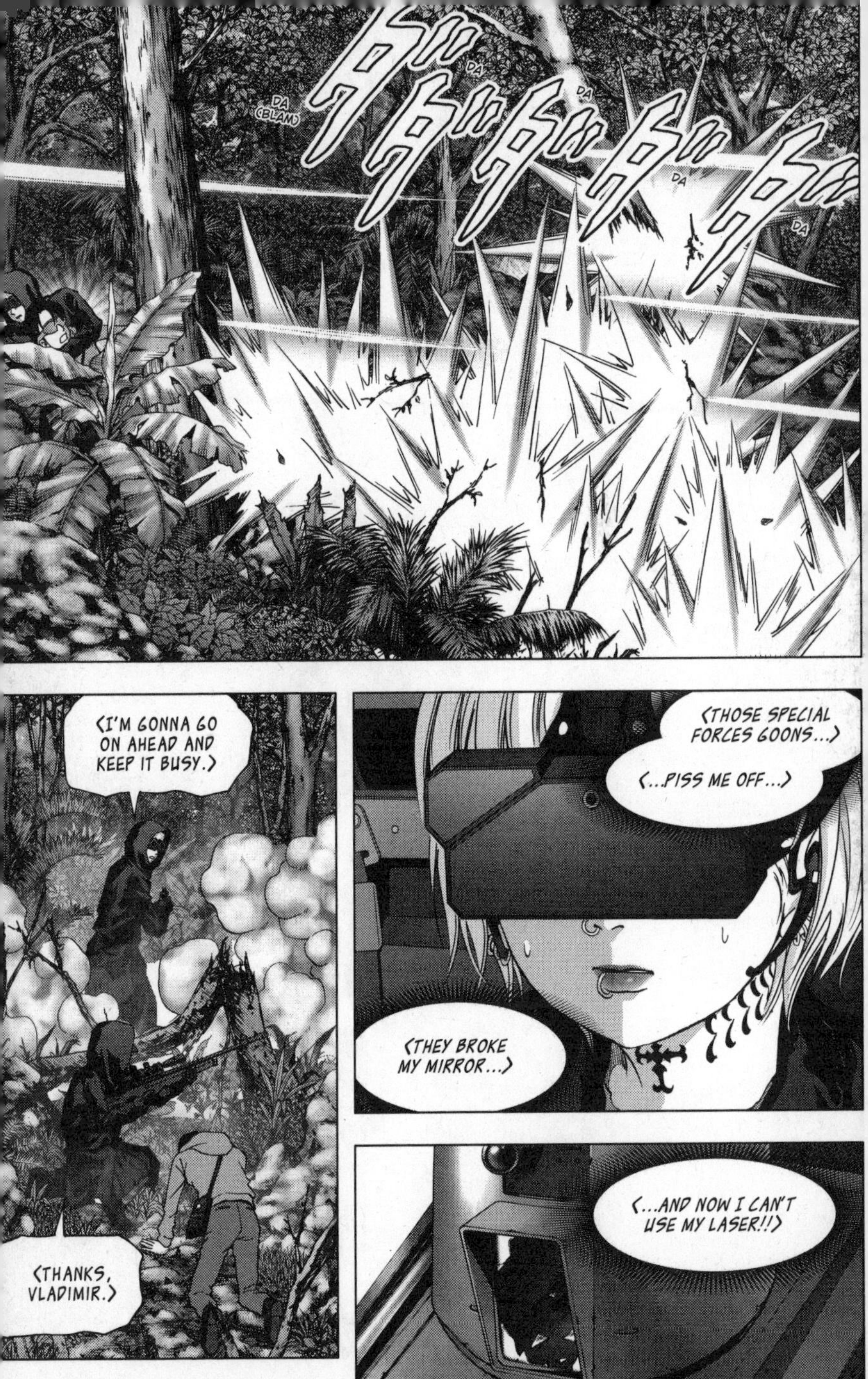
DA
DA
DA
DA (BLAM)
DA
⟨THOSE SPECIAL FORCES GOONS...⟩
⟨...PISS ME OFF...⟩
⟨THEY BROKE MY MIRROR...⟩
⟨...AND NOW I CAN'T USE MY LASER!!⟩
⟨I'M GONNA GO ON AHEAD AND KEEP IT BUSY.⟩
⟨THANKS, VLADIMIR.⟩

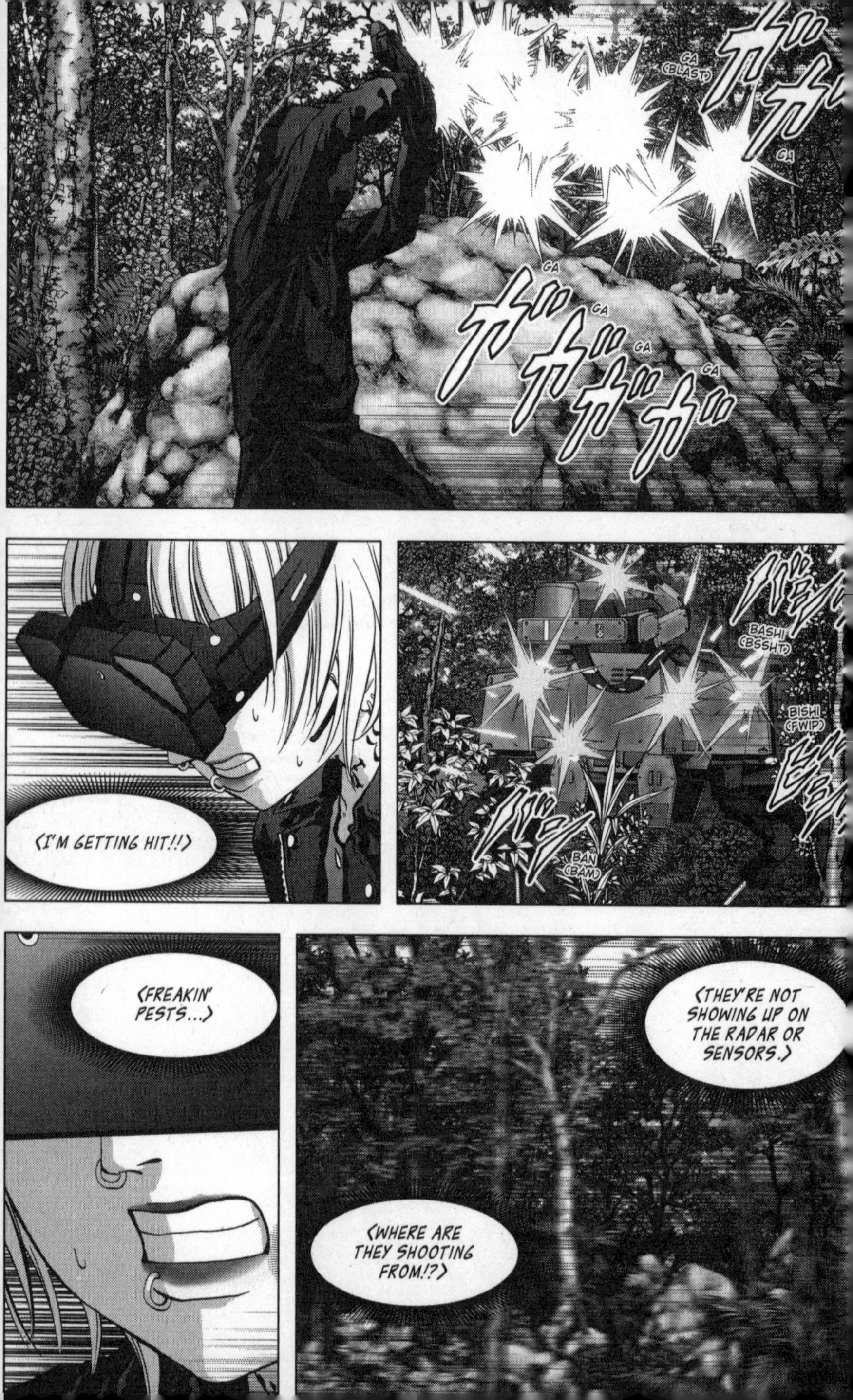
GA
(BLAST)
GA
GA
GA
GA
GA
BASHI
(BSSHT)
BISHI
(FWIP)
BAN
(BAM)
〈I'M GETTING HIT!!〉
〈THEY'RE NOT SHOWING UP ON THE RADAR OR SENSORS.〉
〈WHERE ARE THEY SHOOTING FROM!?〉
〈FREAKIN' PESTS...〉

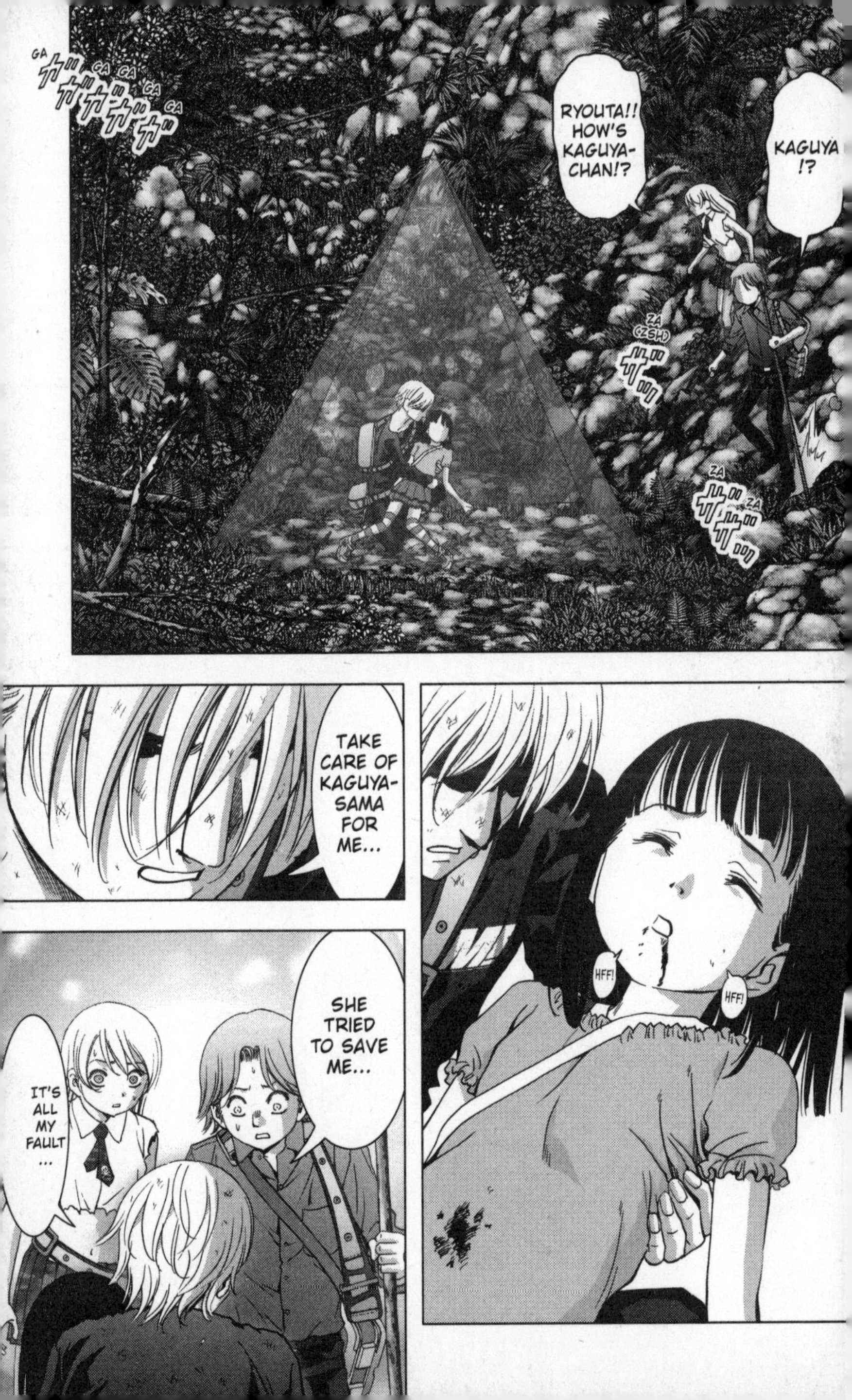
KAGUYA!?
RYOUTA!! HOW'S KAGUYA-CHAN!?
GA GA GA GA GA
ZA (ZSH)
ZA ZA
HFF!
HFF!
TAKE CARE OF KAGUYA-SAMA FOR ME...
SHE TRIED TO SAVE ME...
IT'S ALL MY FAULT...

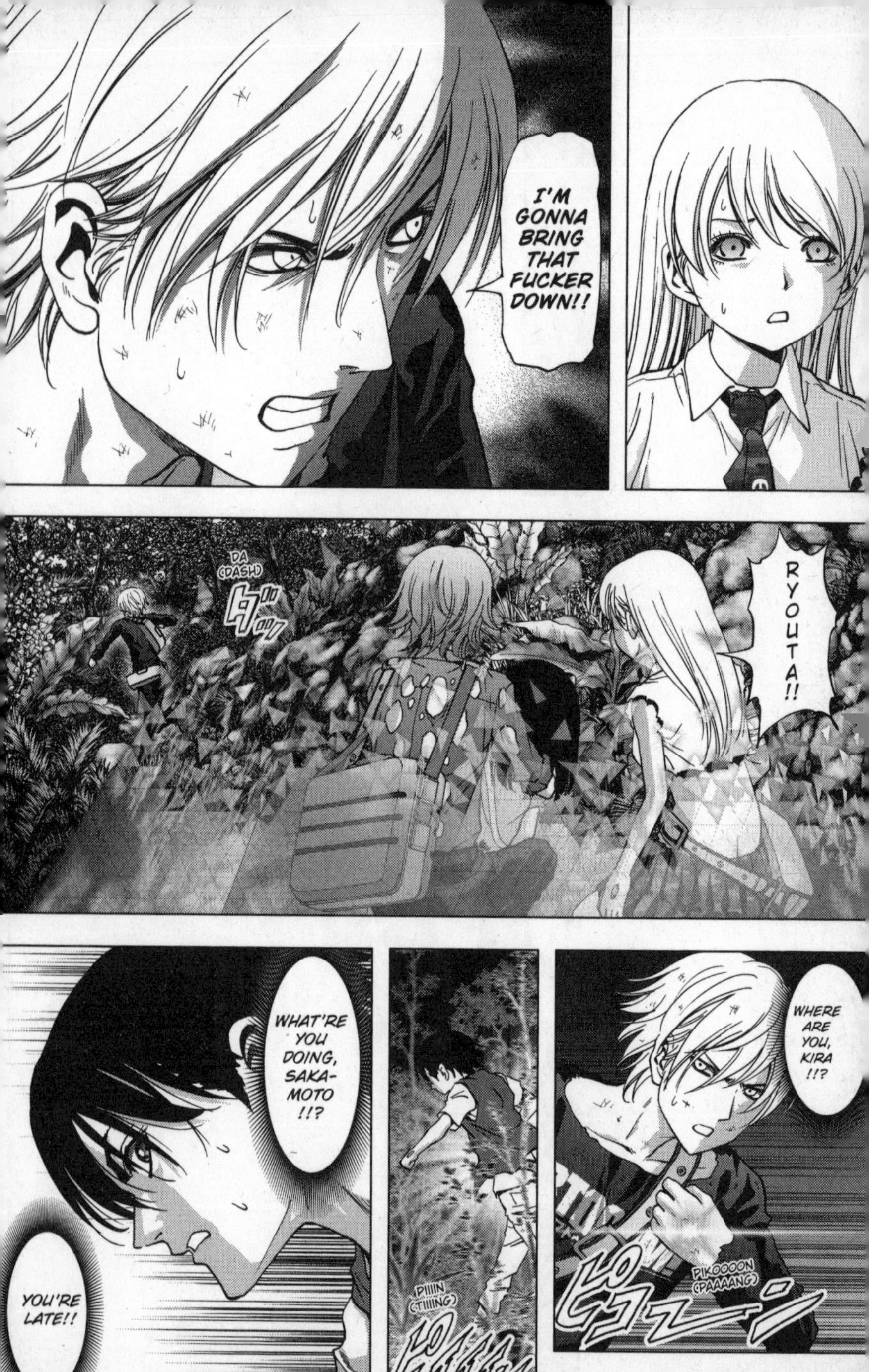
I'M GONNA BRING THAT FUCKER DOWN!!
RYOUTA!!
DA (DASH)
WHERE ARE YOU, KIRA!!?
PIKOOOON (PAAAANG)
PIIIIN (TIIIING)
WHAT'RE YOU DOING, SAKAMOTO!!?
YOU'RE LATE!!

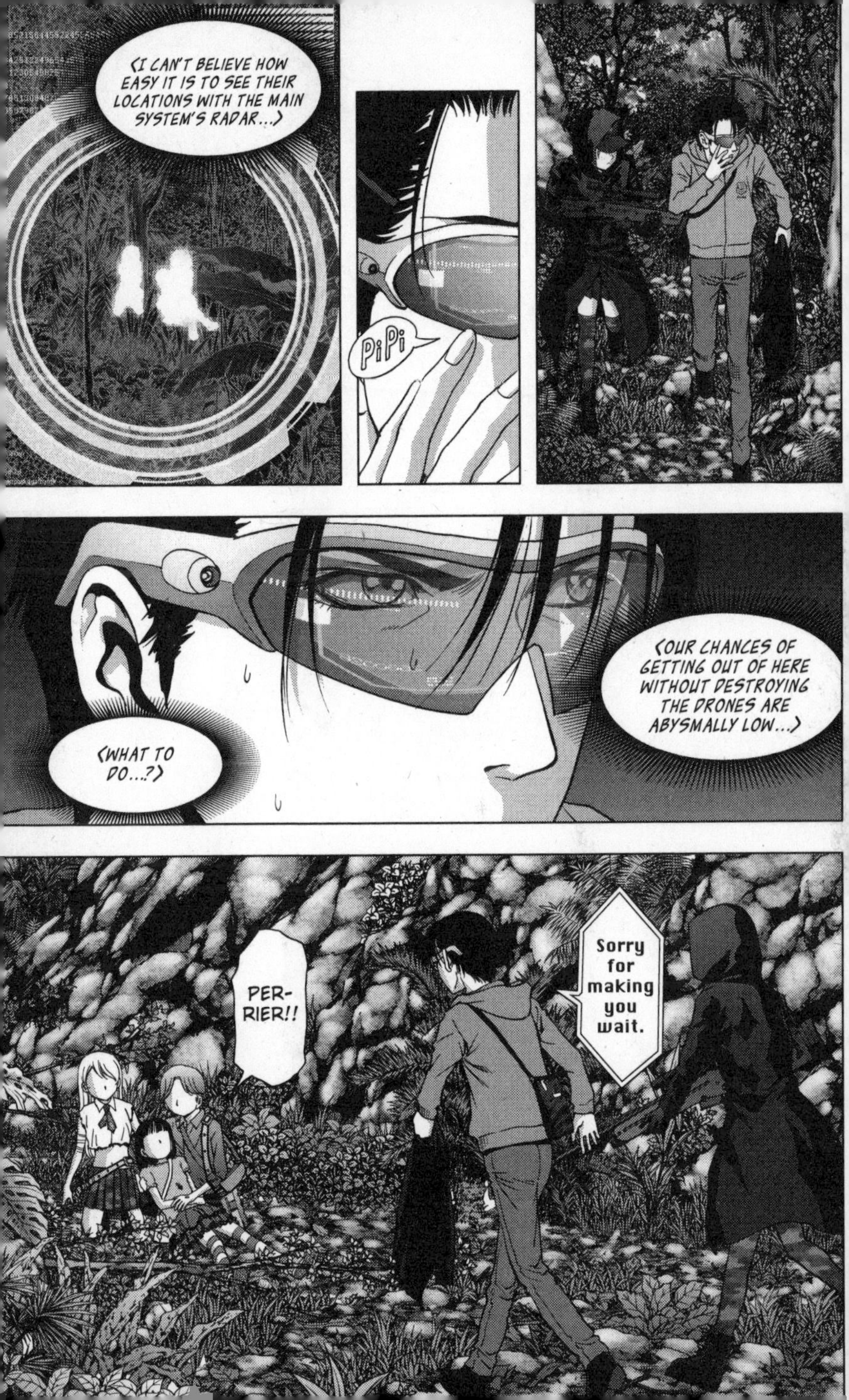
PiPi
<I CAN'T BELIEVE HOW EASY IT IS TO SEE THEIR LOCATIONS WITH THE MAIN SYSTEM'S RADAR...>
<OUR CHANCES OF GETTING OUT OF HERE WITHOUT DESTROYING THE DRONES ARE ABYSMALLY LOW...>
<WHAT TO DO...?>
Sorry for making you wait.
PER-RIER!!

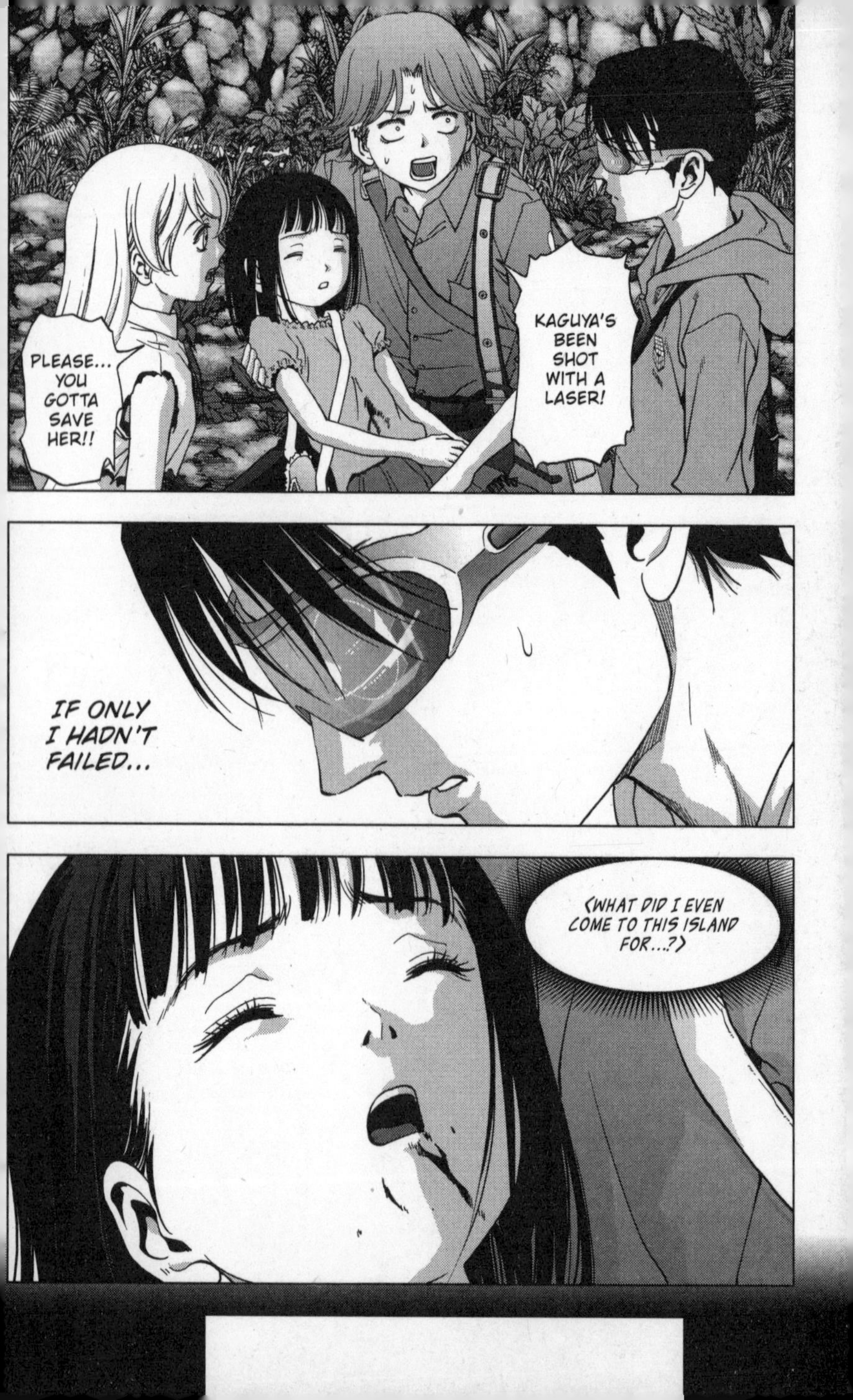
KAGUYA'S BEEN SHOT WITH A LASER!
PLEASE... YOU GOTTA SAVE HER!!
IF ONLY I HADN'T FAILED...
<WHAT DID I EVEN COME TO THIS ISLAND FOR...?>

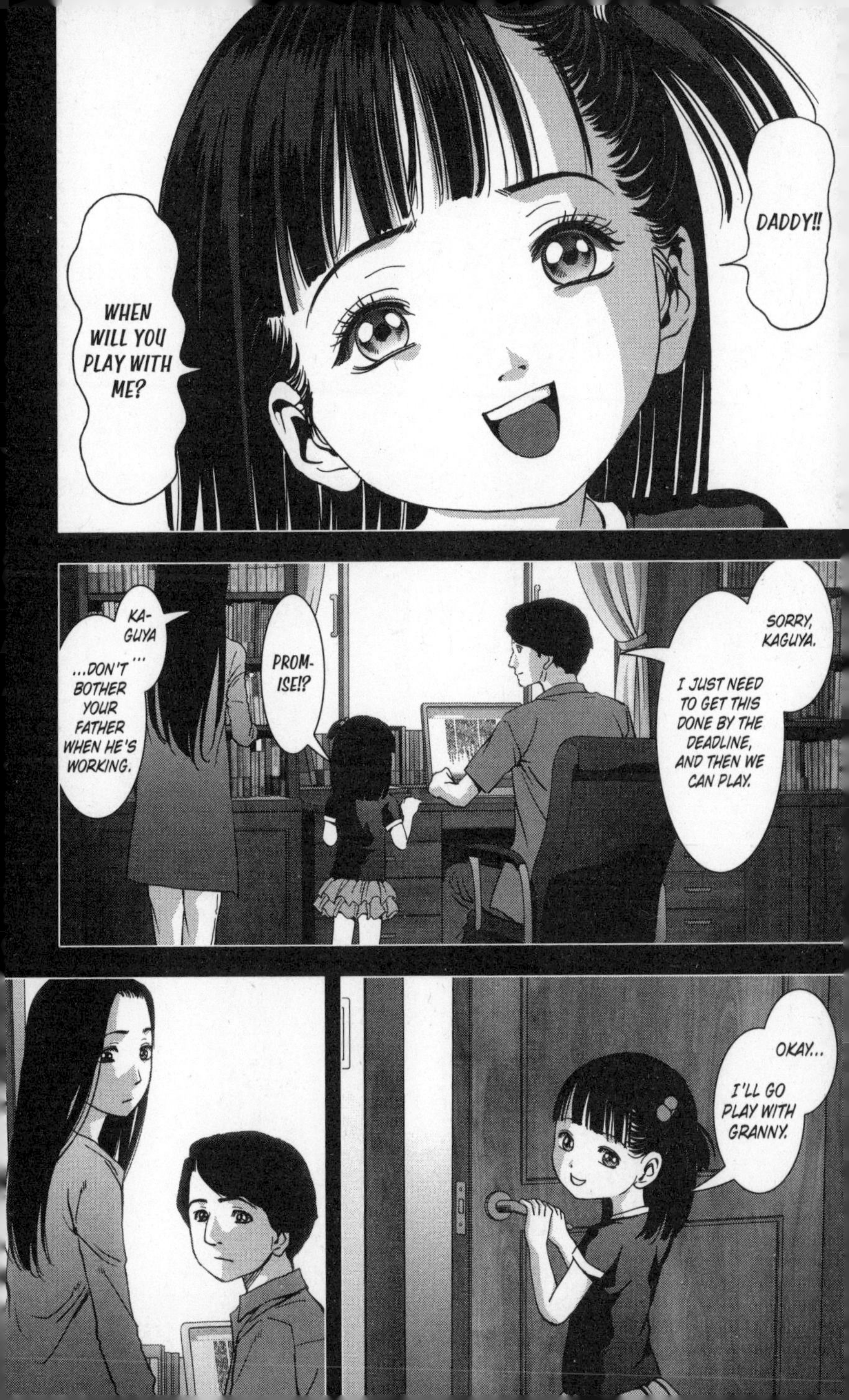
DADDY!!
WHEN WILL YOU PLAY WITH ME?
SORRY, KAGUYA.
I JUST NEED TO GET THIS DONE BY THE DEADLINE, AND THEN WE CAN PLAY.
PROMISE!?
KAGUYA...
...DON'T BOTHER YOUR FATHER WHEN HE'S WORKING.
OKAY...
I'LL GO PLAY WITH GRANNY.

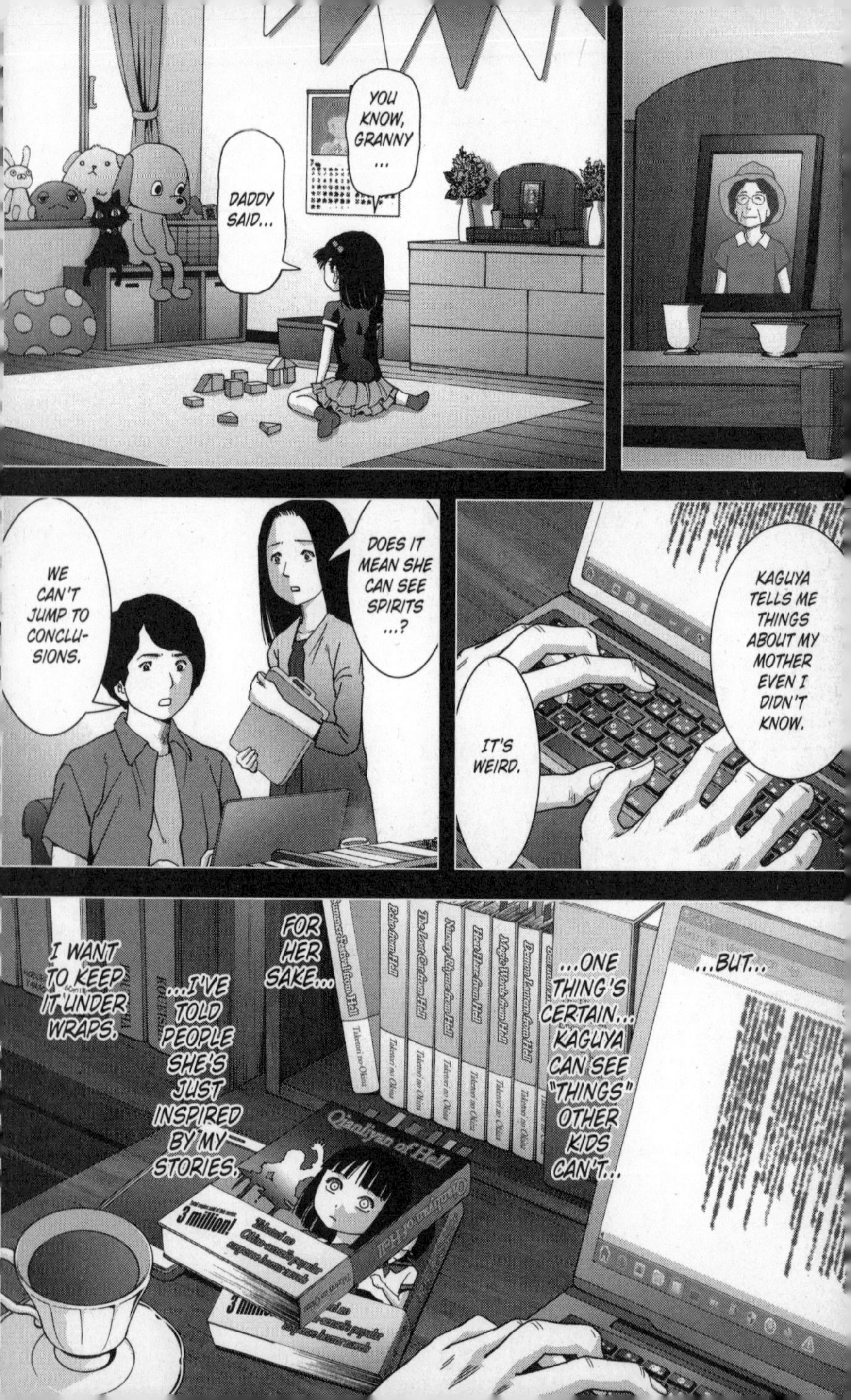
YOU KNOW, GRANNY ...
DADDY SAID...
KAGUYA TELLS ME THINGS ABOUT MY MOTHER EVEN I DIDN'T KNOW.
IT'S WEIRD.
DOES IT MEAN SHE CAN SEE SPIRITS ...?
WE CAN'T JUMP TO CONCLUSIONS.
...BUT...
...ONE THING'S CERTAIN... KAGUYA CAN SEE "THINGS" OTHER KIDS CAN'T...
FOR HER SAKE...
...I'VE TOLD PEOPLE SHE'S JUST INSPIRED BY MY STORIES.
I WANT TO KEEP IT UNDER WRAPS.
Qianliyan of Hell
3 million!

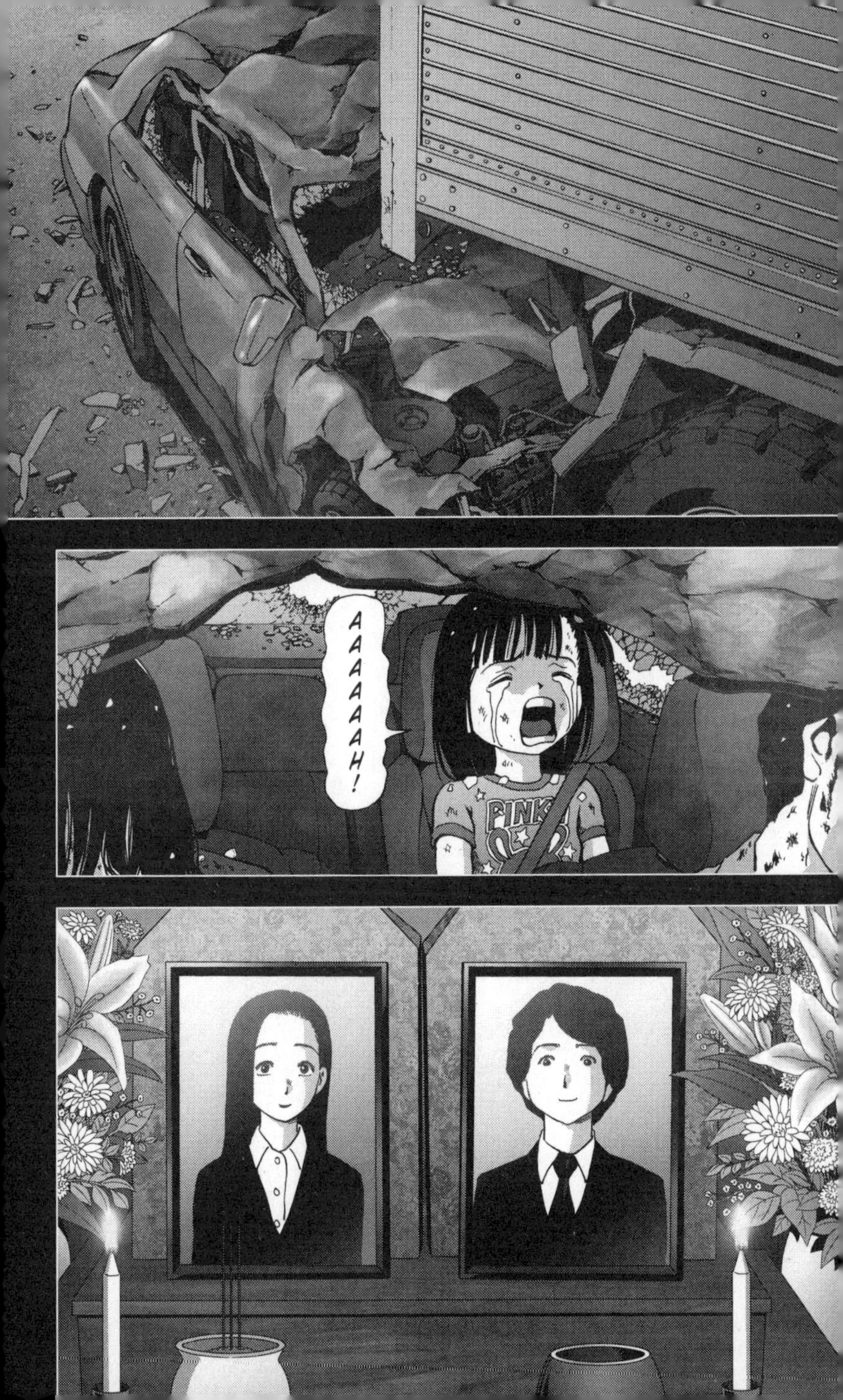
AAAAAAH!

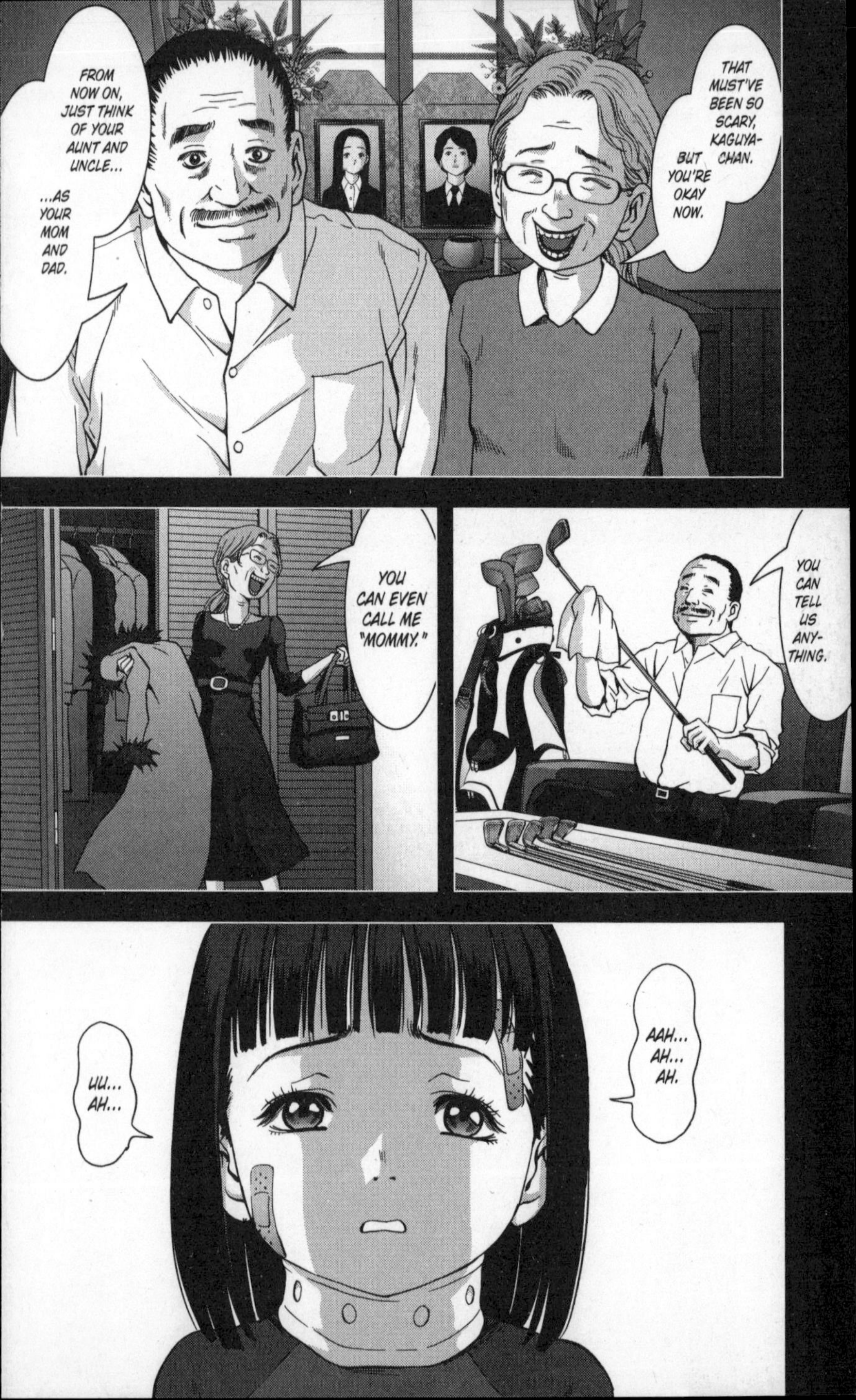
THAT MUST'VE BEEN SO SCARY, KAGUYA-CHAN.
BUT YOU'RE OKAY NOW.
FROM NOW ON, JUST THINK OF YOUR AUNT AND UNCLE...
...AS YOUR MOM AND DAD.
YOU CAN TELL US ANYTHING.
YOU CAN EVEN CALL ME "MOMMY."
AAH... AH... AH.
UU... AH...

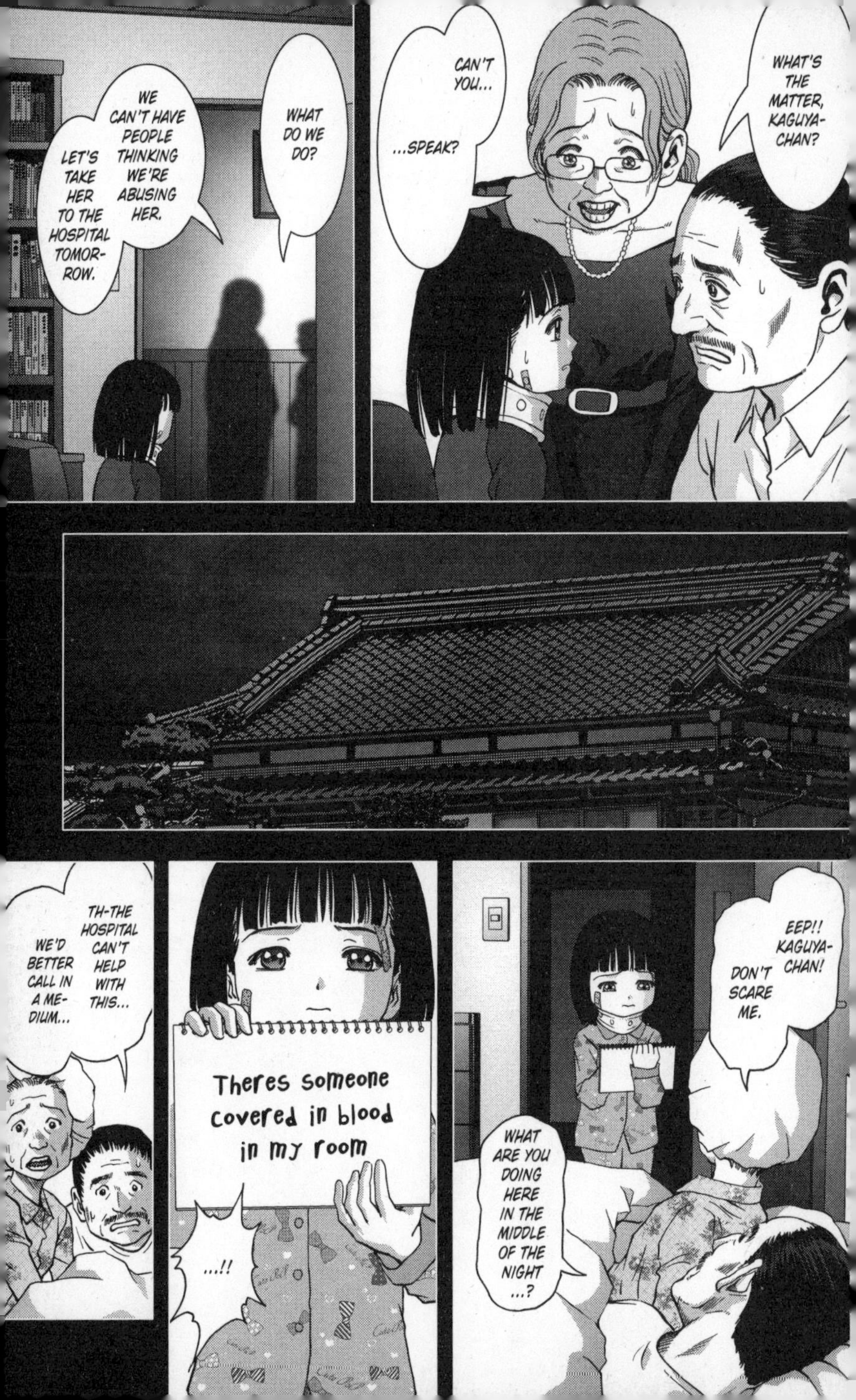
WHAT'S THE MATTER, KAGUYA-CHAN?
CAN'T YOU...
...SPEAK?
WHAT DO WE DO?
WE CAN'T HAVE PEOPLE THINKING WE'RE ABUSING HER.
LET'S TAKE HER TO THE HOSPITAL TOMORROW.
EEP!! KAGUYA-CHAN!
DON'T SCARE ME.
WHAT ARE YOU DOING HERE IN THE MIDDLE OF THE NIGHT...?
Theres someone covered in blood in my room
...!!
TH-THE HOSPITAL CAN'T HELP WITH THIS...
WE'D BETTER CALL IN A MEDIUM...

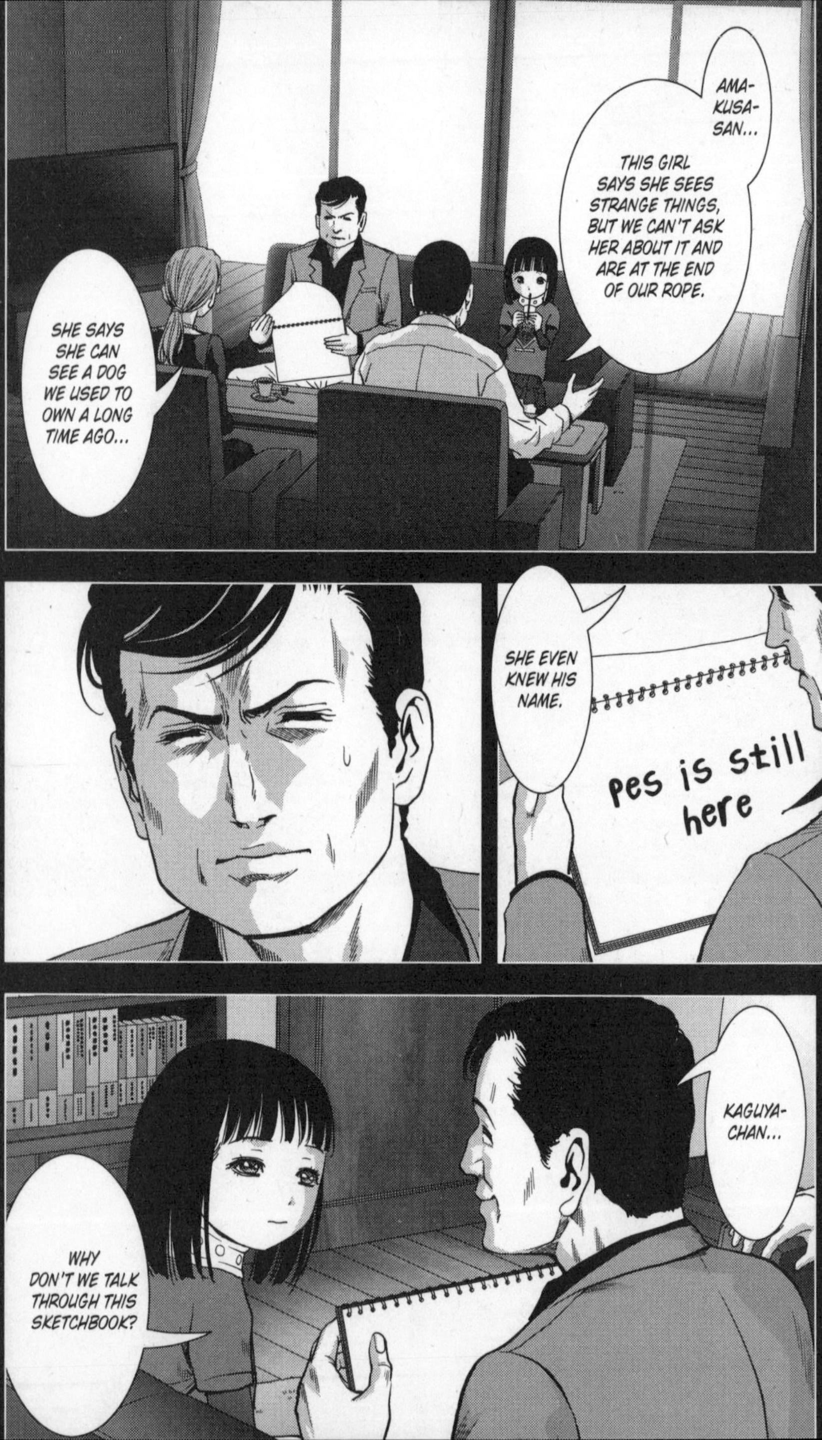
AMA-KUSA-SAN...
THIS GIRL SAYS SHE SEES STRANGE THINGS, BUT WE CAN'T ASK HER ABOUT IT AND ARE AT THE END OF OUR ROPE.
SHE SAYS SHE CAN SEE A DOG WE USED TO OWN A LONG TIME AGO...
SHE EVEN KNEW HIS NAME.
pes is still here
KAGUYA-CHAN...
WHY DON'T WE TALK THROUGH THIS SKETCHBOOK?

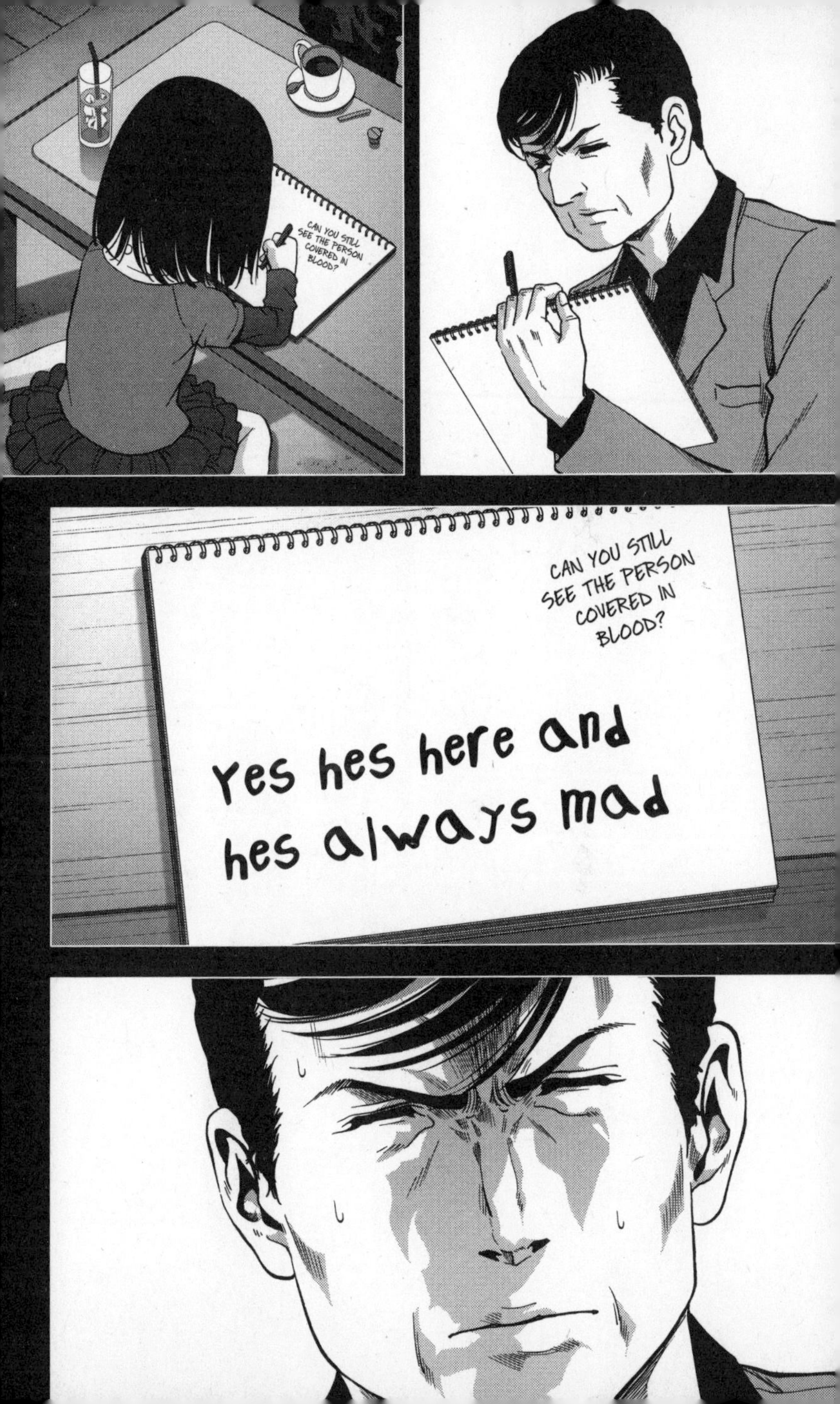

CAN YOU STILL SEE THE PERSON COVERED IN BLOOD?
CAN YOU STILL SEE THE PERSON COVERED IN BLOOD?
yes hes here and hes always mad

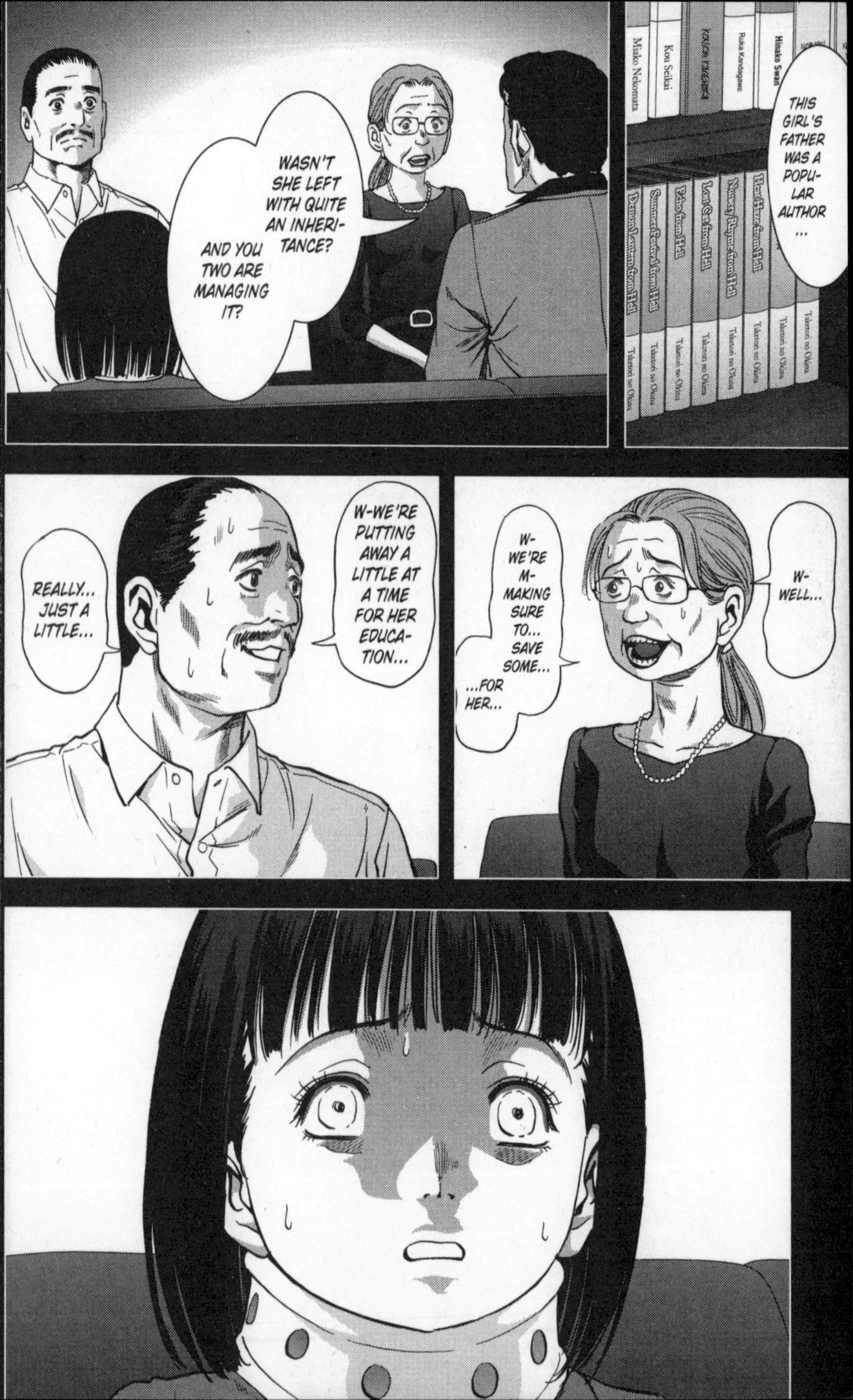
Hinako Swan
Ruka Kandagawa
Kou Seikai
Miako Nekomata
THIS GIRL'S FATHER WAS A POPULAR AUTHOR...
WASN'T SHE LEFT WITH QUITE AN INHERITANCE?
AND YOU TWO ARE MANAGING IT?
W-WELL...
W-WE'RE M-MAKING SURE TO... SAVE SOME...
...FOR HER...
W-WE'RE PUTTING AWAY A LITTLE AT A TIME FOR HER EDUCATION...
REALLY... JUST A LITTLE...

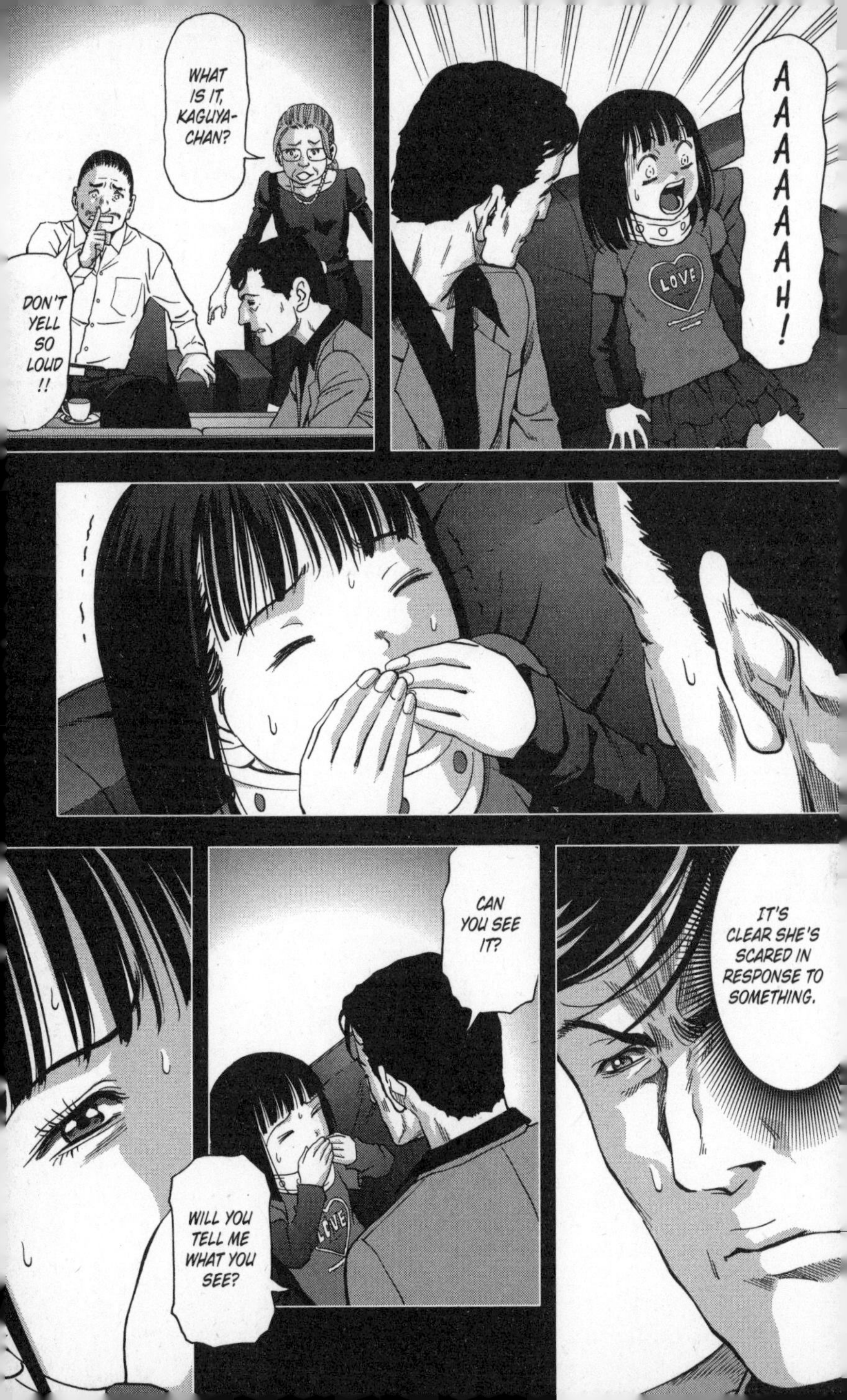
AAAAAAAH!
WHAT IS IT, KAGUYA-CHAN?
DON'T YELL SO LOUD!!
IT'S CLEAR SHE'S SCARED IN RESPONSE TO SOMETHING.
CAN YOU SEE IT?
WILL YOU TELL ME WHAT YOU SEE?

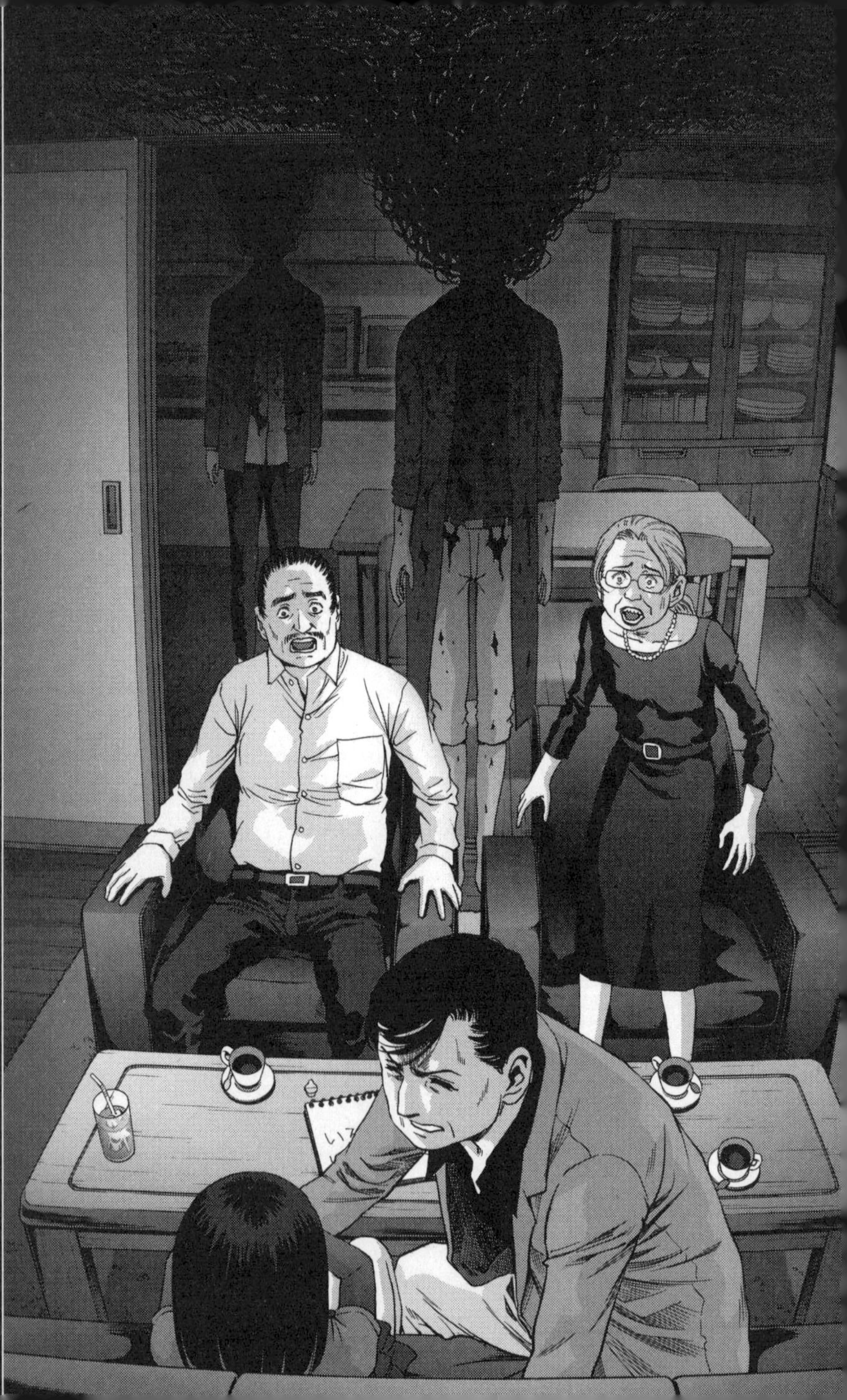

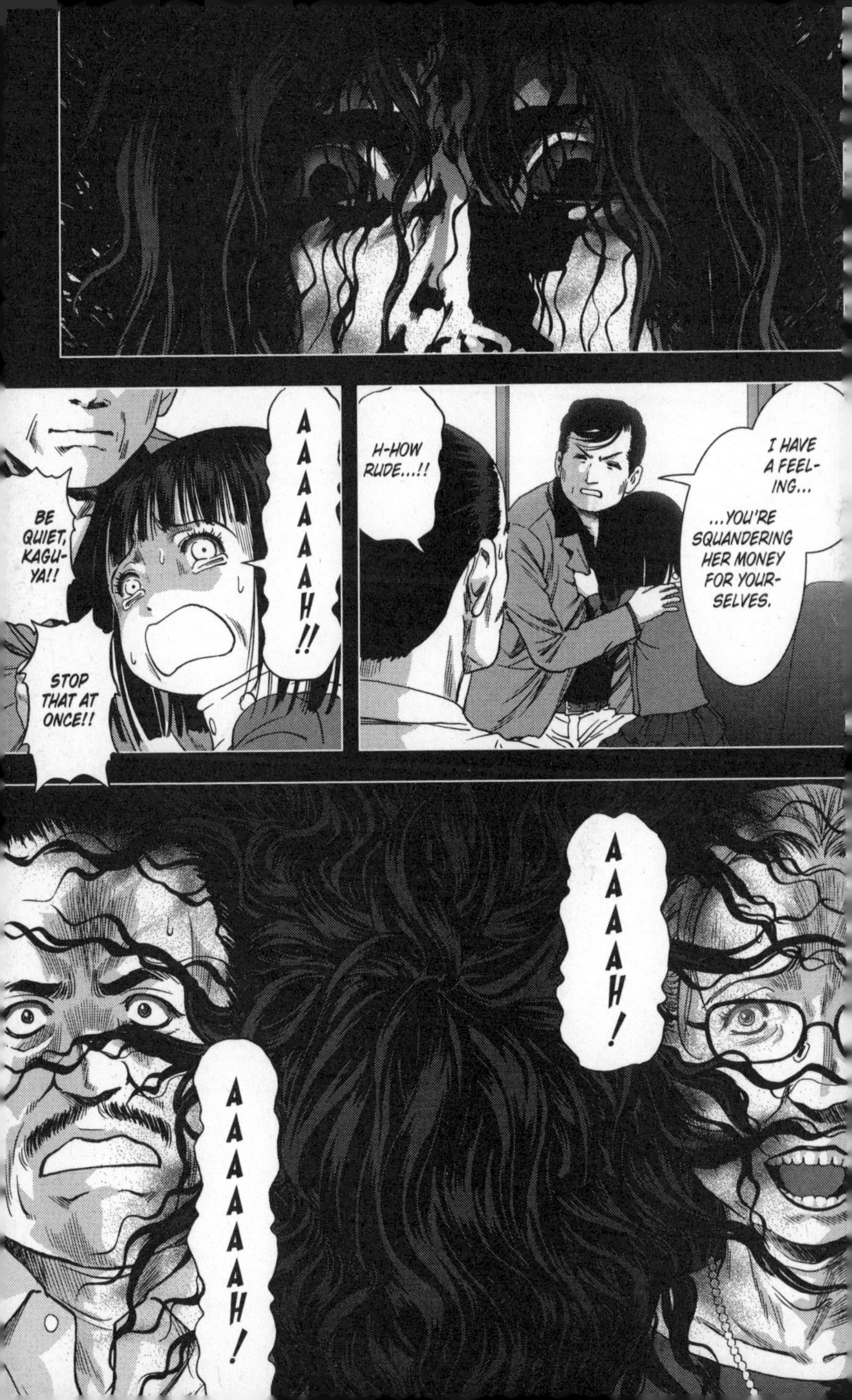
I HAVE A FEEL-ING...
...YOU'RE SQUANDERING HER MONEY FOR YOUR-SELVES.
H-HOW RUDE...!!
AAAAAAAH!!
BE QUIET, KAGU-YA!!
STOP THAT AT ONCE!!
AAAAH!
AAAAAAH!

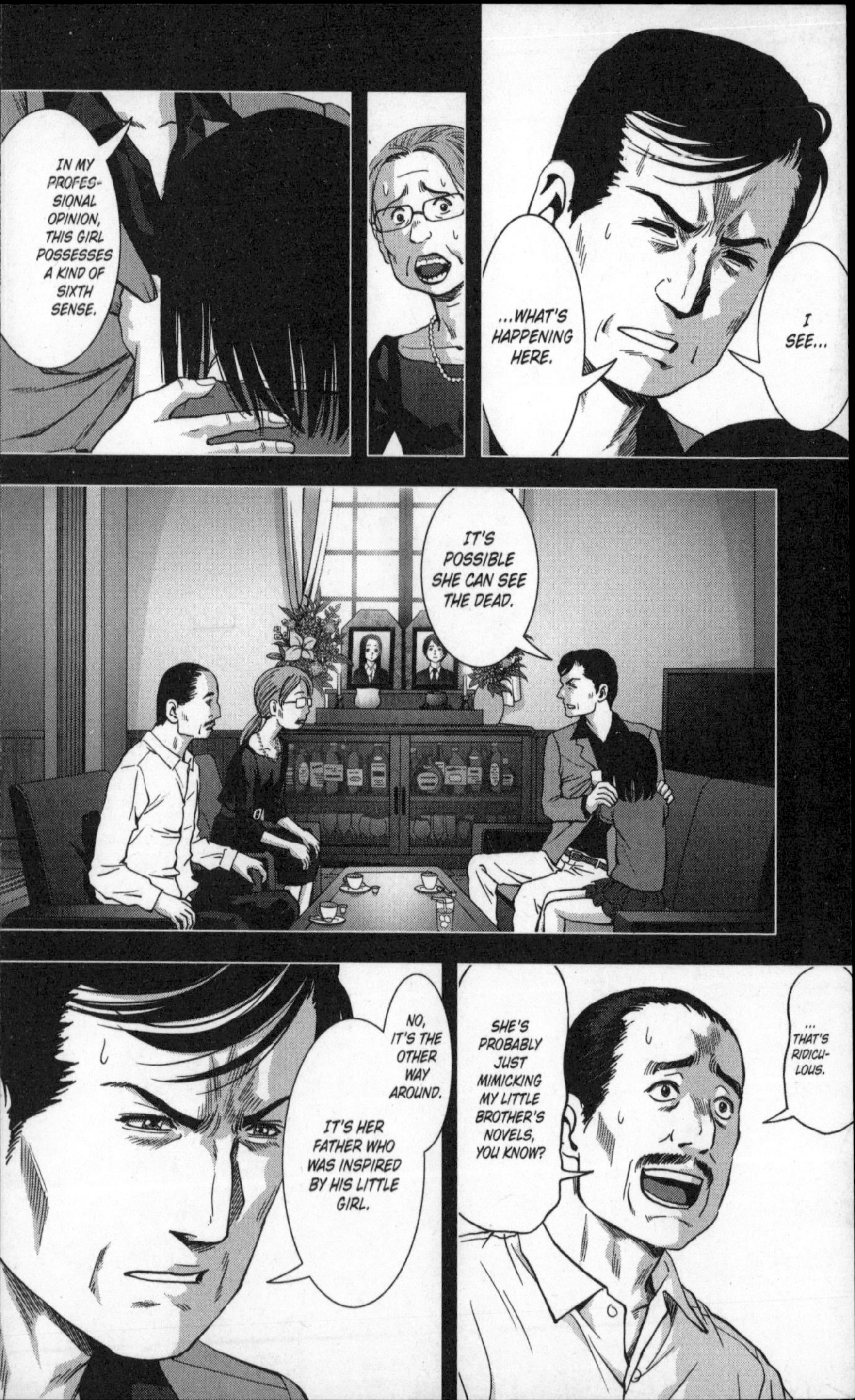
I SEE...
...WHAT'S HAPPENING HERE.
IN MY PROFES-SIONAL OPINION, THIS GIRL POSSESSES A KIND OF SIXTH SENSE.
IT'S POSSIBLE SHE CAN SEE THE DEAD.
...THAT'S RIDICU-LOUS.
SHE'S PROBABLY JUST MIMICKING MY LITTLE BROTHER'S NOVELS, YOU KNOW?
NO, IT'S THE OTHER WAY AROUND.
IT'S HER FATHER WHO WAS INSPIRED BY HIS LITTLE GIRL.

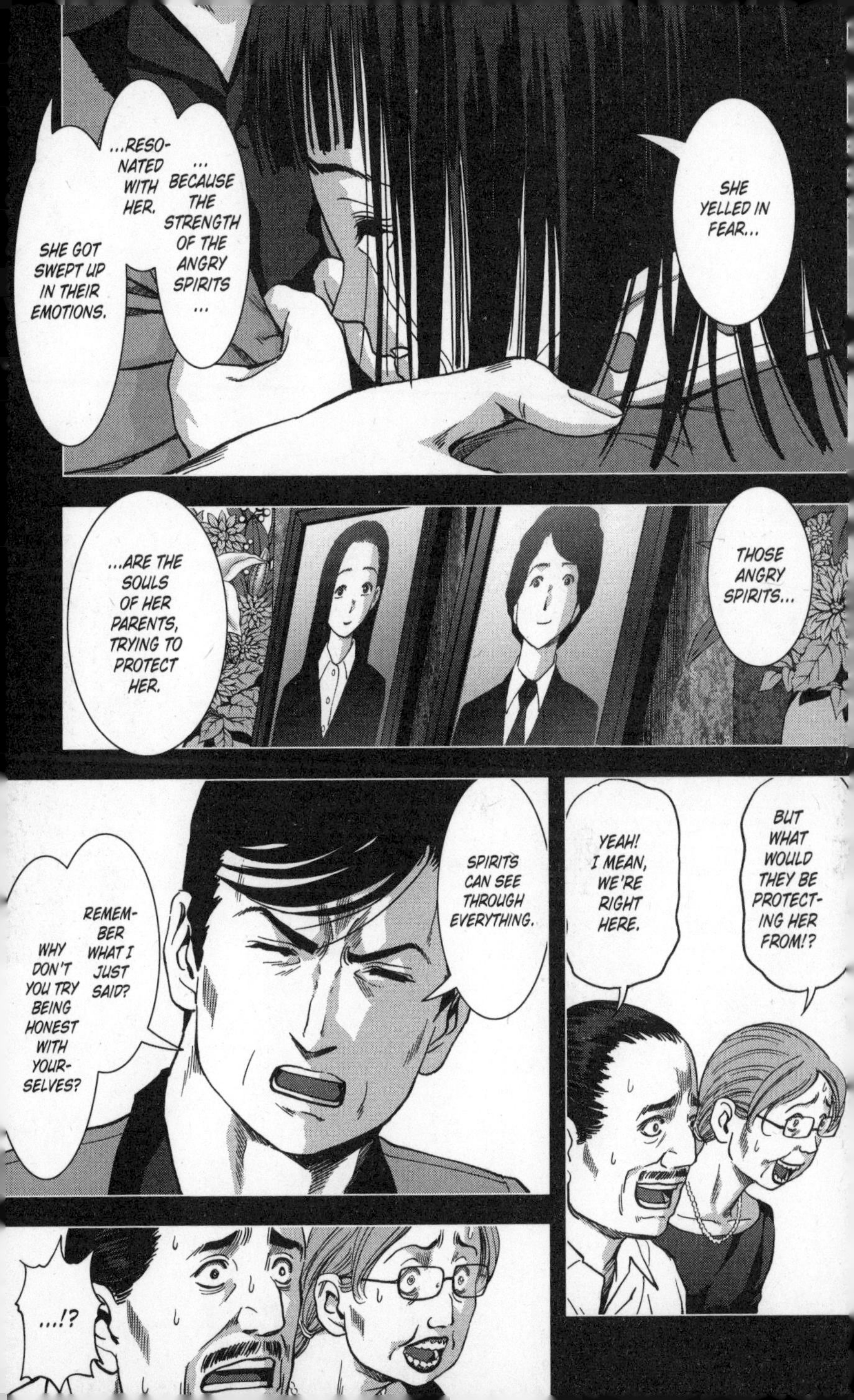
SHE YELLED IN FEAR...
...BECAUSE THE STRENGTH OF THE ANGRY SPIRITS...
...RESONATED WITH HER.
SHE GOT SWEPT UP IN THEIR EMOTIONS.
THOSE ANGRY SPIRITS...
...ARE THE SOULS OF HER PARENTS, TRYING TO PROTECT HER.
BUT WHAT WOULD THEY BE PROTECTING HER FROM!?
YEAH! I MEAN, WE'RE RIGHT HERE.
SPIRITS CAN SEE THROUGH EVERYTHING.
REMEMBER WHAT I JUST SAID?
WHY DON'T YOU TRY BEING HONEST WITH YOURSELVES?
...!?

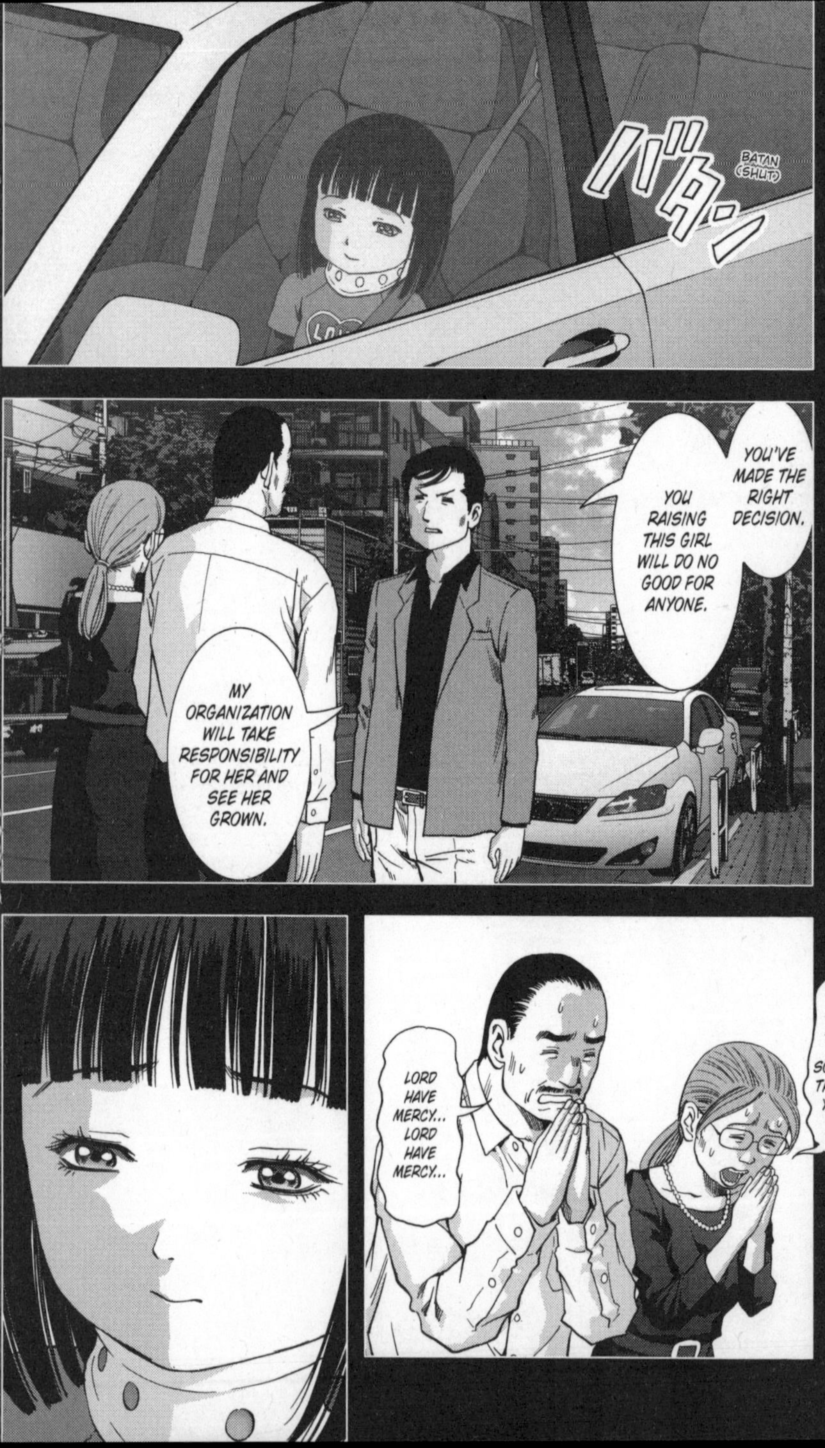
バタン
BATAN (SHUT)
YOU'VE MADE THE RIGHT DECISION.
YOU RAISING THIS GIRL WILL DO NO GOOD FOR ANYONE.
MY ORGANIZATION WILL TAKE RESPONSIBILITY FOR HER AND SEE HER GROWN.
I... I'M SO SORRY. THANK YOU.
LORD HAVE MERCY... LORD HAVE MERCY...

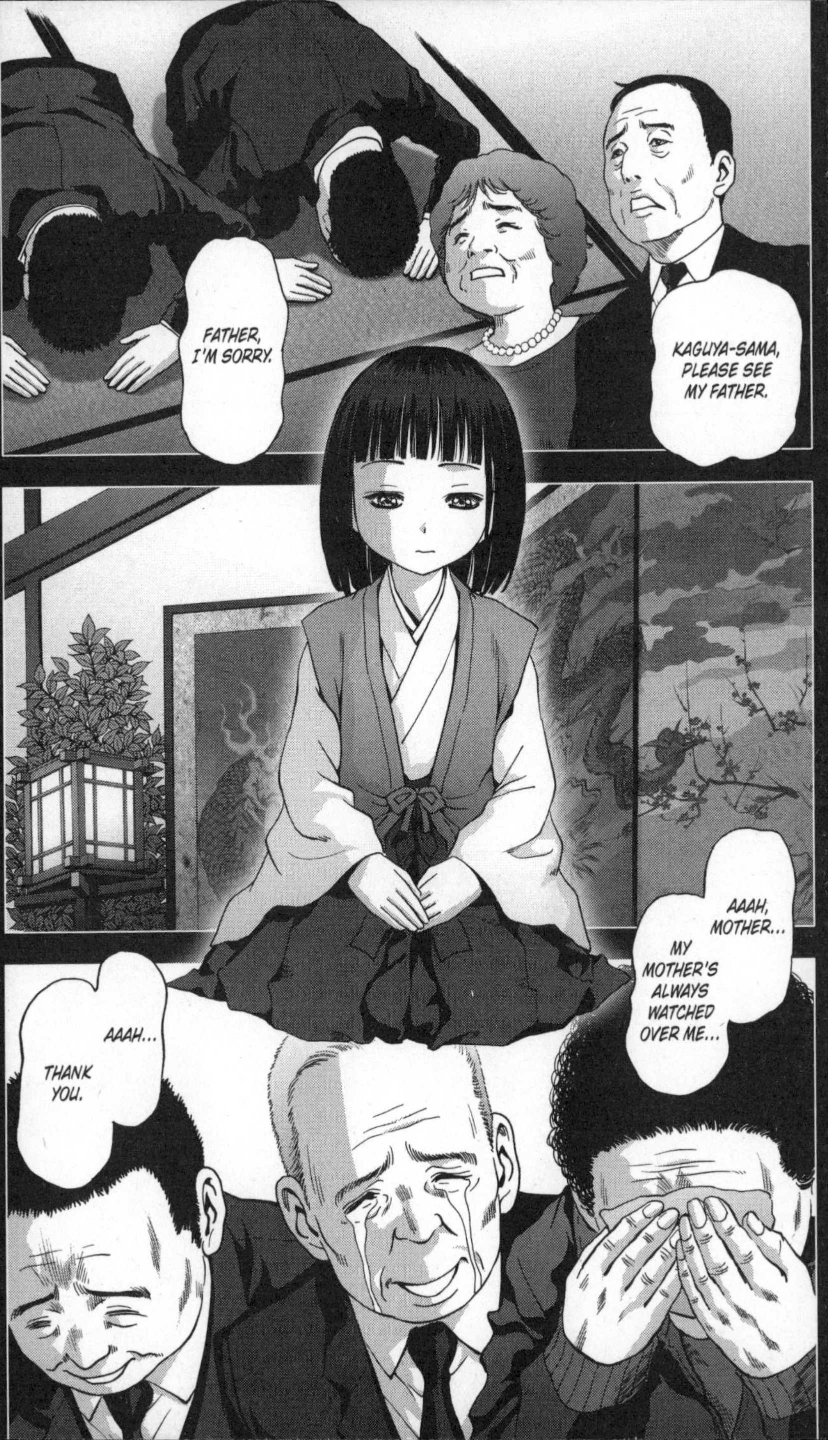
KAGUYA-SAMA, PLEASE SEE MY FATHER.
FATHER, I'M SORRY.
AAAH, MOTHER...
MY MOTHER'S ALWAYS WATCHED OVER ME...
AAAH...
THANK YOU.

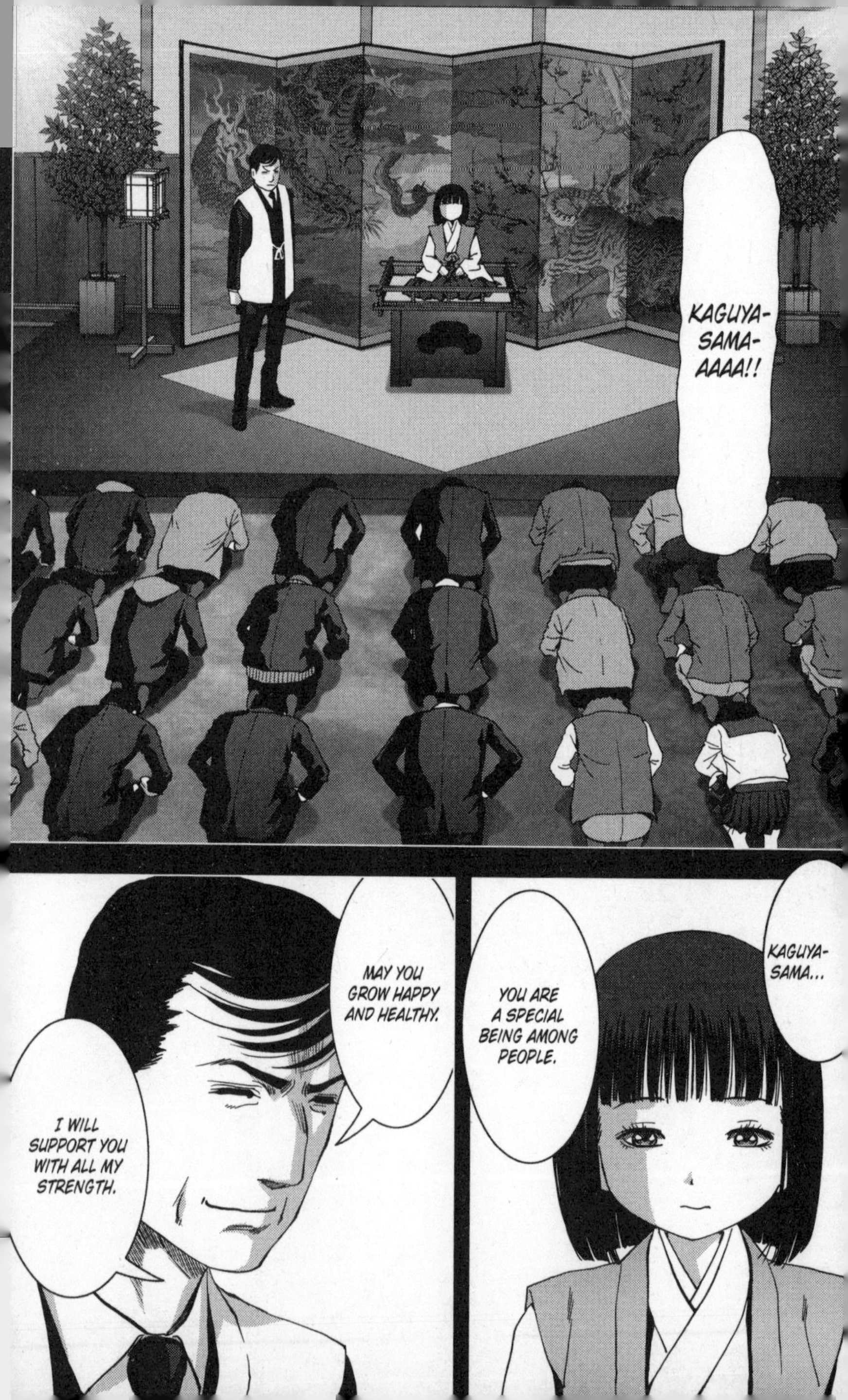
KAGUYA-SAMA-AAAA!!
KAGUYA-SAMA...
YOU ARE A SPECIAL BEING AMONG PEOPLE.
MAY YOU GROW HAPPY AND HEALTHY.
I WILL SUPPORT YOU WITH ALL MY STRENGTH.

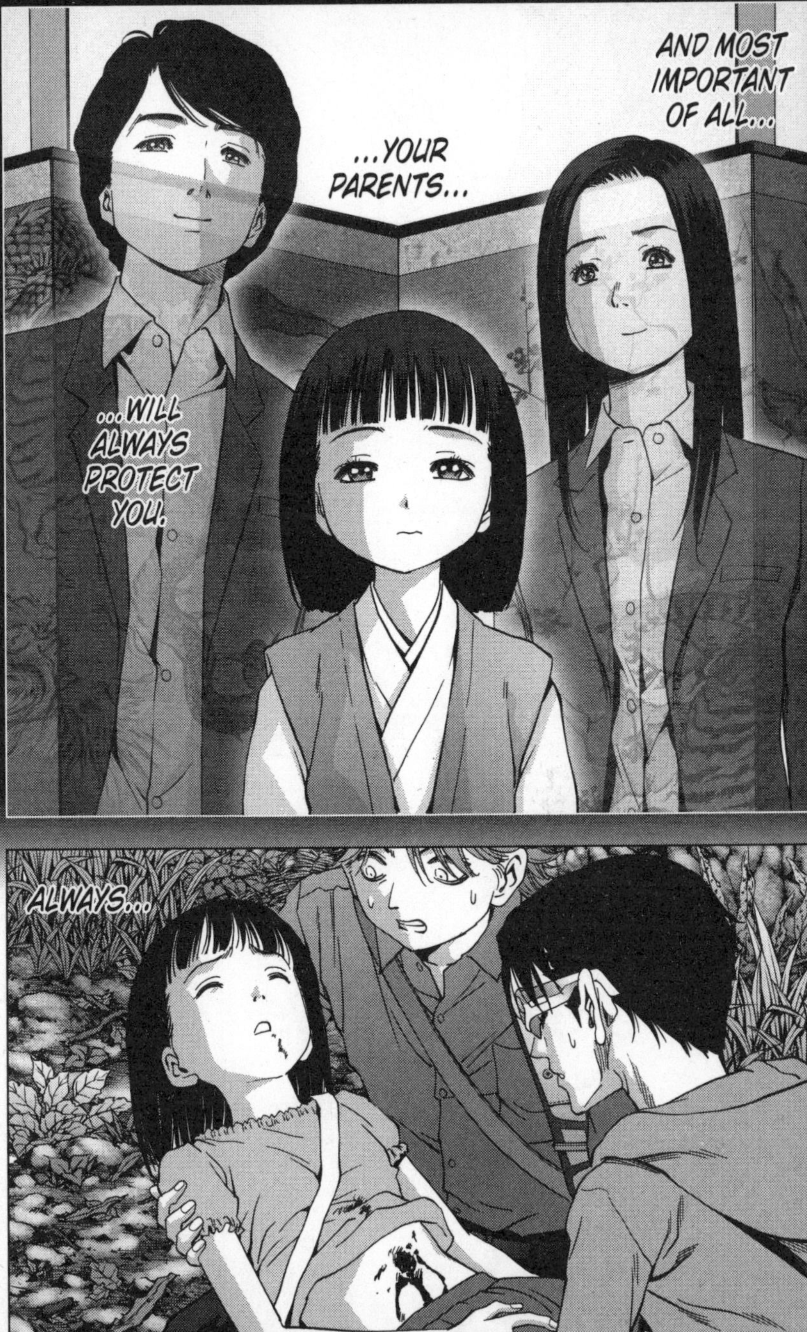
AND MOST IMPORTANT OF ALL...
...YOUR PARENTS...
...WILL ALWAYS PROTECT YOU.
ALWAYS...

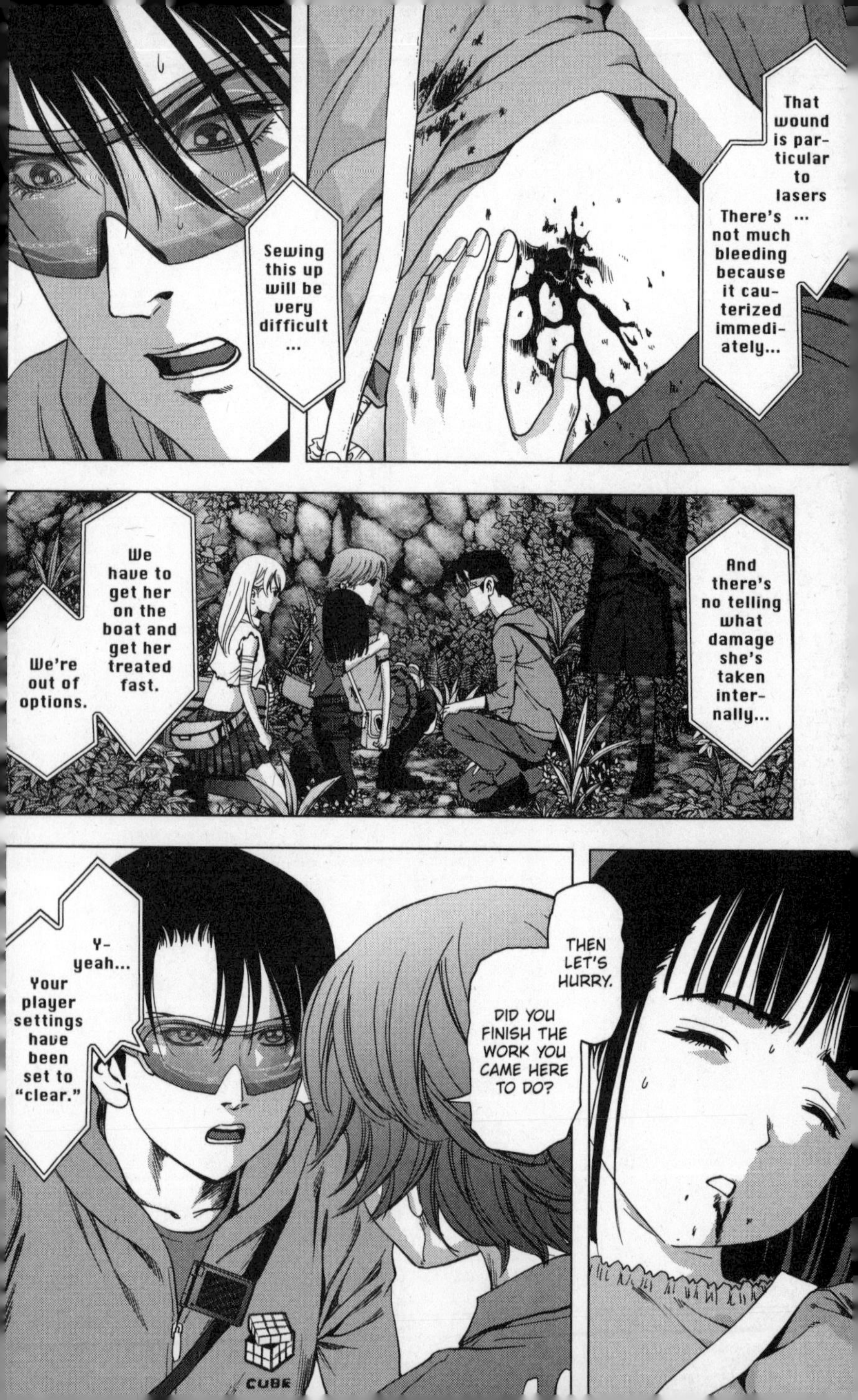
That wound is particular to lasers ...
There's not much bleeding because it cauterized immediately...
Sewing this up will be very difficult ...
And there's no telling what damage she's taken internally...
We have to get her on the boat and get her treated fast.
We're out of options.
THEN LET'S HURRY.
DID YOU FINISH THE WORK YOU CAME HERE TO DO?
Y-yeah... Your player settings have been set to "clear."
CUBE

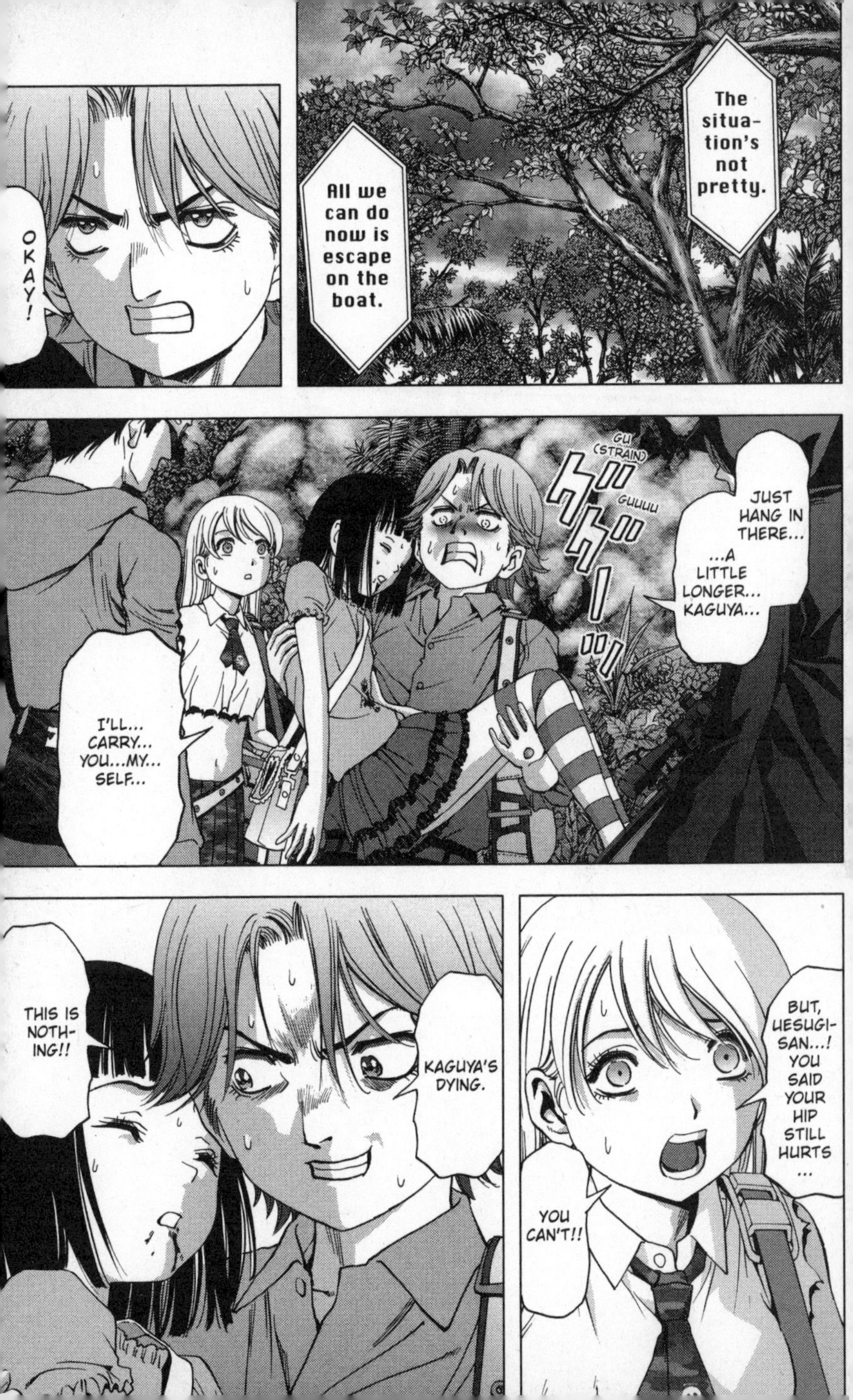
The situation's not pretty.
All we can do now is escape on the boat.
OKAY!
GU (STRAIN)
Guuuu
JUST HANG IN THERE...
...A LITTLE LONGER... KAGUYA...
I'LL... CARRY... YOU...MY... SELF...
BUT, UESUGI-SAN...! YOU SAID YOUR HIP STILL HURTS ...
YOU CAN'T!!
KAGUYA'S DYING.
THIS IS NOTHING!!

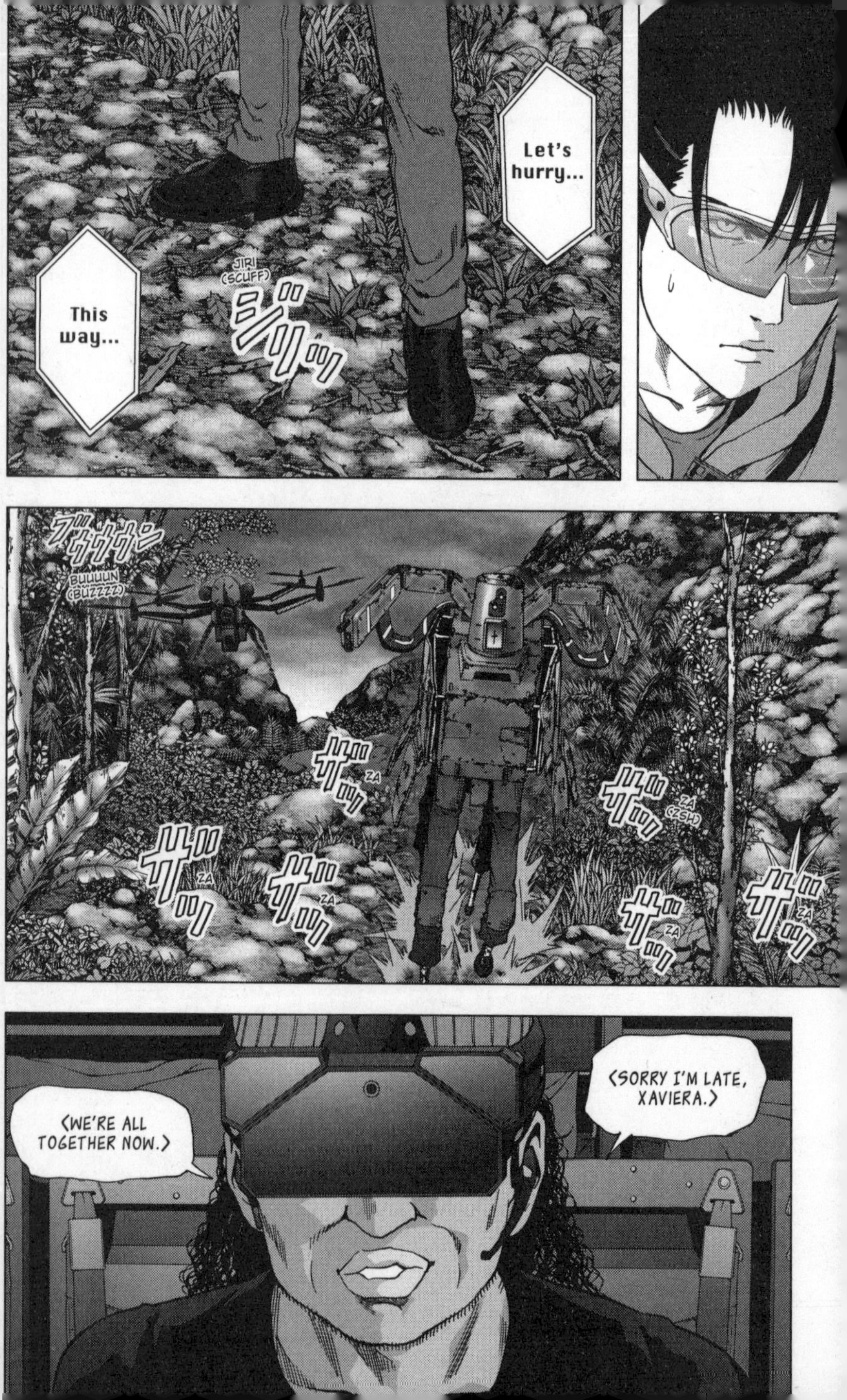
Let's hurry...
JIRI (SCUFF)
This way...
BUUUUN (BUZZZZ)
ZA (ZSH)
ZA
ZA
ZA
ZA
ZA
〈SORRY I'M LATE, XAVIERA.〉
〈WE'RE ALL TOGETHER NOW.〉

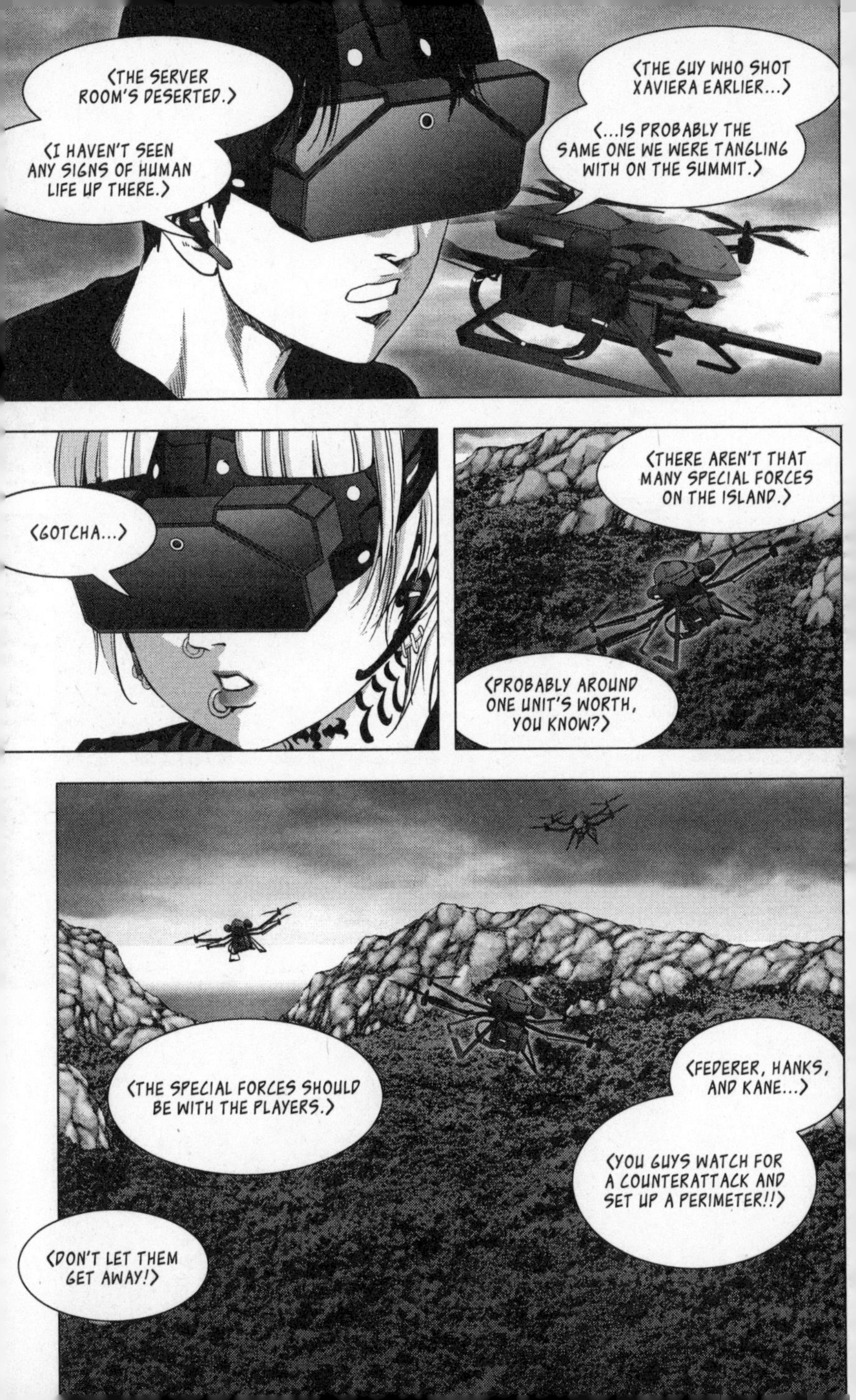
〈THE GUY WHO SHOT XAVIERA EARLIER...〉
〈...IS PROBABLY THE SAME ONE WE WERE TANGLING WITH ON THE SUMMIT.〉
〈THE SERVER ROOM'S DESERTED.〉
〈I HAVEN'T SEEN ANY SIGNS OF HUMAN LIFE UP THERE.〉
〈THERE AREN'T THAT MANY SPECIAL FORCES ON THE ISLAND.〉
〈PROBABLY AROUND ONE UNIT'S WORTH, YOU KNOW?〉
〈GOTCHA...〉
〈FEDERER, HANKS, AND KANE...〉
〈YOU GUYS WATCH FOR A COUNTERATTACK AND SET UP A PERIMETER!!〉
〈THE SPECIAL FORCES SHOULD BE WITH THE PLAYERS.〉
〈DON'T LET THEM GET AWAY!〉

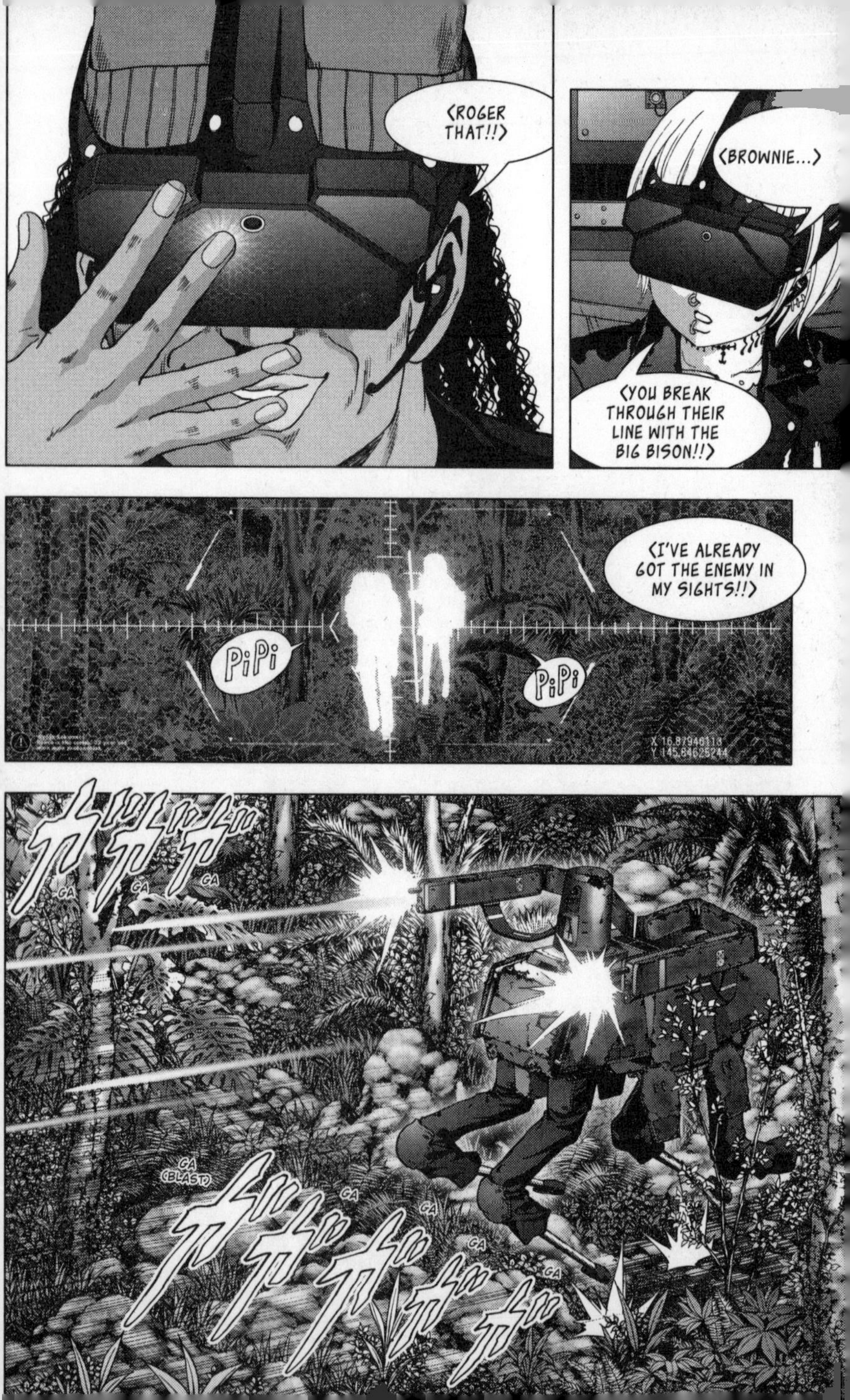

〈BROWNIE...〉
〈YOU BREAK THROUGH THEIR LINE WITH THE BIG BISON!!〉
〈ROGER THAT!!〉
〈I'VE ALREADY GOT THE ENEMY IN MY SIGHTS!!〉
PiPi
PiPi
X 16.87946113
Y 145.84625244
GA
GA
GA
GA
(BLAST)
GA
GA
GA
GA

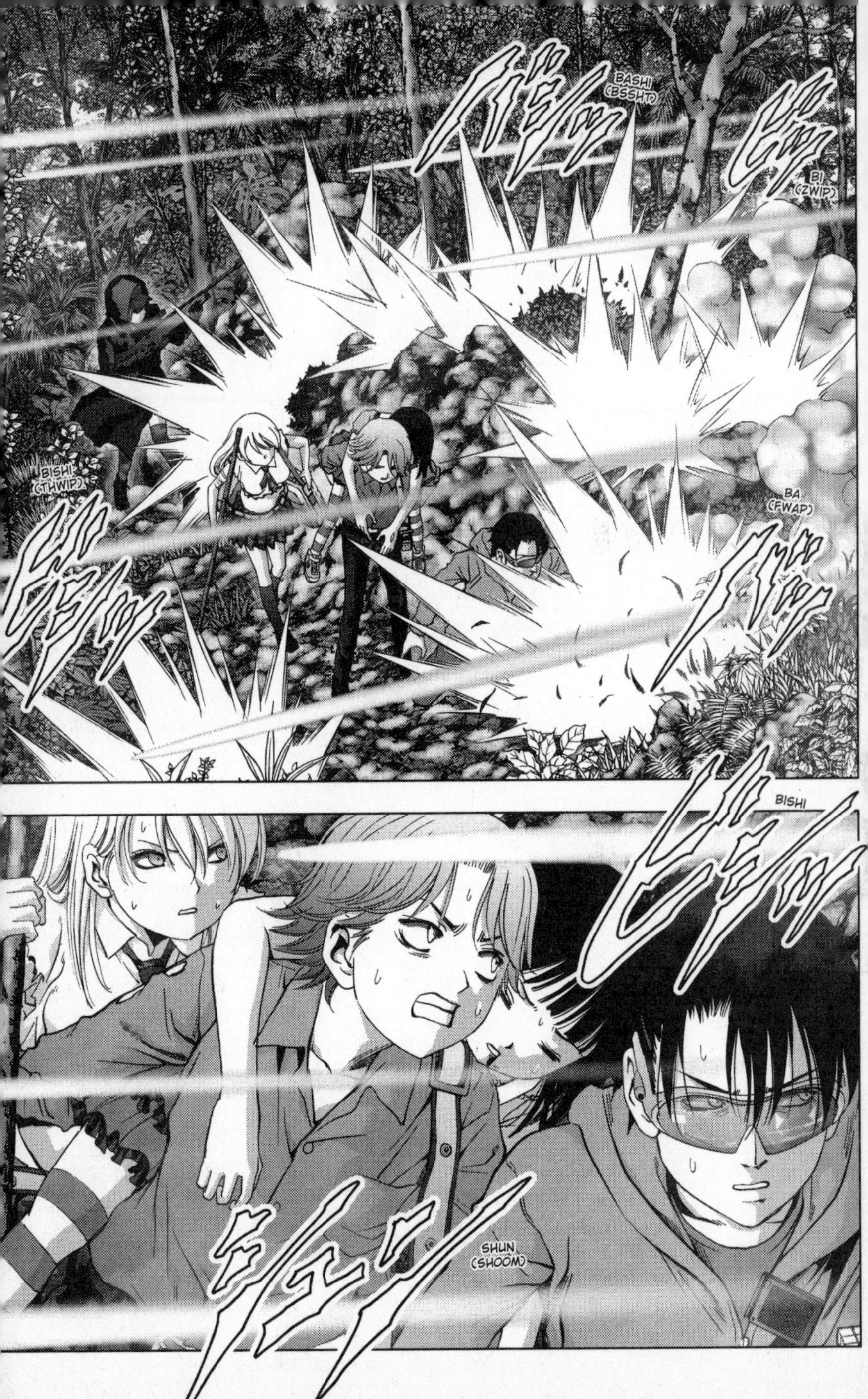
BASHI (BSSHT)
BI (ZWIP)
BA (FWAP)
BISHI (THWIP)
BISHI
SHUN (SHOOM)

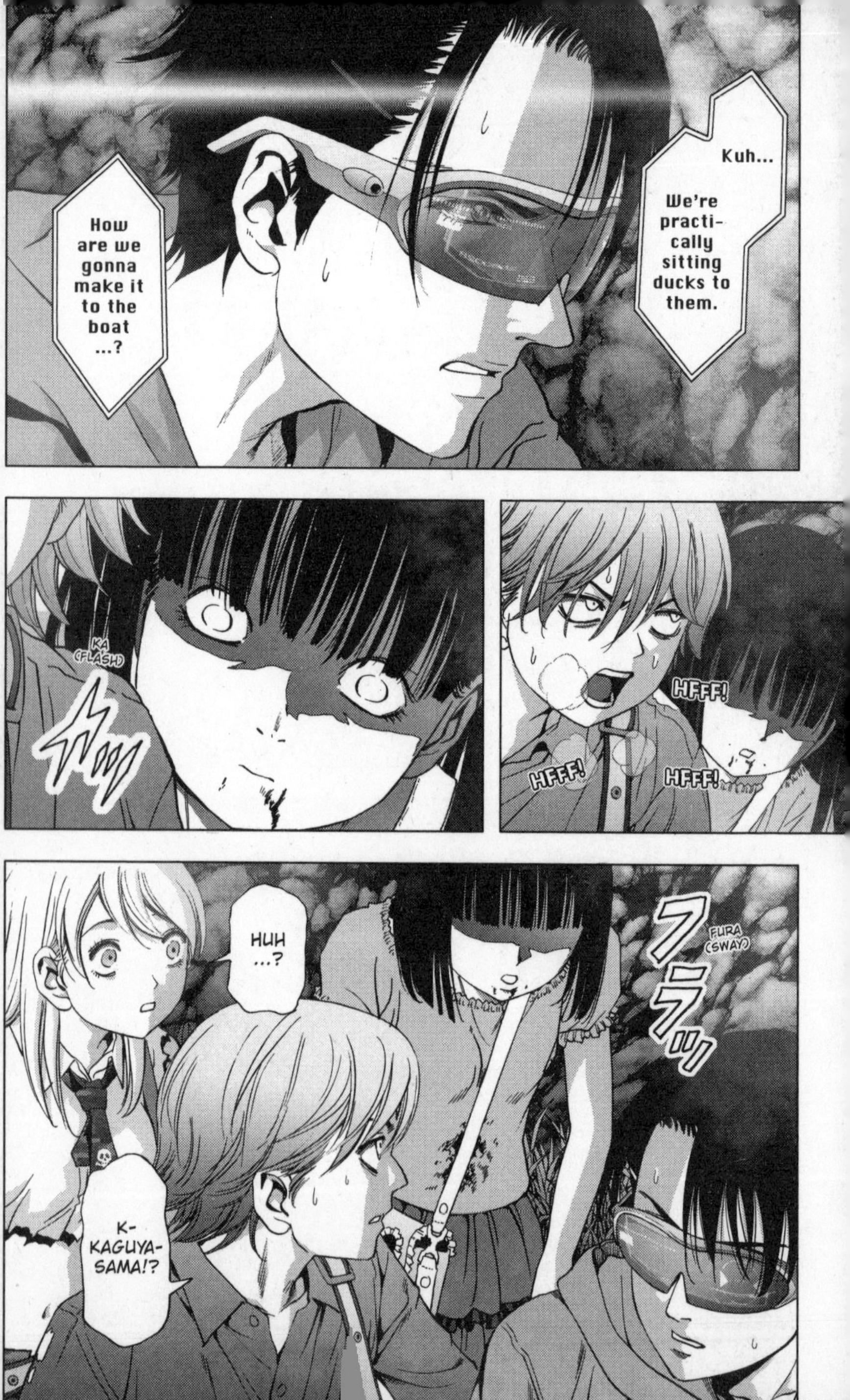
Kuh...
We're practi-cally sitting ducks to them.
How are we gonna make it to the boat ...?
HFFF!
HFFF!
HFFF!
KA (FLASH)
FURA (SWAY)
HUH ...?
K-KAGUYA-SAMA!?

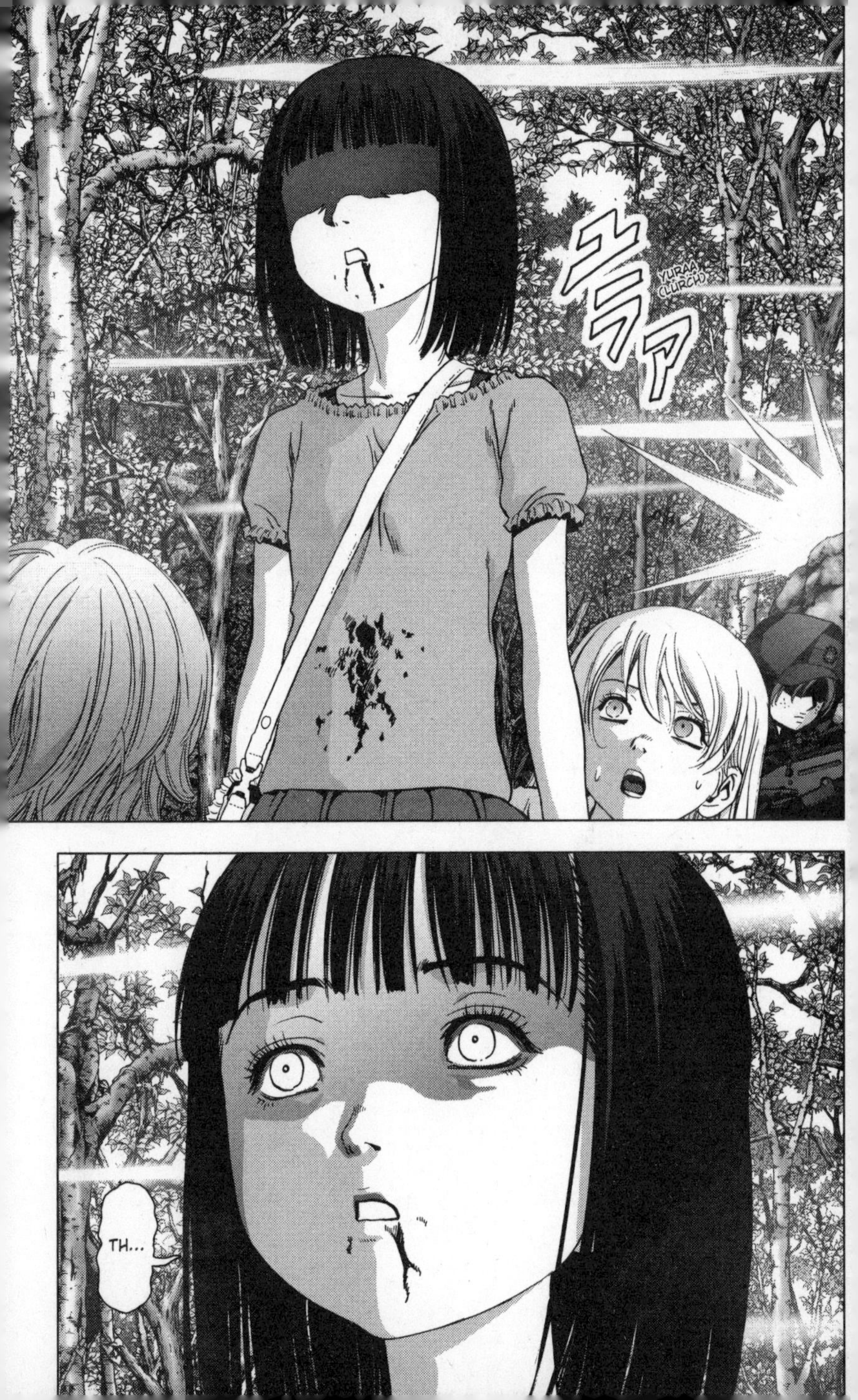
ユラァ
YURAA (LURCH)
TH...

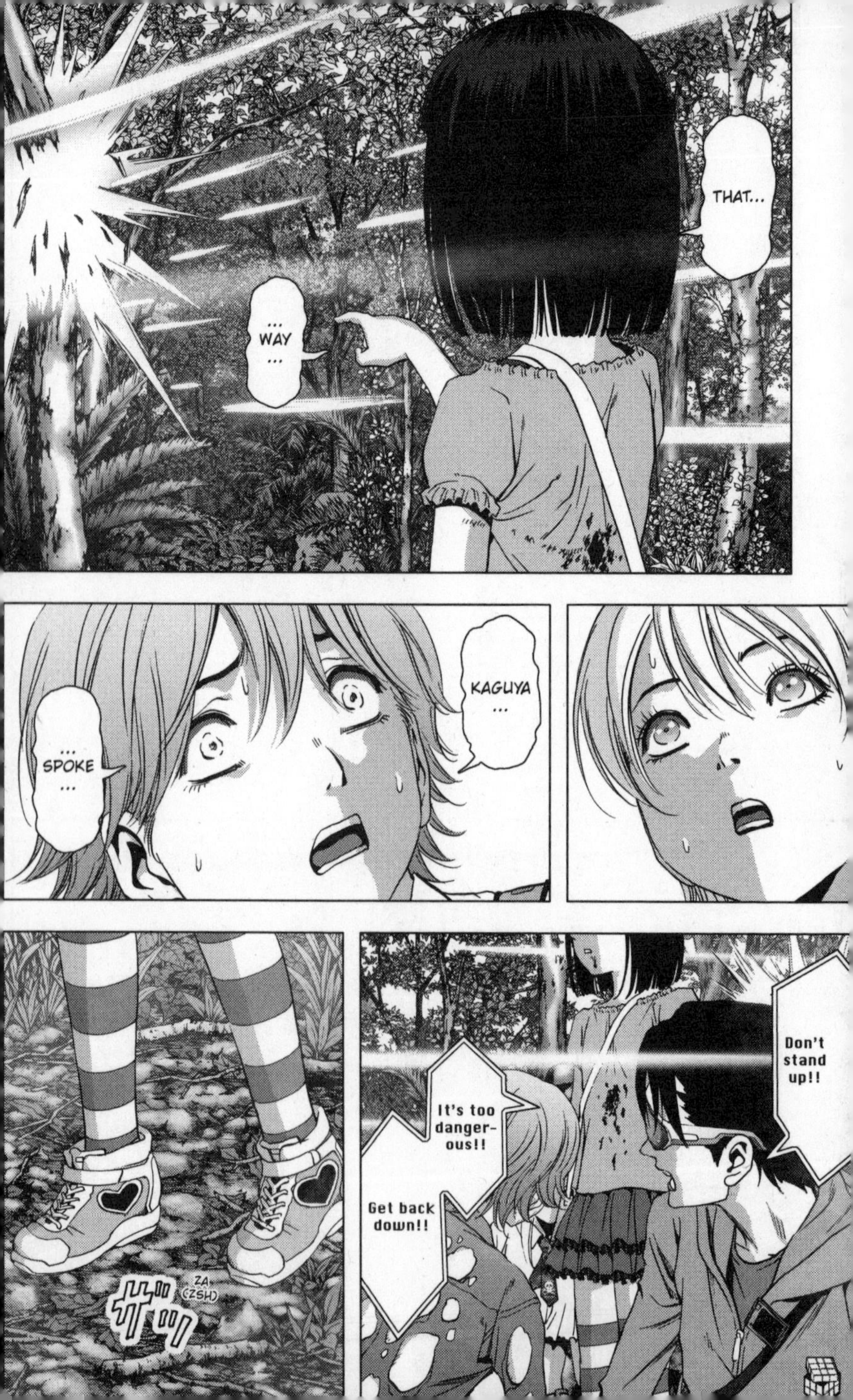
THAT...
... WAY ...
KAGUYA ...
... SPOKE ...
Don't stand up!!
It's too danger-ous!!
Get back down!!
ZA (ZSH)

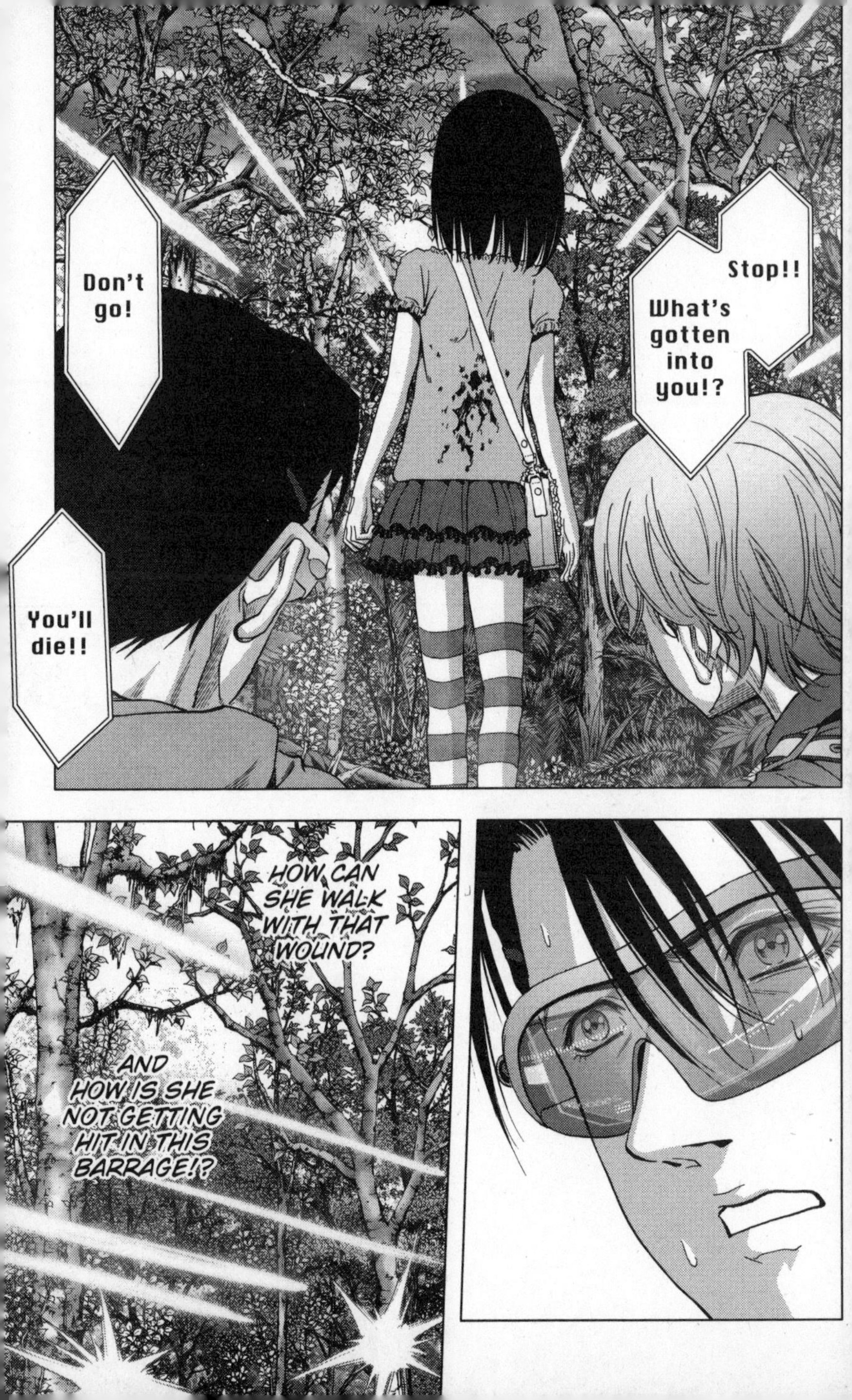
Stop!!
What's gotten into you!?
Don't go!
You'll die!!
HOW CAN SHE WALK WITH THAT WOUND?
AND HOW IS SHE NOT GETTING HIT IN THIS BARRAGE!?

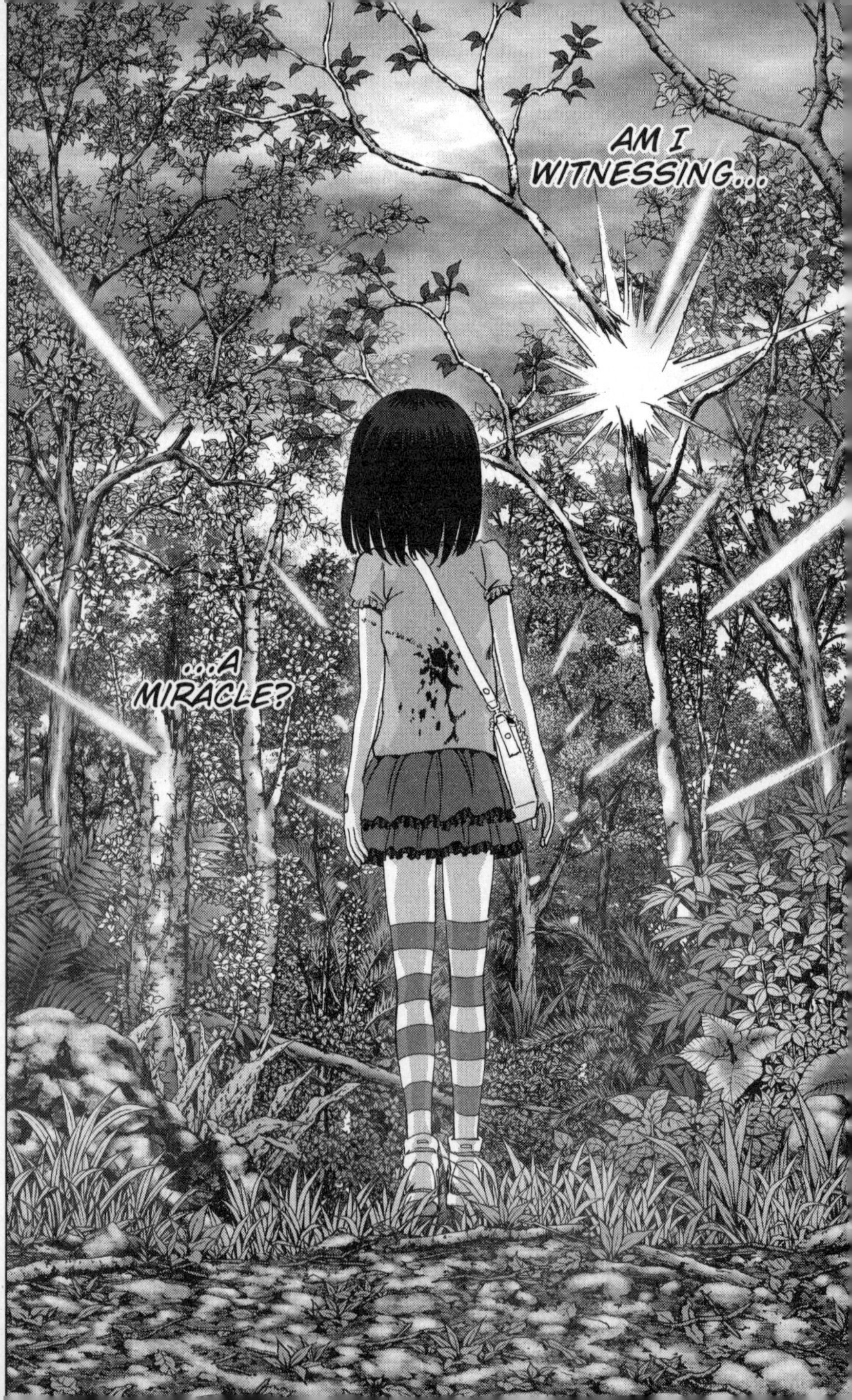
AM I WITNESSING...
...A MIRACLE?

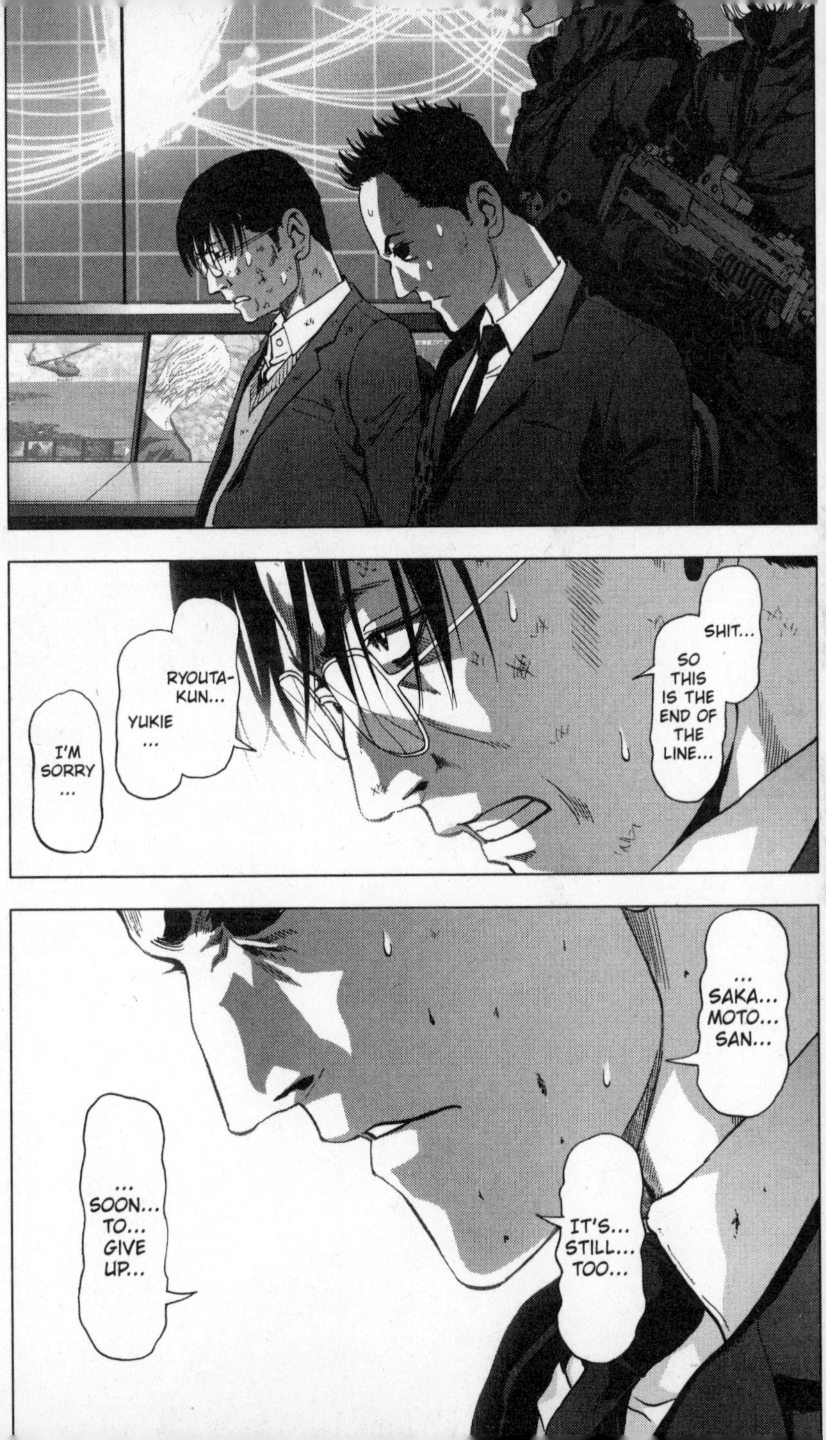
SHIT... SO THIS IS THE END OF THE LINE...
RYOUTA-KUN... YUKIE...
I'M SORRY...
...SAKA... MOTO... SAN...
IT'S... STILL... TOO...
...SOON... TO... GIVE UP...

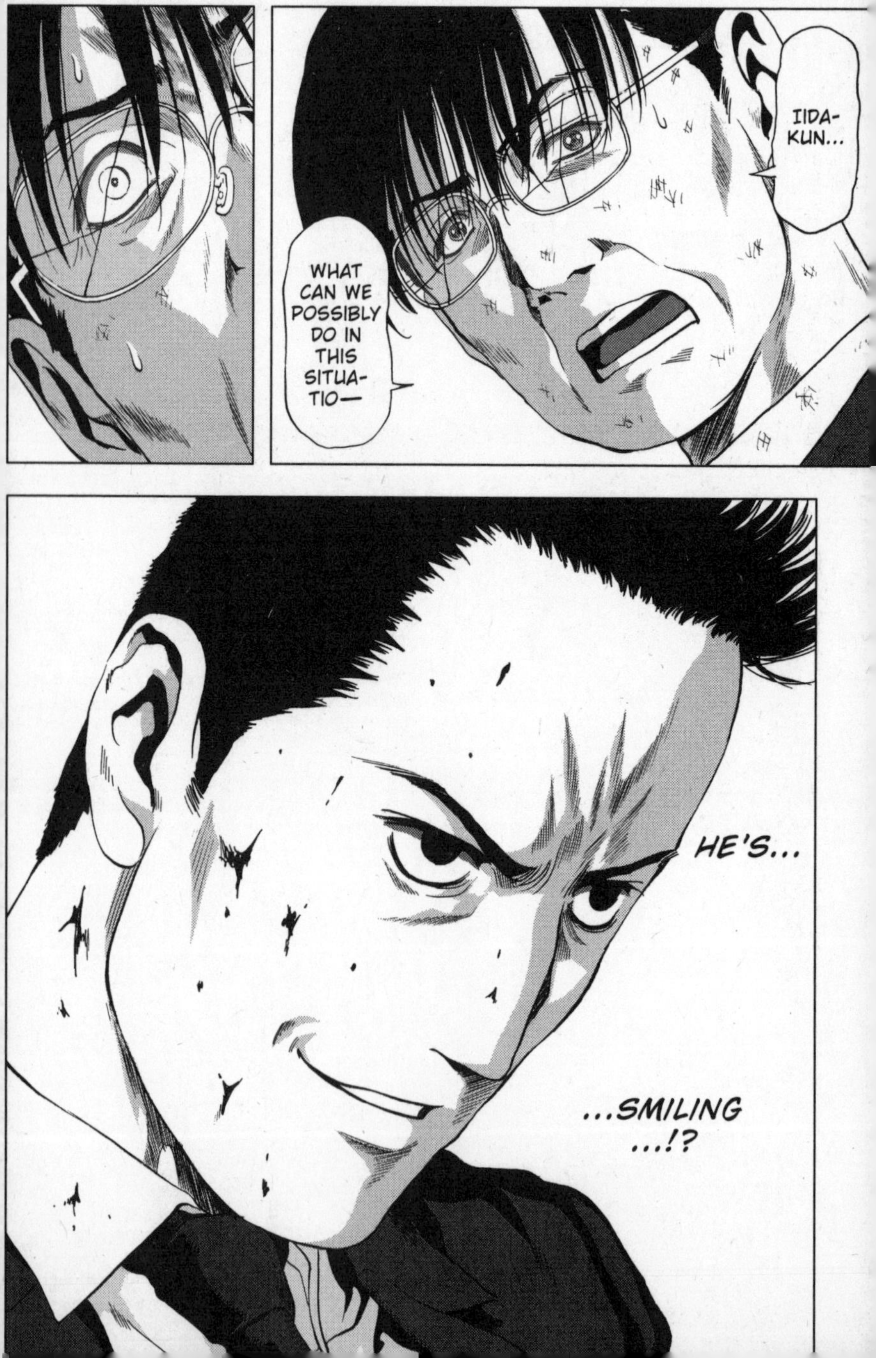
IIDA-KUN...
WHAT CAN WE POSSIBLY DO IN THIS SITUATIO—
HE'S...
...SMILING ...!?

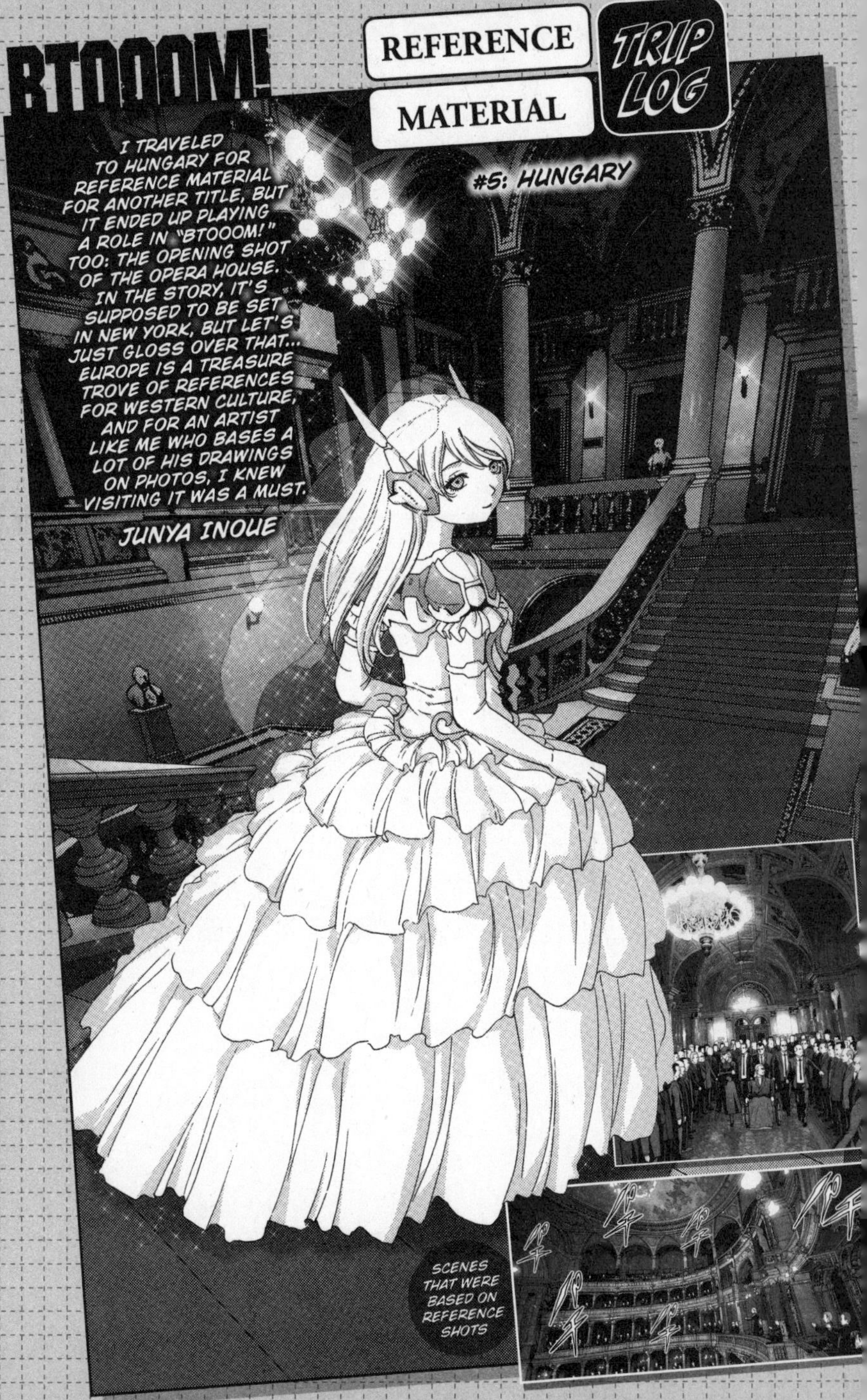
BTOOOM!
REFERENCE MATERIAL
TRIP LOG
#5: HUNGARY
I TRAVELED TO HUNGARY FOR REFERENCE MATERIAL FOR ANOTHER TITLE, BUT IT ENDED UP PLAYING A ROLE IN "BTOOOM!" TOO: THE OPENING SHOT OF THE OPERA HOUSE. IN THE STORY, IT'S SUPPOSED TO BE SET IN NEW YORK, BUT LET'S JUST GLOSS OVER THAT... EUROPE IS A TREASURE TROVE OF REFERENCES FOR WESTERN CULTURE, AND FOR AN ARTIST LIKE ME WHO BASES A LOT OF HIS DRAWINGS ON PHOTOS, I KNEW VISITING IT WAS A MUST.
JUNYA INOUE
SCENES THAT WERE BASED ON REFERENCE SHOTS

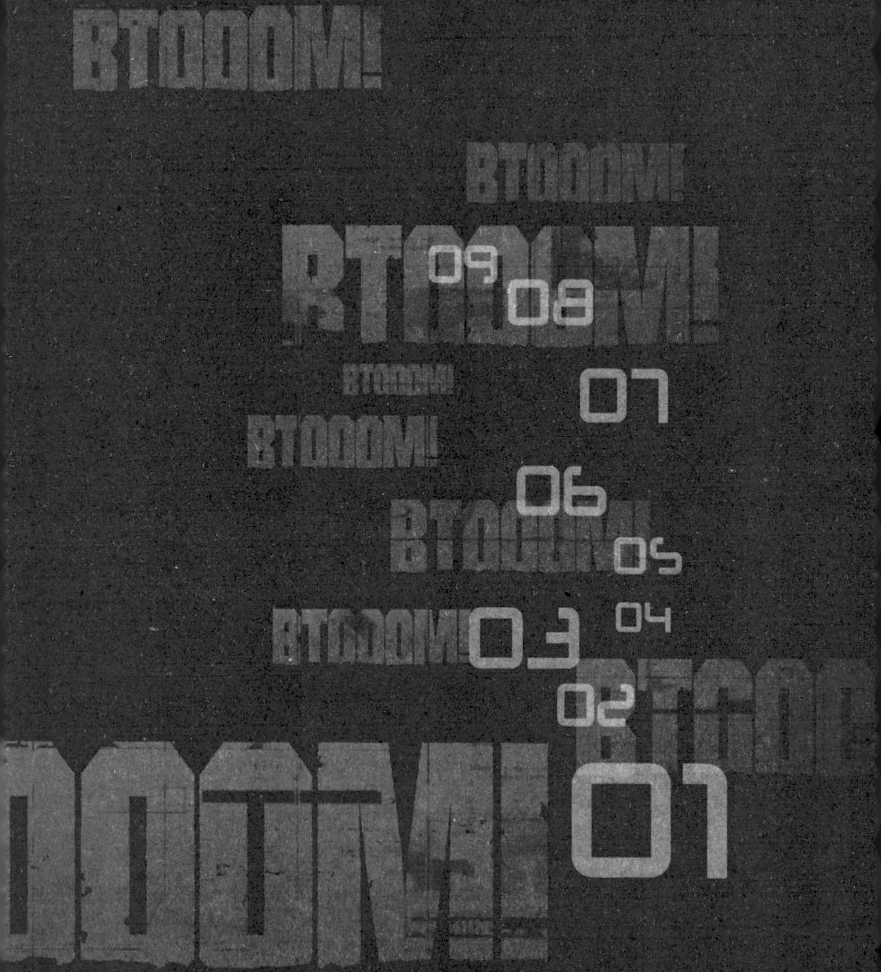
BTOOOM!
BTOOOM!
09
08
07
BTOOOM!
06
05
04
BTOOOM!
03
02
01

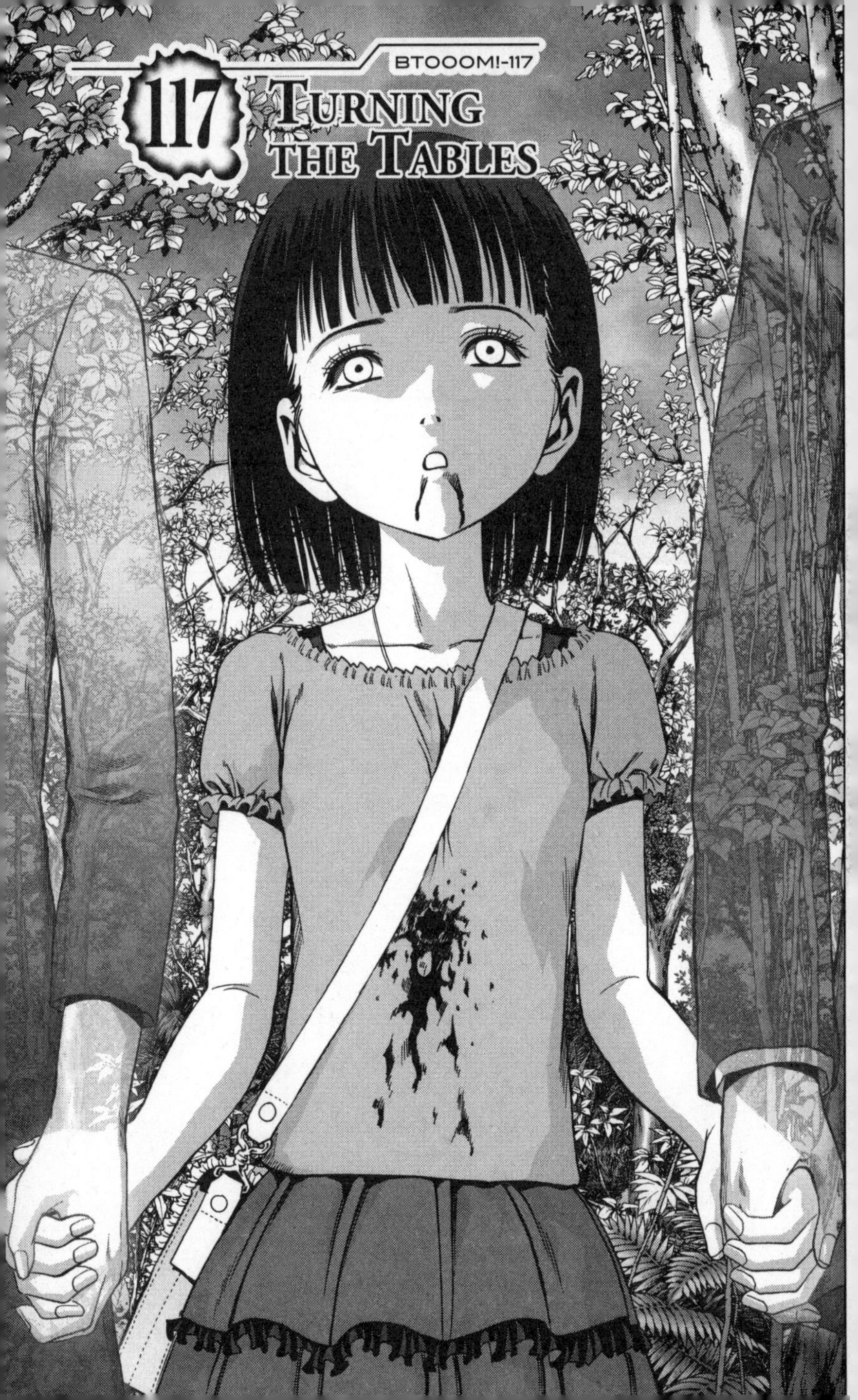
BTOOOM!-117
117
TURNING THE TABLES

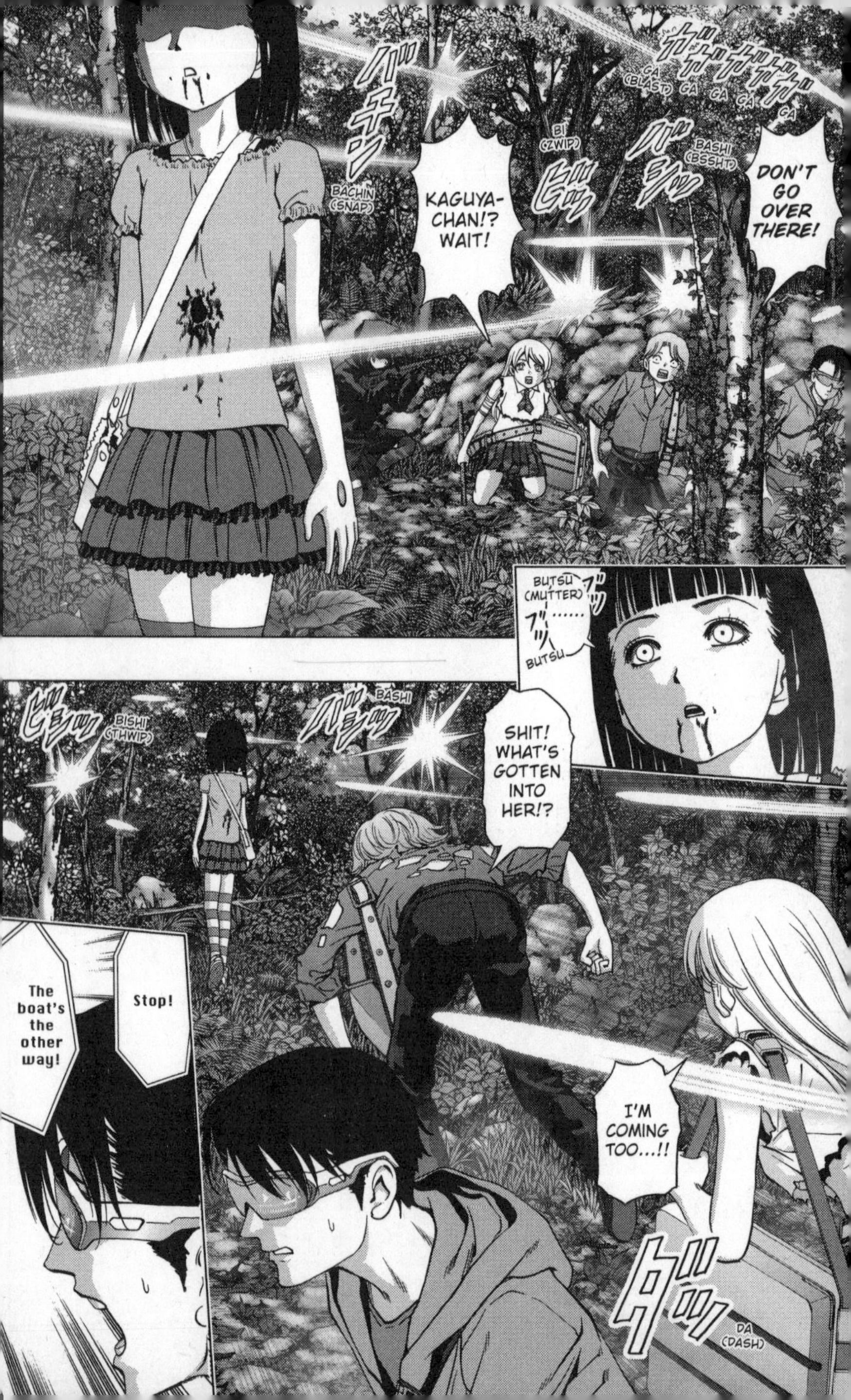
GA (BLAST) GA GA GA GA
DON'T GO OVER THERE!
BASHI (BSSHT)
BI (ZWIP)
KAGUYA-CHAN!? WAIT!
BACHIN (SNAP)
BUTSU (MUTTER)
......
BUTSU
SHIT! WHAT'S GOTTEN INTO HER!?
BASHI
BISHI (THWIP)
I'M COMING TOO...!!
DA (DASH)
Stop!
The boat's the other way!

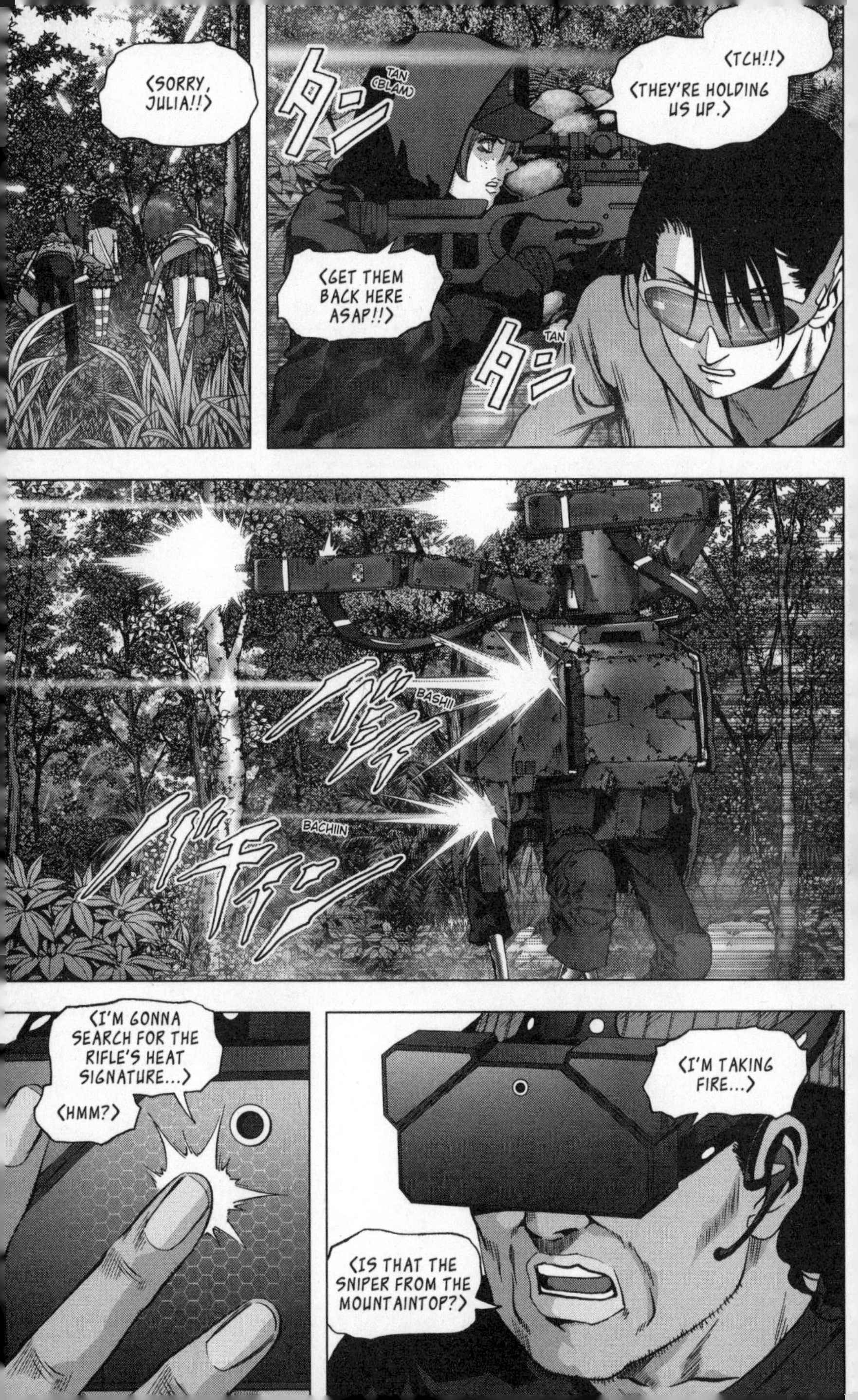

〈TCH!!〉
〈THEY'RE HOLDING US UP.〉
TAN (BLAM)
〈GET THEM BACK HERE ASAP!!〉
TAN
〈SORRY, JULIA!!〉
BASHII
BACHIIN
〈I'M TAKING FIRE...〉
〈IS THAT THE SNIPER FROM THE MOUNTAINTOP?〉
〈I'M GONNA SEARCH FOR THE RIFLE'S HEAT SIGNATURE...〉
〈HMM?〉

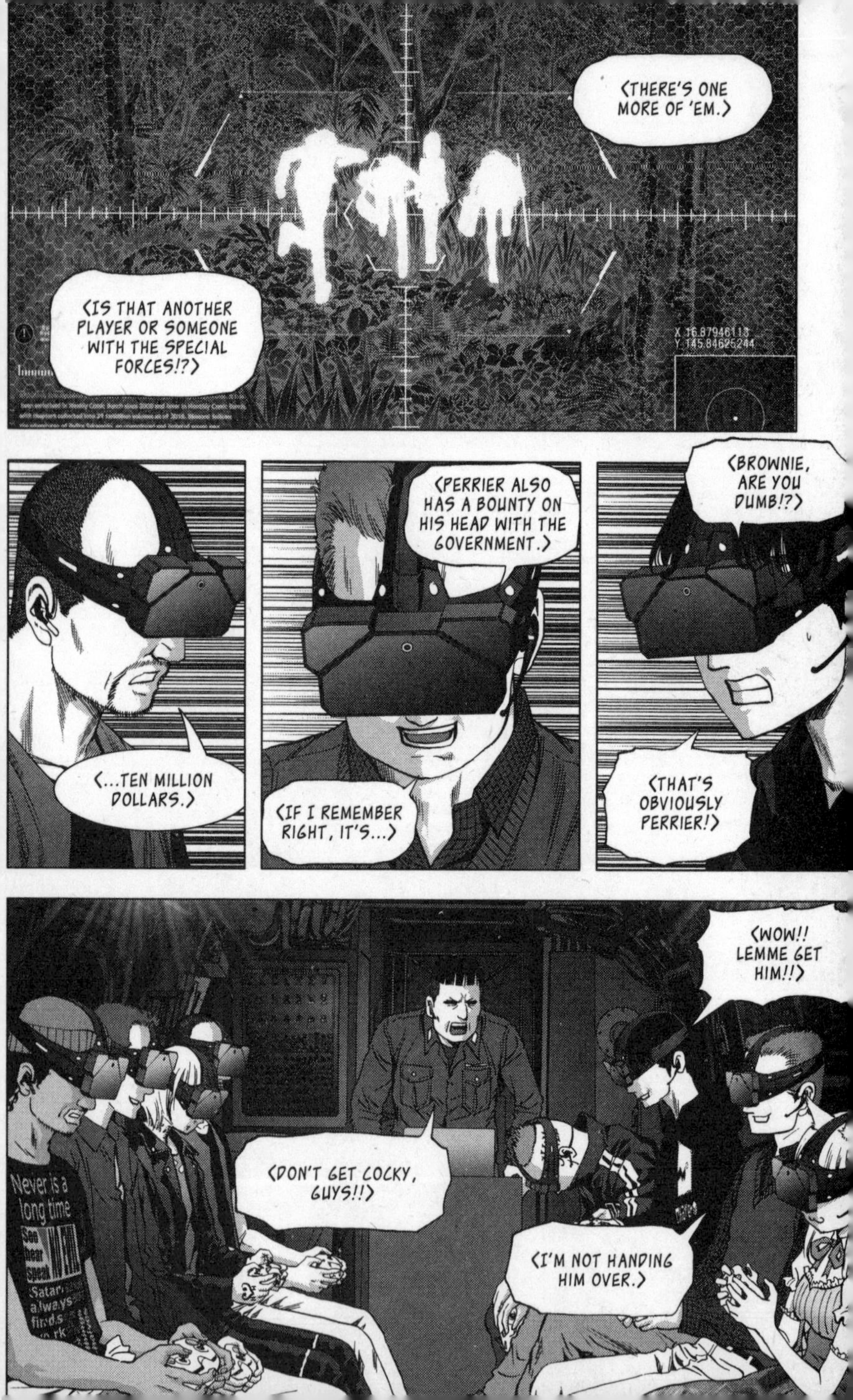
〈THERE'S ONE MORE OF 'EM.〉
〈IS THAT ANOTHER PLAYER OR SOMEONE WITH THE SPECIAL FORCES!?〉
X 16.87946113
Y 145.84625244
〈BROWNIE, ARE YOU DUMB!?〉
〈THAT'S OBVIOUSLY PERRIER!〉
〈PERRIER ALSO HAS A BOUNTY ON HIS HEAD WITH THE GOVERNMENT.〉
〈IF I REMEMBER RIGHT, IT'S...〉
〈...TEN MILLION DOLLARS.〉
〈WOW!! LEMME GET HIM!!〉
〈I'M NOT HANDING HIM OVER.〉
〈DON'T GET COCKY, GUYS!!〉
Never is a long time

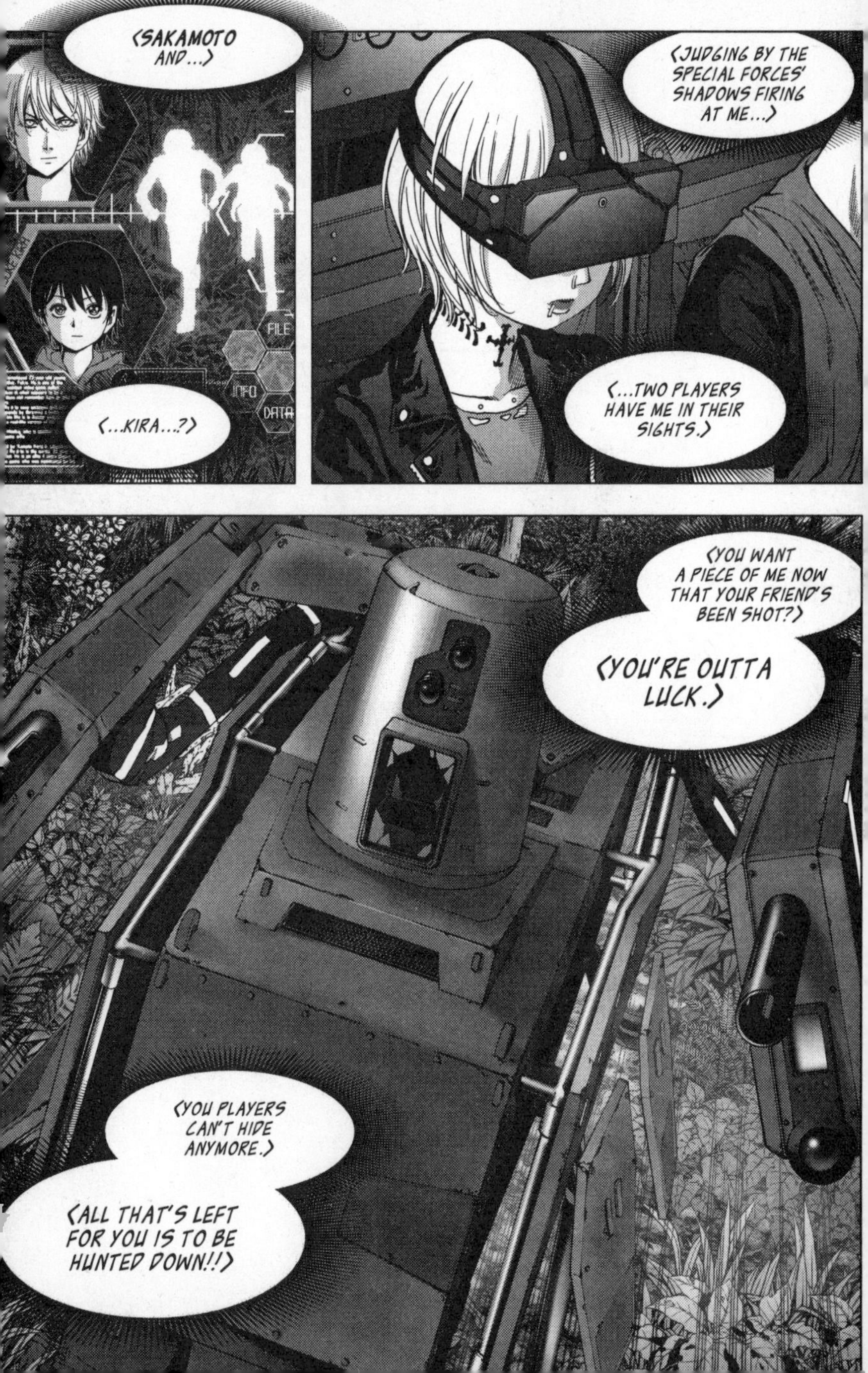
‹JUDGING BY THE SPECIAL FORCES' SHADOWS FIRING AT ME...›
‹...TWO PLAYERS HAVE ME IN THEIR SIGHTS.›
‹SAKAMOTO AND...›
FILE
INFO
DATA
‹...KIRA...?›
‹YOU WANT A PIECE OF ME NOW THAT YOUR FRIEND'S BEEN SHOT?›
‹YOU'RE OUTTA LUCK.›
‹YOU PLAYERS CAN'T HIDE ANYMORE.›
‹ALL THAT'S LEFT FOR YOU IS TO BE HUNTED DOWN!!›

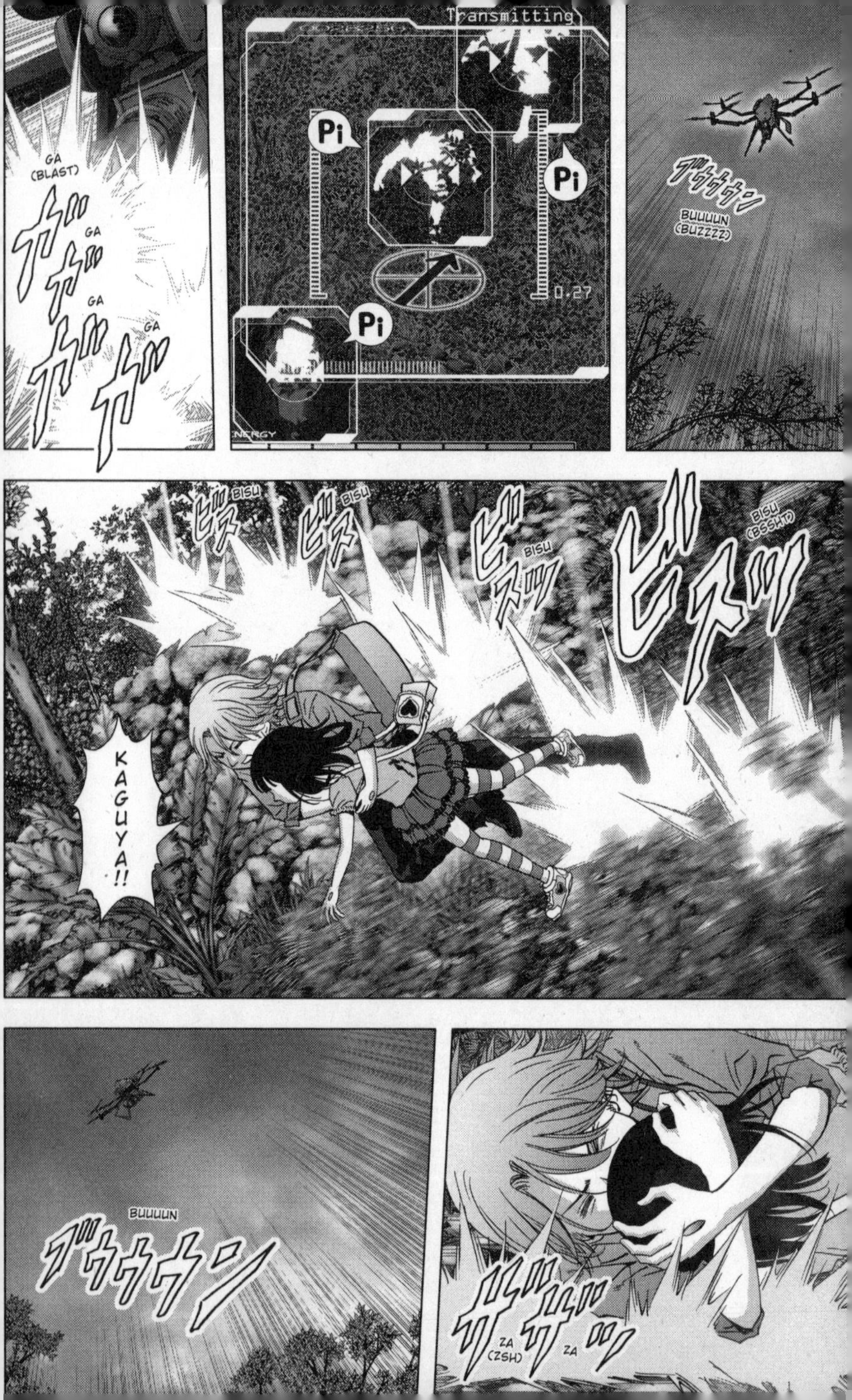

ブゥゥゥン
BUUUUN (BUZZZZ)
Transmitting
Pi
Pi
0.27
Pi
GA (BLAST)
GA
GA
GA
BISU (BSSHT)
BISU
BISU
BISU
KAGUYA!!
ZA (ZSH)
ZA
ブゥゥゥン
BUUUUN

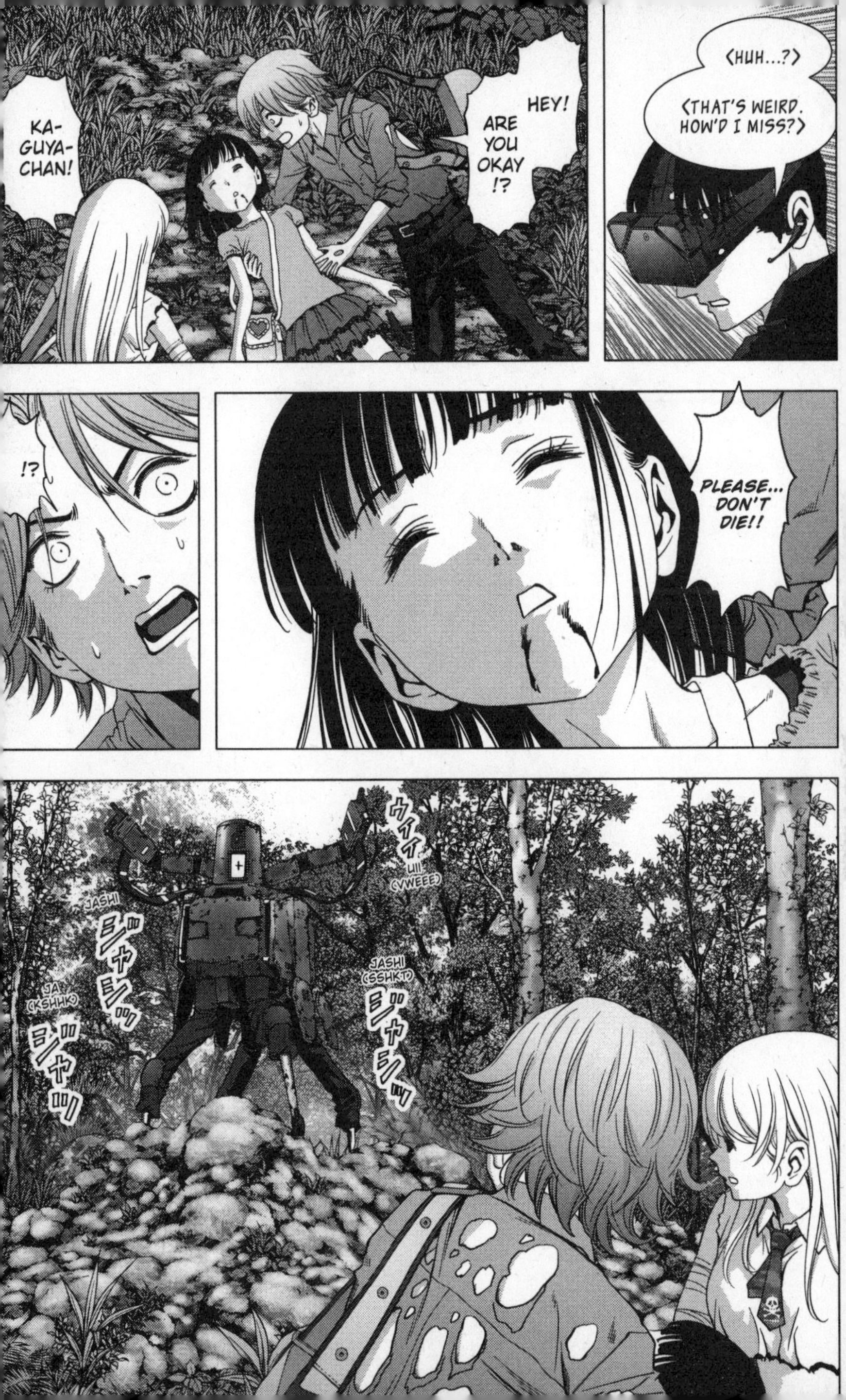
<HUH...?>
<THAT'S WEIRD. HOW'D I MISS?>
HEY! ARE YOU OKAY!?
KA-GUYA-CHAN!
PLEASE... DON'T DIE!!
!?
ウィイ
UII (VWEEE)
JASHI (SSHKT)
ジャシッ
JASHI
ジャシッ
JA (KSHHK)
ジャッ

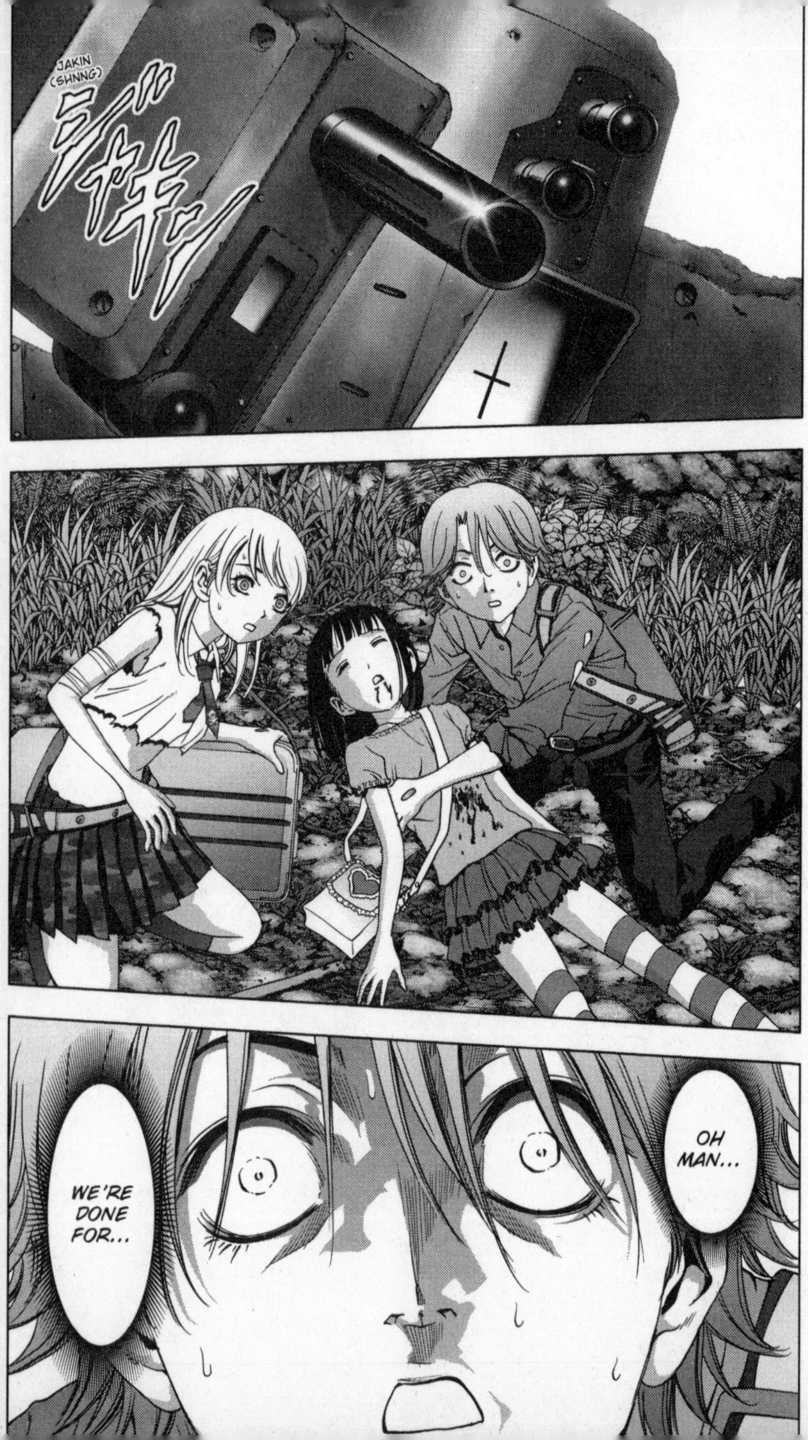
JAKIN (SHNNG)
ジャキン
OH MAN...
WE'RE DONE FOR...

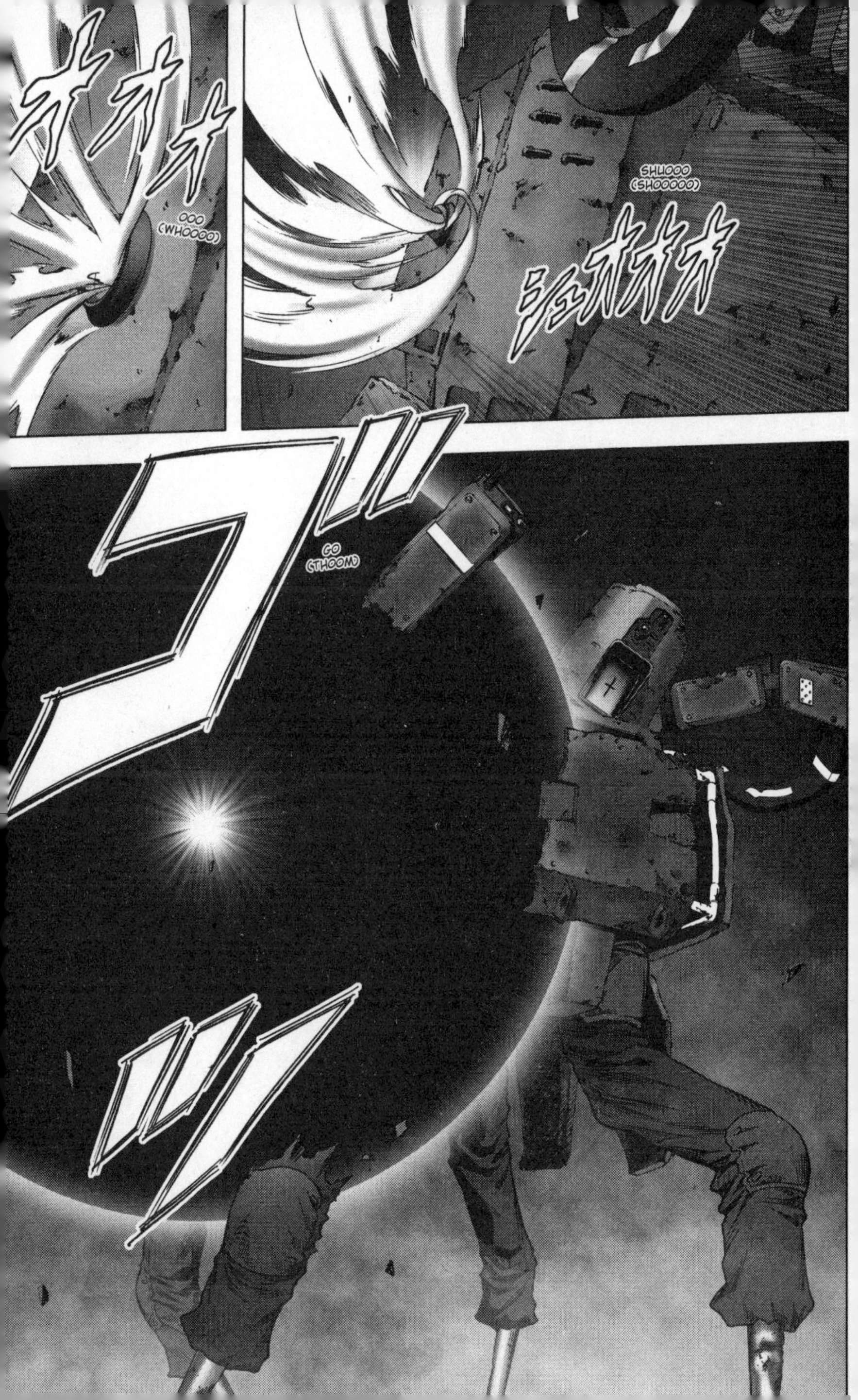
SHUOOO
(SHOOOOOO)
シュオオオ
オオオ
OOO
(WHOOOOO)
ゴッ
GO
(THOOM)

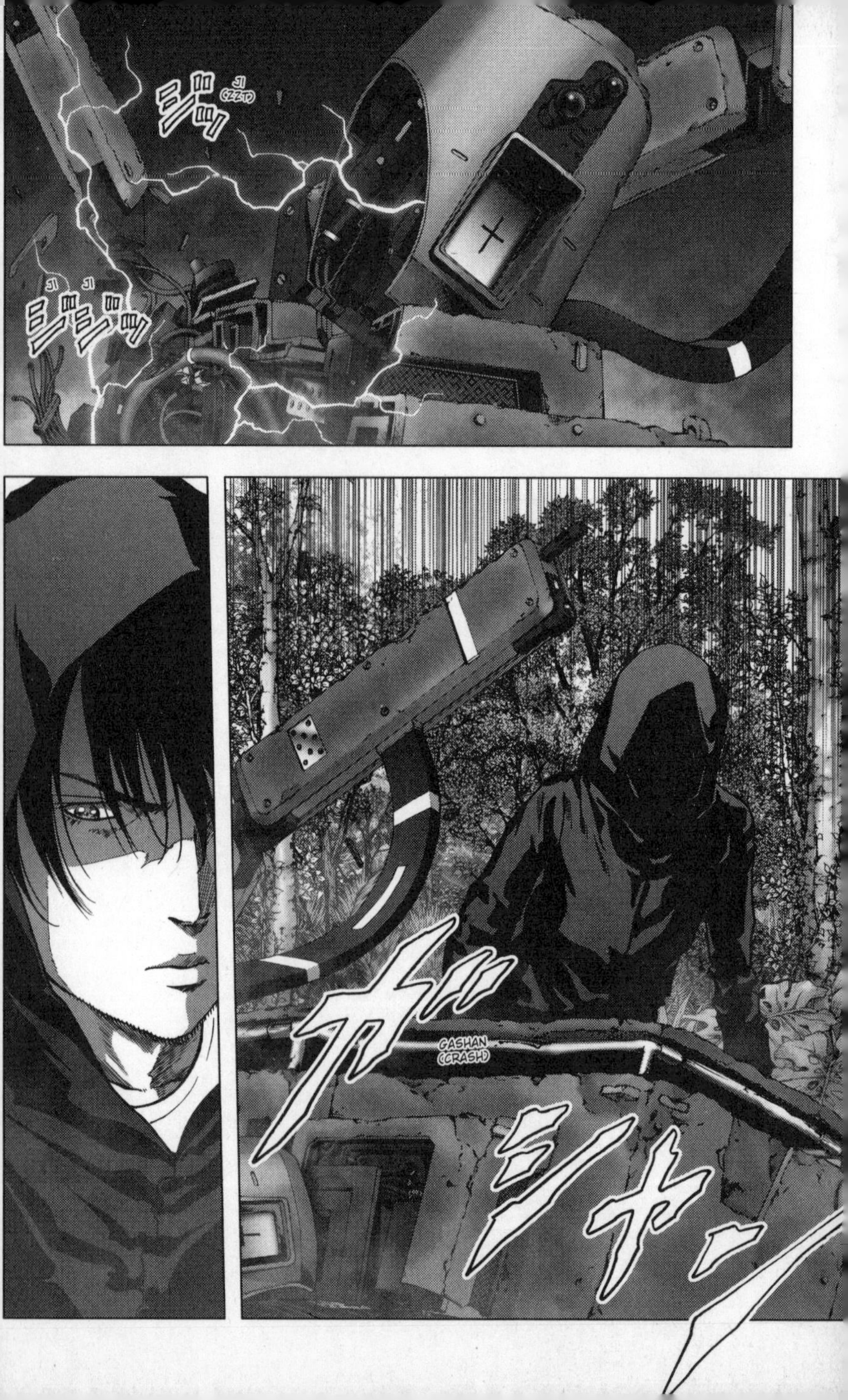
JI
(ZZT)
JI JI
GASHAN
(CRASH)

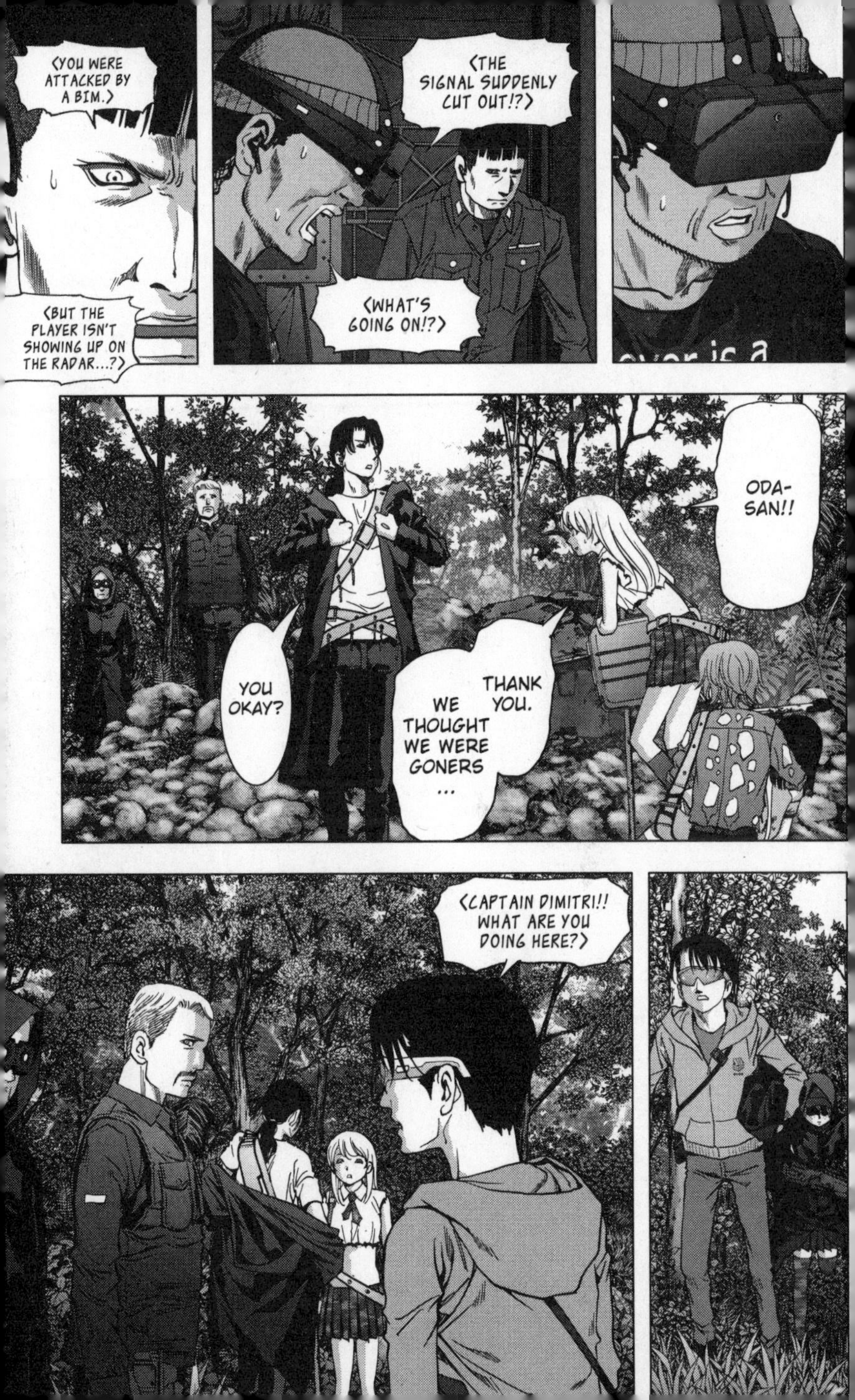
<THE SIGNAL SUDDENLY CUT OUT!?>
<WHAT'S GOING ON!?>
<YOU WERE ATTACKED BY A BIM.>
<BUT THE PLAYER ISN'T SHOWING UP ON THE RADAR...?>
ODA-SAN!!
THANK YOU.
WE THOUGHT WE WERE GONERS...
YOU OKAY?
<CAPTAIN DIMITRI!! WHAT ARE YOU DOING HERE?>

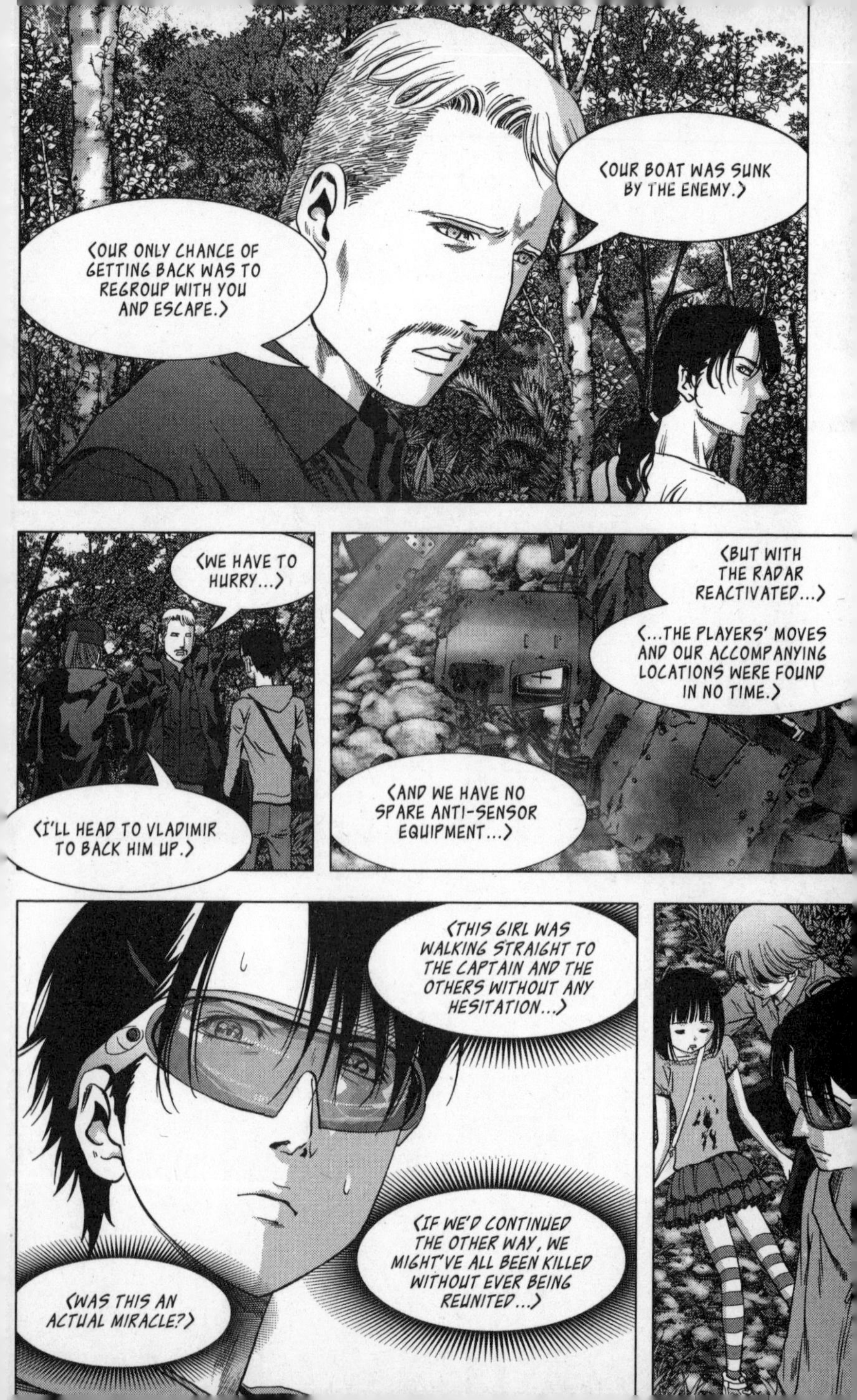
⟨OUR BOAT WAS SUNK BY THE ENEMY.⟩
⟨OUR ONLY CHANCE OF GETTING BACK WAS TO REGROUP WITH YOU AND ESCAPE.⟩
⟨BUT WITH THE RADAR REACTIVATED...⟩
⟨...THE PLAYERS' MOVES AND OUR ACCOMPANYING LOCATIONS WERE FOUND IN NO TIME.⟩
⟨AND WE HAVE NO SPARE ANTI-SENSOR EQUIPMENT...⟩
⟨WE HAVE TO HURRY...⟩
⟨I'LL HEAD TO VLADIMIR TO BACK HIM UP.⟩
⟨THIS GIRL WAS WALKING STRAIGHT TO THE CAPTAIN AND THE OTHERS WITHOUT ANY HESITATION...⟩
⟨IF WE'D CONTINUED THE OTHER WAY, WE MIGHT'VE ALL BEEN KILLED WITHOUT EVER BEING REUNITED...⟩
⟨WAS THIS AN ACTUAL MIRACLE?⟩

⟨FOUND YOU!♡⟩

MEOOOW!

ADS

⟨I CAN'T BELIEVE THEY TOOK OUT BROWNIE... THESE GUYS ARE GOOD.⟩

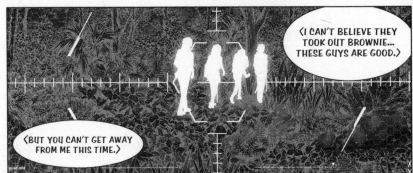

⟨BUT YOU CAN'T GET AWAY FROM ME THIS TIME.⟩

ADS

⟨IT'S MORNING, EVERYONE. TIME TO GO TO BED!♡⟩

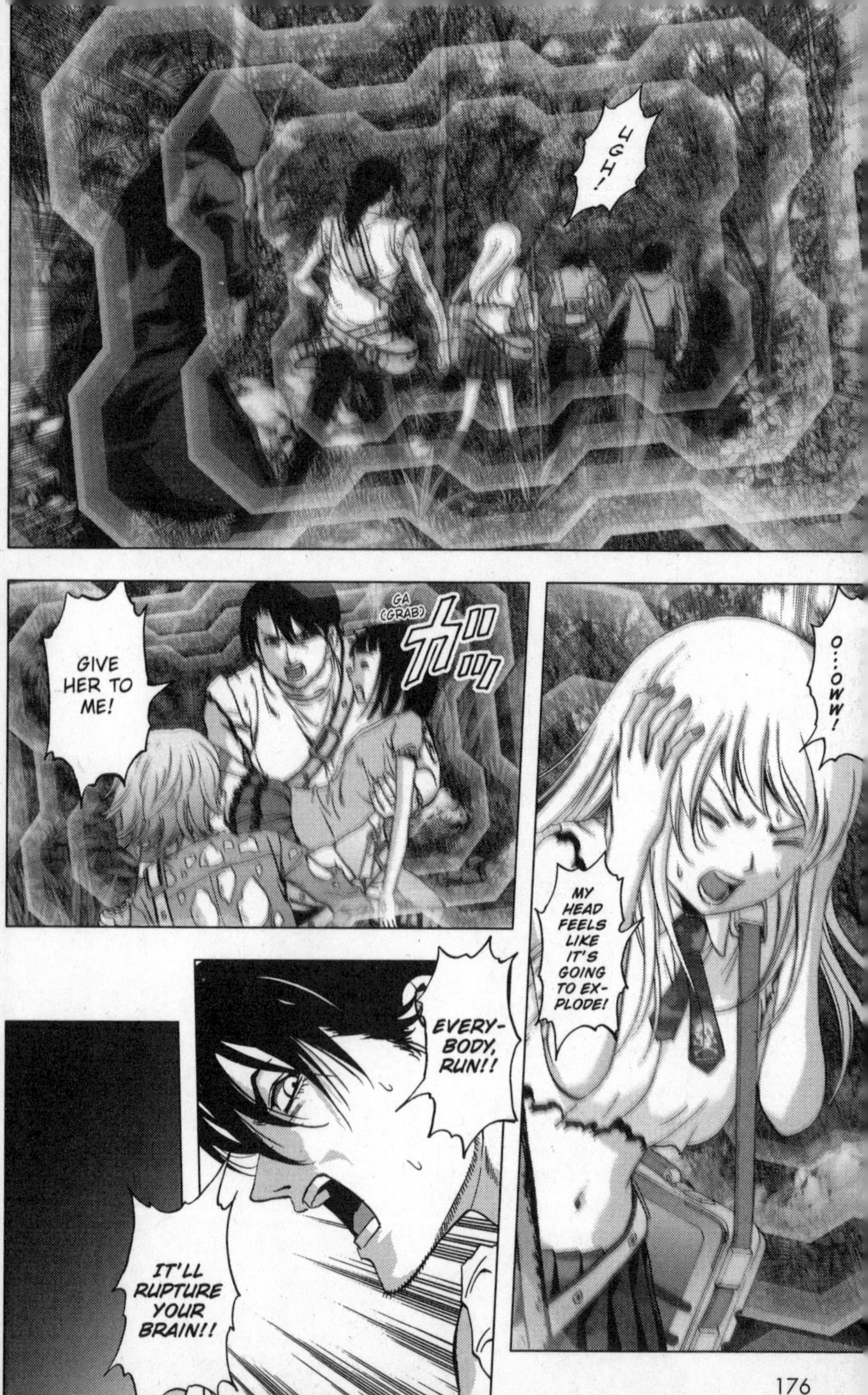
UGH!
O...OWW!
MY HEAD FEELS LIKE IT'S GOING TO EX-PLODE!
GA (GRAB)
GIVE HER TO ME!
EVERY-BODY, RUN!!
IT'LL RUPTURE YOUR BRAIN!!

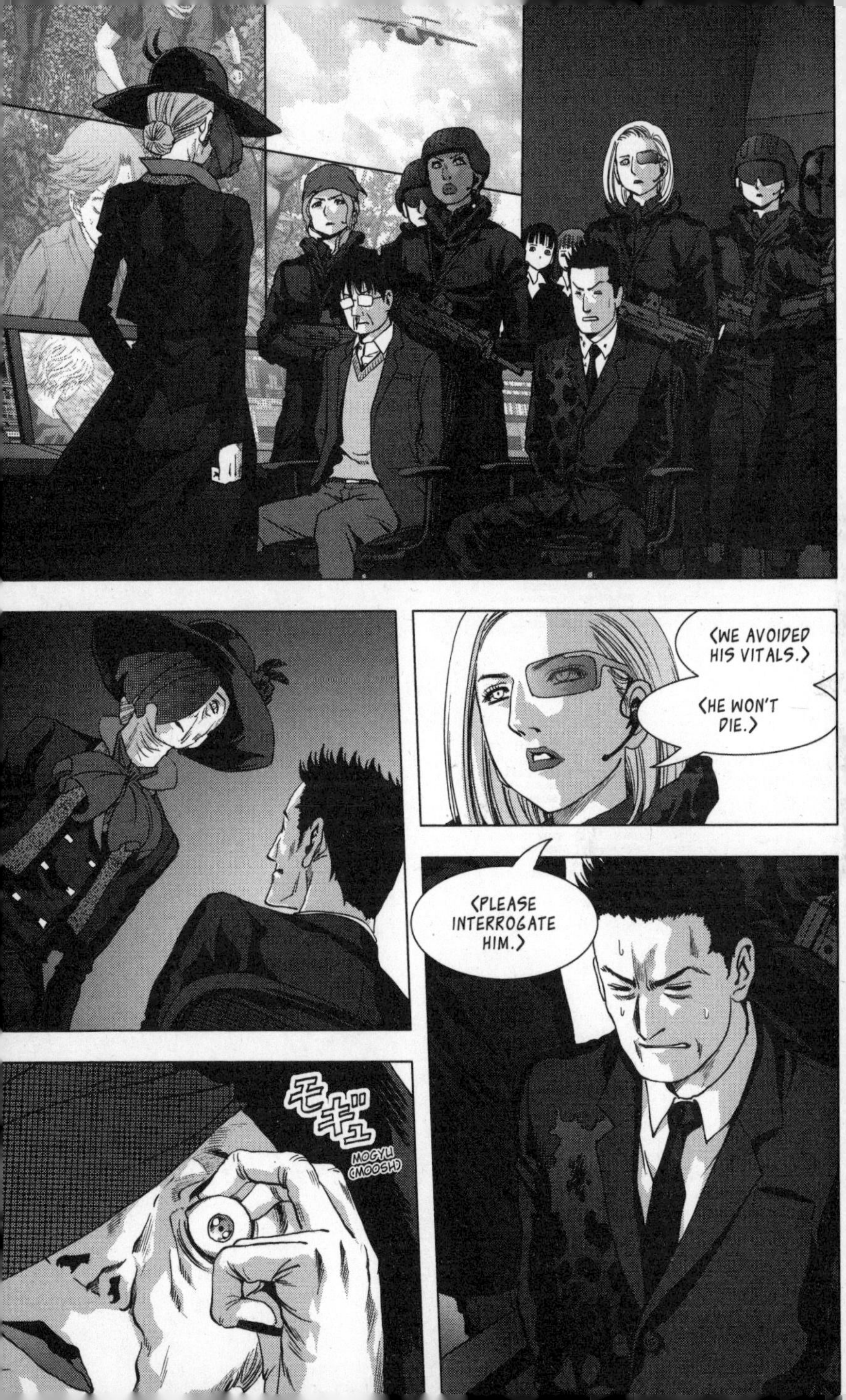
〈WE AVOIDED HIS VITALS.〉
〈HE WON'T DIE.〉
〈PLEASE INTERROGATE HIM.〉
モギュ
MOGYU (MOOSH)

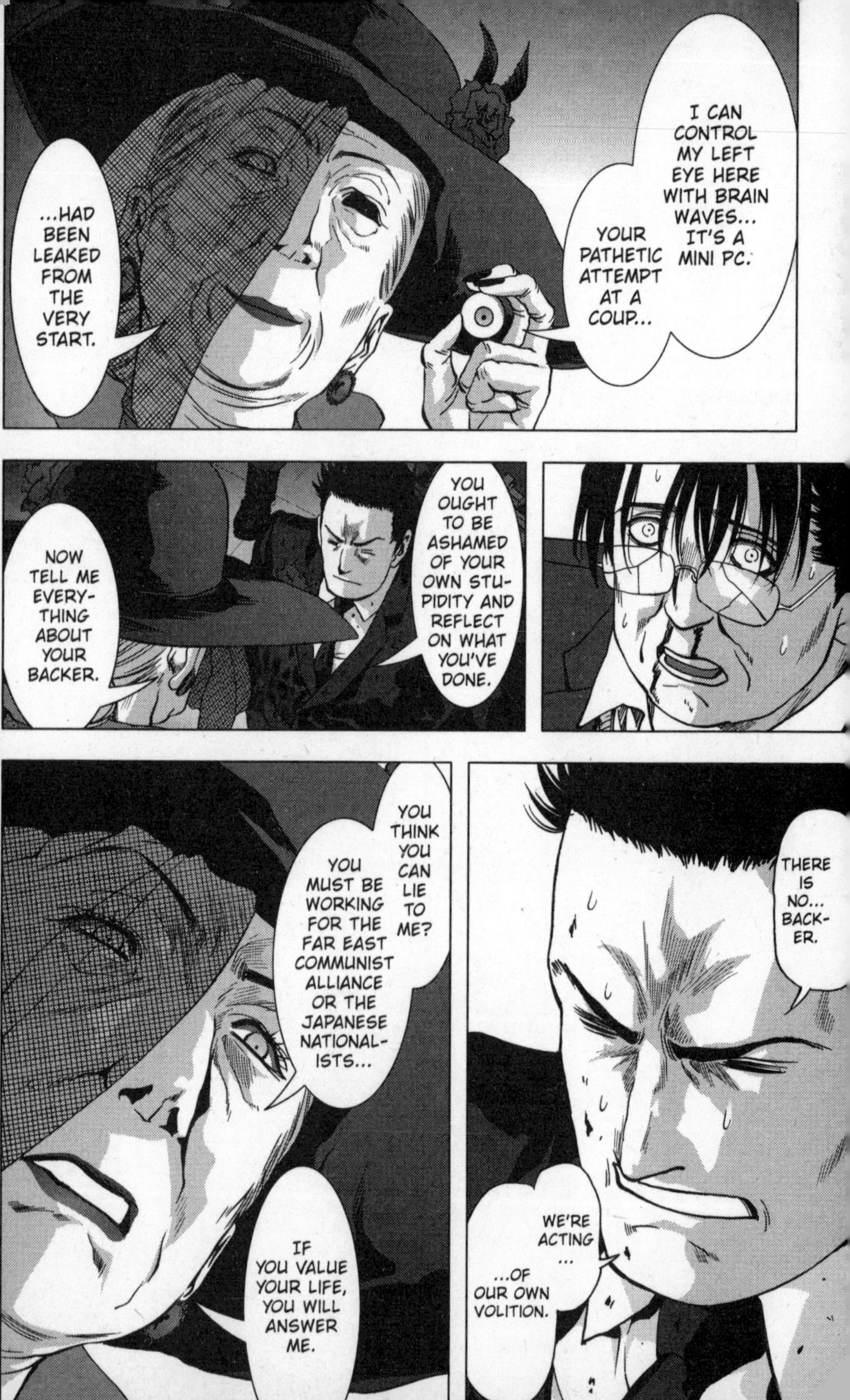
I CAN CONTROL MY LEFT EYE HERE WITH BRAIN WAVES... IT'S A MINI PC.
YOUR PATHETIC ATTEMPT AT A COUP...
...HAD BEEN LEAKED FROM THE VERY START.
YOU OUGHT TO BE ASHAMED OF YOUR OWN STUPIDITY AND REFLECT ON WHAT YOU'VE DONE.
NOW TELL ME EVERYTHING ABOUT YOUR BACKER.
THERE IS NO... BACKER.
WE'RE ACTING ...
...OF OUR OWN VOLITION.
YOU THINK YOU CAN LIE TO ME?
YOU MUST BE WORKING FOR THE FAR EAST COMMUNIST ALLIANCE OR THE JAPANESE NATIONALISTS...
IF YOU VALUE YOUR LIFE, YOU WILL ANSWER ME.

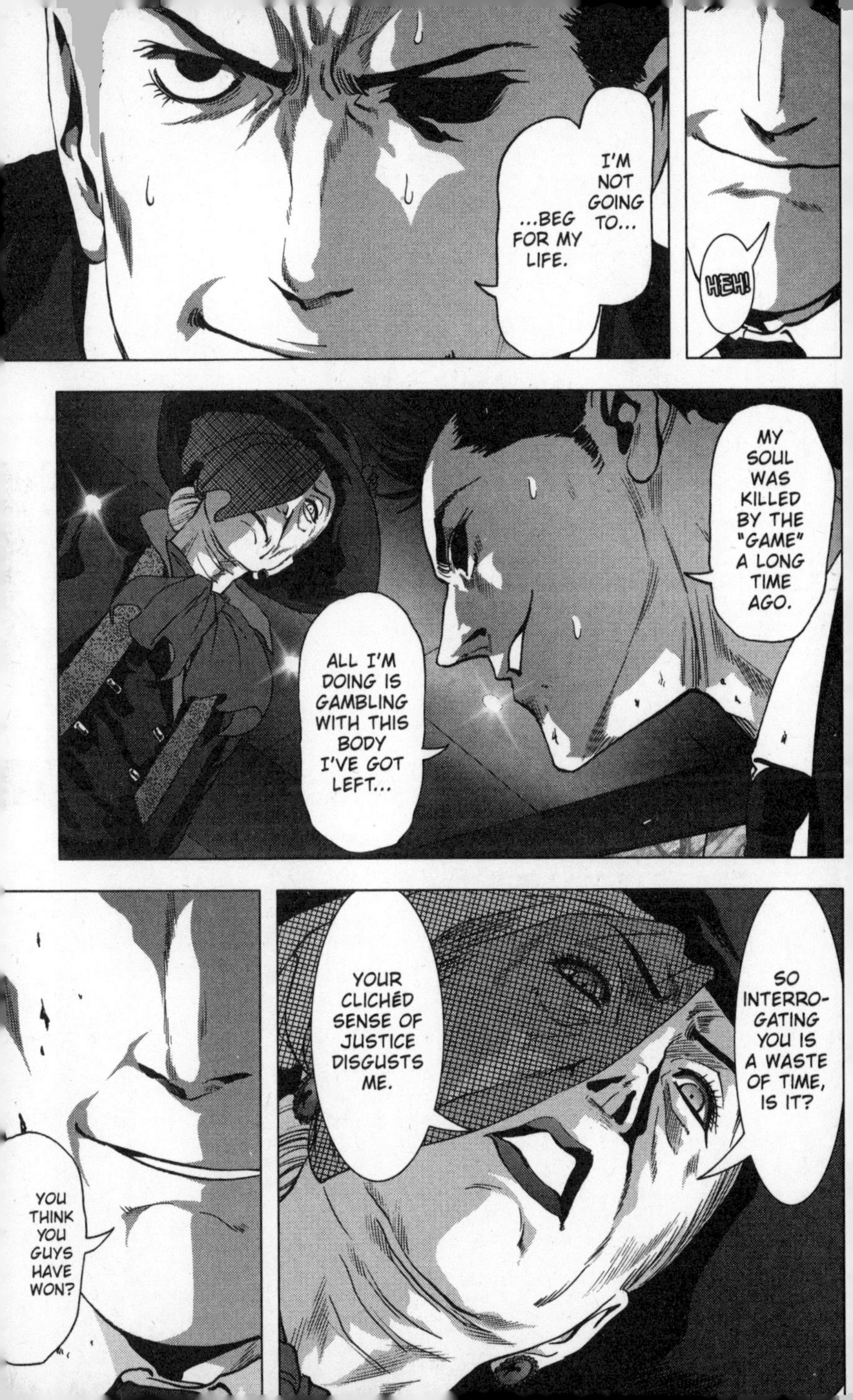
HEH!
I'M NOT GOING TO...
...BEG FOR MY LIFE.
MY SOUL WAS KILLED BY THE "GAME" A LONG TIME AGO.
ALL I'M DOING IS GAMBLING WITH THIS BODY I'VE GOT LEFT...
SO INTERRO-GATING YOU IS A WASTE OF TIME, IS IT?
YOUR CLICHÉD SENSE OF JUSTICE DISGUSTS ME.
YOU THINK YOU GUYS HAVE WON?

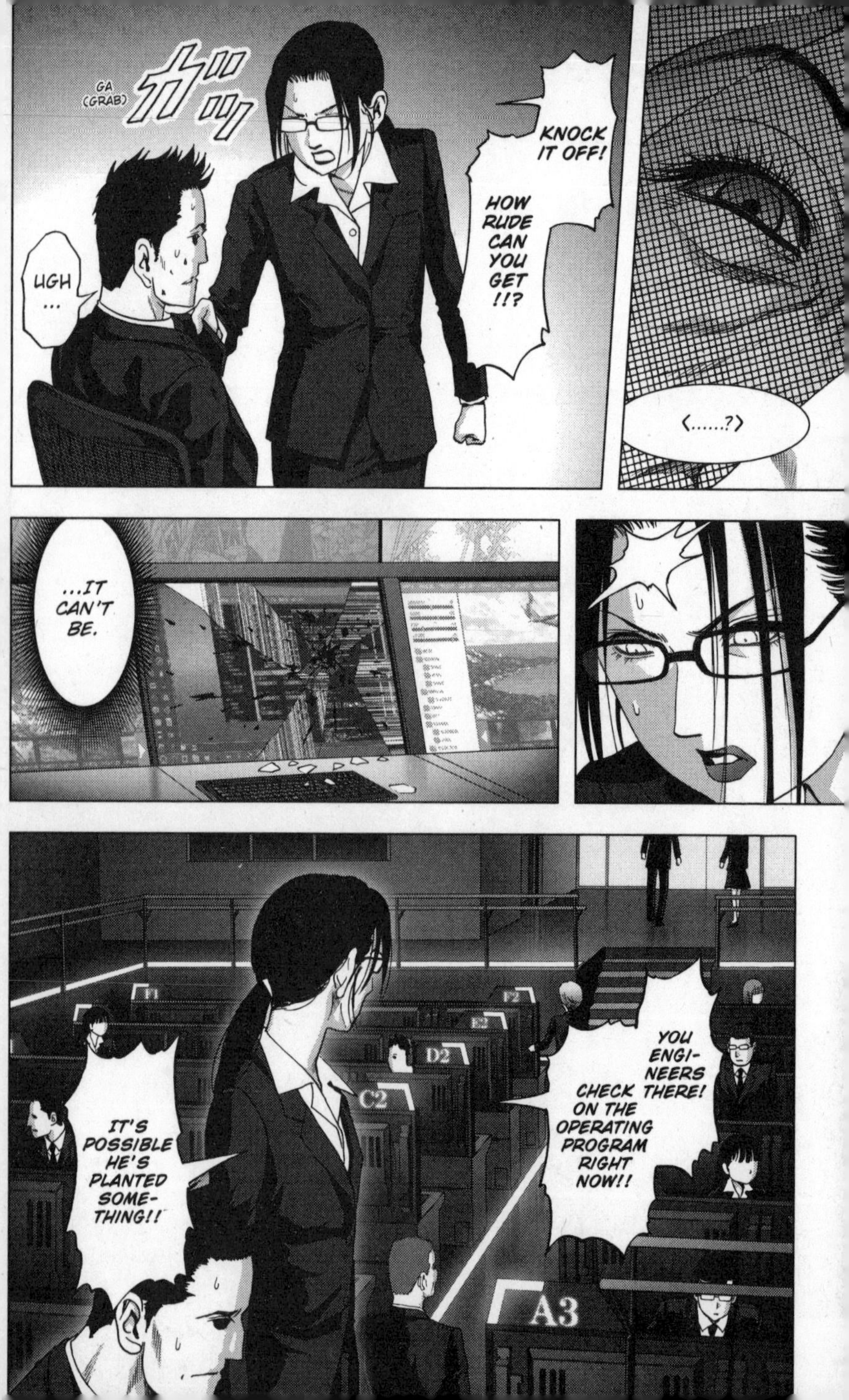
⟨......?⟩
KNOCK IT OFF!
HOW RUDE CAN YOU GET!!?
GA (GRAB)
UGH ...
...IT CAN'T BE.
YOU ENGINEERS THERE! CHECK ON THE OPERATING PROGRAM RIGHT NOW!!
IT'S POSSIBLE HE'S PLANTED SOMETHING!!
F1
F2
E2
D2
C2
A3

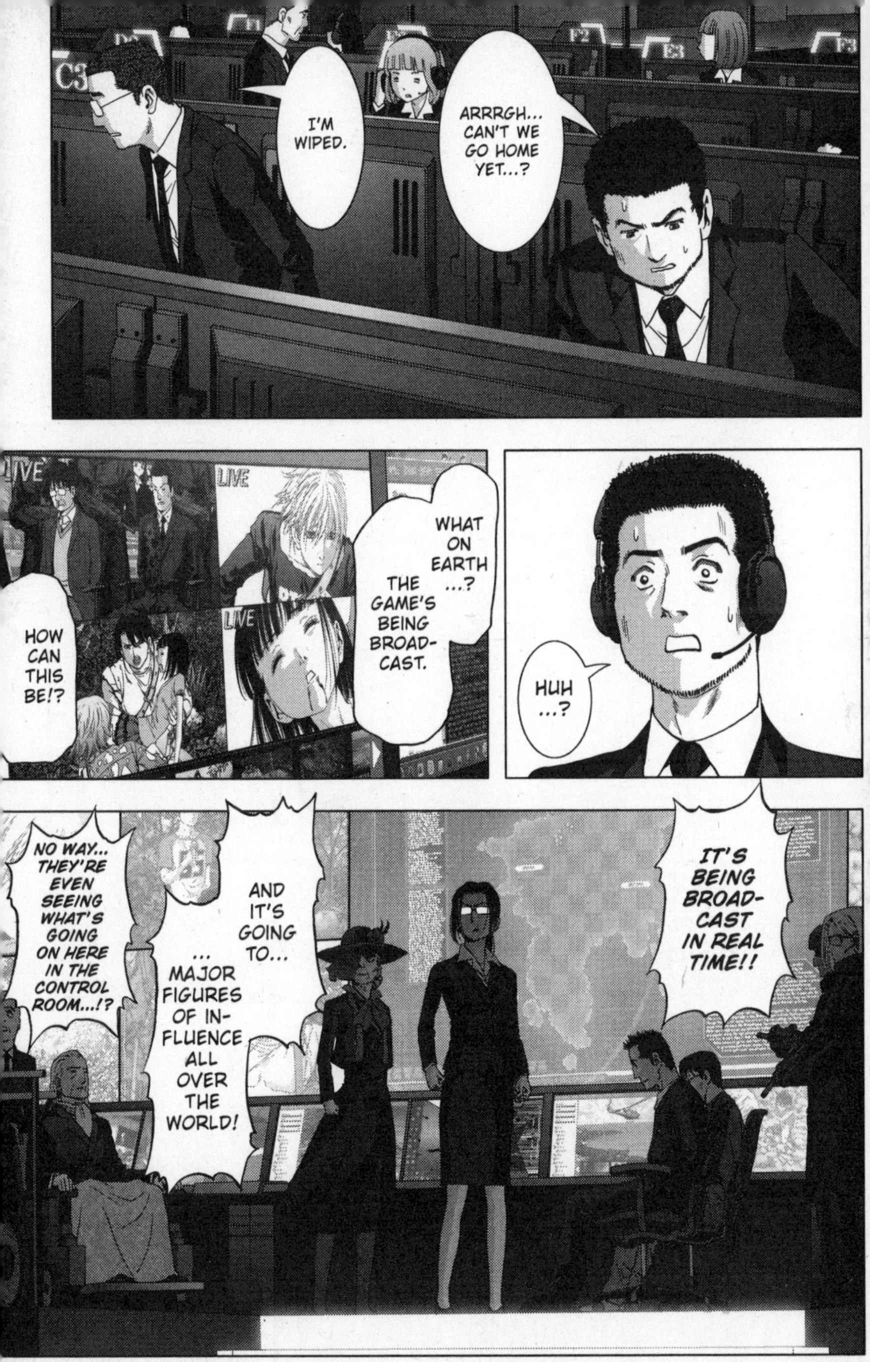
ARRRGH... CAN'T WE GO HOME YET...?
I'M WIPED.
HUH ...?
WHAT ON EARTH ...?
THE GAME'S BEING BROAD-CAST.
HOW CAN THIS BE!?
IT'S BEING BROAD-CAST IN REAL TIME!!
AND IT'S GOING TO...
... MAJOR FIGURES OF IN-FLUENCE ALL OVER THE WORLD!
NO WAY... THEY'RE EVEN SEEING WHAT'S GOING ON HERE IN THE CONTROL ROOM...!?

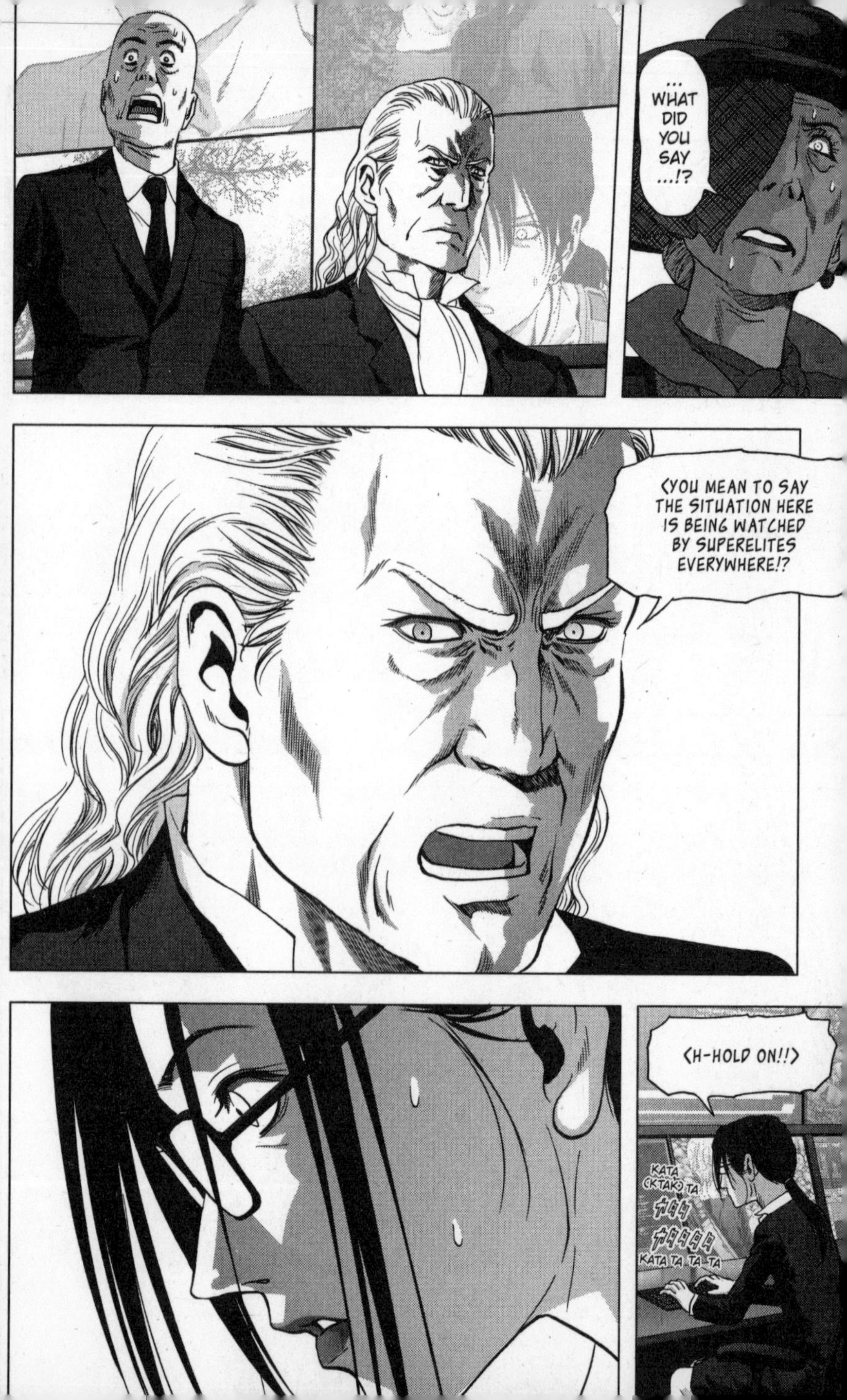
...WHAT DID YOU SAY ...!?
‹YOU MEAN TO SAY THE SITUATION HERE IS BEING WATCHED BY SUPERELITES EVERYWHERE!?
‹H-HOLD ON!!›
KATA (KTAK) TA
KATA TA TA TA

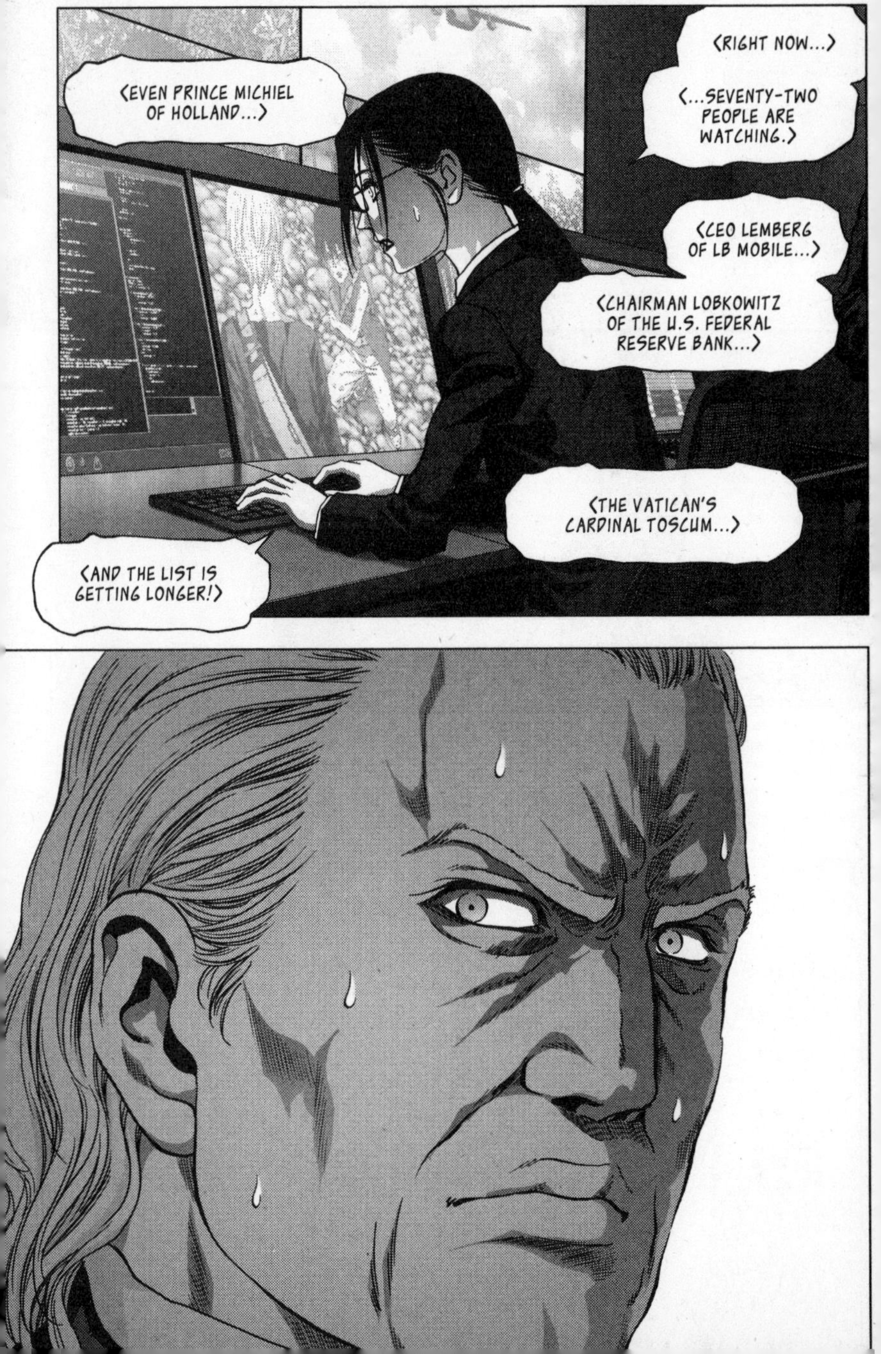
⟨RIGHT NOW...⟩
⟨...SEVENTY-TWO PEOPLE ARE WATCHING.⟩
⟨CEO LEMBERG OF LB MOBILE...⟩
⟨CHAIRMAN LOBKOWITZ OF THE U.S. FEDERAL RESERVE BANK...⟩
⟨THE VATICAN'S CARDINAL TOSCUM...⟩
⟨EVEN PRINCE MICHIEL OF HOLLAND...⟩
⟨AND THE LIST IS GETTING LONGER!⟩

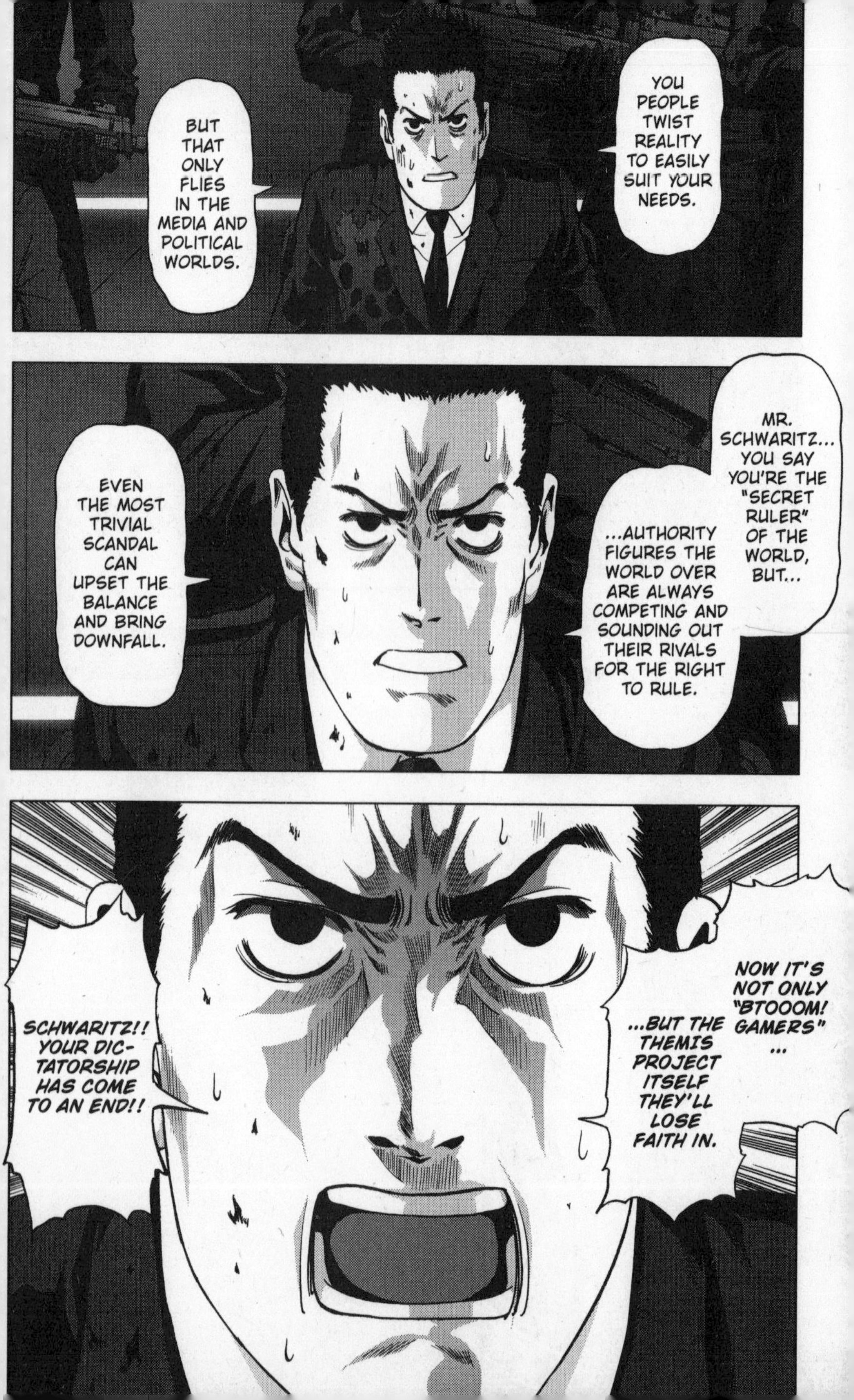
YOU PEOPLE TWIST REALITY TO EASILY SUIT YOUR NEEDS.
BUT THAT ONLY FLIES IN THE MEDIA AND POLITICAL WORLDS.
MR. SCHWARITZ... YOU SAY YOU'RE THE "SECRET RULER" OF THE WORLD, BUT...
...AUTHORITY FIGURES THE WORLD OVER ARE ALWAYS COMPETING AND SOUNDING OUT THEIR RIVALS FOR THE RIGHT TO RULE.
EVEN THE MOST TRIVIAL SCANDAL CAN UPSET THE BALANCE AND BRING DOWNFALL.
NOW IT'S NOT ONLY "BTOOOM! GAMERS" ...
...BUT THE THEMIS PROJECT ITSELF THEY'LL LOSE FAITH IN.
SCHWARITZ!! YOUR DIC-TATORSHIP HAS COME TO AN END!!

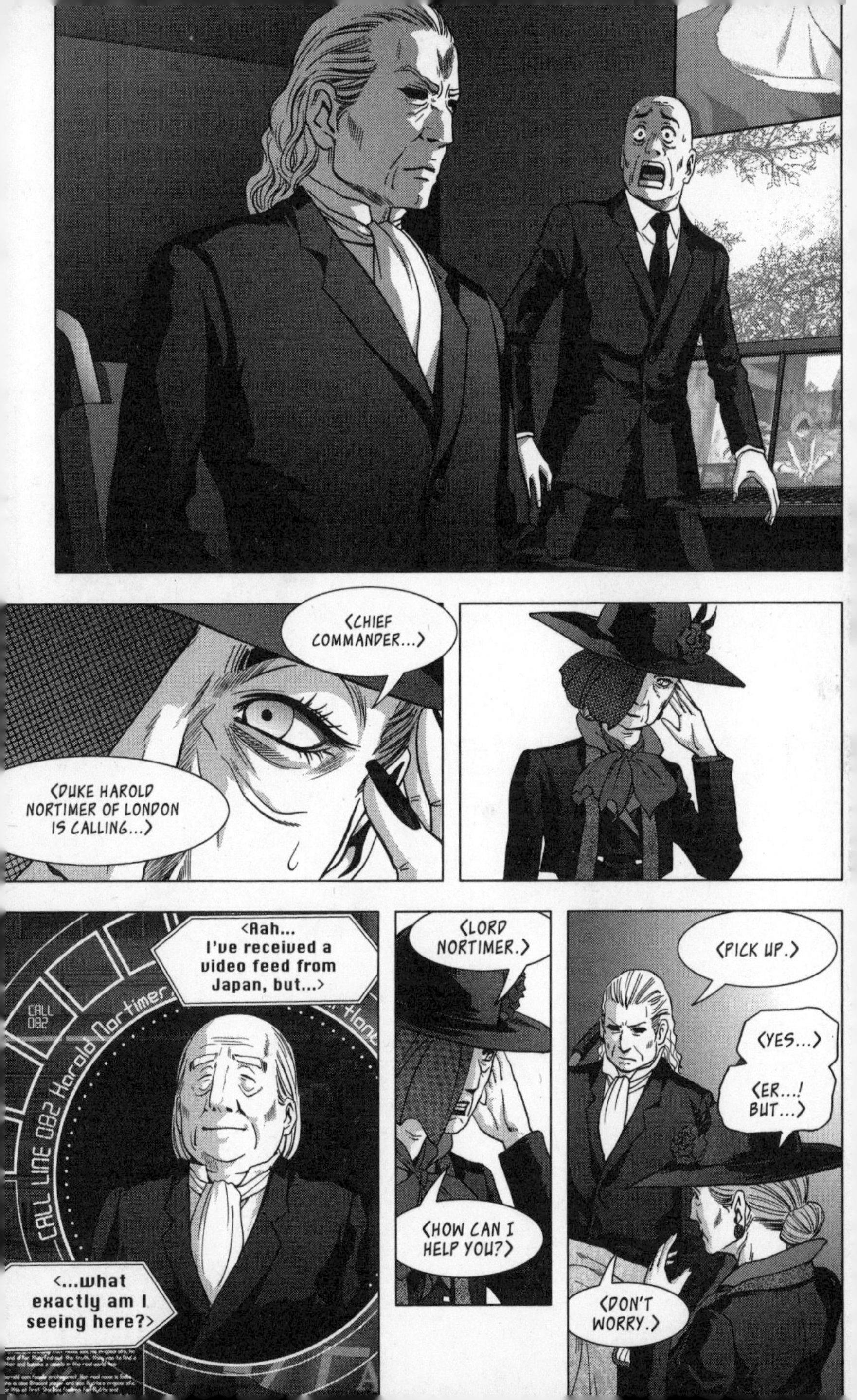
<CHIEF COMMANDER...>
<DUKE HAROLD NORTIMER OF LONDON IS CALLING...>
<PICK UP.>
<YES...>
<ER...! BUT...>
<DON'T WORRY.>
<LORD NORTIMER.>
<HOW CAN I HELP YOU?>
<Aah... I've received a video feed from Japan, but...>
CALL 082
CALL LINE 082 Harold Nortimer
<...what exactly am I seeing here?>

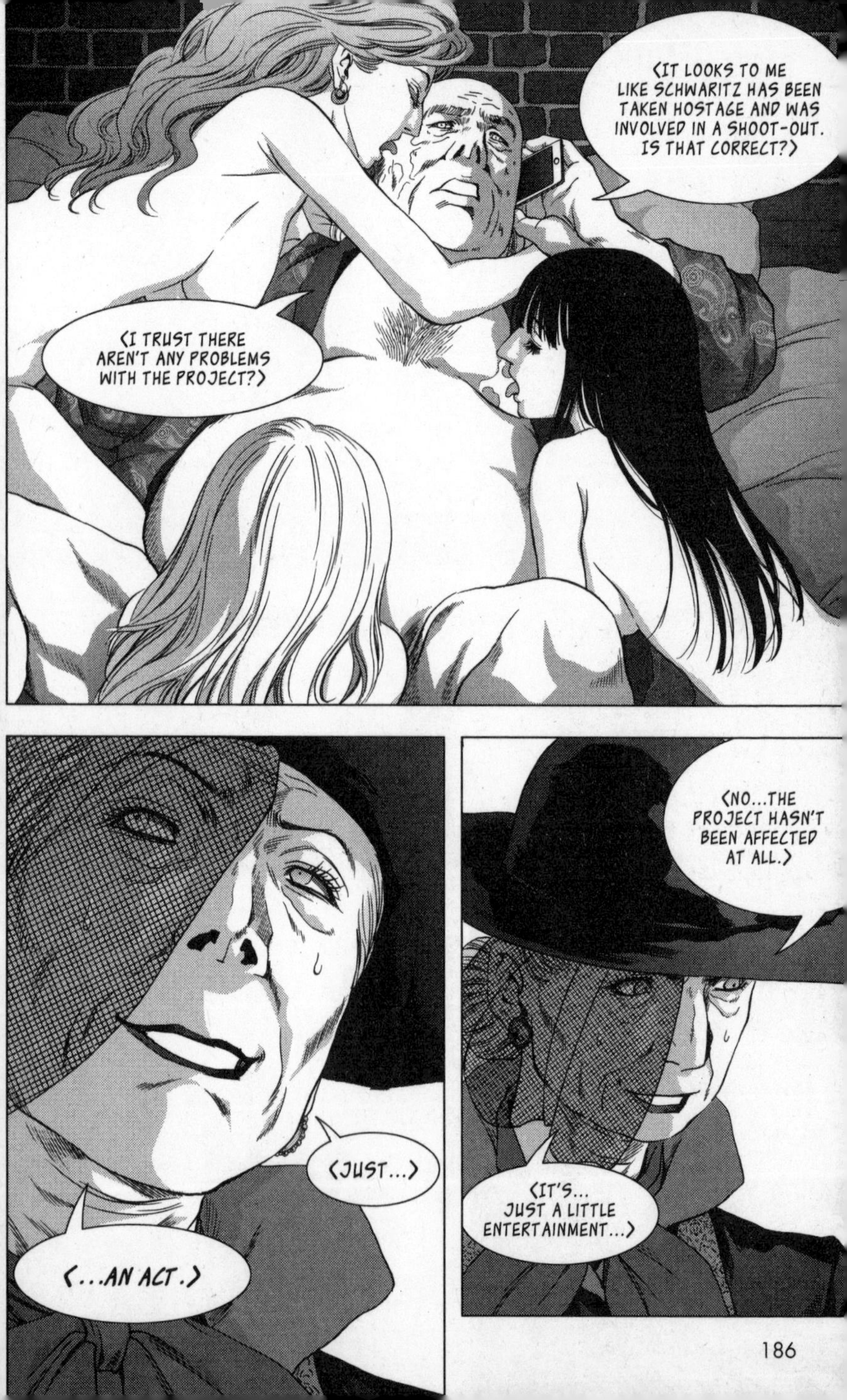
<IT LOOKS TO ME LIKE SCHWARITZ HAS BEEN TAKEN HOSTAGE AND WAS INVOLVED IN A SHOOT-OUT. IS THAT CORRECT?>
<I TRUST THERE AREN'T ANY PROBLEMS WITH THE PROJECT?>
<NO...THE PROJECT HASN'T BEEN AFFECTED AT ALL.>
<IT'S... JUST A LITTLE ENTERTAINMENT...>
<JUST...>
<...AN ACT.>

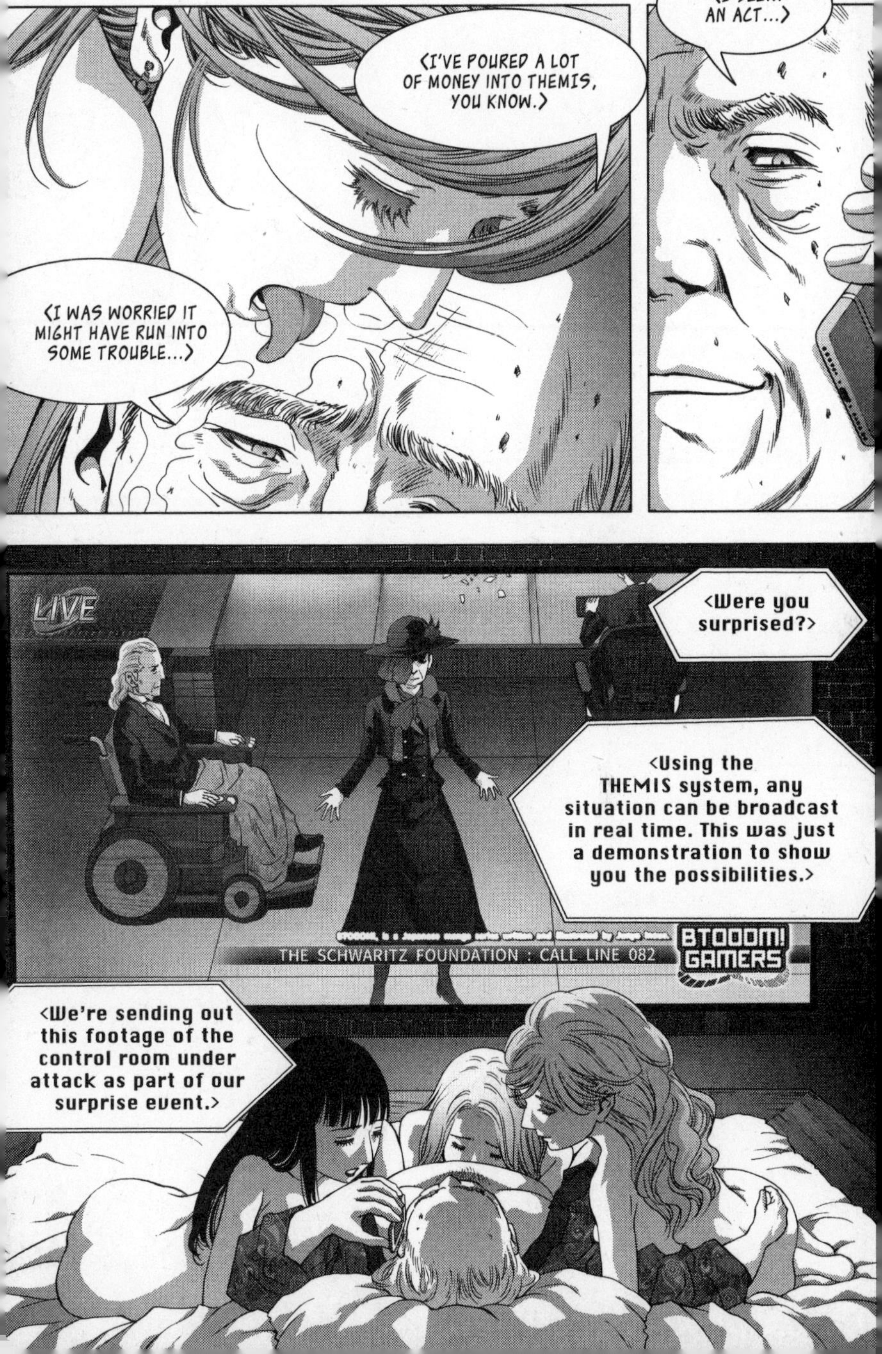
⟨I SEE... AN ACT...⟩
⟨I'VE POURED A LOT OF MONEY INTO THEMIS, YOU KNOW.⟩
⟨I WAS WORRIED IT MIGHT HAVE RUN INTO SOME TROUBLE...⟩
LIVE
<Were you surprised?>
<Using the THEMIS system, any situation can be broadcast in real time. This was just a demonstration to show you the possibilities.>
THE SCHWARITZ FOUNDATION : CALL LINE 082
BTOOOM! GAMERS
<We're sending out this footage of the control room under attack as part of our surprise event.>

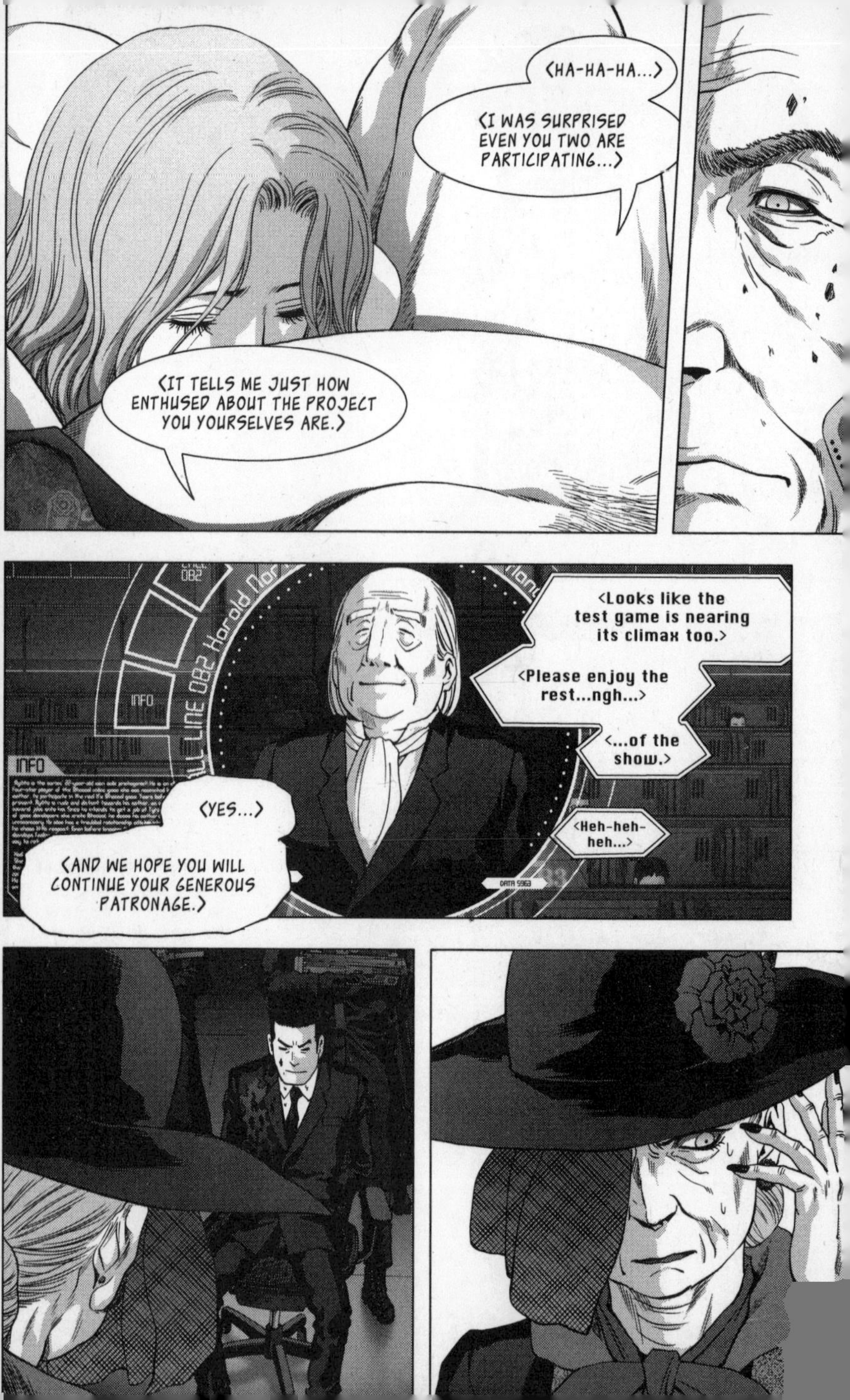

⟨HA-HA-HA...⟩
⟨I WAS SURPRISED EVEN YOU TWO ARE PARTICIPATING...⟩
⟨IT TELLS ME JUST HOW ENTHUSED ABOUT THE PROJECT YOU YOURSELVES ARE.⟩
⟨Looks like the test game is nearing its climax too.⟩
⟨Please enjoy the rest...ngh...⟩
⟨...of the show.⟩
⟨Heh-heh-heh...⟩
⟨YES...⟩
⟨AND WE HOPE YOU WILL CONTINUE YOUR GENEROUS PATRONAGE.⟩

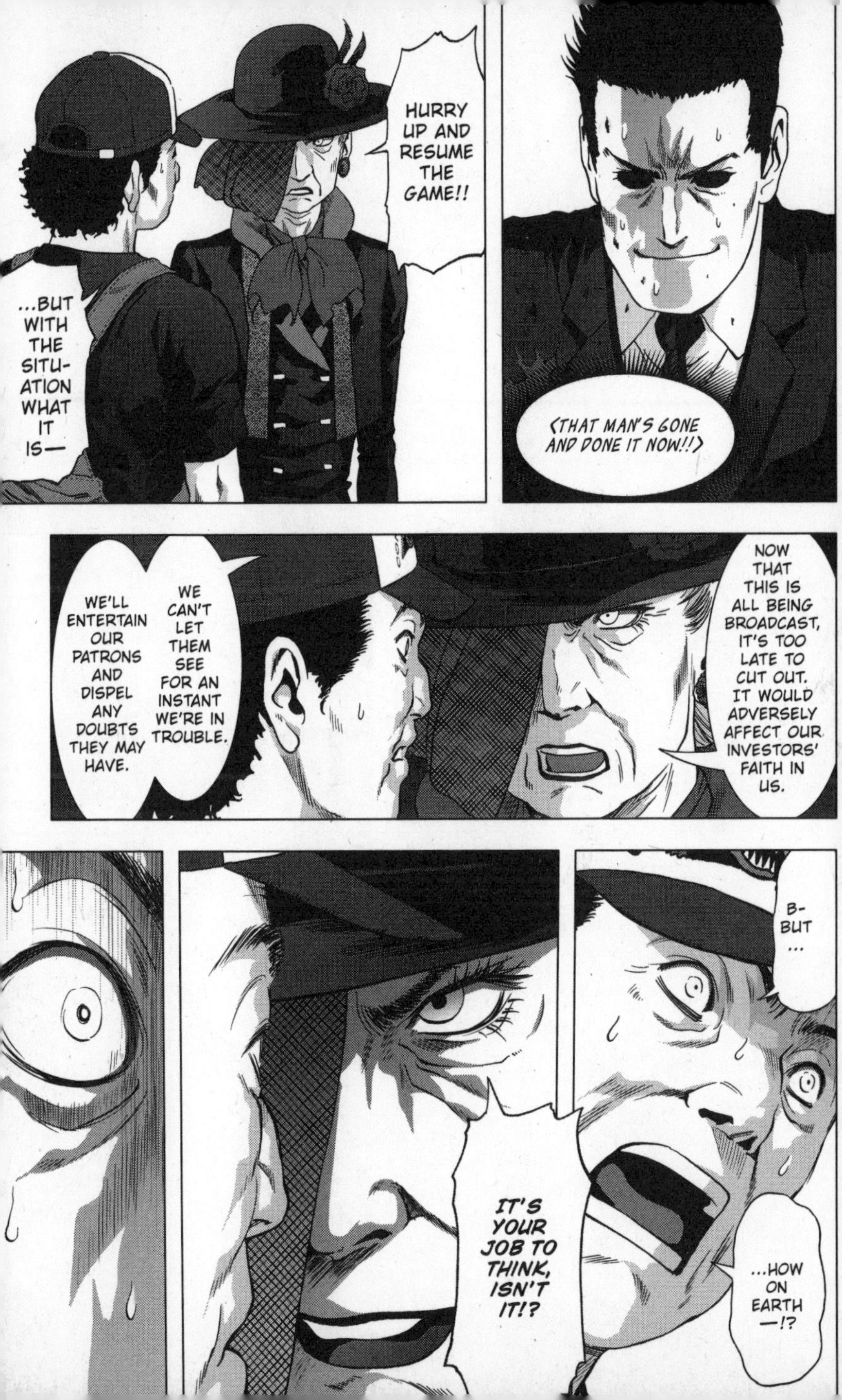
<THAT MAN'S GONE AND DONE IT NOW!!>
HURRY UP AND RESUME THE GAME!!
...BUT WITH THE SITU-ATION WHAT IT IS—
NOW THAT THIS IS ALL BEING BROADCAST, IT'S TOO LATE TO CUT OUT. IT WOULD ADVERSELY AFFECT OUR INVESTORS' FAITH IN US.
WE CAN'T LET THEM SEE FOR AN INSTANT WE'RE IN TROUBLE.
WE'LL ENTERTAIN OUR PATRONS AND DISPEL ANY DOUBTS THEY MAY HAVE.
B-BUT...
...HOW ON EARTH—!?
IT'S YOUR JOB TO THINK, ISN'T IT!?

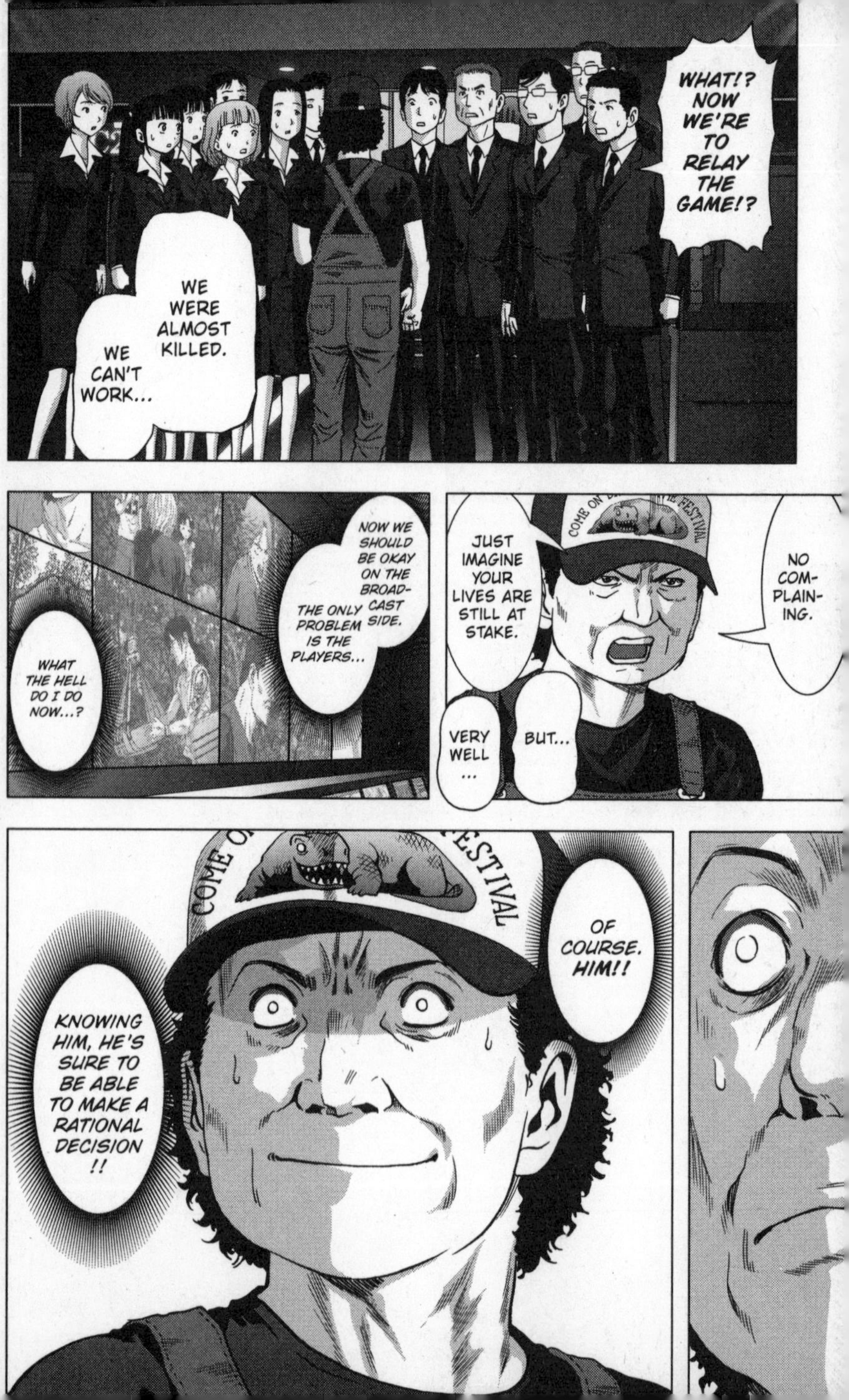
WHAT!? NOW WE'RE TO RELAY THE GAME!?
WE WERE ALMOST KILLED.
WE CAN'T WORK...
NO COMPLAINING.
JUST IMAGINE YOUR LIVES ARE STILL AT STAKE.
BUT...
VERY WELL ...
NOW WE SHOULD BE OKAY ON THE BROADCAST SIDE.
THE ONLY PROBLEM IS THE PLAYERS...
WHAT THE HELL DO I DO NOW...?
OF COURSE. HIM!!
KNOWING HIM, HE'S SURE TO BE ABLE TO MAKE A RATIONAL DECISION !!

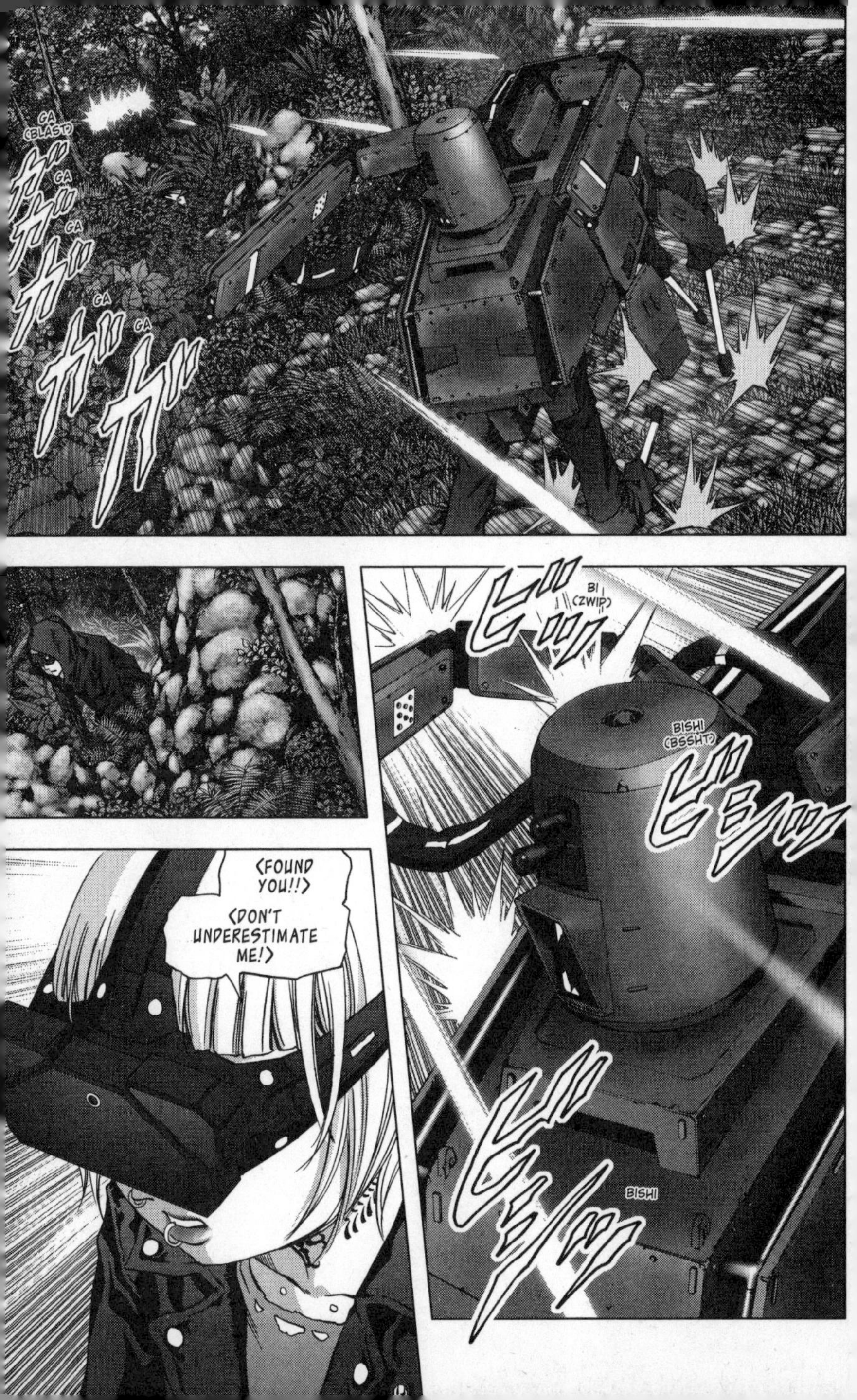

GA (BLAST)
GA
GA
GA
GA
BI (ZWIP)
BISHI (BSSHT)
BISHI
<FOUND YOU!!>
<DON'T UNDERESTIMATE ME!>

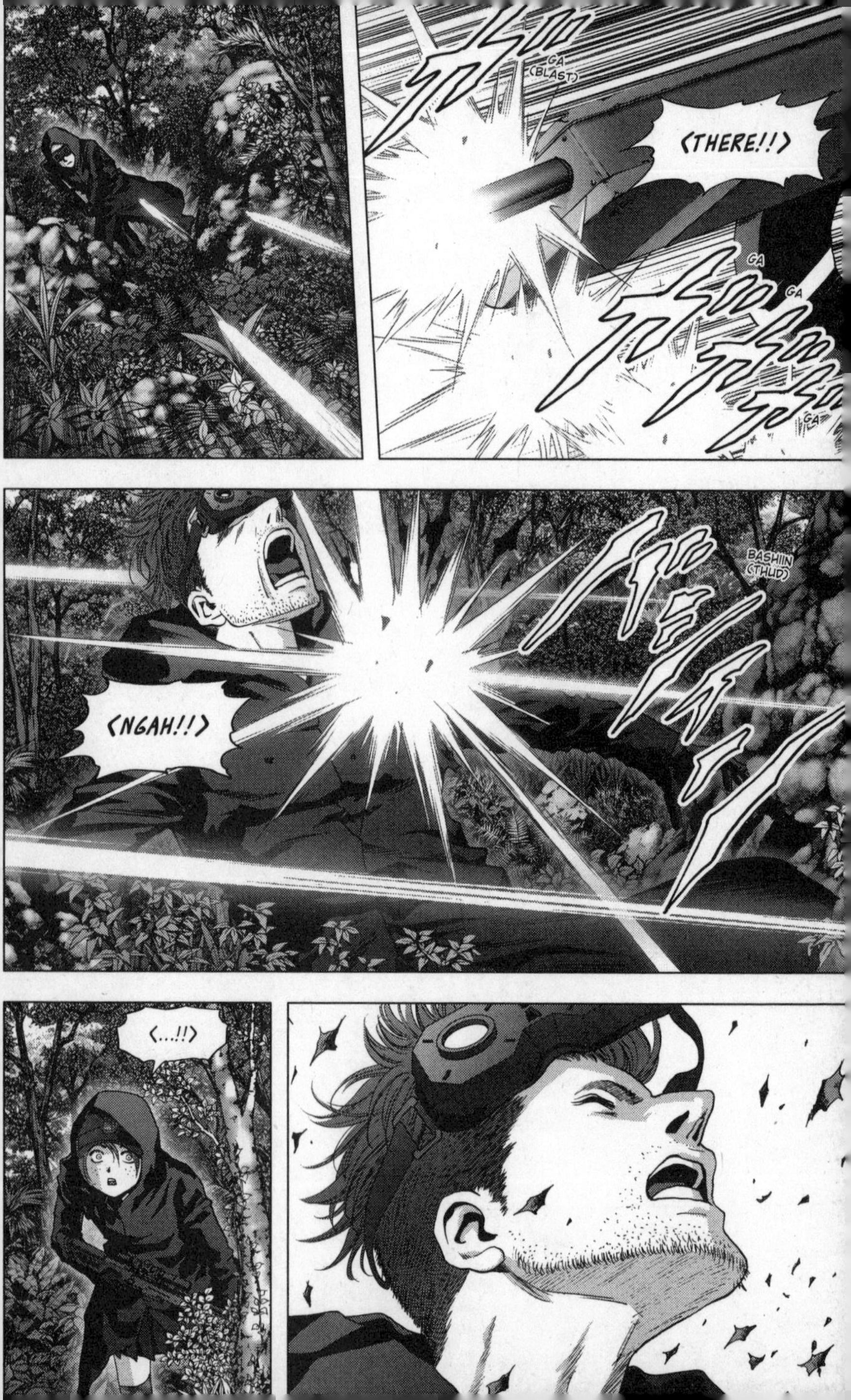
GA (BLAST)
<THERE!!>
GA
GA
GA
BASHIIN (THUD)
<NGAH!!>
<...!!>

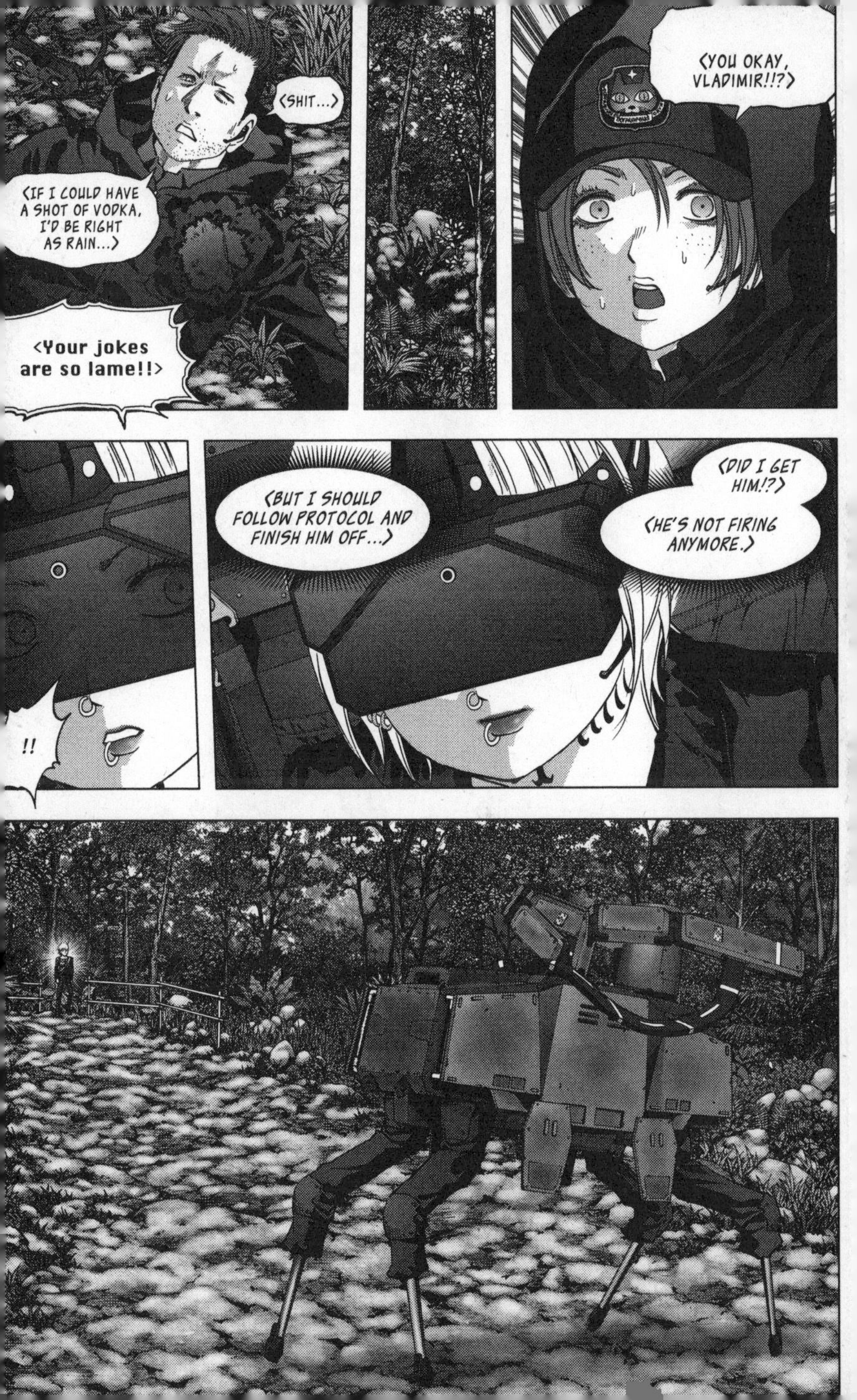
<YOU OKAY, VLADIMIR!!?>
<SHIT...>
<IF I COULD HAVE A SHOT OF VODKA, I'D BE RIGHT AS RAIN...>
<Your jokes are so lame!!>
<DID I GET HIM!?>
<HE'S NOT FIRING ANYMORE.>
<BUT I SHOULD FOLLOW PROTOCOL AND FINISH HIM OFF...>
!!

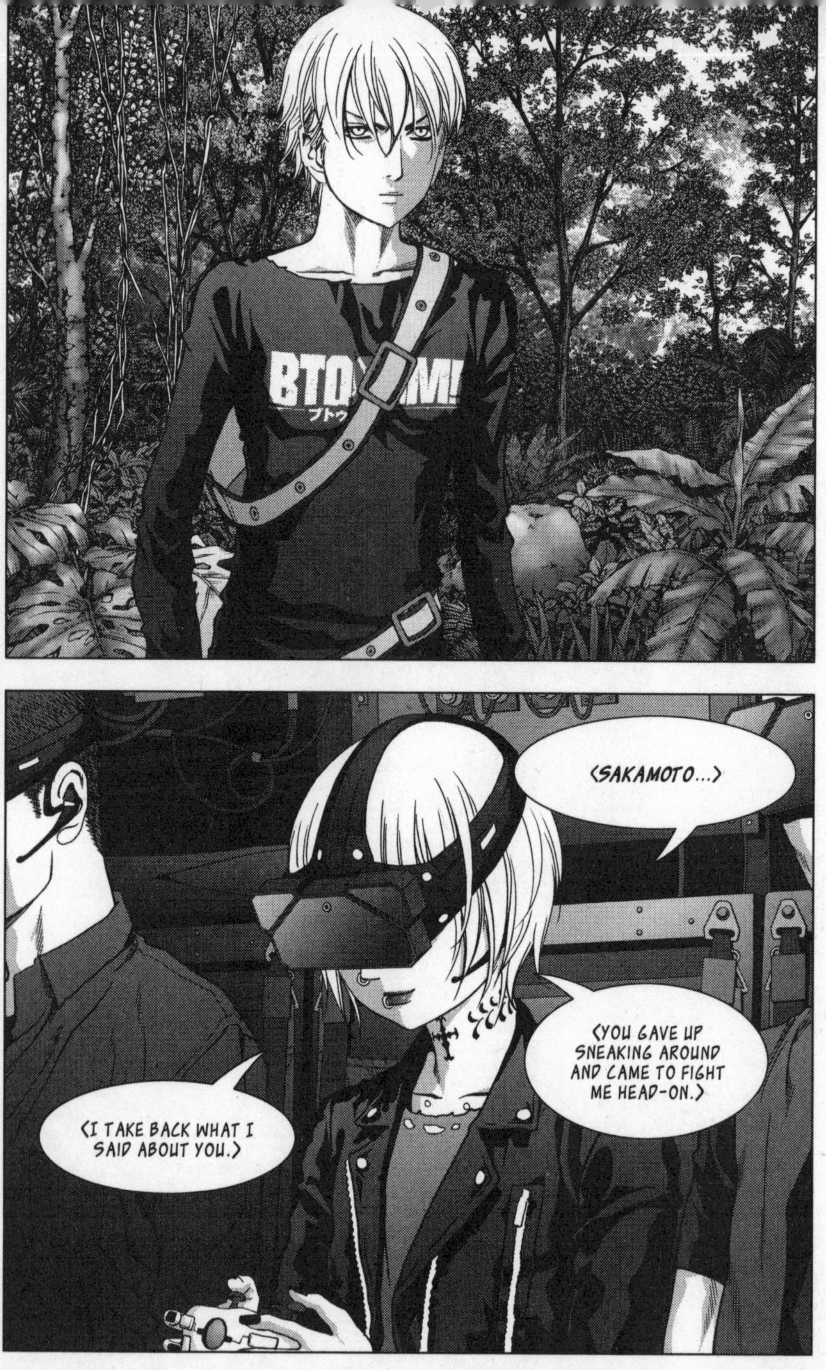
‹SAKAMOTO...›
‹YOU GAVE UP SNEAKING AROUND AND CAME TO FIGHT ME HEAD-ON.›
‹I TAKE BACK WHAT I SAID ABOUT YOU.›

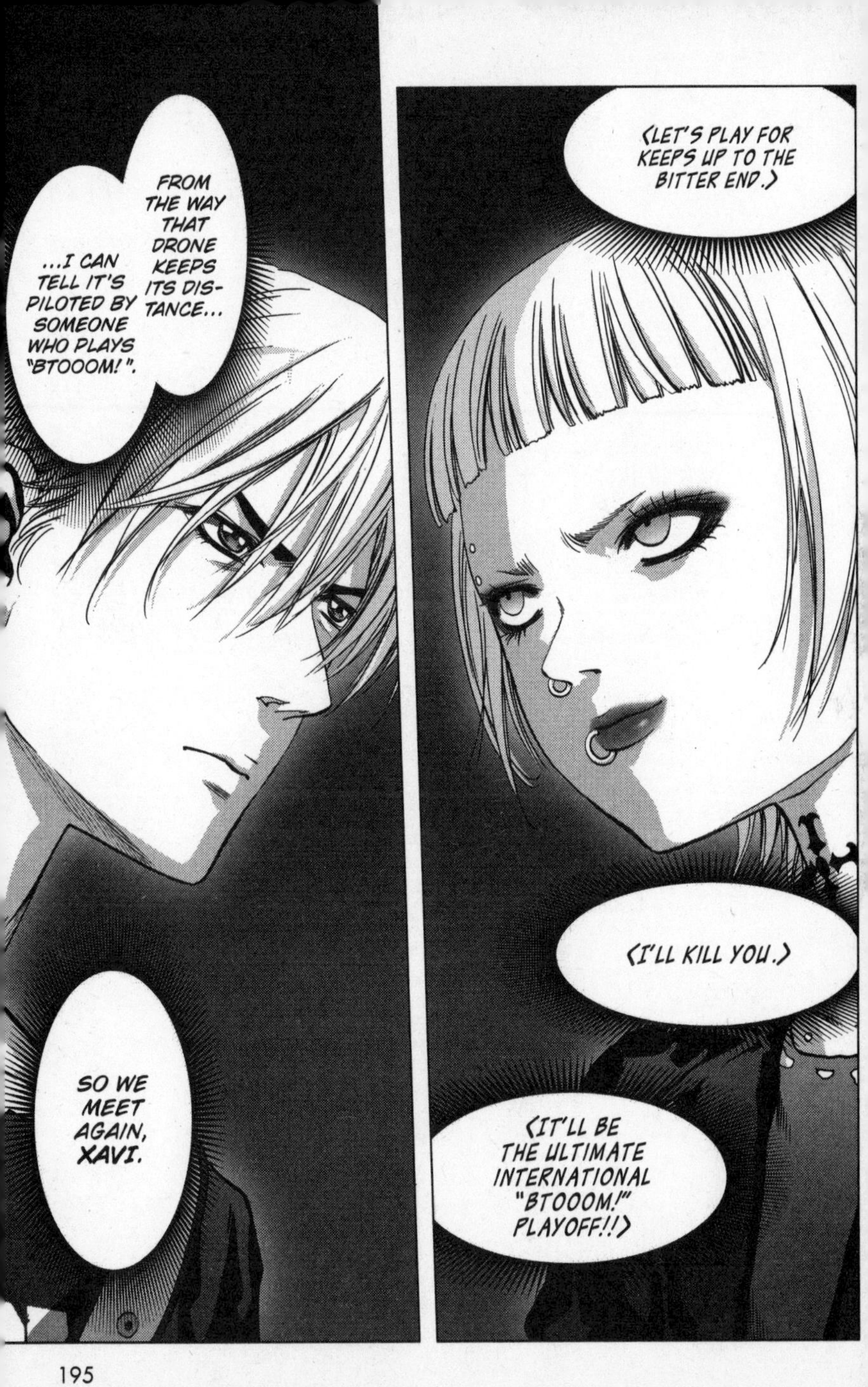

<LET'S PLAY FOR KEEPS UP TO THE BITTER END.>
<I'LL KILL YOU.>
<IT'LL BE THE ULTIMATE INTERNATIONAL "BTOOOM!" PLAYOFF!!>
FROM THE WAY THAT DRONE KEEPS ITS DIS-TANCE...
...I CAN TELL IT'S PILOTED BY SOMEONE WHO PLAYS "BTOOOM!".
SO WE MEET AGAIN, **XAVI**.

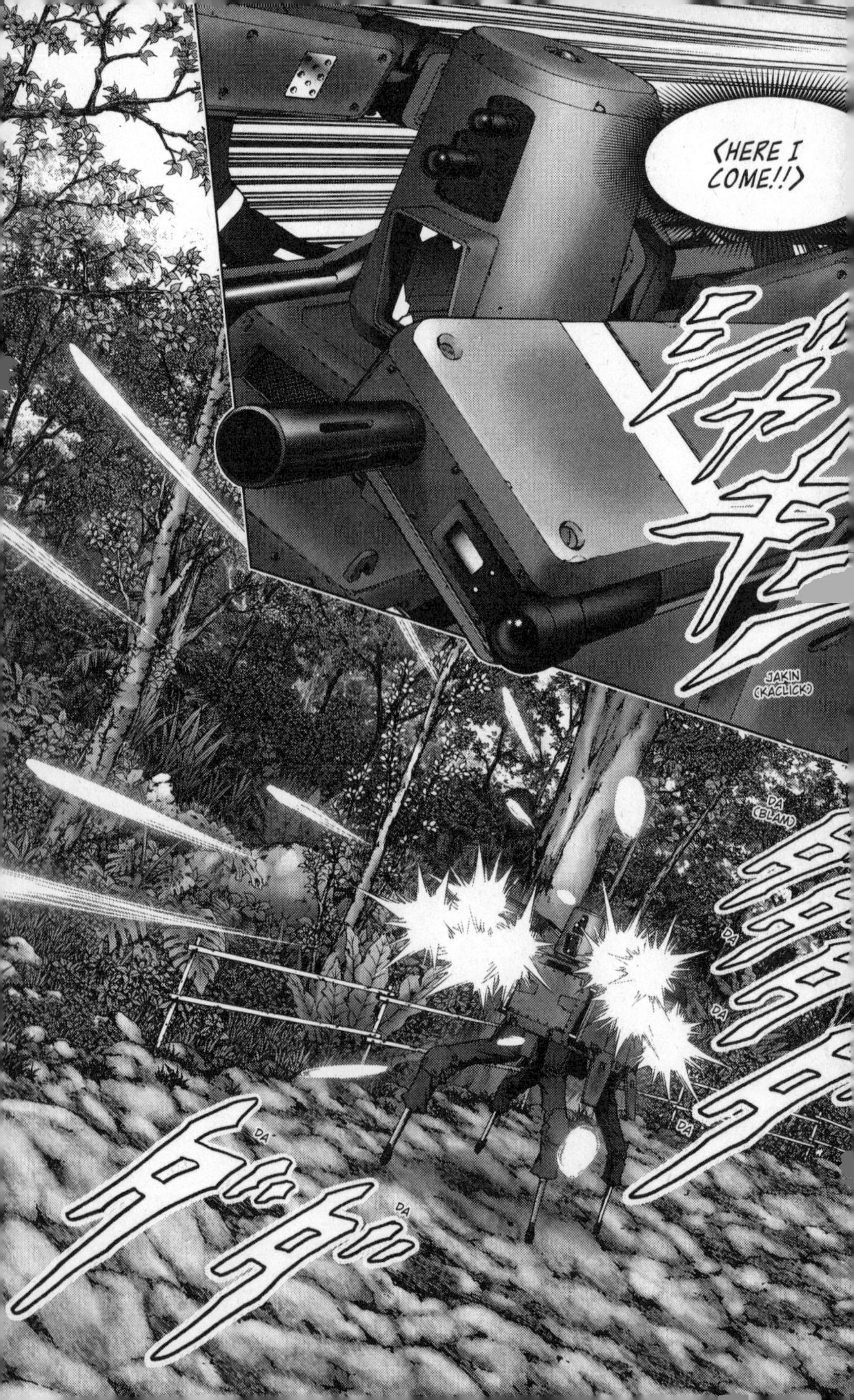
<HERE I COME!!>
JAKIN (KACLICK)
DA (BLAM)
DA
DA
DA
DA
DA

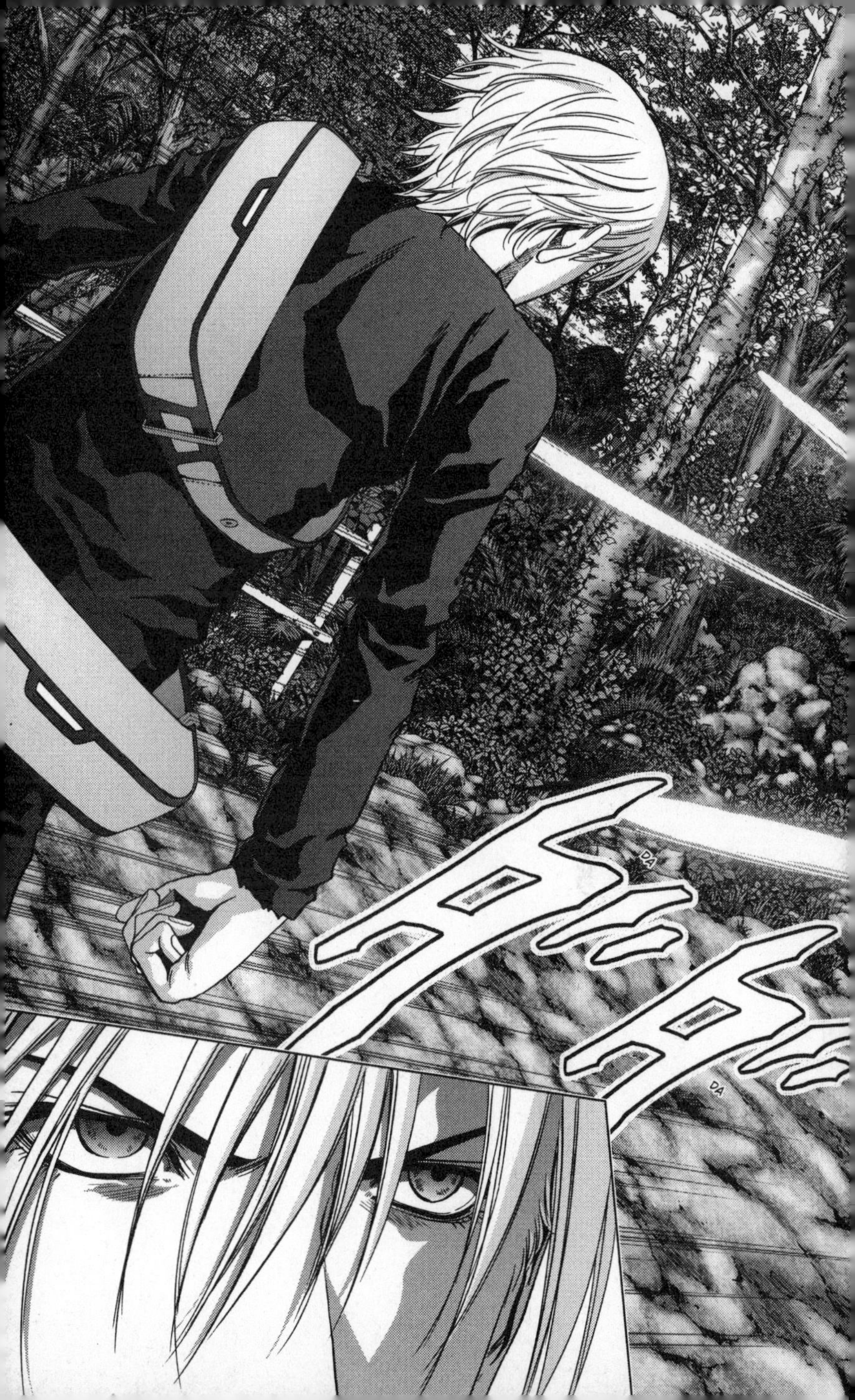
DA
DA

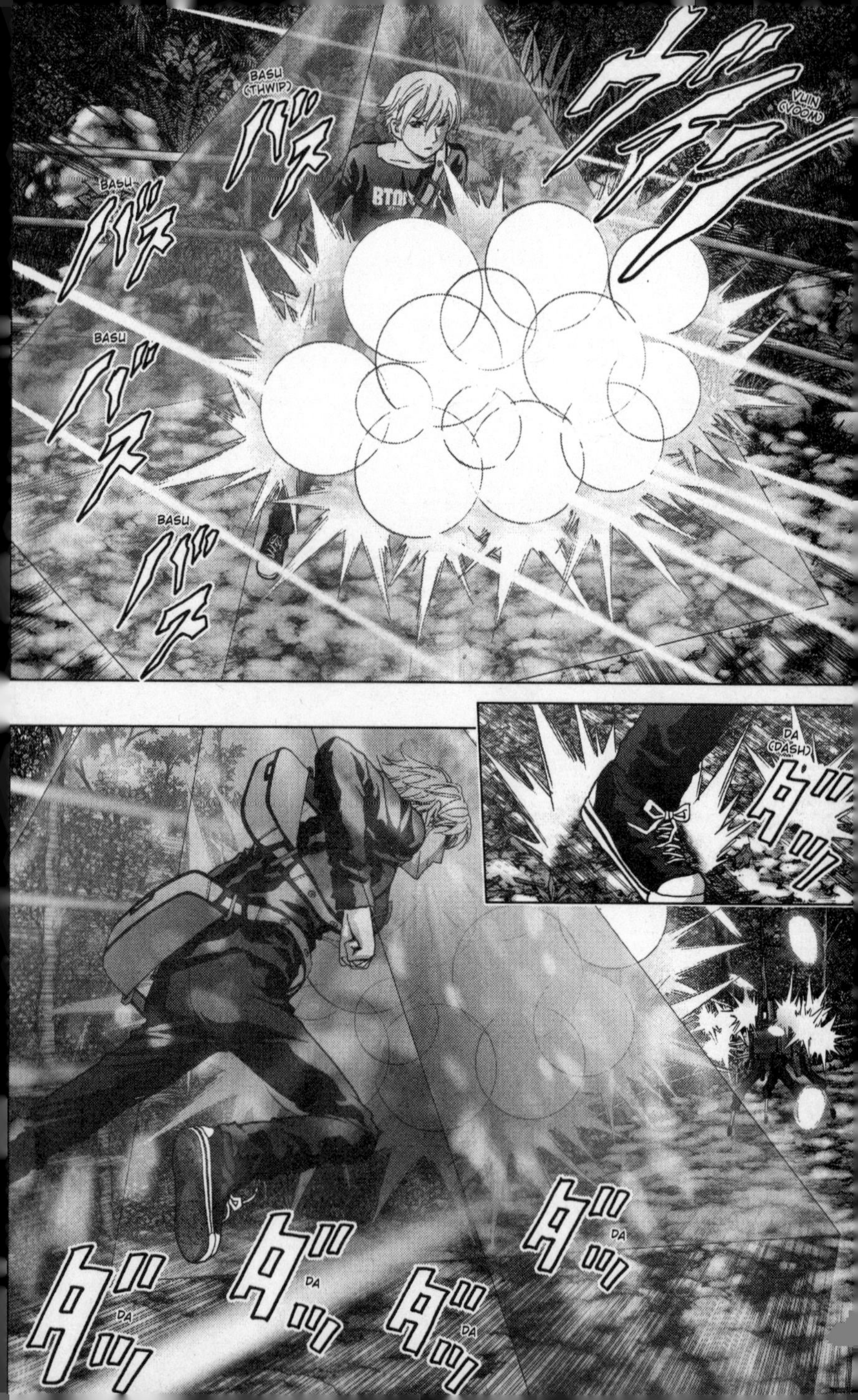
VUIN (VOOM)
BASU (THWIP)
BASU
BASU
BASU
DA (DASH)
DA
DA
DA
DA

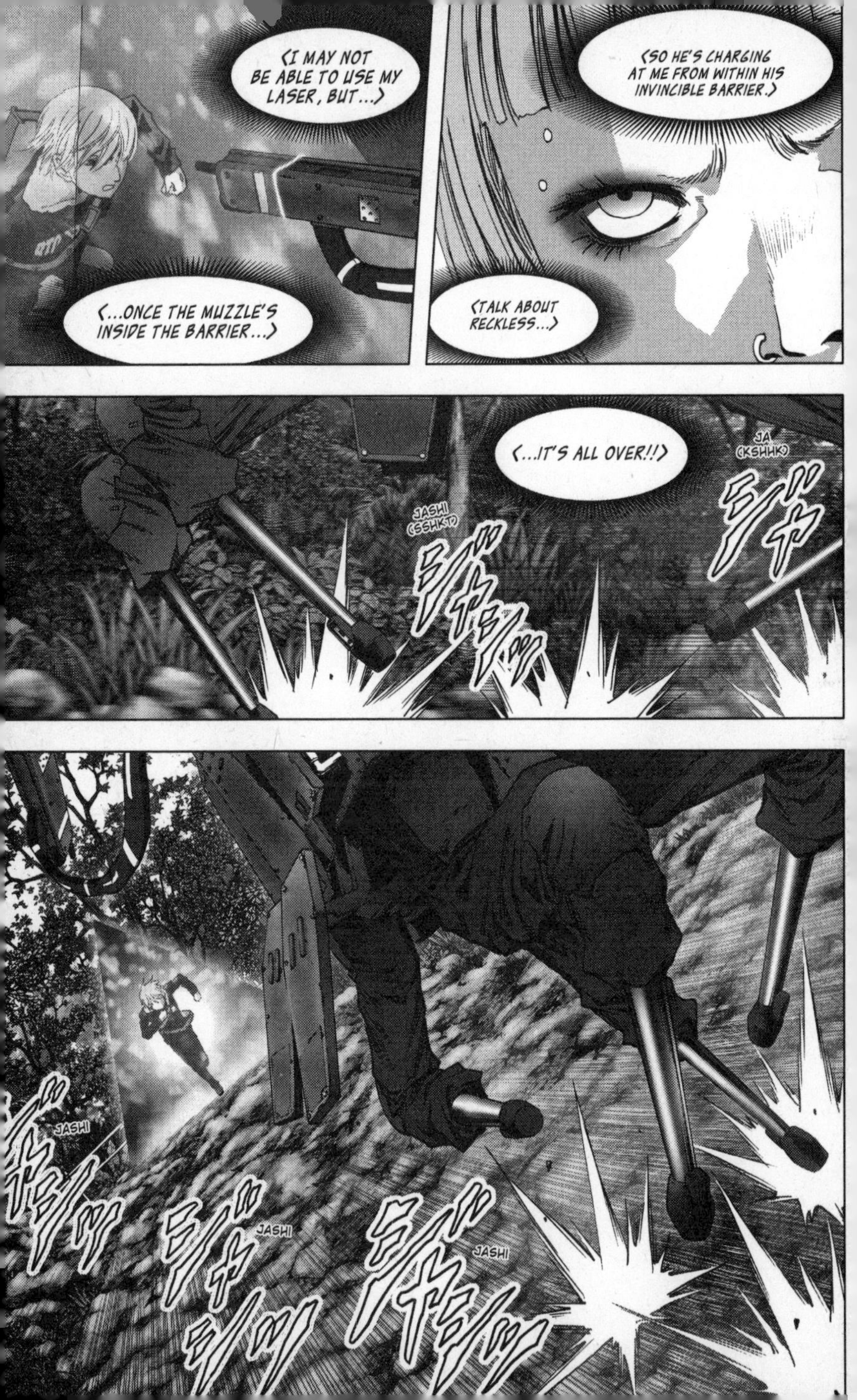
<SO HE'S CHARGING AT ME FROM WITHIN HIS INVINCIBLE BARRIER.>
<TALK ABOUT RECKLESS...>
<I MAY NOT BE ABLE TO USE MY LASER, BUT...>
<...ONCE THE MUZZLE'S INSIDE THE BARRIER...>
JA (KSHHK)
<...IT'S ALL OVER!!>
JASHI (SSHKT)
JASHI
JASHI
JASHI

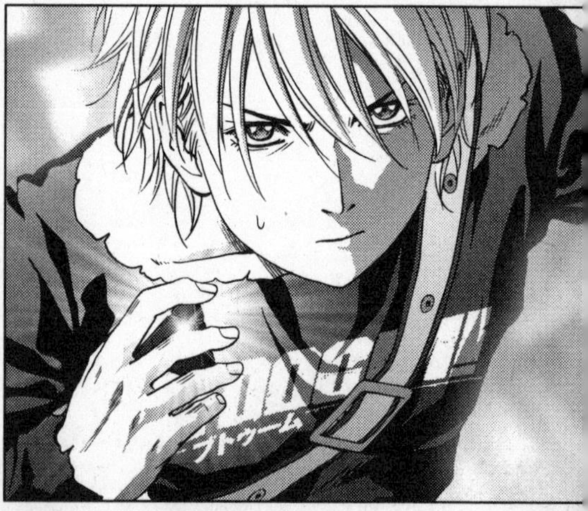

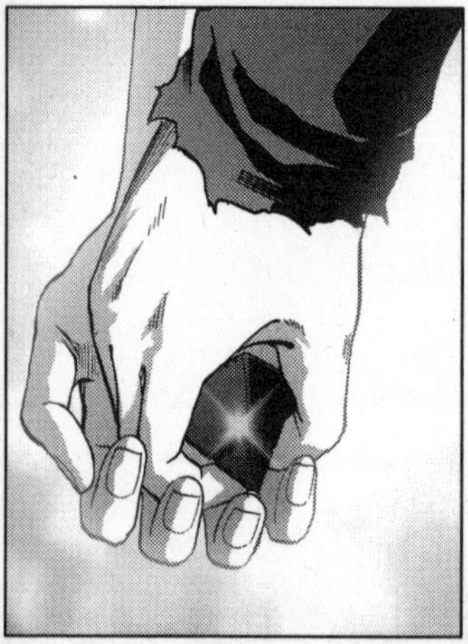

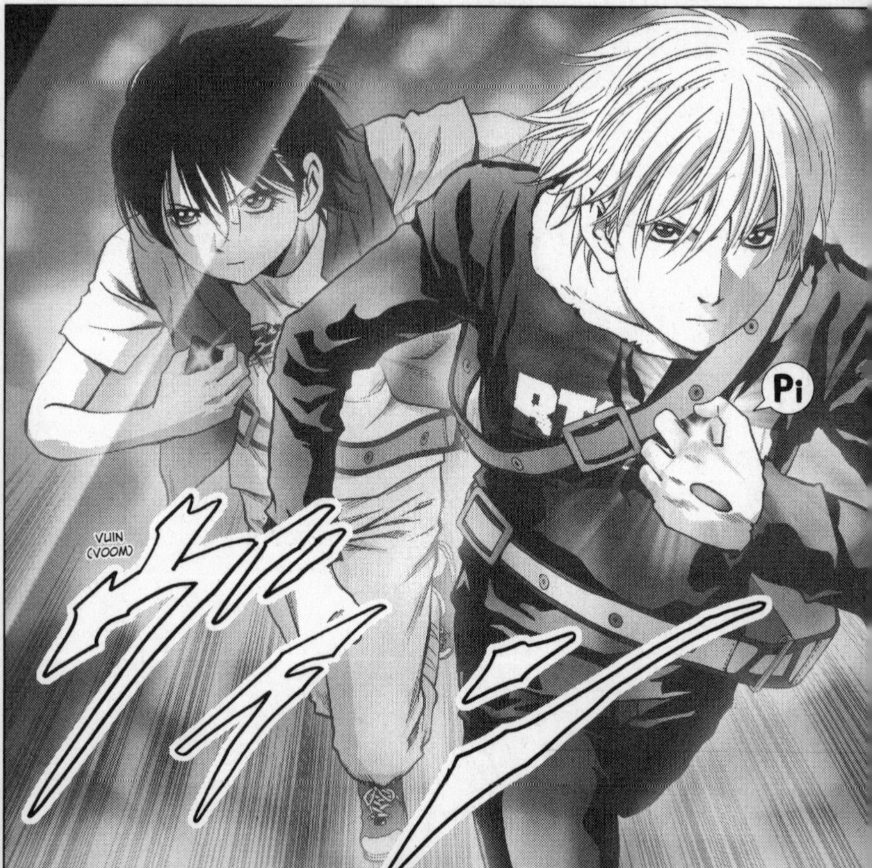
Pi
VUIN
(VOOM)

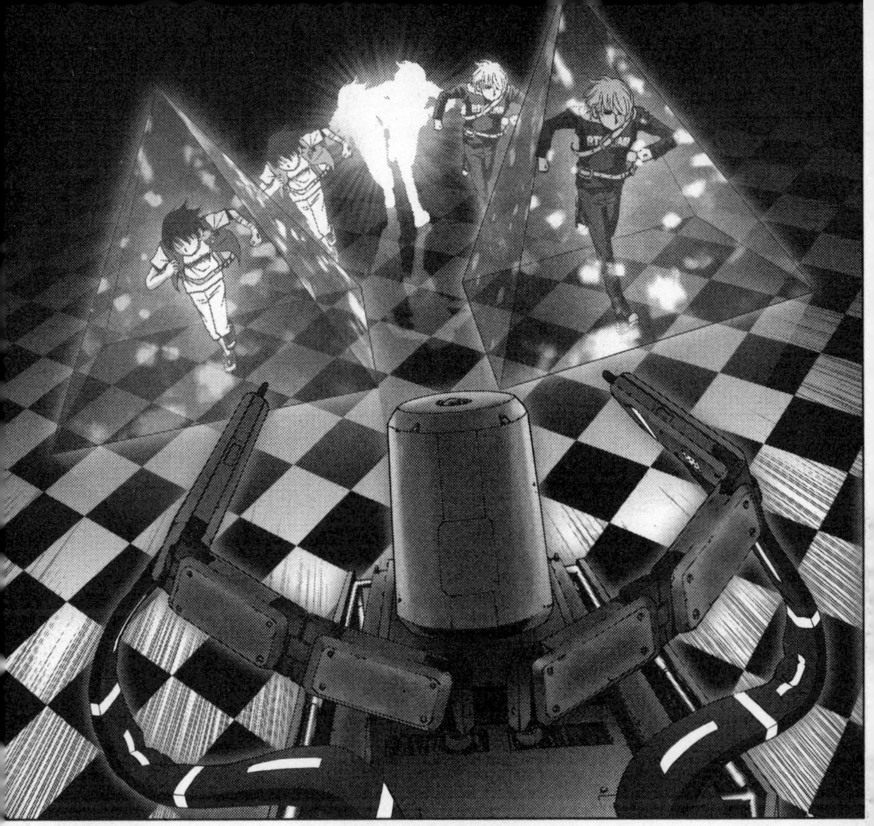

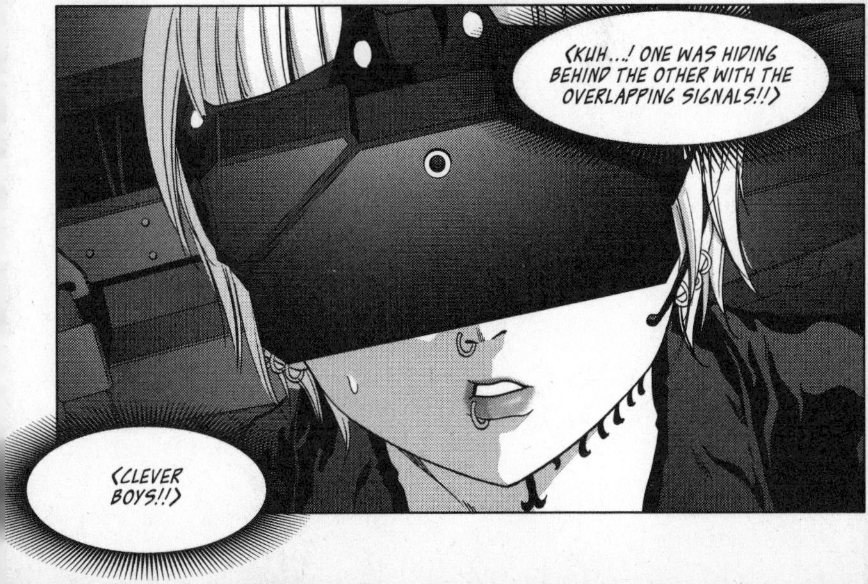
<KUH...! ONE WAS HIDING BEHIND THE OTHER WITH THE OVERLAPPING SIGNALS!!>
<CLEVER BOYS!!>

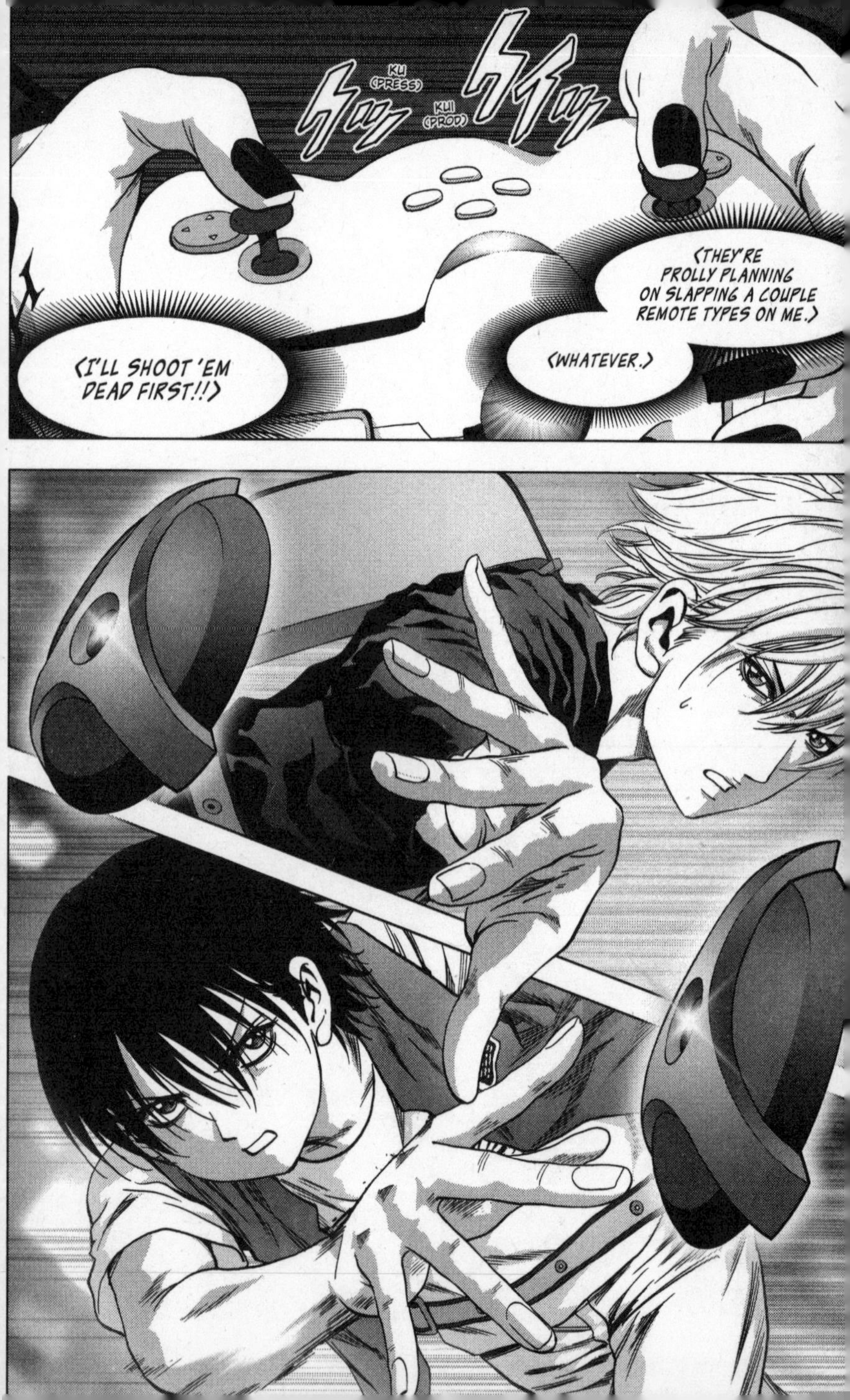
KUI (PROD)
KU (PRESS)
⟨THEY'RE PROLLY PLANNING ON SLAPPING A COUPLE REMOTE TYPES ON ME.⟩
⟨WHATEVER.⟩
⟨I'LL SHOOT 'EM DEAD FIRST!!⟩

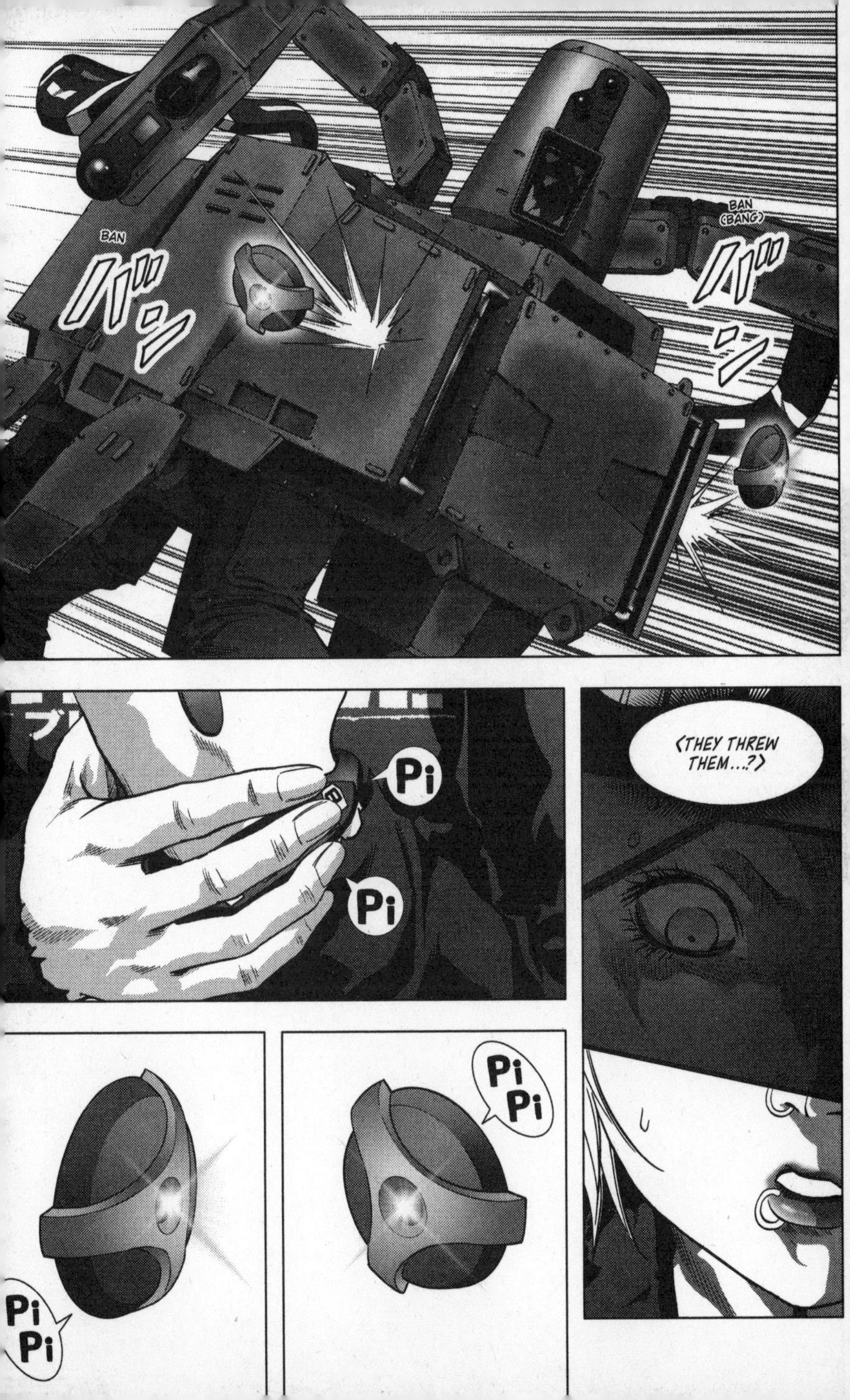
バン
BAN (BANG)
バン
BAN
<THEY THREW THEM...?>
Pi
Pi
Pi Pi
Pi Pi

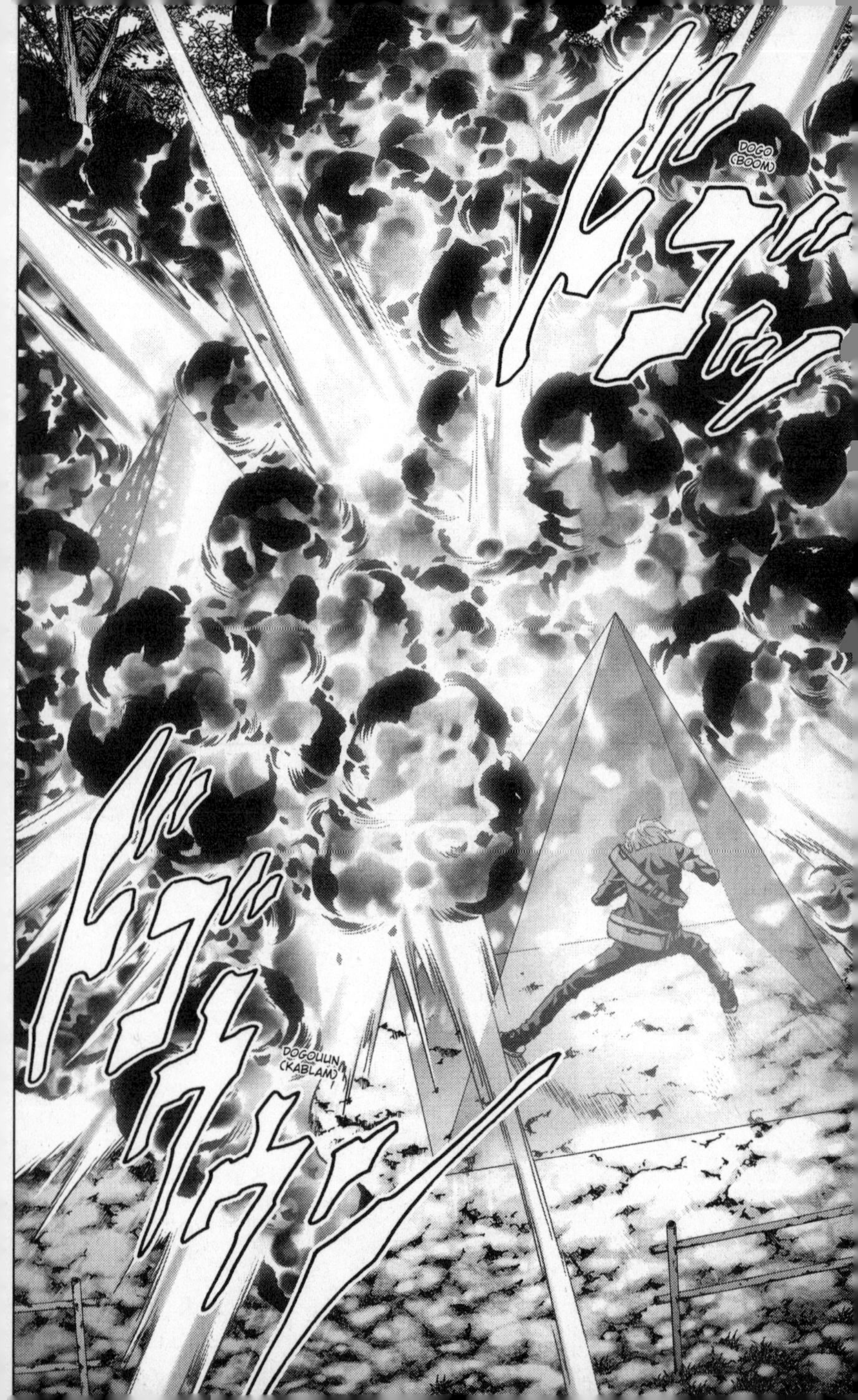
DOGO (BOOM)
DOGOUUN (KABLAM)

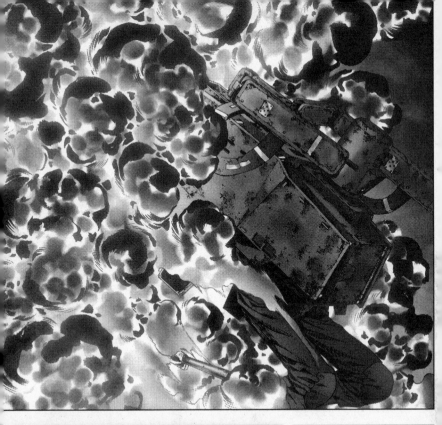

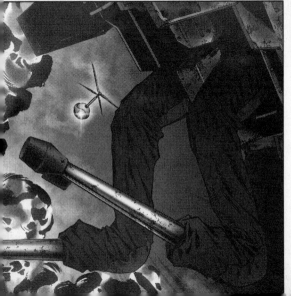

⟨I BET THEY'RE TRYING TO THROW ME OFF.⟩

⟨BUT UNLESS YOU STICK THEM RIGHT ON ME, I WON'T BREAK.⟩

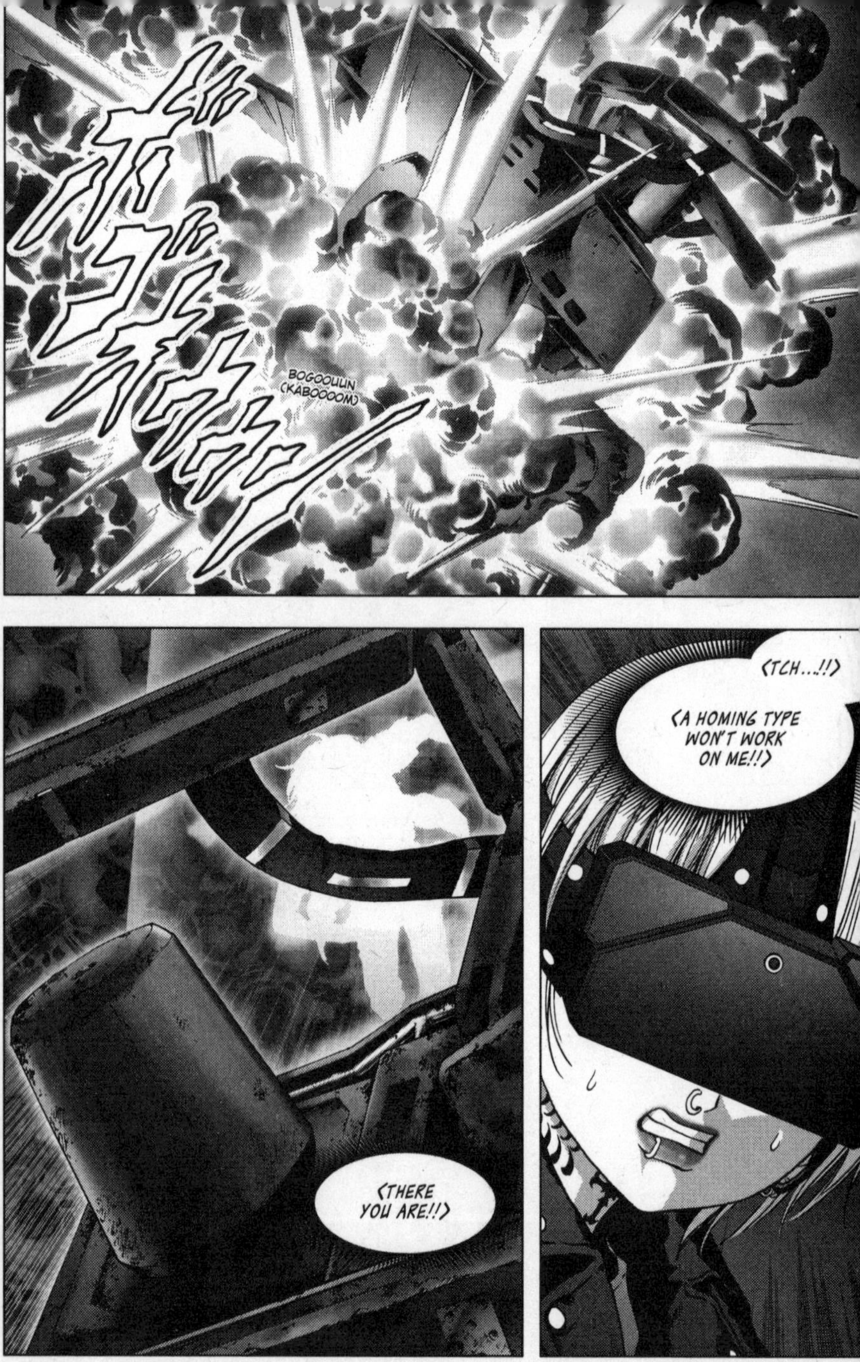
BOGOOUUN
(KABOOOOM)
<TCH...!!>
<A HOMING TYPE WON'T WORK ON ME!!>
<THERE YOU ARE!!>

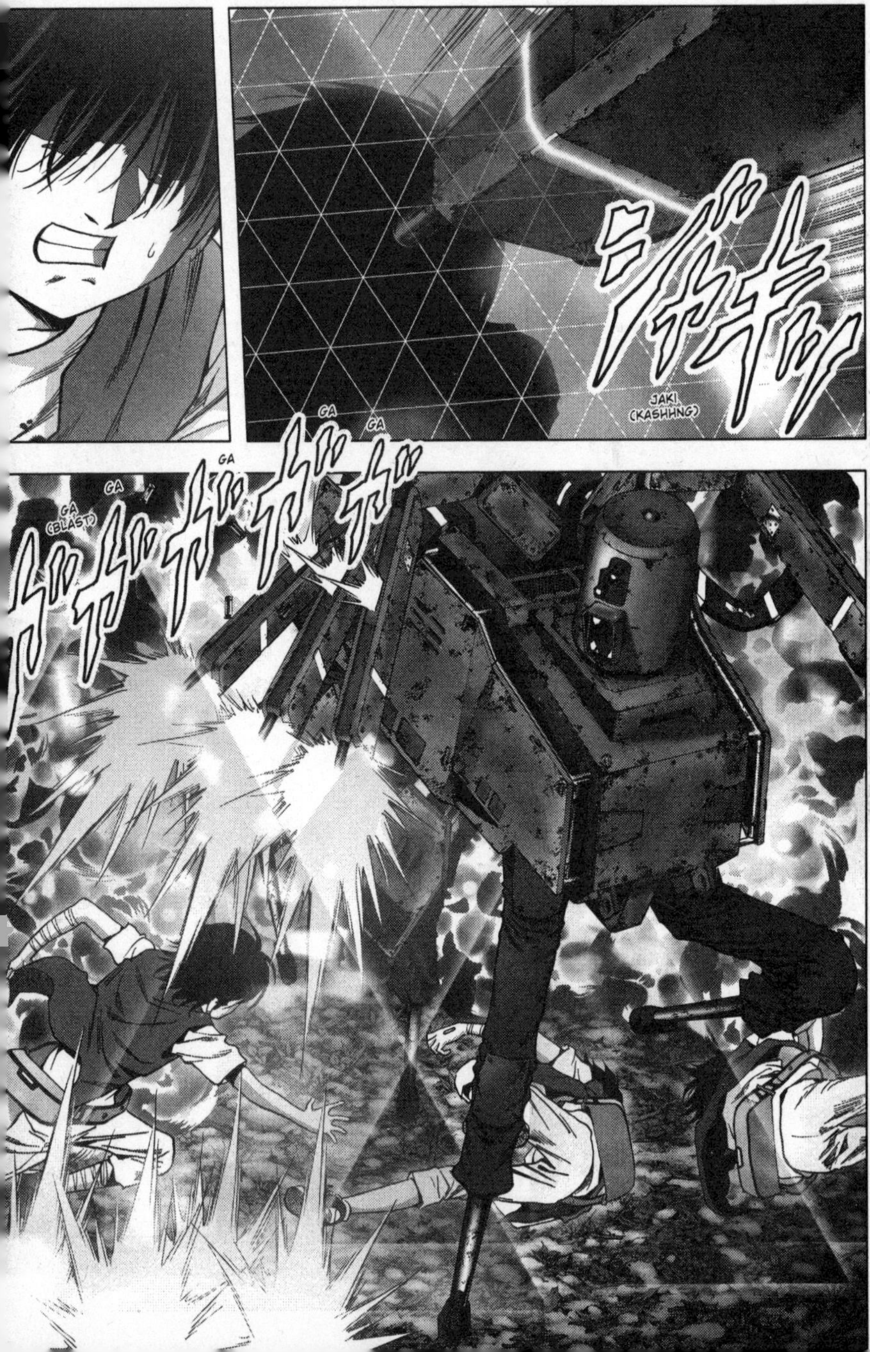
JAKI
(KASHHNG)
GA
(BLAST)
GA
GA
GA
GA

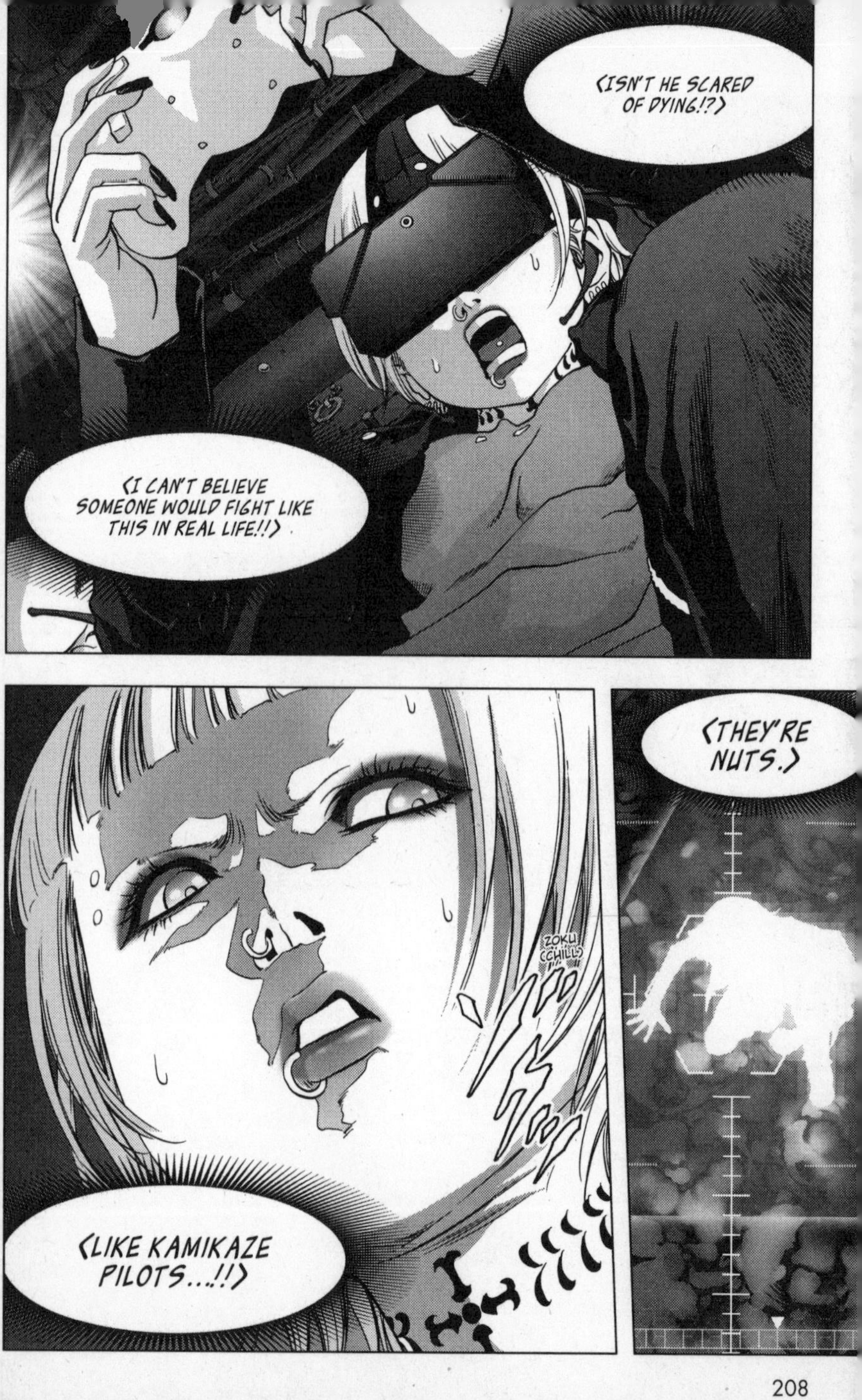

<ISN'T HE SCARED OF DYING!?>
<I CAN'T BELIEVE SOMEONE WOULD FIGHT LIKE THIS IN REAL LIFE!!>
<THEY'RE NUTS.>
ZOKU (CHILL)
<LIKE KAMIKAZE PILOTS...!!>

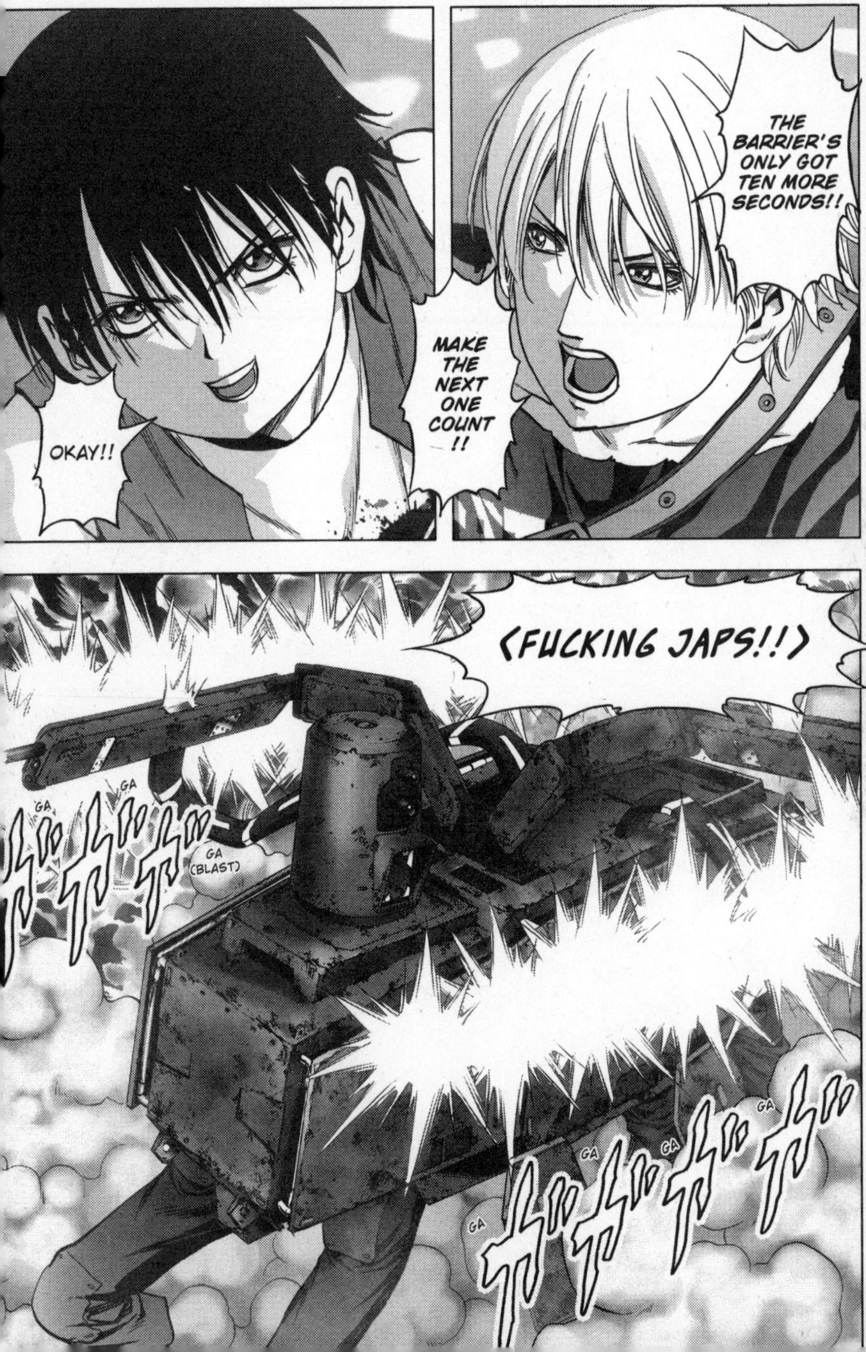

THE BARRIER'S ONLY GOT TEN MORE SECONDS!!
MAKE THE NEXT ONE COUNT—!!
OKAY!!
‹FUCKING JAPS!!!›
GA GA GA GA
GA GA GA (BLAST)

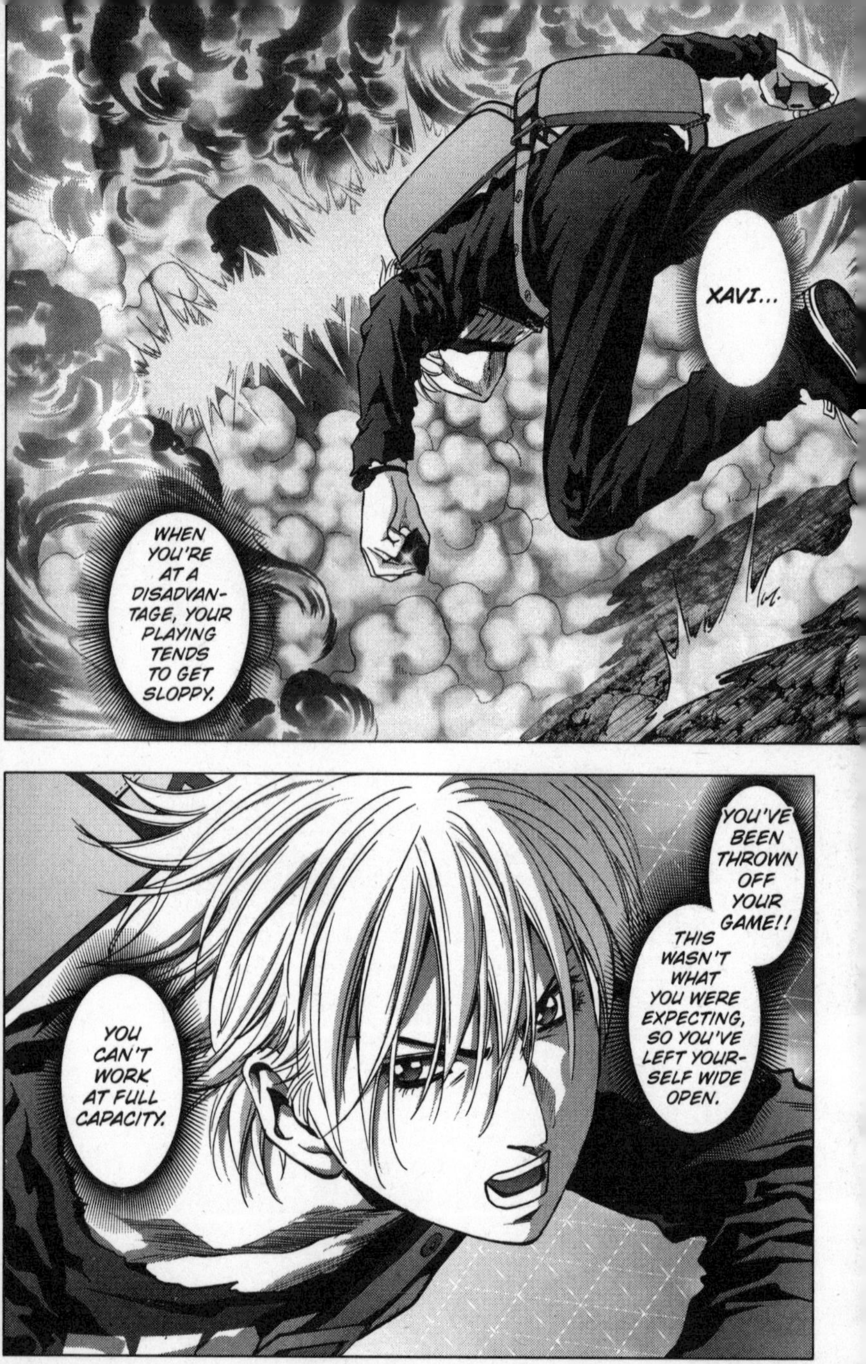
XAVI...
WHEN YOU'RE AT A DISADVAN-TAGE, YOUR PLAYING TENDS TO GET SLOPPY.
YOU'VE BEEN THROWN OFF YOUR GAME!!
THIS WASN'T WHAT YOU WERE EXPECTING, SO YOU'VE LEFT YOUR-SELF WIDE OPEN.
YOU CAN'T WORK AT FULL CAPACITY.

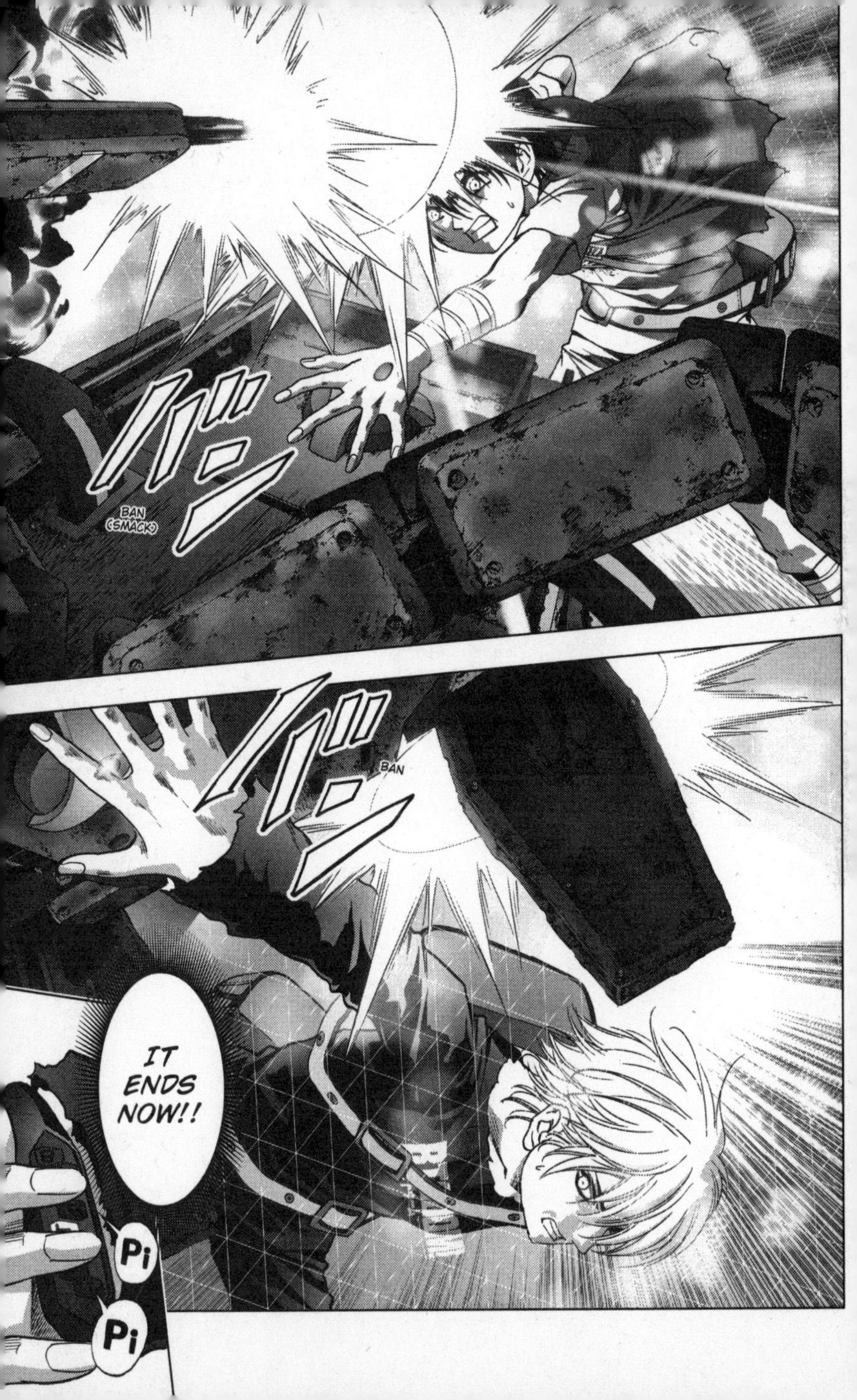
バン
BAN (SMACK)
バン
BAN
IT ENDS NOW!!
Pi
Pi

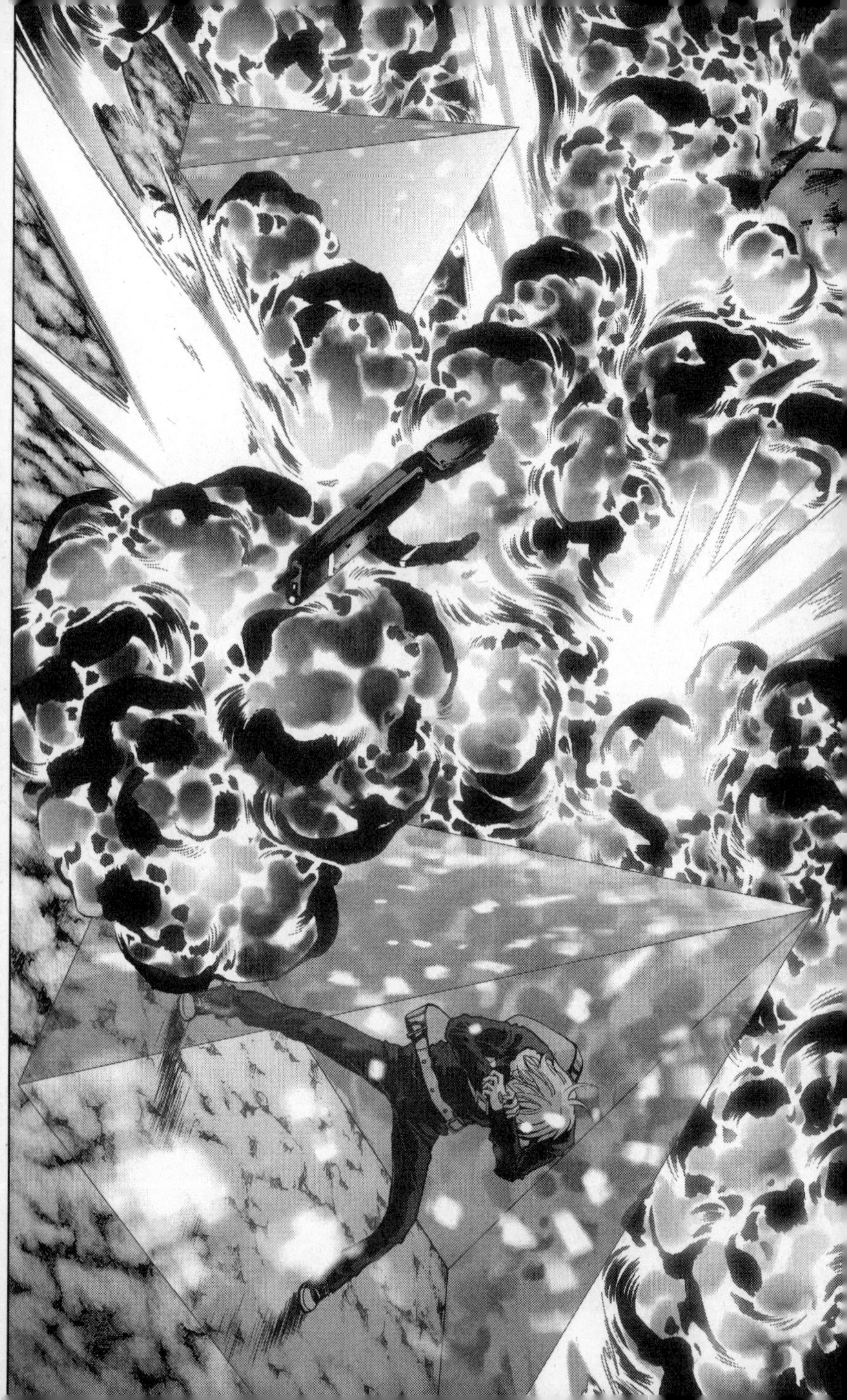

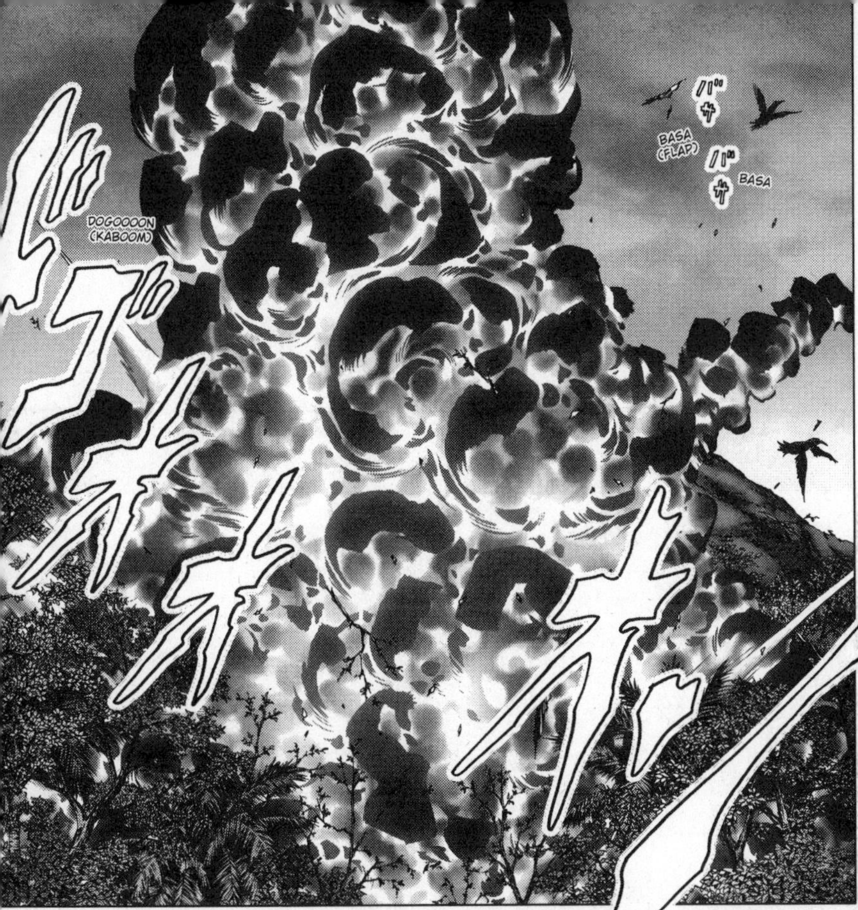
バサ
BASA (FLAP)
バサ
BASA
DOGOOOON (KABOOM)

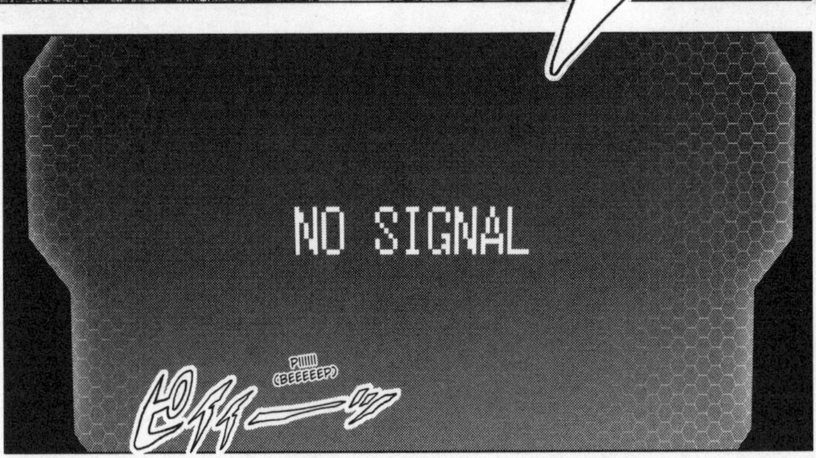
NO SIGNAL
PIIIII (BEEEEEP)

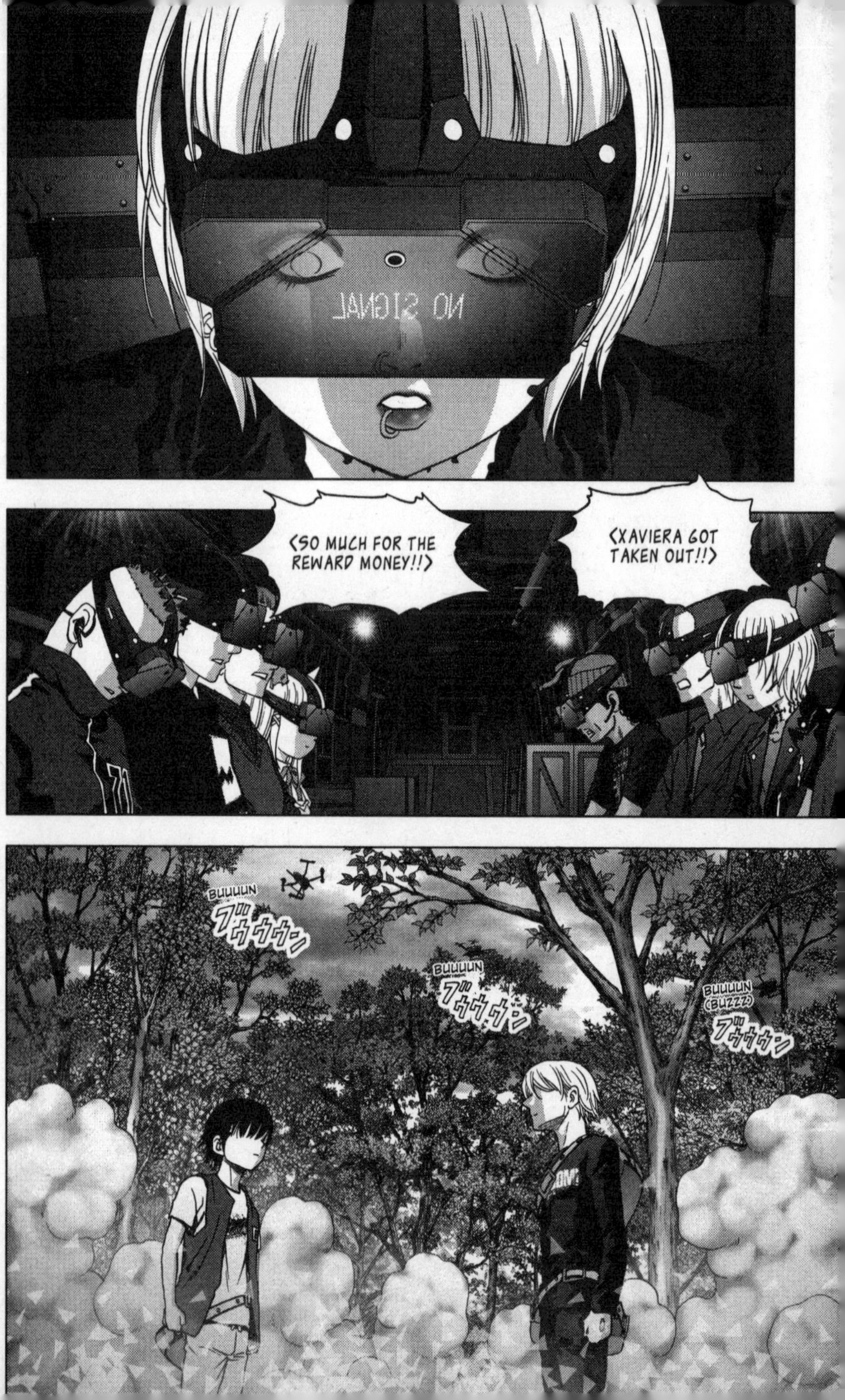
NO SIGNAL
<XAVIERA GOT TAKEN OUT!!>
<SO MUCH FOR THE REWARD MONEY!!>
BUUUUN (BUZZZ)
ブゥウウン
BUUUUN
ブゥウウン
BUUUUN
ブゥウウン

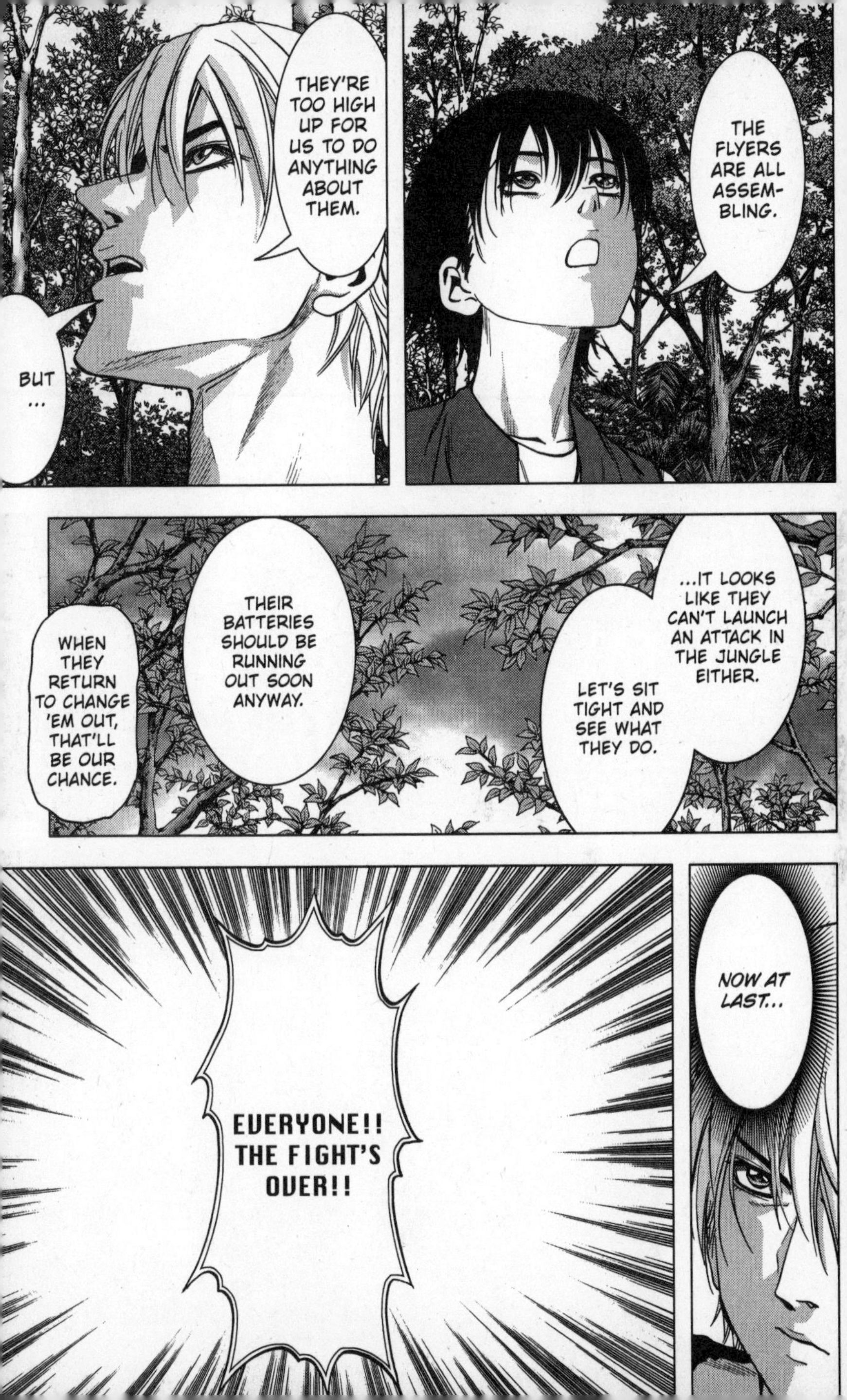
THE FLYERS ARE ALL ASSEM-BLING.
THEY'RE TOO HIGH UP FOR US TO DO ANYTHING ABOUT THEM.
BUT ...
...IT LOOKS LIKE THEY CAN'T LAUNCH AN ATTACK IN THE JUNGLE EITHER.
LET'S SIT TIGHT AND SEE WHAT THEY DO.
THEIR BATTERIES SHOULD BE RUNNING OUT SOON ANYWAY.
WHEN THEY RETURN TO CHANGE 'EM OUT, THAT'LL BE OUR CHANCE.
NOW AT LAST...
EVERYONE!! THE FIGHT'S OVER!!

!?

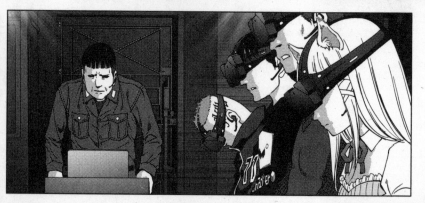

SORRY TO ALWAYS PUT A WRENCH IN THINGS, BUT... THIS IS TAKANO-HASHI.

WHAT I'M ABOUT TO TELL YOU IS WHAT THE SCHWARITZ FOUNDATION THEMSELVES WANT. SO YOU ARMY LOT SHOULD LISTEN UP TOO.

〈...?〉

216

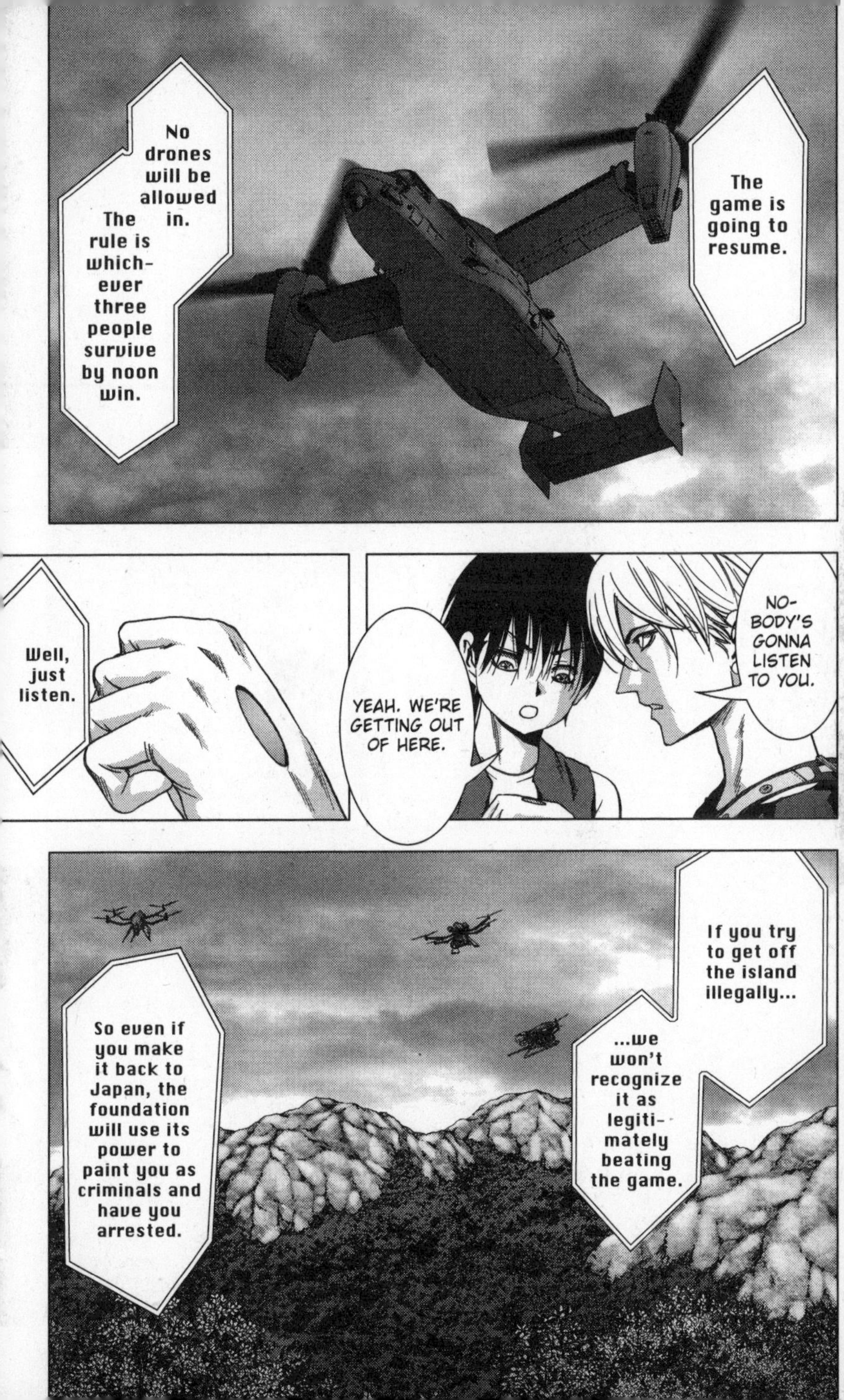

The game is going to resume.
No drones will be allowed in.
The rule is whichever three people survive by noon win.
NOBODY'S GONNA LISTEN TO YOU.
YEAH. WE'RE GETTING OUT OF HERE.
Well, just listen.
If you try to get off the island illegally...
...we won't recognize it as legitimately beating the game.
So even if you make it back to Japan, the foundation will use its power to paint you as criminals and have you arrested.

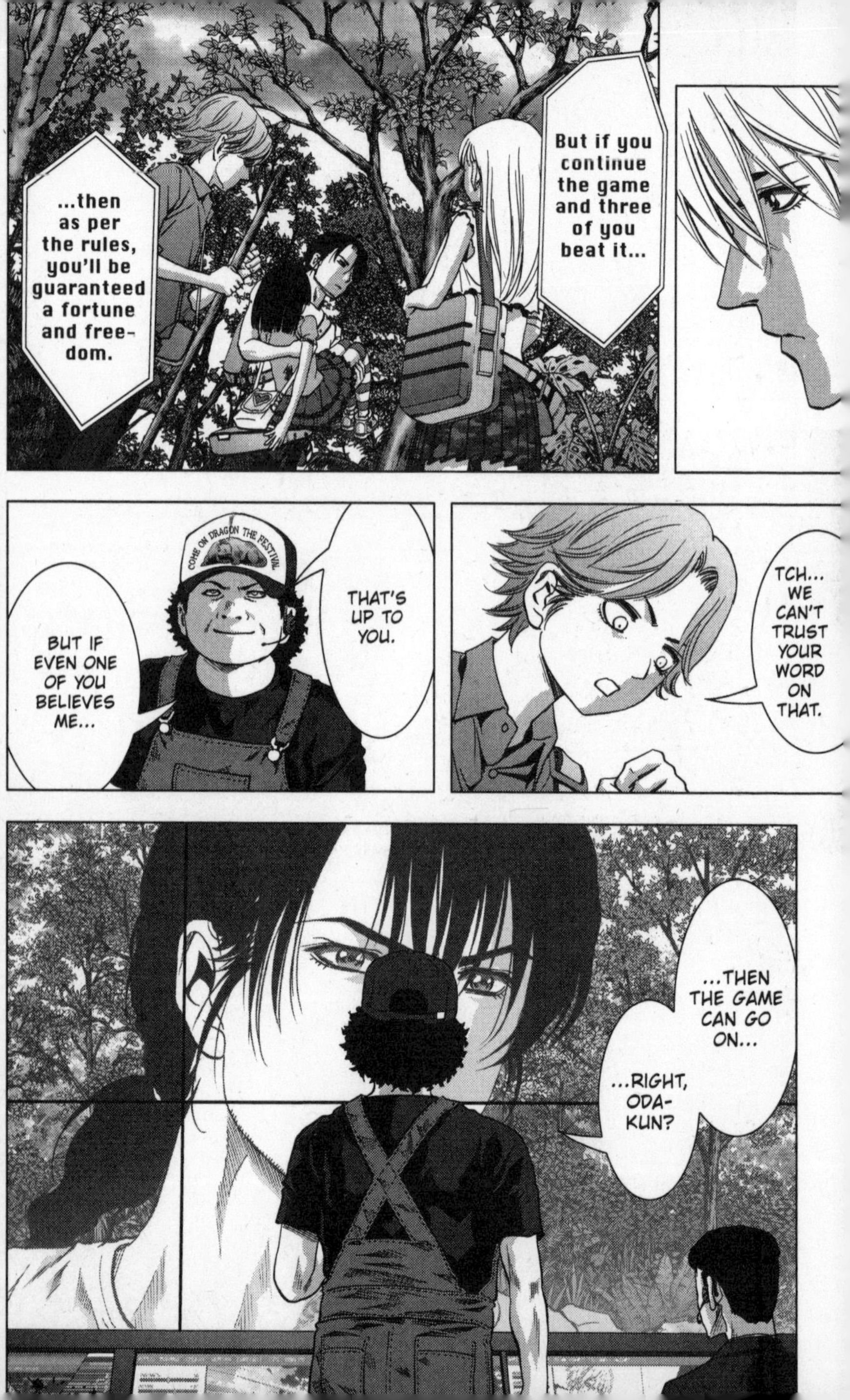
But if you continue the game and three of you beat it...
...then as per the rules, you'll be guaranteed a fortune and free-dom.
TCH... WE CAN'T TRUST YOUR WORD ON THAT.
COME ON DRAGON THE FESTIVAL
THAT'S UP TO YOU.
BUT IF EVEN ONE OF YOU BELIEVES ME...
...THEN THE GAME CAN GO ON...
...RIGHT, ODA-KUN?

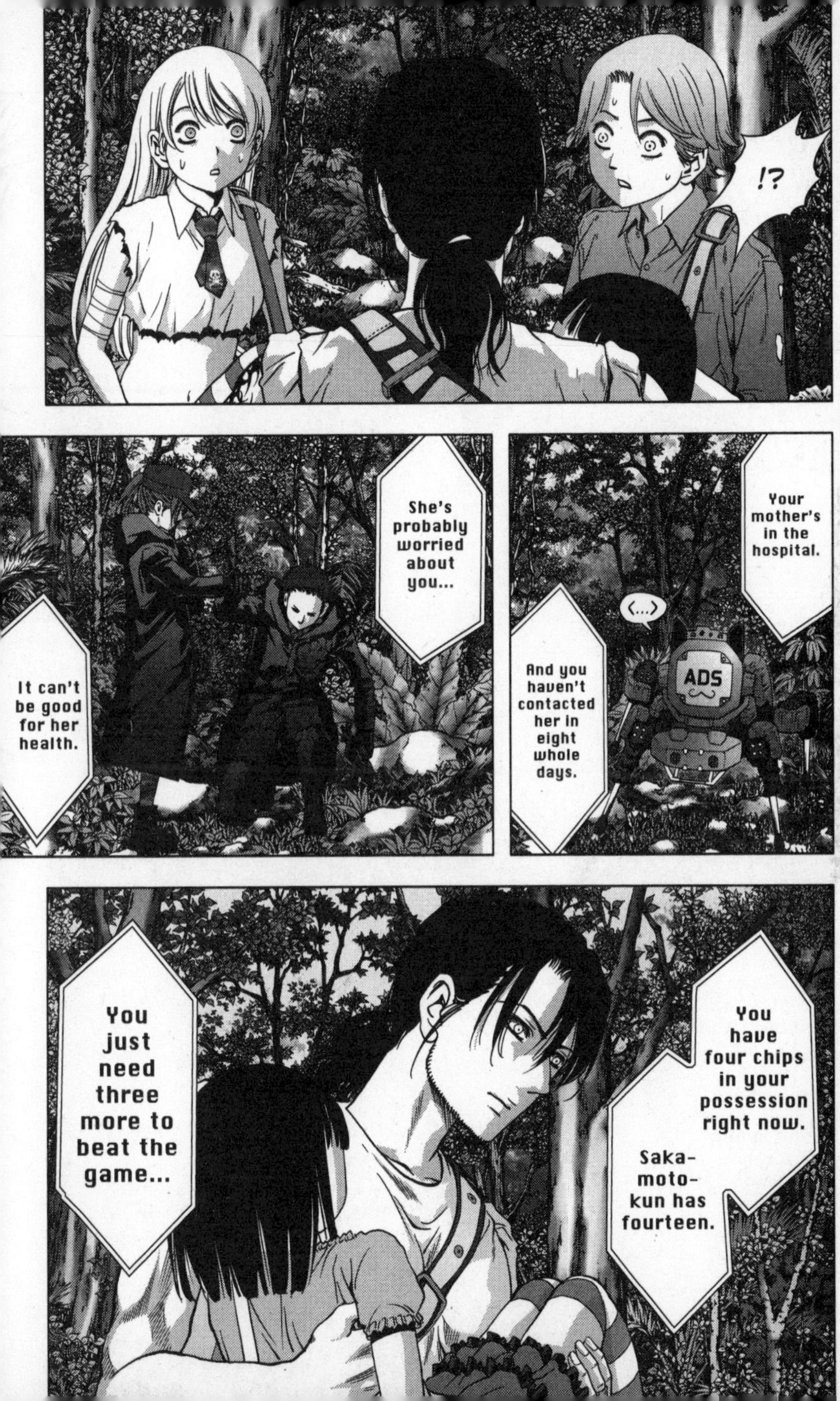
!?
Your mother's in the hospital.
(...)
And you haven't contacted her in eight whole days.
She's probably worried about you...
It can't be good for her health.
You have four chips in your possession right now.
Saka-moto-kun has fourteen.
You just need three more to beat the game...

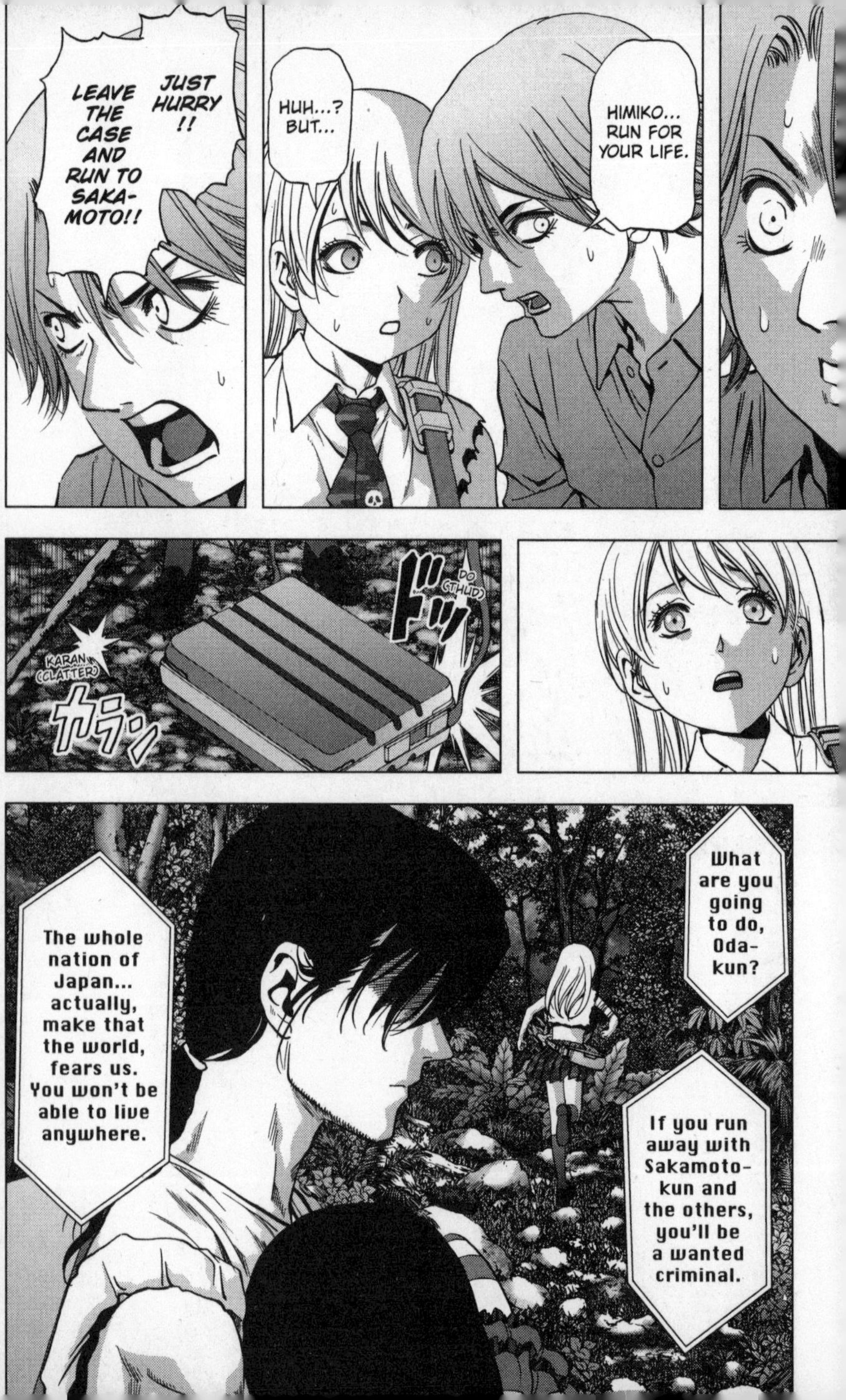
HIMIKO... RUN FOR YOUR LIFE.
HUH...? BUT...
JUST HURRY!!
LEAVE THE CASE AND RUN TO SAKAMOTO!!
DO (THUD)
KARAN (CLATTER)
What are you going to do, Oda-kun?
If you run away with Sakamoto-kun and the others, you'll be a wanted criminal.
The whole nation of Japan... actually, make that the world, fears us. You won't be able to live anywhere.

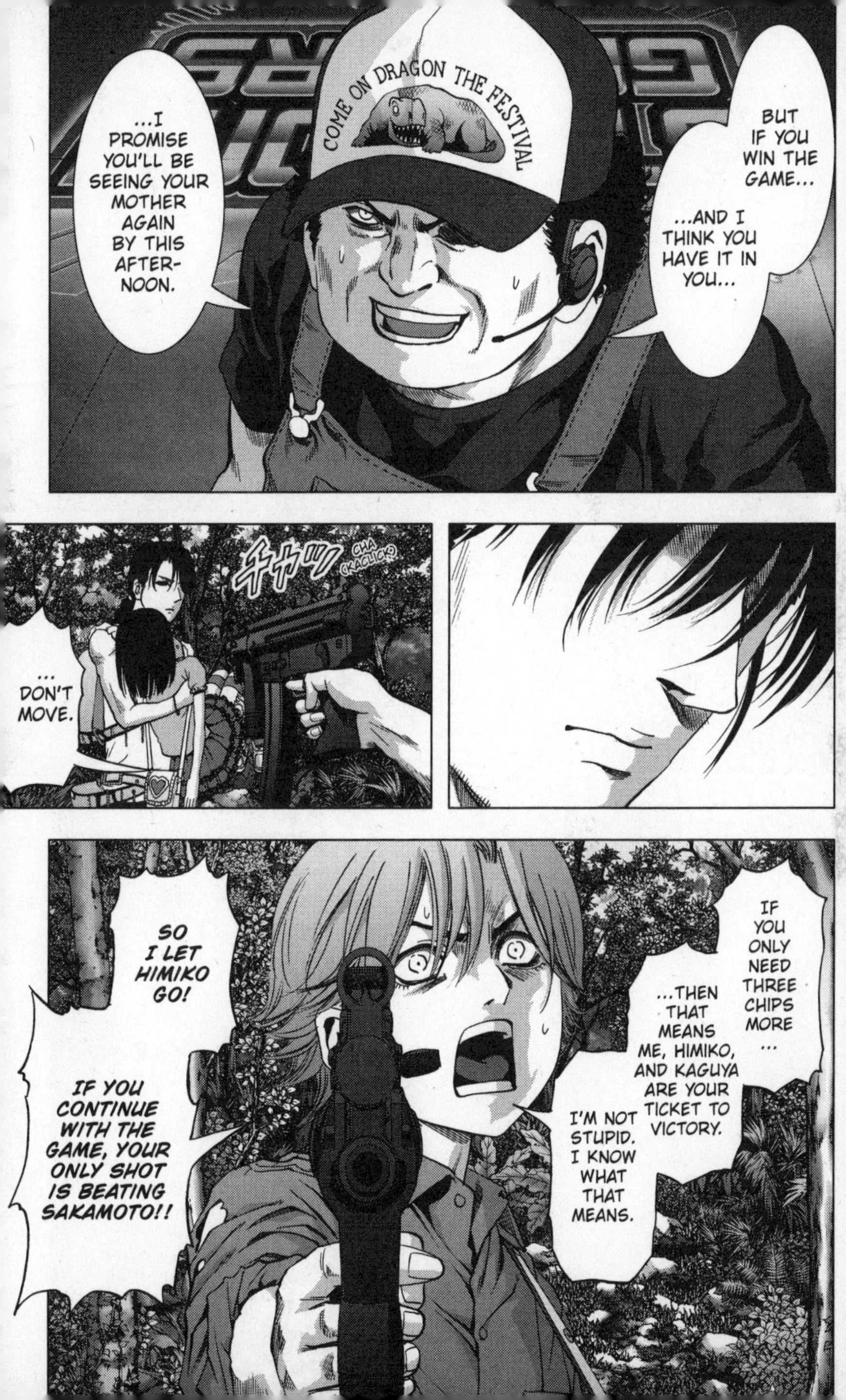
COME ON DRAGON THE FESTIVAL
BUT IF YOU WIN THE GAME...
...AND I THINK YOU HAVE IT IN YOU...
...I PROMISE YOU'LL BE SEEING YOUR MOTHER AGAIN BY THIS AFTER-NOON.
チャッ CHA (KACLICK)
...DON'T MOVE.
IF YOU ONLY NEED THREE CHIPS MORE ...
...THEN THAT MEANS ME, HIMIKO, AND KAGUYA ARE YOUR TICKET TO VICTORY.
I'M NOT STUPID. I KNOW WHAT THAT MEANS.
SO I LET HIMIKO GO!
IF YOU CONTINUE WITH THE GAME, YOUR ONLY SHOT IS BEATING SAKAMOTO!!

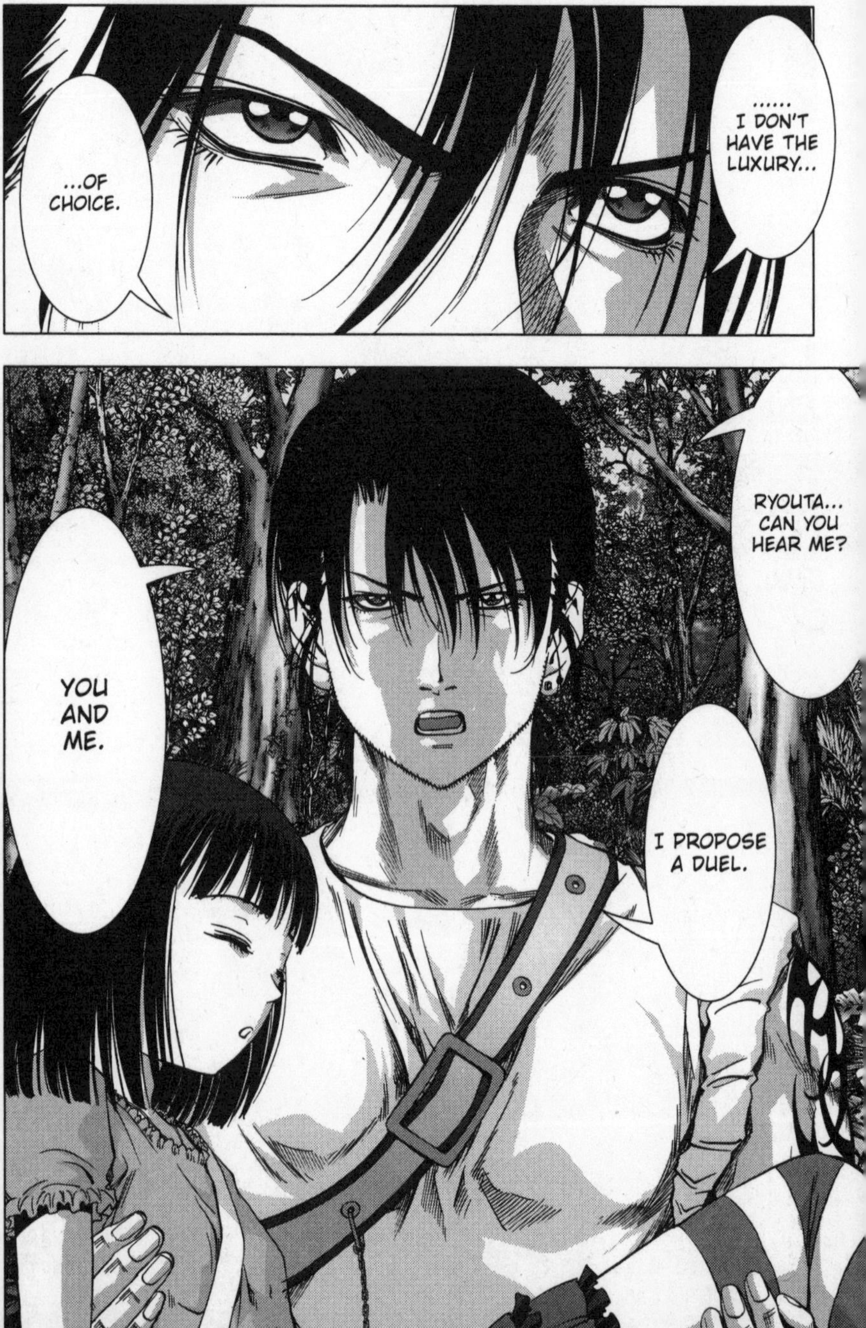
...... I DON'T HAVE THE LUXURY...
...OF CHOICE.
RYOUTA... CAN YOU HEAR ME?
I PROPOSE A DUEL.
YOU AND ME.

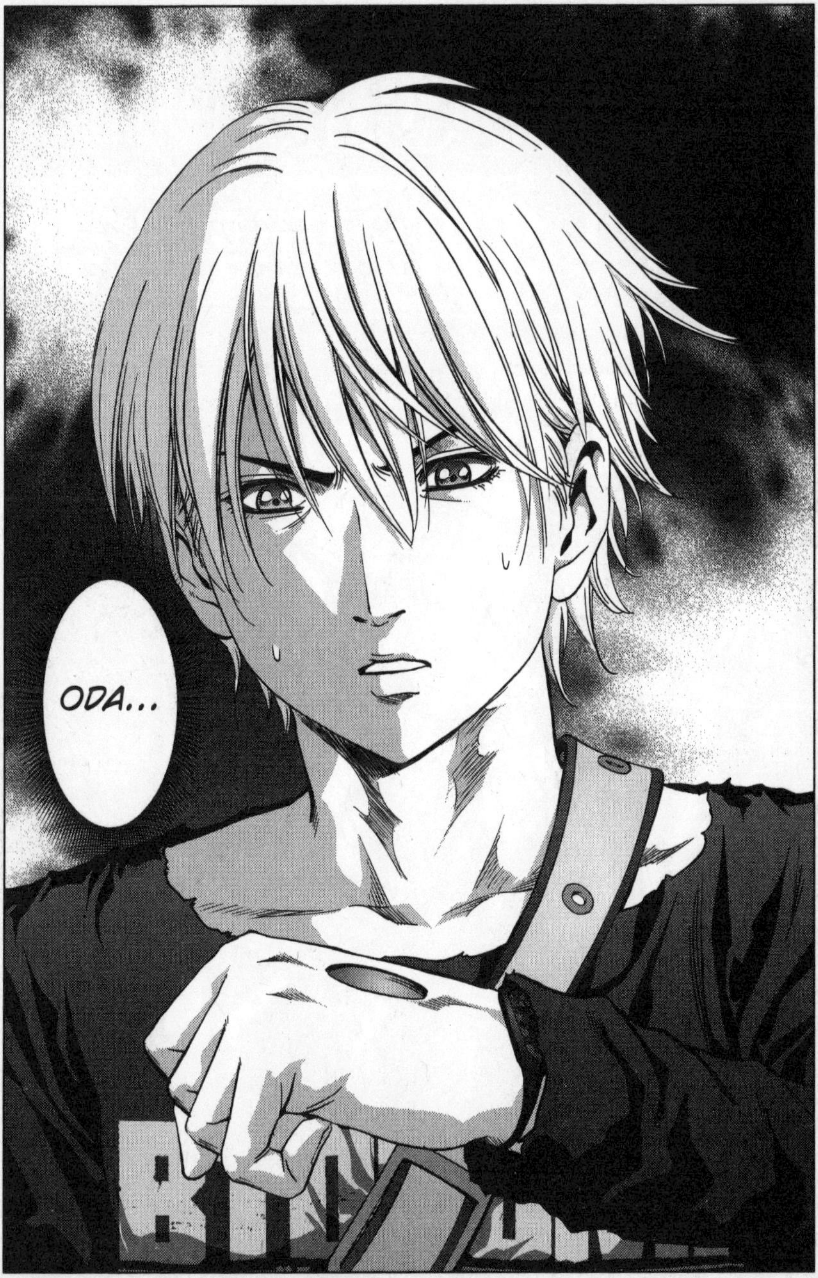
ODA...

TO BE CONTINUED IN BTOOOM! ㉖ Light & Dark

BTOOOM! 25

JUNYA INOUE

Translation: Christine Dashiell

Lettering: Phil Christie

This book is a work of fiction. Names, characters, places, and incidents are the product of the author's imagination or are used fictitiously. Any resemblance to actual events, locales, or persons, living or dead, is coincidental.

BTOOOM! © Junya INOUE 2009. All rights reserved. English translation rights arranged with SHINCHOSHA PUBLISHING CO. through Tuttle-Mori Agency, Inc., Tokyo.

English translation © 2019 by Yen Press, LLC

Yen Press
1290 Avenue of the Americas
New York, NY 10104

Visit us at yenpress.com
facebook.com/yenpress
twitter.com/yenpress
yenpress.tumblr.com
instagram.com/yenpress

First Yen Press Edition: June 2019

Yen Press is an imprint of Yen Press, LLC.
The Yen Press name and logo are trademarks of Yen Press, LLC.

The publisher is not responsible for websites (or their content) that are not owned by the publisher.

Library of Congress Control Number: 2013497409

ISBNs: 978-1-9753-2898-6 (paperback)
978-1-9753-2899-3 (ebook)

10 9 8 7 6 5 4 3 2 1

WOR

Printed in the United States of America